Donald B. Meyer

The Protestant Search for Political Realism, 1919-1941

GREENWOOD PRESS, PUBLISHERS
WESTPORT, CONNECTICUT

The Library of Congress has catalogued this publication as follows:

Library of Congress Cataloging in Publication Data

Meyer, Donald B
    The Protestant search for political realism, 1919-
1941.

    Bibliography: p.
    1. Church and social problems--United States.
2. Protestant churches--United States. 3. Niebuhr,
Reinhold, 1892-1971. 4. Christianity and politics.
I. Title.
[HN39.U6M45 1973]   261.7   72-12314
ISBN 0-8371-6698-5

Originally published in 1960
by the University of California Press,
Berkeley and Los Angeles

Reprinted with the permission
of the University of California Press

First Greenwood Reprinting 1973

Library of Congress Catalogue Card Number 72-12314

ISBN 0-8371-6698-5

Printed in the United States of America

To Genevieve

Acknowledgments

I am grateful to the following for permission to quote from books held in their copyright: Reinhold Niebuhr (*Does Civilization Need Religion?*); Lisa Rauschenbusch (Walter Rauschenbusch, *Christianity and the Social Crisis*); Harper and Brothers (Reinhold Niebuhr, *An Interpretation of Christian Ethics*, A. J. Muste, *Non-Violence in an Aggressive World*, Kirby Page, *The Abolition of War*, and Devere Allen, ed., *Pacifism in the Modern World*); The Macmillan Company (Harry Ward, *The New Social Order*); Rinehart and Company (Sherwood Eddy, *The Challenge of Russia* and *Russia Today*); Charles Scribner's Sons (George Coe, *A Social Theory of Religious Education*, Harry Ward, *In Place of Profit*, and Reinhold Niebuhr, *Moral Man and Immoral Society*, *Reflections on the End of an Era*, *Christianity and Power Politics*, and *The Nature and Destiny of Man*). I am grateful also to the editors of the *Christian Century* for permission to quote from the files of that magazine.

In its original form this book was a thesis written in the Department of History, Harvard University, under the title "The Protestant Social Liberals in America, 1919–1941." To Arthur M. Schlesinger, Jr., I owe thanks for his warm interest at every stage of its composition.

My wife shared the emotions of revision and publication—no small thing.

D. M.

Contents

I

The Height of the Times

This book is not about typical men. Protestant ministers intent upon politics between 1919 and 1941 were a minority of their profession; those who were strong political liberals a minority smaller still. A Baptist pastor defending socialism, a Presbyterian pastor working for industrial democracy, an Episcopal pastor manning picket lines, a Methodist pastor serving the United Front: such men were living out purposes only dimly felt by others. They did not represent Protestant ministers as a whole; certainly they did not represent the Protestant congregations. Often they spoke for only a handful, were disavowed by more, and were ignored by most.

They were, if not typical, symptomatic. They registered points of pressure, significant not only for themselves but for their unheeding fellows. What occupied them was not a matter of their own invention. It is possible to argue that religion and politics should not be associated in some one particular way or another; it is not possible to prove they need be in no association whatever. They are related everywhere; only the consciousness with which the relationship is faced and realized varies. The pastors studied in this book were those of fullest consciousness. For most of them,

1

deliberate, systematic attention to politics and questions of social organization was their primary professional occupation, precisely as men of religion. They thought of their interest, in fact, as the heart of their religious evangel, as a "gospel," the social gospel.

The basic subject of this book is not their politics, however, or even the relationship they wished between religion and politics. It is religion itself. In the years between the wars, social-gospel history became much more than a series of attempts to put religion into social practice. It was the record of a crisis in the religion itself. Every step in the search for practical translation meant a deepening of self-consciousness about the nature of the original idealism. By 1934 the decisive issue was no longer how to bring the ideal to reality, but whether the old idealism was truly Protestant, truly Christian, indeed truly religious. In Reinhold Niebuhr, with whom the problem of politics came to a climax, the social gospel found its climactic critic. Beginning as a criticism of society, the Protestant social concern ended as a criticism of religion. To record the evolution of this religious self-consciousness under the pressure of politics is the main topic of this book.

The pastors in whom this self-consciousness developed were reformers and, as such, were indebted to an age of reform. Many of their ideas they owed to men around them. This had been true among the earlier social-gospel leaders, between the Civil War and the First World War. Edward Bellamy and Henry George, Richard Ely and Simon Patten, Lester Ward and Herbert Croly, Populists and Progressives and socialists all had formulated economic, political, and social ideas more fully and clearly than the pastors, as Thorstein Veblen, John Dewey, and spokesmen for the New Deal were to continue to do. The pastors were therefore a kind of register of the penetration of the religious community by ideas from more secular headquarters. The social gospel could be regarded as, in a sense, reform with a Protestant gloss, the gloss interesting but inessential. Reform first, religion second.

On the other hand, the social-gospel pastors set reform in a context larger and often more explicit and systematic than, generally, did the others. At the same time, few lay reformers of the late nineteenth and early twentieth centuries, including even those who rejected religious dimensions, failed to show some signs of religious roots and morale. Thus, it would be possible to regard reform as the social gospel unconscious of its religious debts. Religion first, reform second.

The problem of debts and priorities is not a subject of this book. The examples of Weber and Tawney surely prove that such a problem can be studied. Social-gospel study has already been much advanced by the research of Henry May, James Dombrowski, Aaron Abell, Charles Hopkins, and above all by the scholarship of H. Richard Niebuhr.[1] It remains to be seen whether, as recent interest in religious history deepens, the balance is fated to swing to assigning religion priority in all things. In this book neither the degree to which Protestantism was penetrated by and indebted to reform nor the degree to which reform was indebted to Protestantism is of controlling interest; rather the interest is with religion itself, as challenged by politics. Not origins, but the climax, guides the tale.

For idealists, one of the crucial moments arrives when they begin to think systematically, not only of the end they wish to serve, but also of the means, and then, still more critically, under the stress of hope or anxiety, begin to make choices among the means. Much of the labor of the social-gospel idealists, from Washington Gladden's first work in the 1870's to Walter Rauschenbusch's *Theology for the Social Gospel*, published in 1917, had gone into defining, defending, and preaching their vision of the ideal goal. By the end of the First World War, however, the pastors had come to be dominated by questions of strategy, and so they were to remain, moving from hope to anxiety, for the next twenty-three years. Between 1919 and 1941, their major debates turned on the problem of power. How could the vision be brought to pass? Who would bear it to victory? Pastors confronted politics directly, as the means to victory. In so doing, they exposed themselves to the pressures that every idea faces in action. Politics was to be not only a means, but also a testing of the ends.

The self-consciousness forced out under this testing ultimately took the form of theology. The crises of the social gospel in the last years before Pearl Harbor were fought out in theological terms. One of my aims is to set that theological debate in context, rather more than to elaborate all the terms of the debate itself. Its context, even more than its content, was the decisive feature of the debate; here the fact that I am discussing religious reform is of major pertinence. Touching the heart—the task of "gospel" —is involved one way or another with touching the patterns of social power—the task of politics: this was the insight that men of the social gospel had always in mind. As a consequence they could not raise political questions without also raising questions of the "heart"—or, if that honorable, lost word miscarries, of the "whole" man. Once under pressure, the search for an ideal association between religion and politics demanded gradually more explicit inspection of the association between self and society, as well as between man and God. It was to be in the struggles of the social gospel that American Protestantism resumed, after long neglect, religion's incessant inquiry into the nature of human nature.

In the process of resuming this inquiry, certain assumptions of the social gospel were brought to light, giving the religious debate a more than parochial Protestant interest. Bearers of a purportedly universal ideal, the pastors eventually came to exhibit how profoundly American culture had sustained them in those ideals. They were critics of the American economy and American society, but only deep expectations about the special qualities of American society had allowed them to criticize in the first place. Without such expectations, criticism would have been meaningless. These expectations became an essential part of the defense of their liberal religion. Subordinate versions of these were the expectations the pastors revealed about their own churches. Far more than the lay liberals, the pastors were committed to institutional homes. The churches "held" their leaders far more than any universities, journals, professional societies, or informal groups did or could. The pastors' positions were closer to those of the party politician than to those of the "unattached" idealist. One of the most difficult problems for the pastors was how to balance their tradition with their criticism. This rich entanglement of their idealism with assumptions about their churches—

as major social organizations of American life—and about American society at large lent their theological struggles so large a resonance.

The Protestant spirit has become progressively less understood since the noontime of laissez faire. The social-group pastors, if they did not add to positive understanding, at least helped clarify some of the conditions that contributed to the loss of understanding, not only among outside observers but among Protestants as well. They were part of a process of self-rediscovery. They were forced to try to understand not only their society and politics but themselves and their tradition as well, and came in the end to debate their own reconstruction as well as the reconstruction of the society. They ended up measuring not only American business, labor unions, Republican politics in the 'twenties, New Deal politics in the 'thirties, and American foreign policy throughout, but also the yardstick itself—that is, the meaning of religion—by which they measured American society and man's social existence generally.

In the emergence of this new self-consciousness, two moments in the period between the wars had symbolic importance. At one point, at the beginning, the social-gospel pastors had the chance to hope. They expressed broad optimism unguardedly, as it seemed they were being offered their chance of victory. For a great many Americans—and not only the pastors—history seemed "open" in 1919. There are perspectives, of course, from which every moment can be seen to have its openness. Philosophy of history aside, however, from the standpoint of the working world some seasons do seem to offer particularly critical, particularly fine opportunities for choices that will shape the future. A Protestant theologian who will figure in this study, Paul Tillich, has described such occasions as *kairos:* the times are full. If men have prepared for them, the times can decisively grasp and shape the conditions of their lives. Kairos does not come through plan; it comes through "grace," a sum of forces far beyond the scale for men to control. Once it arrives, men are granted the chance to become—never absolutely and never permanently but more than before—their own destiny. The year 1919 seemed such a chance.

Thirteen years later the pastors had reason to despair. They were forced to face tests they had never before imagined, were pinned against their hopes by harsh reality, and were forced thus to explore their deepest commitments.

The mood of 1919 was national. Wartime unity had broken, but a wartime height of energy still prevailed. Groups that had been submerged in the common effort reasserted their interests with the supercharge of war-born frustration, expansion, and fervor. At war's end, the nation had at hand great new industrial facilities developed to meet the demands of the crusade. It had, from the performance of government agencies, striking experience of what rationalized, over-all planning might achieve in every sphere. It had, in a public accustomed to filling great abstractions with living emotions, reservoirs of volatility available for the service of new abstractions.

From their wartime jobs as government administrators, consultants, and contractors, businessmen carried the will to rationalize into the code agreements and trade associations reshaping American industry behind its ideological façade of competitive laissez faire. The wartime practice of calculated and economy-wide concessions to all segments of economic interest—capital, labor, government, management, farmer, consumer—sharpened the image of the new business leader, the enlightened businessman, who had only begun learning his way with Hanna and then Theodore Roosevelt and the Eastern Progressives. Charles Schwab, John D. Rockefeller, Jr., and Dwight Morrow no more thought of the business world as a jungle in which it was each man's duty to behave as a lion than they thought of it as a cooperative Eden unified by love. Older traditions of business leadership reëmerged also, of course. Whether or not they were willing to discard jungle sociology for association among themselves, the older lions were quite determined that new parties were not to be admitted to the agreements. Drawing in the fashion of the times upon the reservoir of free emotion, proponents of the open shop transformed their rallying cry into something more acceptable: the open shop became the "American" plan.

Obviously, when all parties came out asserting themselves to excess, not all could win. Something of a test of strength emerged in 1919, and was to hold good for the next eighteen years. The AFL found itself fattened from wartime, at the peak of its at least numerical strength, and under the prodding of William Z. Foster undertook new conquests. By November, 1919, the strikers at U. S. Steel were routed; by 1921 the AFL had lost more than one million members. Railroad men, who had won the Adamson eight-hour law in 1916 and had enjoyed much favor under Secretary McAdoo, rallied in 1919 to Glen Plumb's plan for public ownership of the industry. Not only did they lose; by 1922 Attorney General Daugherty was to fling his injunction in the face of the shopmen quite as though instructed by the spirit of Richard Olney.

On one far political wing, strange sects emerged from the wartime shambles of the Socialist party, in a series of fissions to the left, at the end of which both a Communist and a Communist-Labor party stood beyond the Socialist party itself. In the Midwest a collection of small local organizations, without concern for Marxist credentials, seemed to testify to the survival of the old agrarian insurgency. These groups had no precise opposite numbers on the right. Right-wing enthusiasm organized into watchdog societies of professional patriotism, without independent political pretensions; their true opposites were not the Communists so much as those unknown exponents of direct action who mailed bombs in brown paper to the eminent and staged the symbolic holocaust in Wall Street. Excess flourished in each direction: behind the excessive witch-hunting of Attorney General Palmer were a few excessive witches; behind the excessive paranoia of the political left were excessive persecutions.

And yet it appeared, in a way, after all the fervor and the saving messages, as though the only saving message that could win general assent was the one that could restore the unity—the saving message of "normalcy." Out of the enthusiasm there emerged Warren Harding. The literary men had always understood that this was the ultimate pattern; with no discernible pause for indecision, Dos Passos, Mencken, Lewis, Cummings, Hemingway, and the rest simply renewed and intensified a moral and spiritual secession from the pieties of American culture already underway a great many years before. The literary men were perhaps the only ones to preach their saving postwar evangel in something like willing sectarian isolation.

From the record it would seem that enthusiasm burned no higher anywhere than within the leadership of the Protestant churches. In 1919 and 1920 Protestantism spoke with a degree of confidence and self-assertion befitting only men who felt themselves at the opening of a new era—and themselves responsible for its opening. The Presbyterians in fact called it that; they needed $35,000,000 for their New Era Movement, and had 87 ½ per cent of it subscribed by May. The Disciples of Christ had begun by a successful expansion of their own prewar Men and Millions Movement. The name was apt: an aura of statistics hung about the fervor as clouds of glory. When the Methodists remembered that the first year of peace would coincide with the birthday of their missions, they undertook what was at the time statistically the largest single enterprise ever mounted by a Protestant denomination in the history of the country—the Centenary of Methodist Missions. By June, 1919, the Methodist Episcopal Church and the Methodist Episcopal Church South had, between them, collected subscriptions for $140,000,000. For three summer weeks at the state-fair grounds in Columbus, Ohio, one million persons paid admissions and helped celebrate the hundred years of missionary conquest.[2]

The Methodist Centenary remained the largest single undertaking of a Protestant denomination only because it became clear that the pattern of the world's redemption was to be not denominational but truly Christian-wide, a business not of the churches but of, at last, the Church. How high the ecumenical spirit blazed can be measured: in one of the few general assemblies on record in which the body of delegates from the floor acted over and beyond its official shepherds, the Presbyterian Church, USA, also at Columbus in 1918, issued a general invitation, to whichever sister communions would listen, to discuss, prepare for, and be prepared to consummate a plan for general, organic Protestant union. Such an invitation could not be buried in the official report. Upon instruction of the delegates the invitation was put upon the wires instantly, without cooling of the heart, to the delegates of four other denominational assemblies then in session. Meantime, while committees, ad interim committees, and subcommittees of the churches took up the Presbyterian offer, home and foreign missionary leaders of the churches undertook one supreme united response to the challenge and opportunity of the new day: the Interchurch World Movement was born. At first, talk was of $300,000,000, then of $500,-000,000. The final figure was one billion dollars, $335,000,000 to be subscribed in the first few years, the rest later. The program exalted the imagination: Interchurch proposed to survey ". . . all the facts about the religious, social, moral, physical and economic environments of humanity through the world [so that] from these facts a unified program shall be worked out in which all can concur." The chairman of the Chicago committee, Herbert C. Willett, summed up the use to which these facts were to be put: "The program of the Interchurch World Movement includes nothing less than the complete evangelization of all of life."[3]

Clearly modeled on the wartime bond drives, the gigantic fund-raising programs of Protestantism just after the First World War marked a peak of Protestant morale, a peak of fever. Churchmen had preached the war as it had not been preached by other voices; they had confirmed its moral and even divine character, and they took from it an obsessive image of righteousness united with power. Although the obsession remained throughout the decade ahead, fever alone lent the leaders a conviction that union of righteousness and power did already exist in the Protestant churches themselves. Interchurch collapsed within eighteen months. It had financed a famous report on the labor conditions at Judge Gary's United States Steel; there were those to say that Judge Gary could not reconcile the report with support for Interchurch and that the report, therefore, and the collapse were not without their deep inner connections.[4] In any

event, Interchurch collapsed. Other money drives of the denominations remained on paper. By the middle of the 'twenties still
other financial statistics indicated that the missionary nerve of
the nineteenth century celebrated at Columbus was withering.

Many diagnoses of the errors of Protestant leadership were offered in the ensuing decade; perhaps the simplest bore against the
illusion of unity. If the wartime agencies had offered opportunity
and morale to the ecumenical liberals, the war itself had massive
symbolic interest for the distributors of *The Fundamentals,* which
liberal exegesis and logic could not have hoped to dissolve.
Liberal churchmen had preached the war as a definitive stage in
the evolutionary crusade of democracy against autocracy, but
premillennialist chrurchmen could serve it up in opposite fashion
to congregations susceptible to literal-symbolic proof for their
apocalyptic texts. Only barely did the enthusiasm of 1919 drown
out the rumblings of schism that mounted to open battle in the
fundamentalist wars of 1922 to 1927. Earliest and most severely
riven were the Presbyterians, in 1918 crying "union" over the
telegraph, in 1923 crying "heretic" at Harry Emerson Fosdick
as he was driven from his pulpit.

In its immediate postwar fervor, in fact, Protestantism was at
the beginning of a time constituting the precise opposite of what
the leaders of Interchurch and money drives imagined: instead
of a simplified era of final triumph, Protestantism was entering a
period of complexity and defeat—the most complex in its American experience, marked by some of its most serious defeats. A
single general fact lay behind this and provided context for everything else: Protestantism could no longer easily, even to itself—
and this was the nub—count upon its historic position as an
accepted, senior partner in the national culture. In the decade
ahead, all wings of the Protestant churches were mobilized into
some kind of defensive reaction. Fundamentalists, tragically but
inevitably in symbiosis with the Ku Klux Klan, attempted to resist
a new culture. Liberals, led by Fosdick, attempted to adapt themselves to it. The attempts of both groups were resisted; both
groups fell under the fire of a new sophistication that took exception to the entire tradition of Protestant evangelical culture. An

almost Aristotelian fatal flaw was at work in the strength of 1919, which resulted in definite tragedy in two issues.

First, the investment in the war came to tragedy. The war had come as a surprise. Its appearance in Europe in 1914 had been a shock, and Protestant leaders, like the American public, opposed American entry in very high moral tones. But as American entry began to be argued as a national necessity, Protestant leaders were presented with a supreme challenge to the policy of partnership in the culture. With the declaration of war, their answer was to identify even more than totally with national policy, transferring the same high tone justifying peace to the justification of war, preaching the war not simply as national but also as religious necessity. This, the greatest of the Protestant prophets, Walter Rauschenbusch, could not do; it engendered in those who did the extra overtone of desperation, an overeagerness in their alignment of the Word with the world, that in recollection was to haunt the liberals of the 'twenties and provoke in them those acute pangs of revulsion that marked a first tentative step toward the idea of maintaining righteousness even at the cost of the old partnership. The wartime assertion of partnership had been something of a tour de force; regrets, recantations, and retractions of the war sermons began within two years of the armistice.

Further, the most stunning Protestant triumph of 1919 became Protestantism's most tragic burden. The Volstead Act and the Eighteenth Amendment climaxed generations of Protestant agitation, which presumed the old partnership of evangelical church and national culture. But the churches could not patrol their victory. Within a matter of years, sophisticated scorn and indifferent resentment characterizing both the new intelligentsia and a new popular culture had been crystallized by Prohibition. To a large circle of spectators, especially from metropolitan and industrial labor, Prohibition reawakened the disastrous image of a coercive Protestant—if not, still worse, clerical—moralism laying hands directly upon the power of the state. Because no groups within the churches were free to criticize Prohibition, because it constituted a new orthodoxy to which liberals as well as conservative evangelicals were committed, the "noble experiment" never

failed to distort and compromise decisions on other issues demanding their own uncompromised solutions—church finance,
church policy, theology, cultural accommodation, above all the
social gospel. The distorting effect carried outside into some of
the major institutions and patterns of American life, especially the
Democratic party. For the Democratic party in the North there
could be no rest until the triumph of 1919 was brought to defeat,
a defeat in which the prestige of Protestantism was entangled.

In a word, the victory at armistice and the victory of Prohibition were both hollow.

Like the missionary enthusiasts, like the ecumenical Interchurch enthusiasts, like the fundamentalists, like the Prohibition-
ists, the prophets of the social gospel emerged from the war fired
with their own sense of coming fulfillment. They had always been
a small minority, but they had thought of themselves as a vanguard minority; now the scene was set for the general march.
The social-service commission of the Northern Baptists, meeting
in Denver in May, 1919, declared roundly that "it is not a question
whether there shall be some radical changes and thoroughgoing
readjustments in the social order"; the only question concerned
the manner of change, whether through conflict or through reason
reinforced by religious idealism. The Baptists adopted the report
of the commission.[5] At its special postwar convention, the Federal
Council of Churches adopted an expanded and more pointed
version of the 1912 Social Creed; the social-service commission
drew up a report, *The Church and Social Reconstruction,* which
was mailed to the 100,000 pastors of the nation. The council's
Commission on War and the Religious Outlook produced a
volume, *The Church and Industrial Reconstruction,* systematically formulating the social passion into a general directive for
future action. At the Episcopal general convention of 1919, the
Joint Commission on Social Service presented a full-dress factual
survey, both sophisticated and urgent, reviewing the contemporary state of affairs in the labor movement, theories of industrial and social reorganization, and the relevant duties of
Protestantism in general, Episcopalianism specifically.[6] Eminent
leaders of the church from prewar days laid new stress on the

social evangel, such as William Adams Brown, mild, moderate, unprogrammatic, in his lectures to industrial secretaries of the Y.W.C.A., "Christianity and Industry," and Charles Reynolds Brown of Yale Divinity School, in his Depauw lectures where he hearkened to a democratic spirit in industry like that in politics.[7] New leaders such as Henry Sloane Coffin, soon to head Union Theological Seminary, suggested in *A More Christian Industrial Order* that "some form of public control of essential industries" might be required. In *Democratic Christianity* and *Church Finances and Social Ethics*, the new Methodist bishop for Pittsburgh, Francis J. McConnell, sketched out the crucial role to be played by the church in the press of society toward fulfilled democracy. Perhaps the most sweeping announcement of Christian duty came from Harry F. Ward of the Methodists, whose manifesto of 1919 was endowed with the simplest and most final of watchwords: *The New Social Order.* "The signs are clear . . . that we have arrived at one of those conjunctions of economic pressure and idealistic impulse, which occasion fundamental changes in the organization of life." [8] Facts, history, criticism, and argument, the book fused all in its sense of imminence.

It was not as though the prophets were alone. Liberal, political, and social enthusiasm was part of the postwar release, and its at least verbal sanctions were to be found in the utterances of the man who seemed to hold in his hands as much power to raise history to a new level as any man in memory. In 1919 Woodrow Wilson was occupied with the League of Nations and permanent peace—and these also were visions of liberal enthusiasm. But Wilson further gave character to the visions of social reconstruction and industrial democracy. In his messages of May 20 and December 2, 1919, to Congress, Wilson announced, in a survey of the industrial scene, ". . . we cannot go any further in our present direction." The real community of interest, he said, that did exist between capital and labor had been frustrated in action, and could be made manifest

> . . . only in a new organization of industry . . . The object of all reform in this essential matter must be the genuine democratization of industry, based upon a full recognition of the right of those who

work, in whatever rank, to participate in some organic way in every decision which directly affects their welfare or the part they are to play in industry.[9]

It was true that the Industrial Board set up in February as an attempt to extend the War Industries Board into peacetime had been disbanded by May. It was true that the Industrial Conference of October, called to spark an atmosphere of community and coöperation between capital and labor, broke up within days on the intransigence of both sides. Nevertheless, high words were on record from high places, like principles laid down in encyclicals. Even if what Harry Ward meant by "industrial democracy" was not what Wilson meant, even though the high words concealed a whole spectrum of disagreement, nevertheless what Wilson meant and everyone felt was that the question lay open; principles did exist, and society awaited, plastic, will-inviting, to be molded.

So the prophets were not alone. Such an organ of secular liberalism as the *Nation*, following the pronouncements of Presbyterians, the Federal Council, Methodist bishops, and Catholic bishops, welcomed ". . . this vast social force . . . apparently upon the point of arousing itself. It would be hard to overestimate the impetus which [they could give] to any project of industrial or political reform." Twenty-one years later, another editor of the *Nation* was to protest identification of the Second World War with the cause of "Christian civilization"; Christianity stood on both sides. Christianity had nourished dictatorship as well as democracy; the war was secular.[10] But, except among dogmatic Marxists and the International Workers of the World, secular liberals in 1919 did not take it as dogma that religion always conserved, that religion was in fact always the partner of the standing order and could be nothing else. Events of the year 1919, whatever the 'twenties were to bring, seemed to be justifying enthusiasm. A new era of international relations under preparation in Paris; the greatest strike of the times—that of the steel workers—held up to public scrutiny, by an agency of the churches, against private opposition; the promise of church-wide mobilization for nation-wide action; a fountain of prophecy from the religious presses; a melodramatic strike among the textile workers of Lawrence, Massachusetts, carried to last-minute victory by a handful of Protestant ministers: these were the things the prophets saw. No matter how soon the sense of frustration began to gather, or how early the warmth began to cool, the fact that the passion had risen to the occasion without reserve was perhaps the essential. Forty years of apprenticeship had prepared the prophets for such an occasion, and perhaps it would not have been their part to question in skepticism or cool detachment, let alone to ask whether their preparation ought to have been for such occasions at all.

For the social gospel, perhaps the single tragedy of the year was that its greatest spokesman was not alive on Armistice Day. Walter Rauschenbusch had died, in Rochester, New York, only a few months before. This was the man who had gathered the mission into a final evangel, preaching it more glowingly and with more reasoned faith than any other of his generation of Protestant leaders. In two earlier books, *Christianity and the Social Crisis* (1907) and *Christianizing the Social Order* (1912), as well as in *A Theology for the Social Gospel* (1917), Rauschenbusch had supplied the social passion with a sense of destiny.[11] He had raised the prospect of a decisive turning point in history, where Christianity would move from ideal to reality, from sentiment to responsibility. There is no understanding Rauschenbusch, or the social gospel, unless it is understood that he conceived this turning point literally. For sixteen centuries, ever since the captivity of the primitive Church to its own political triumph under Constantine, the essence of the Christian word had been neglected. At the end of those sixteen centuries, in the twentieth century, it was being rediscovered, preached, harnessed, and put to work. It would mean a real difference, in politics, in economics, in society generally. The new field for Christian action was the social system; it was society that was to experience Christian conversion.

This word was not lost with the death of Rauschenbusch at a vigorous fifty-seven. Yet immeasurable pathos attached to the fact that Rauschenbusch himself had died a troubled man, invaded by an uneasiness he had no time to plumb.[12] This unhappiness was itself a phenomenon of the social gospel: it betrayed a spiritual vulnerability to politics. Rauschenbusch had allowed himself to believe in history. He had not, however, been able to reconcile himself to the war on any basis, and it had struck deep into the soul. It was entirely possible, therefore, that he might not have shared the enthusiasm of 1919. If he had lived to face the 'twenties, he might have drawn from his own disturbance a new, darker, more complex morale.

As it was, the life and works of Rauschenbusch gave enthusiasm a final, formal sanction. Of his last book, despite its cautions and darker edges, it was said: "Professor Rauschenbusch has given us the last word on the new social order. Men received his book as though a modern Isaiah had spoken . . . In thousands of pulpits men took heart." [13]

What was the explanation for Rauschenbusch's stature? He preached his word winningly. He managed to gather up much of the moral emotion of Progressivism and give it explicit, even systematic, religious sanction. Yet neither his rhetorical nor his symbolic power really measured his significance, for in addition to these Rauschenbusch had an important logical point. It can best be understood in light of an obvious question he opened up himself: why, after all, had Christianity never succeeded in mastering society?

There were many answers. In the spirit standard to liberal Protestantism, Rauschenbusch saw the long history of Christianity since Constantine in the wrong hands. The true faith consisted of the teachings of Jesus, but all types of authority had come in to smother them: ecclesiasticism and dogma, fanaticism and ritualism, philosophers and popes, emperors and kings. They had used Christianity, not applied it. In addition, there was also the effect of sin to be calculated. Rauschenbusch's concept of sin was never remarkably clear, and never well correlated with other factors in human nature and history. Nevertheless, it could not be denied in sentimental optimism that some tendencies in human nature did resist the Word.

Such explanations as these had weight, but one more reason outranked them all. Actually, in saying that the true evangel of Christianity had been ignored, Rauschenbusch was not expressing his full view, for it was more typical of him to say that Christianity had in fact managed to spread its faith. The true Word had not been forgotten so much as it had not been implemented.

> . . . the Church has often rendered invaluable aid . . . against some single intolerable evil, but [and here lay the crux] it has accepted as inevitable the general social system under which the world was living at the time, and has not undertaken any thorough-going social reconstruction . . . It is this diffused spirit rather than the conscious purpose of organized Christianity which has been the chief moral force in social change.[14]

Diffused spirit was not enough. Something more was needed, something that had never before been available. "To undertake the gradual reconstruction of social life consciously and intelligently would have required a scientific comprehension of social life which was totally lacking in the past. Sociology is still an infant science." [15] This being true, even with the best will in the world, philosophers, popes, kings, and good Christian laymen could not have carried out the ultimate reaches of the teachings of Jesus. They had lacked social science; they had lacked sociology.

The insights of modern social science were the logical foundations of Rauschenbusch's optimism. It was new knowledge that opened the way to a Christianized social order. Comprehension of society as evolving, as process, indefinitely plastic, subject to choice, will, and decision, gripped Rauschenbusch's imagination with something of the same power that swayed earlier evangelical imaginations confronted by America as a great new field for missions. "Without such a conception of the evolution of social institutions any larger idea of social regeneration could hardly enter the minds of men." [16] Rauschenbusch went on to say that "the modern socialist movement is really the first intelligent, concerted and continuous effort to reshape society in accordance with the laws of social development." But it was not necessary

for his fellow prophets to adopt his personal socialism to feel
the fullness of the times. Society was the target, the system was
the mission.

Of course the idea of a Christian society was not new, as
Geneva, the Puritan Commonwealth, and Puritan Massachusetts,
to recall only the most pertinent, proved. In fact, once the words
"Christian society" are uttered, it is remembered that the ideal,
in form, had never been absent. For every society of Christians
there had been Christian apology. The difference between the
"Christianized social order" envisioned by Rauschenbusch and
the Christian social order of the medieval thousand years was
plain, however. For Rauschenbusch, the Christianized social order
would display in all its parts the touch of human will. Christian
apology did not make the order Christian; only Christian action
could. To take a word from the Christian sociology that Rauschenbusch, Americanized Baptist from a German Lutheran past, discarded, there were no "Orders" at all. Natural law was not Christian sociology. The difference between the Christian order of
Geneva and the order of Rauschenbusch was also plain. Whatever the adequacy of their social engineering, the men of Geneva
had not lacked confidence in their will. They applied it to every
part of their social world. But the men of Geneva had not understood the teachings of Jesus, by which the will ought to be
directed. They had used the wrong blueprints. Jesus had
preached a social order touched in all its parts by love, permitting,
sustaining, fostering in its members the life that Jesus taught the
heart to lead. The decisive new Word breaking into history was
a Word of command upon both will and love, to enter all society,
as power.

Never given to bold expectations without later qualifications,
Rauschenbusch hedged, at least by implication, on his hopes for
the immediate rewards to be won from the new insights: "Sociology is still an infant science." Yet, like the men to whom his enthusiasm was indebted—the sociologists and pragmatists of the
late nineteenth century, with the philosophers of the Enlightenment behind them—Rauschenbusch had assumed that infancy
meant inevitable fulfillment. If it would take time to develop

the infant science, and more time to apply it universally, still the decisive stage had already been reached. The process itself was equivalent, almost, to the goal. The religious symbol for the goal was the "Kingdom," in Rauschenbusch's usage, that lay ahead as a universal society but was also, as the Bible had it, "within," as imaginative, present possession. Rauschenbusch believed that the turning point had been reached, and for him this did not mean that society stood far from its salvation but as close as every individual who has made his "decision."

Rauschenbusch did not believe society could be Christianized merely by the power of the Word alone. Preaching was not politics. Nor was social science politics. In the 1920's, and still more in the 1930's, the pastors would search for some adequate conjunction of the Word with power. The search often would be futile, and the Word would end up still floating in abstraction. Perhaps more often the search would be dangerous, the Word imperiled by its alliances. Trust in the validity of the Word itself was so strong, however, that the search was always for the same thing: politics aimed directly at religion, ultimately politics that was in itself religious.

In order to measure the morale with which the pastors first embarked on their search in the postwar world, we cannot do better than glance briefly at the report of the Federal Council of Churches, *The Church and Industrial Reconstruction*. It is always useful to know whether and how the imagination of powerful individuals like Rauschenbusch can be assimilated on less inspired levels. In the council's report, prophecy underwent its apparently inevitable modern fate by being put in the hands of a committee, the council's Committee on the War and the Religious Outlook. Directly engaged in producing the report were Alva Taylor, social-service secretary of the Disciples of Christ; President W. H. P. Faunce of Brown University, who had delivered a social-gospel oration before the Northern Baptists in 1919; F. Ernest Johnson of the Federal Council's social-service commission; W. E. Hocking, philosopher at Harvard; Frank Crouch of the council; J. Howard Melish, Episcopal clergyman in

Brooklyn; and H. N. Shenton, Columbia University sociologist.
The committee issuing the report included Harry Emerson Fosdick; Charles Gilkey and Shailer Mathews of the University of
Chicago; Francis J. McConnell, destined to be one of the great
postwar leaders of Methodism as well as of the social gospel;
Charles Macfarland of the council; John R. Mott, Y.M.C.A.
leader; Frank Mason North of the council; and Henry Churchill
King of Oberlin. The actual drafting of the report was the work
of Samuel McCrae Cavert, secretary of the committee as well as
of the Federal Council of Churches.

Written as a *Summa,* an American counterpart to the Arch-
bishops' "Inquiry" in England, the report was offered as a comprehensive general directive to social-gospel agents at large. In
style it achieved a kind of neutral transparency, without heat,
without rhetorical shorthand, without intensity, literal and un-
literary to a fault. In this, it was similar to many high social-gospel
tracts, due not merely to its birth by committee, but to the faith
in method, in light, in science, to a confidence that all crucial
turning points had already been passed. The very organization of
the report expressed this confidence, beginning in scholastic
fashion with first principles, moving to deductions, then specifying practical implications in detail. In scholastic fashion, the
concrete data found in the report served illustrative rather than
inductive purposes. None of this violated an old evangelical
orientation: the report had no historical dimension. As always for
the evangelical, the time was "now," that perpetual present when
the absolute deed of salvation can always occur. All historical
overview of the vast problems discussed was consigned to an ap-
pendix by Frank Crouch, "The Historic Attitude of the Church to
Economic Questions."

In an attempt to make explicit what, in many social-gospel
tracts, was left vague, the report opened with a discussion of the
religious grounding of social principles. God is the Lord of all
life, of both worlds, material as well as spiritual. "Mankind in all
its relations, therefore, must be organized according to the will
of God, as revealed in Christ. The entire social order must be
Christianized. The world as a whole is the subject of redemp-

tion." [17] With the authority of the Bible scholar Shailer Mathews behind the committee, the Biblical foundation for this view required no argument.

In Jesus' teaching on the Kingdom, three principles could be found. As a child of God, the human—his personality—was of sacred worth. Brotherhood was the primary and proper relation between man and man. The law for all social behavior was that of loving service. In these principles it was clear that Jesus conceived of the Kingdom as organic: individual salvation or self-development alone was impossible. Each man had to find his place in the organic kingdom before he could attain his true destiny as a child of God: ". . . personality can fulfill itself only in a social setting, its values be realized only in fellowship." [18]

The authors of the report, using their tests—personality, brotherhood, service—one by one proceeded to measure the economic system. The system did not pass its tests. Through irregular employment, inadequate wages, insufficient leisure, child labor, and long hours for women, the system stunted personalities. Inviting and depending upon a spirit of division and conflict—between capital and labor, within capital itself, within labor itself, and within the general public—it violated brotherhood. Finally, in its emphasis upon motives of self-interest, the economic system violated the spirit of service, engendering parasitical groups within the society and allowing its affairs to be managed autocratically rather than democratically.

This was a sweeping and, in some ways, penetrating criticism of the tradition of Amercian laissez-faire capitalism, and some men might have drawn radical conclusions. But at this point the committee drew a distinction: capitalism means on the one hand, it said, certain technical arrangements, such as large-scale factory production, the wage system, and ownership of the means of production by a few. It means on the other hand, however, certain moral and spiritual attitudes. Could, then, the spirit be changed without revolutionizing the technical forms? Could, in other words, the social gospel avoid a head-on anticapitalist position?

The report indicated that it could. Thus, although "property for power," concentrated in a few hands, deserved the sharpest criticism, "property for use" deserved respectful consideration. Similarly, the sufferings of labor were not necessarily the result of the wage system itself; freedom for the worker might be possible even within the terms of the wage system. Again, although competition had brought many evils, it might have value when set in context of some new ethical code, such as that of medicine or other professions. In general, if the inner spirit of the system could be transformed, common good replacing individual good, profit of the personality replacing material profit, the merely technical features of the system might deserve continued life.

How could such a transformation be brought about? "The Christian answer is that love is created by love. It is a self-perpetuating virtue, creating the same attitude in others." [19] This was a scholastic first principle only. The committee, intent upon realism, pointed out that Christians would meet with three sorts of men: those already guided by Christian motive, those who sought the same ideal social end but from different motives, and those of outright unsocial will. With the second, typified by labor movements, the Christian could and should coöperate. As to the third, the Christian should be consistent. His attitude toward the war of classes should be the same as his attitude toward international wars, for instance. Temporary use of second-best procedures was sometimes necessary—struggle was sometimes required—but of course struggle should be carried on without violence, within the limits set by law.

> Christianity does not deny that there is radical evil in human nature. Indeed, it emphasizes it. But it refuses to accept it as final. It is there to be changed and it can be changed, if only for a long enough time and in a thorough enough way we bring to bear upon it the principles of Jesus.[20]

The theory here was hardly precise. Asserting that "love creates love," then turning about to ask what love must do when it has not created love, the report simply anticipated years of confusion and debate. It would be on the question of the means appropriate to an ethic of love that the social gospel would first irreparably split. The obscurity in the report was a function of the larger unreadiness among its authors to press forward in clarification of the very rationale of the social gospel. Technical forms and inner spirit were not independent of each other: although the report did not deny this, it did not advance comprehension of their interdependence. The origins and character of the critical elements in the situation—motives—were not explained in terms of the interdependence. Was the unsocial will of men of the third category, with whom love was not enough, related to the structures of the system? Did the technical forms of the system pose no barriers to the influence of love? Then—reversing perspective —how did it happen that some men were evidently so free of the influence of the system that they could count on the purity of their own motives? The report only postponed such questions. It was still carried by enthusiasm for the ends.

The committee handled difficulties about the nature of the ultimate ideal by distinguishing immediate from more distant goals. Among immediate goals specified were items standard in Progressivism and liberalism: public-works programs and un-employment insurance, minimum-wage and maximum-hour codes, child-labor laws and laws regulating the work of women— all eventually realized nationally by the New Deal. A somewhat more striking immediate goal was expanded unions with collective bargaining, also eventually realized under the New Deal. For a longer future, however, the committee anticipated democratic industrial management through "works councils," together with redistribution of profits through profit-sharing and taxation. This began to undercut the distinction between the spirit and the technical forms of the system. In fact, the more distant the anticipated future, the more it seemed that the forms as well as the spirit were to be changed: ". . . some form of cooperation in the ownership of productive wealth is the completest expression of social control and is the ultimate goal most in keeping with the Christian ideal of brotherhood." [21]

An extension of terms already established by Progressives, Populists, and other moderate reformers, this nevertheless deserved to be called a "radical" vision. The committee was extremely cautious about "public ownership"—that is, formal state control of the economy. It was suspicious of the centralization of power in state socialism. Was it suggesting the outlines of a "democratic socialism"? It would be impossible to be certain, since in these visions of the longer future it became particularly difficult to ascertain the committee's ideas about the relationships between spirit and technical forms, between ethic and structural power. Thus, exactly why should power centralized in the state be dangerous, if the general sway of love had been established? Was it possible that the structure of centralized power had dangerous influences upon spirit? If that was so, was it not necessary to do justice to the reasons for such influences before counting on love as a reliable method? Again, the report was posing, not solving, problems.

A final question remained. What should the Christian do now, whatever the course of others? The answer was simple. Whether as employer, investor, employee, consumer, citizen, he should take the first step. "For the Christian to adopt higher social standards before others are willing to do so may involve financial loss and sacrifice, but to be ready to sacrifice for the good of mankind is an essential part of the Christian way of life . . ." [22] The role of the church was to help the individual be ready by embodying in its own life its own social ideal of brotherhood and loving service, thus helping its children to carry the free life of personality into the economic world.

Certain things about this conclusion were noteworthy. The committee neither asserted nor doubted the inclination of the Protestant congregations, in their actual social, economic, and political character, to undertake this task. It simply assumed such an inclination. Religious motives could be trusted to come first. In addition, the committee never questioned that good will would mean good method. Among Christians at large every individual could do something in his immediate station in life to advance social salvation. The sacrifices made by a businessman or a consumer, for instance, would mean more than his own personal spiritual enhancement; they would also contribute to solving the problems of the system. Men of good will would not, moreover, find themselves at loggerheads on questions of rational and technical method. If only men wanted them, right answers were available for everything.

In the 'twenties, and still more in the 'thirties, social-gospel leaders were to find themselves forced for the first time to face the possibility that Protestant congregations were not, after all, of suitable character to bear the ideal to victory. Also, there was the possibility that technical answers to moral problems of social organization were not always clear and immediately available or, when available, not necessarily moral.

In sum, the cool transparency of the report was misleading. Less clear in theory, less stable in assumptions than its authors thought it to be, the report was adapted to the mood of 1919 but not to the twenty years ahead. Like Rauschenbusch, the committee drew its confidence from a vision of expanding order; the very fact of the possibility of such a vision, the fact of its apparently rational, technical plausibility, gave strength to its plausibility as a political reality. That it was a spiritual possibility was not the business of the men of the social gospel to doubt.

Yet this concept of their evangel as a vision of expanding order hid from the eyes of the Protestant pastors a critical fact in their own origins. The social gospel had begun as much in fear of loss as in hope of gain, as much in anxiety as in hope. Behind the confidence of 1919 had worked a shock of limitation. The ambiguity of these origins helped sustain the ambiguity of the whole later enterprise of the social passion.

II

The Heritage

In the generation after the Civil War, Protestants still felt
themselves thoroughly at home. In their politics, their economics,
their ethics, their culture, they believed themselves in an assured
and ancient partnership with their society. America was a
Protestant country, marked throughout by the touch of religious
will. Differences in the sociology of this conviction were of small
account. Patterns of natural law, "the great ordinances of God
for the social organization of man," might be regarded as fixed
norms, to which the society nicely conformed. More positivis-
tically, the society might be regarded as the product of Protestant
men creating the forms of godly life. In either instance, Protestant
energy was understood to have inspired and to be maintaining the
community. The community was accepted as both the test of
good men and their sum.

The fields that the old religious energy was accustomed to patrol
no longer comprised the total society. Whole new reaches—above
all, those of industrialism—were not being permeated by the old
ethic and the former sanctions with even a small degree of the
power Protestantism had exercised in the farms, villages, market
towns, and merchant cities. Religious apology for these emerging

reaches was naturally quick to appear. The forms of industrial power were defended as simply further extensions of Protestant energy—proper fruits of the Protestant ethic at work. In the clerical argument for laissez faire,[1] dating from before the Civil War, there was, it is true, seed for that later degenerate flowering, the doctrine of the independence and autonomy of the economic sphere, as preached, for instance, in the 1920's by the National Association of Manufacturers.[2] By this doctrine, economic life rested upon "laws" of its own independent of religion altogether. This relegation of religion to a separate, circumscribed sphere constituted the fundamental heresy of the industrial world. Deeper apologies for industrial capitalism sought to avoid this. The laissez-faire market could be justified as a field for moral as well as economic and demibiological competition, as a proving ground for both the spiritually and the materialistically fit, as the Puritans had justified their own more closely controlled markets. But to this atomization of society into competitive units, various "gospels" were generally added, in obedience not to logic but to tradition, to prudence, and even—at least in part—to human solidarity. The gospel of wealth, the gospel of stewardship, and even the gospel of service that was to appear in the 'twenties, were all efforts to preserve the fabric, or at least the illusion, of a society unified by morality, of a culture informed by religious meaning and morale.[3]

Industrialism, however, called all apologies into question more vividly than had the economies of the past. The great labor strikes of the 'seventies, 'eighties, and 'nineties testified to the breakdown of harmony, to the rise of forces beyond containment. The early articulate reaction of Protestant spokesmen to the labor strife of that period concentrated upon its violence and disorder. This was anarchy, and it was to be dealt with according to the moral logic of social order. Let the strikers be taught patience, humility, thrift, diligence, and, above all, good order. If necessary, let them taste force. This response came from orthodox quarters—though not from all orthodox quarters—in what seemed a perfectly logical application of traditional views of sinful human nature. It came also from liberal quarters. Henry Ward Beecher, leading preacher of his day and champion of evolution in theology, stood as a warning against any temptation to think that liberal religion drew men into liberal politics. On the contrary, religious liberalism had gone much further than orthodoxy in trying to devise a religious description of the facts of the industrial age, without trying to change them. Liberalism usually provided a more intelligible, less disturbing rationale for the standing order than did orthodoxy. Beecher did not fall short of blessing force.[4]

In this "hard" response was fear of anarchy from below; it would be sentimental to imagine that the social-gospel pastors never felt it. It persisted clearly into the 'twenties. But from the time of Washington Gladden's first statements on the labor question in 1876, another emotion was apparent as well. The new industrial society was frustrating evangelism. It was placing too many men out of religious reach.

Gladden, a country boy, had come in to preach in Brooklyn. He knew the mill laborers of North Adams and Springfield and the strikers of the Ohio Hocking Valley. Gladden's later congregations were always of the comfortable middle class; in Columbus not the strikers but their bosses were his flock. Nonetheless, Gladden had known the others, he had tried to reach them, and he was aware of them as men with legitimate grievances against the system—grievances that numbed them to the meaning of his message. Rauschenbusch also as a youth had bathed in the open air of the older world, and then spent eleven years at the little Baptist church on West 45th Street, in the area known as Hell's Kitchen. Leaving to spend the rest of his life in the academy, he had with him a modern picture of damnation against which to compose his theology for the modern heaven. Harry Ward held his pulpit in the "stockyards" church of Methodism, on Union Avenue in Chicago, before going on to Oak Park and then into the academy. Although Reinhold Niebuhr's Bethel Evangelical Church in Detroit was by no means a proletarian parish, he knew the workers at the Ford plants during his thirteen years of service, and did not forget them once he moved on to Union Theological Seminary. Perhaps more than any others, these four men marked stages in the creative logic of the social gospel, and they all had their experience with the frontiers of evangelism. There were many others, early and late: Herbert Casson in Lynn from the 'seventies, Charles Stelzle of the Bowery from the 'nineties, Norman Thomas preaching Presbyterianism on the East Side before the First World War. Kirby Page, on the European battle fronts of 1916 and 1917, lived through still another, new-style frustration, one that was eventually to become as critical for the social gospel as industrialism. The Protestant ministry came, and largely continued to come in the 1920's and 1930's, from older preserves of American society, from unspoiled villages and small Protestant towns, and their shock in early manhood, upon recognition of the new world, was an experience steadily repeated.[5] The social gospel had perhaps more than its fair share of academic leaders, of immaculate theorists, of church executives, and of pastors insulated in middle-class parishes, but there was also some sense of the evangelical frontiers to leaven abstract theory.

Evangelism foundered on the condition of certain men—the men of North Adams and of Hell's Kitchen, of Pittsburgh and of Homestead. Society was cutting men off from the Word; certain areas of the culture could not be reached. Institutional churches, settlement houses, and missions in the new urban chaos were late-nineteenth-century efforts to touch the new audiences, but this was not sufficient strategy for Christianizing the social order. John Wesley's old tactics for the workers of England were rejected. Wesley made no attacks on the society of which his miners and millworkers were presumably members; Wesley drove, straight to the individual heart, to transmute it, then left it where he found it to work out its social, earthly fate as it would. Wesley certainly had clear notions as to what this fate, following conversion, would be. The converted wage earner would work his way out to middle-class freedom. But this followed rather than preceded the fact that he drove directly through the social barriers.[6]

Not new religious theory inspired the social-gospel but a kind of global intuition of the situation Protestantism faced in its scale, its depth, and its structural character. Accidental factors alone would have been enough to turn pastors into new channels. Wesley's proletarian audiences, for instance, had been tuned to

Protestant rhetoric and English traditions. In America, many of
the new masses not only had no Protestant or American memories
but hardly knew the English language. What preaching could
reach them? No Protestant church ever succeeded in its foreign-
language missions. None reaped important harvests from its
institutional churches or its settlement houses.

Early social-gospel leaders were uneasy about disorder from
below and about the limits upon evangelism defined by the new
industrial labor classes. They were uneasy in another way too,
which divided them more decisively from liberal apologists for
the new order. From the standpoint of the past, anarchy in the
late nineteenth century was advancing as much from above as
from below. By no means adequately justified within the old
moral logic, men of immense new power and organizations of
unprecedented scale and influence had appeared within the community. The context for the Protestantism of individualistic piety
—whatever its theology—was not only a social economy in which
each generation could expect to rise, but was also a social economy
in which the classes that had risen could expect to hold their
positions. In the dazzling heroes of the gospel of success, men
could find individualistic economy justified, but they also found
established security threatened.

The wish for stability was perfectly apparent in the early
social gospel. The books of Gladden breathed the cool, benign
pieties of the comfortable parishes of Springfield and Columbus;
he preached for protection of the parish as well as for redemption
of the *proles*. Many churchmen rallied to Edward Bellamy's
nationalism; the projection, in Bellamy's coldly formal, static
utopianism, of a middle-class dream of security, inspired by growing anxiety and insecurity, cannot now be overlooked. The new
order for which Rauschenbusch yearned amounted to a universalization of the culture of the Protestant town. He, like the others,
assumed a high degree of identity between the prudential interests
of that culture and the interests of the humanitarian-evangelical
heart.[7] There was a deep investment of doctrine in an established
community. In their most extreme demands, social-gospel leaders

would continue to take this investment for granted, count on it, take from it much of their courage.

This defensive interest does not "explain" the social gospel, however, for the churchmen were defending not simply the achievements of a tradition but its principles as well. Actually, they were engaged in trying to carry their tradition through to completion.

As fortification for their claim that Christian faith meant self-conscious direction of society, the social-gospel pastors were fortunate enough to have nineteenth-century German Bible scholarship at hand.[8] This scholarship seemed to show a much greater interest on the part of Jesus Christ in the salvation of society than the churches of individualistic piety had realized. Shailer Mathews' *The Social Teachings of Jesus* (1897) and Francis Greenwood Peabody's *Jesus Christ and the Social Question* (1900) were the two best-known American works claiming direct gospel foundations. Here and there men discovered that Jesus had been a socialist and that the gospel text contained the outlines of one or another explicit reorganization of the economy. For the most part it was enough that the teachings of Jesus be understood to contain measures by which to judge the social order.

American clergymen contributed relatively little to this scholarship. The deeper rationale for their rejection of laissez faire lay in their own history. Both liberal and orthodox Protestantism in America had emphasized the will. Established powers over and above and outside the individual—preëminently established churches and the paternal state—had been rejected as alien to a Protestant philosophy of authority, obstacles to the expression of power by the individual. This long-range drive had worked to disintegrate Calvinist theocratic authority internally, in New England even more than in other Calvinist lands, and thereafter had served to encourage the individual to act on his own, alert against false powers and privileges from without even more than against false voices from within.

This was the very foundation of laissez faire. But laissez faire was not a logically ultimate conclusion to such a morale, for it drew a line beyond which the will was not supposed to go, a line logically and wholly arbitrary. Where official church and paternal state had imposed harmony before, theories of "natural" harmony were substituted; this, after all, was celebration of only a negative triumph in the logic. Laissez faire restricted the will and would hold men of the holy imagination only so long as it guaranteed its own fruits. It was beginning to fail to do so. In the great strikes, and in the monopolization of power and opportunity, natural harmonies were sounding dissonance. In calling for deliberate, self-conscious direction of the whole social economy, the social-gospel leaders were true to the heart of their longer tradition. Let the will be extended once more, in a final advance, upon society as a whole.

As support for this cry, the social science of the nineteenth century was more important than Bible scholarship. Not enough work has yet been done to measure the immediate Protestant backgrounds of many of the social scientists themselves. If Lester Ward, setting forth the concept of social control quite directly, rejected all religious dimensions in his ethics, many of his professional colleagues did not. With Rauschenbusch the alliance became prophecy—a climax, not a betrayal, of the Protestant religion of will.[9]

Shaping the vision of a new social order, then, was a mixture of motives. Behind the exalted sense of possibility lay much more than pure vision alone—anxiety, prudence, and temporary defeat. In giving themselves over to a language of pure religious idealism, the pastors veiled these origins, with the effect of obscuring their own interests from themselves.

This can be seen in the council's report, *The Church and Industrial Reconstruction*, in which three different kinds of criticism of the economic system were quite distinct. The first might be called analysis of alienation—the alienation of man from man, of man from God, and of man from himself. Forced by the system to act on lower rather than higher motives, men were alienated from their true selves. Forced to treat their fellows as commodities, tools, and means, men were alienated from each other. Alienated in these ways, men were alienated from the essential processes of being—that is, from God. Here the system was judged by the religious test of the absolute worth of personality, and here most of the rhetoric of the social gospel clustered.

The second kind of criticism might be called analysis of disorder. The report, as had the early leaders, often criticized "competition" as an offense against love. Actually, competition was a euphemistic designation for evils of another sort. Conflict, violence, and open coercion were shocking in themselves. Beneath the surface of hope and enthusiasm lay the disquieted feeling of potential anarchy. This concern for order rarely appeared in straightforward frankness, however, but was taken up in the personalist analysis of alienation. Its influence could be seen plainly in the committee's formal isolation of the problem of the methods for social change. All the early prophets had so isolated it, often in considerable perturbation. The formal solution to the problem was to make the end of conflict simultaneous with the end of impersonality and alienation. Thus to work immediately against conflict could be identical with working immediately for the personalized social order. No hard choices had to be made. The possibility that conflict might have a role in serving the ideal could be ignored. The further possibility could also be ignored —that restoration of order might be attractive enough to be acceptable without being perfect enough to embody the personalist ideal.

A third type of analysis fell somewhere between the other two. If the first—alienation—might be called psychological, and the second—disorder—might be called political, this third level was plainly economic and was concerned with injustice. Here the system was charged with its failure to provide men with money, with goods, with work itself. Statistics of income distribution, of real wages, of annual incomes, of hours, and of unemployment had appeared in many earlier social-gospel manuals, bulletins, and books, and would continue to do so. Sometimes the crux of everything was assumed to reside in this third level. The dean of Yale Divinity School, Charles R. Brown, said: "We all know that

if every man had all that he earns by actual service rendered
to society by the labor of hand or brain, and if no man had any
more than he earns . . . the whole industrial question would be
settled." [10] On this level everything came under a judgment of
rights, function, fair shares.

In its casual, un-self-conscious, even unconscious, amalgamation
of all three ideals, the council's report faithfully repeated a leading
pattern of the early social-gospel mind. That mind expressed itself
most readily in terms of the personalist ideal, conceiving its obstacles in terms of motive, calculating its tactics in terms of
motive, defining its ends in terms of motive. This allowed for
a certain formal intellectual consistency. To solve the problem of
motive, presumably, was to solve all problems. By definition, love
meant order and justice. Since love solved everything, the fact
that the social gospel had been inspired in the first place partly
by apprehension of disorder and limitation as well as by idealistic
hope could be forgotten. But order might well be restored short
of both justice and love. Even justice might be achieved short of
love. The social gospel had not made distinctions between these
three measures of social achievement; they were fused unconsciously, as in the council's report. This unconsciousness was
the leading fact. It left open the possibility that visions of mere
order and mere justice could be given absolute religious sanction
unknowingly. The possibility came true. By 1932, the differences
between order and justice and, even more important, between
justice and love, had entered into the debate in which the social
gospel disintegrated.

The search for realistic politics stemmed in part from these
ambiguities in the original idealism of the social gospel, and the
search helped force those ambiguities into the open.

Before the First World War the prophets largely believed that
in proclaiming the Word they were proclaiming inevitable reality.
God was love, God was in life, and life was essentially an evolutionary process working toward unification of ideal and real.
Behind these identities of holy imagination was fact—the fact
that they were not identities in fact. But a generation for whom

Darwin could be taken to confirm what religious liberals had long been ready to believe—the progressive power of immanent process—could only have felt eventual harmony rather than present tensions to be the more fruitful theme of their preaching. Again, Rauschenbusch summed up an era, declaring the idea of evolutionary social fulfillment the single greatest insight of the modern Christian mind (although Jesus had anticipated it). In this, as in all else, he was more complex and subtle than his formulas usually indicated, the evolutionary process including, for him, support of a third party and of labor unions. But until the war it had rarely seemed necessary to face the realities of power directly.

They had to be faced sooner or later, however. Society had power over spirit. Evangelism was being frustrated. Laissez-faire capitalism did not allow Christian living. A tug of war was going on between preaching and the system. These were the central insights of the social-gospel pastors, and to act upon them implied changes in evangelical strategy.

The wrestle of Francis Greenwood Peabody with the problem of strategy in 1900 revealed how politics would have to be faced, despite all efforts to avoid it. In *Jesus Christ and the Social Question*, Peabody insisted firmly that Jesus' method was the conversion of the individual heart in direct, personal evangelism. Such direct conversion must remain the method; what had to be changed was simply its content—from the old gospel of individualistic piety and salvation to the social gospel. Once men were converted to the correct gospel, right social relations would emerge. This, Peabody said, rather than a strategy of large-scale social reorganization independent of such conversion, was the Christian method of change.[11]

These were, clearly, not all the alternatives. What would the men so converted eventually do? At some point they would be sufficient—in numbers, wisdom, power, and spirit, presumably— to undertake those reforms of the system to which their personal conversion called them. As converted men, they would make best use of their resources to reshape the system, and thereby they would, willy-nilly, bring all those still unconverted, still corrupted by the old system, under the influence of the new. Peabody had no ground whatever for rejecting such social action of the converted as un-Christian. To have pushed his own logic to its conclusion would have been to demand a universal, unanimous conversion, which was what the social gospel had seen was impossible in the first place.

Peabody's real anxiety was to insist that the change wrought in men by a reform in their social environment was not equivalent to the change wrought by Christian conversion. But he had failed to confront the idea that ultimate Christian conversion might, in some instances and in some ways, have to wait upon earlier changes in the society. In this failure not only Peabody, but all the early social-gospel leaders, were exposed to a climactic danger. The prophets could not persist in believing the method of personal conversion a substitute for large-scale change and politics. In trying to make their peace with politics, however, they were left tempted to carry into politics their ultimate religious aims, and to identify politics and social conversion with religious conversion of the heart.

The temptation to adopt "environmental" strategy was strong from the start, primarily because the social gospel had risen in response to the system's power to frustrate evangelism. By 1919, attempts like Peabody's to restrict the faith to the old-fashioned techniques of individual evangelization, to restrict it from politics, were being rejected, and so long as the amalgamation of love with justice and order remained uninspected, the climactic danger remained alive. Logically, the turn to politics involved several problems of strategy. One might have been called "dialectical": how to adjust as between individual conversion and broad manipulation of the environment; another, "sociological": how to recognize the most likely candidates for immediate individual conversion under present conditions; and another, "chronological": when and how the tactics of social change could and should be supplemented and completed by individual conversion.

No such distinctions had appeared, hidden as they were in the glow of the purely religious rhetoric and in the faith in the inevitability of God's process. One more thing contributed. In deploring the alienation caused by the system, were the pastors thinking of all men? Was the alienation of the labor market universal? Was the alienation of great wealth and autocratic power universal? Similarly, were disorder and injustice everywhere pervasive? The evil symptoms of the system seemed rather to cluster at the poles. What lay between? Chapters iii and iv study the social-gospel approach to the poles—capital and labor. Chapter v will indicate how these efforts to get into some sort of realistic relationship with these two centers of alienation were heavily conditioned by what the pastors assumed of the middle. Perhaps here, between the poles, were people already converted, or at least not yet corrupted by the system.

In this hope the intention of the social gospel in its wrestle with politics was revealed. What was sought was a conjunction of righteousness and power, a fusion of the Word with politics, and it was this search that led onto the rocks. Criticism of a religion that could inspire such a search came to constitute a main feature of the new self-consciousness of the 'thirties.

Where were the men who were to live out this tale? By 1919 they had won some reasonably stable positions for themselves in the church community, and it is helpful to have some sense of what these positions were, and of their limits. They suggest a measure both of the realism of the prophets and of their problems.

The social gospel was inherently nondenominational. But the problem facing all Protestants whose guiding concerns transcended denominational boundaries was that the most effective facilities and most available channels for evangelism and action were still denominational. To begin this checklist with denominational homes is therefore the fairest way of indicating the outreach of the social gospel in the 'twenties, even though in almost every instance social-gospel impulses submerged traditional divisions. It is not really necessary to know that Walter Rauschenbusch, for instance, was a Baptist in order to understand Rauschenbusch. That he was a Baptist is of interest simply as proof that the Baptists could support one of the greatest of the prophets despite the fact that the Baptist clergy gave proportionately few men to the social gospel.

The Northern Methodist Church, on the other hand, was favorable ground. Methodism had long combined evangelical energy with organizational strength, and theologically the Methodist principle of leaving the test of faith to personal experience saved the church from the worst of the struggles over liberalism. Partly because of this tradition, combining warmth of heart with efficiency, Methodist pastors still had some sense of mission as Methodists that was compatible with the more general mission of the liberal social gospel. Rauschenbusch had paid them a special compliment, which they repeated more than once:

> The Methodists are likely to play a very important part in the social awakening of the American churches . . . They have rarely backed away from a fight when the issue was clearly drawn between Jehovah and Diabolus . . . Their leaders are fully determined to form their battalions on the new line of battle, and when they march the ground will shake.[12]

Rauschenbusch's use of the future tense had been right, for Methodist pastors had not been first in the fight. They appeared where Methodists, gradually developing some middle-class and liberal congregations, first came into steady contact with the unhappier symptoms of the new economic order. If then they drew on the perfectionism that had spread widely in comfortable Methodist circles before the Civil War, they like the other prophets were responding to danger as well. Ferment began in the 'nineties. Denominational magazines began to discuss the sociology of Jesus. Frank Mason North spearheaded Methodist attention to the problems of the swelling cities. Beginning in 1892, the New York East Conference introduced reports on social questions and continued to emit reports until by the early days of the New Deal it was adopting the most extreme positions of any regular official church body in Protestantism. Members of New York East in these early days were North, who was later to serve as president of the Federal Council, and Bishop Herbert Welch, first president of the Methodist Federation for Social Service. This was a nice demonstration of the sociology of the social gospel. New York City, although a center of Methodist revivals before the Civil War, was being lost as a typical Methodist —and indeed Protestant—preserve, and here the ferment centered. It was not close to the heart of popular Methodist culture.

Welch and North, together with Worth Tippy and Ernest Zaring in Ohio and Harry Ward in Chicago, envisioned an "attempt to do for our day what the early temperance societies and the Abolition Society did for their era," and formed the Methodist Federation for Social Service in December, 1907.[13] The federation became prophetic headquarters within Methodism, an outpost against Diabolus, and itself a storm center, a line of battle, eventually the most extreme of the institutional personalities of the social gospel. Most of the Methodist prophets were associated with it in some way: Bishops Herbert Welch, Edgar Blake, Francis J. McConnell; editors Dan Brummit and Halford Luccock of the *Christian Advocates*, L. O. Hartman of *Zion's Herald*, George Elliott of the *Methodist Review;* teachers and officials, including H. F. Rall and Georgia Harkness of Garrett, E. S. Brightman of Yale, Charles McConnell of Boston; settlement workers, such as Mary McDowell, Lucy Meyer, and Helen Murray; preachers of the leading churches of Methodism, such as Ernest Fremont Tittle of Evanston, Charles Webber of New York, and G. Bromley Oxnam of Los Angeles. These were not the men who made the federation what it was, but they supported it, fought for it when necessary, preserved for it a rare liberty and prestige. None of them followed it when its work carried it into strange ways, but they defended its original courage.

The federation was the work of one man above all. From his stockyards church on Union Avenue, Chicago, Harry Ward moved to Euclid Avenue in Oak Park, a model of the new suburban civilization at that moment when its attitude toward the "system" had not been fixed. From Oak Park, Ward went to Boston University, then to Union Theological Seminary in New York where he remained until 1944. From 1912 he served as executive secretary of the federation. The visible shift of federation perspective, from a prewar emphasis upon reform, social service, and the socialization of evangelism, to emphasis upon outright opposition to capitalism as such was Ward's shift. He moved from the stockyards church and a settlement house, symbols of service, to the American League Against War and Fascism, symbol of revolution.

The federation prepared reports for the quadrennial conferences of the denomination, held its own conferences—the quadrennials in Evanston, 1922, 1926, 1930, constituting leading events of the social gospel—and published its own small paper, *Social Service Bulletin.*[14]

The federation had freedom in the church. It was an authorized agent of the denomination, hence "official," yet it received no financial support from the denomination and its administration was autonomous. It was thus nearly invulnerable to coercion from official leaders. This freedom was important, but it also meant a precarious existence. Dependent wholly upon the contributions of its individual members, its budget was never large —$15,000 in 1923 was a peak. In 1933 it nearly foundered.

The Methodist Board of Temperance, Prohibition and Public Morals drew vastly greater support in all ways from the church at large. The federation's freedom was due in truth to a kind of indifferent neglect. Its position was like that of the Methodist prophets generally. Self-conscious, articulate, often provided with great churches and high offices, they were atypical within their own church. They spoke from an urban Methodism, a highly educated Methodism, in a church yet predominantly of village and town and of a ministry whose training primarily remained that of earlier days. The strength of the passion within Methodism arose in part from this fact, that the areas of most intense social-gospel challenge were not typically Methodist areas, and thus were free.

Episcopalianism spawned by all odds the largest number of church groups devoted to the social passion.[15] The American branch of the Church Association for the Advancement of the Interests of Labor (CAIL) was founded in 1887, on a British model, chiefly by Bishops Henry Potter and Frederic Huntington, and William Dwight Porter Bliss. Four years later, also on a British model, the Christian Social Union was formed, with Potter and Huntington again leaders. It was as secretary of the union that Bliss preached his Bellamy-ite socialism up and down the land for ten years. In 1901 the General Convention authorized a commission to study labor organizations. The 1910 convention converted this body into a Joint Commission on Social Service, and in 1913, with Frank M. Crouch appointed full-time secretary, the Joint Commission was made permanent. With this, the Social Union disbanded. The 1919 convention enlarged the Joint Commission into a Department of Social Service, with Charles Lathrop as secretary. When an industrial secretary, Charles Gilbert, was appointed in 1926, the Church Association disbanded.

Official Episcopal support for the social gospel did not surpass that of other denominations, however, and the leading Episcopal social-gospel groups were not official. The Church Socialist League had appeared shortly before the war, founded by Bernard Iddings Bell of Chicago and Franklin Spaulding, Paul Jones, and Vida Scudder of Wellesley. As it developed, the primary work of the league was to defend Jones, bishop of Utah, from attacks on his pacifism in 1917 and 1918. Like the Socialist party itself, this small league, split on the war, died in the early 'twenties. Its successor, the Church League for Industrial Democracy (CLID), was founded in New York in 1919 and survived tenaciously. In William B. Spofford it had an active and flavorful executive secretary, who was also managing editor of the *Witness*. Spofford was concerned with direct contact with labor, attended labor conventions, and visited strikes. The CLID was not a neutral investigating agent; it paid for advertisements in support of the striking railroad shopmen in 1922, and helped support the United Textile Workers in Passaic in 1926. Spofford did not control the CLID as Ward controlled the Methodist Federation, however; unlike Ward, when Spofford entered the League Against War and Fascism in the 'thirties, he could not carry the organization with him.[16] By 1921 the CLID held a choice 400 of the church; its president, Bishop Charles Williams of Michigan, was in many ways the denomination's leading prophet. Williams, unlike many in the CLID, was of the liberal, not the high-church, wing of the denomination. Edward Parsons, bishop of California, succeeded to the presidency upon Williams' death in 1924. Dean Ladd of the Berkeley Divinity School remained a member, despite pressure from his trustees to resign. Other members and officers were Paul Jones, bishop without a diocese following his resignation from Utah; Percy Stickney Grant of New York; J. Howard Melish of Brooklyn; Vida Scudder; and Mary Van Kleeck of the Russell Sage Foundation. Late in the 'twenties membership reached 1,500, of which some 650 were associates from other denominations.

Socialist and generally high-church, the CLID represented a variant upon the passion found in no other group. A kind of duplication of socialist, high-church activities carried on for decades in England, it exhibited the living tie between American and English Anglicanism. The imitation lacked what the English model had—an active political movement by which it could check and clarify its evangel: English liberal politics and eventually the British Labour party. Consequently, in its conferences with labor and business leaders, in its operating vocabulary, in its chosen heroes on the American scene, the CLID blended with the rest of the passion completely. It had, or chose, no chance to drive its socialist orientation beyond the general pieties of the passion. Where the CLID differed was in its theological grounding; following Episcopal doctrines of the Incarnation and of the church, high-church prophets stood apart from the mainstream; the doctrine of the church in particular excused these prophets from much of the wrestle and torment of the evangelical passion concerning the role of the church and the church community in pursuit of the social ideal that is. The CLID was from the beginning acutely conscious of itself as sect within the church; its actions and hopes were not persistently based upon the assumption that its standards had necessarily to be adopted soon within the congregations. It was perhaps for this reason that the CLID remained a handful of members. Otherwise, in the denomination at large, the Episcopal witness was indistinguishable from others, and in fact relatively quiescent in the postwar period. In a way it was the Methodist situation in reverse. As exceptions within the denomination, the Methodist urban and Eastern churches and offices bequeathed a certain freedom. Including many industrial managers, the Episcopal laity offered fewer such enclaves to its pastors. Early Episcopal leadership was beginning to provoke conservative lay reactions. Dean Ladd of Berkeley was one who survived pressure; Paul Jones did not. Mercer Johnson, Percy S. Grant, Irwin St. John Tucker, and Harold Brewster were others translated into the secular world under pressure.

Congregationalists had given leaders to the passion early and continued to give them in the 'twenties.[17] The relative lack of "official," institutional expression was due more to the constitutional nature of Congregationalism than to the standing of the social gospel. The denomination had a Department of Social Relations, with Hubert Herring as secretary. The 1925 social creed of the Congregationalist National Council was one of the few official declarations of special note. A product of a committee of the Social Service Commission, the 1925 declaration was offered to all Federal Council denominations for discussion, and was used by the Reformed Church as a model for its creed of 1926 and by the Methodists in 1928. Passed despite suggestions that it might "alienate the manufacturers of Connecticut who are friends of the Congregational church," the report denounced unlimited freedom of private property, called for unemployment and old-age insurance and the eight-hour day, defended collective bargaining, and demanded a share in management for labor. The only new official denominational organization of significance in the 'thirties was to be the Congregationalist Council for Social Action, the old social-service commission revamped and expanded. In fact, the Council for Social Action came to constitute the one really official denominational agent in social-gospel history in a position to try for thoroughgoing evangelization of its own church.

An official department, commission, or board was standard in other denominations. The Disciples had a Board of Temperance and Social Welfare, with Alva Taylor as secretary. The Northern Baptists had a Division of Social Education; Samuel Zane Batten, second only to Rauschenbusch among the Baptist prophets, was director until his death in 1924, and John W. Elliott succeeded him. The Northern Presbyterians had a Department of City, Immigrant and Industrial Work. All of them official, none of these bodies began to compare with the semiofficial Methodist Federation. No denomination spawned groups similar, in separate sectarian rigor, to the Episcopal CLID until late in the 'thirties.

With the death of Batten, the Baptists did not seek an official leader of dominating social-gospel character. The Baptist department came to deal with Prohibition, recreation, and sumptuary morality. Despite the fact that the Northern Baptists included many laboring men, usually skilled or semiskilled, the denomination's tradition of congregational independence made it difficult to organize any official agencies; in addition, the church, closer to its individualistic evangelical origins, had fewer liberalized sectors than others. Its character allowed a Rauschenbusch or a Batten to survive but not to organize church purposes.

The Northern Presbyterian department was not in fact a social-gospel agency at all. The denomination, worst shaken in the fundamentalist controversy, could not afford one for political reasons, and the department held to a kind of inner-mission evangelism and charity. The showplace of Presbyterian social interest remained the Labor Temple in New York, directed by Edmund Chaffee after the war, but the denomination had cast it off onto its New York synod. Atypical pulpits could rarely flourish within the tighter organization of Presbyterianism, and so long as the glory of Presbyterianism continued to consist in part of a loyalty to orthodoxy greater than that of the Congregationalists, the field for the social gospel among its pastors tended to be stony. All this was compounded wherever its congregations shifted toward the conservatism of high urban social status.

The Disciples board carried on mild education within the denomination. Its secretary, Alva Taylor, ranked high in social-gospel circles, not as a Disciples officer, but as a writer and worker beyond the jurisdiction of his secretaryship. Midwestern, nonurban Disciples had fewer of the kinds of experience that had inspired the social gospel among others. Nevertheless, with a tradition of broad, nondogmatic witness, without tight organization, the Disciples could allow social-gospel energy to course out beyond their own body, above all into the greatest of all social-gospel organs, the *Christian Century*.

In the Evangelical Synod of North America, an authorized Commission on Christianity and Social Problems dated from 1921, a social creed from 1925. The Reformed Church in the United States maintained a commission to organize local groups and socialize church education. Both the Evangelical Synod (the church of Reinhold and Richard Niebuhr) and the Reformed Church were strongly ecumenical in spirit; both belonged to the Federal Council, and both were traditionally open to theological liberalism. The ferment of the social gospel ran high in both ministries; on what few statistical tests there were, the pastors of the Evangelical Synod and the Reformed Church were rivaled among the major denominations only by the pastors of Northern Methodism.[18] Of all the denominations descended from the Continent, of non-English-speaking origins, these two alone gave men to the social gospel.

Elsewhere historical, social, and theological conditions combined to present the social gospel a barren field. Thus Lutheranism as a whole, and not merely Missouri Synod Lutheranism, persisted in its historic reluctance to engage upon affairs of the state and the world and until late in the 'thirties gave no leaders to the cause.[19] Among Southern Baptists fundamentalism, extreme congregationalism, extreme rural constituencies, and casual clerical training combined to inhibit the social passion completely. Southern Methodism and Southern Presbyterianism, combining the first and often to a degree the third and fourth factors, began to yield up leaders only in the 'thirties.

On social and economic grounds, then, denominational character might limit fields of action, might particularly obscure or expose certain emphases, might suggest variations in tactics or rhetoric, but such character was not reflected in the basic problems of the social gospel examined here. The social-gospel pastors spoke out of a shared and common need, and for them the social gospel was intended to shape a new church.

In the century past, shared and common need had often inspired shared and common Protestant efforts: interdenominational preaching, common labor, and mutual forbearance on the frontier; organized common assault upon liquor; interdenominational expansion of Sunday schools. Once successful, such efforts often fell back into denominational patterns, but they revealed what lay at the heart of the evangelical century—a drive outward as well as inward, the imperative to missionize, the vision of the world as Church. By the last third of the century, common effort had become habitual, as genuinely a part of Protestant structure as denominationalism, usually as response to the demand for extended, if not "entire," sanctification. The social gospel constituted simply the broadest concept of the challenge—the challenge of the social system—and it had risen together with the movement issuing in the Federal Council of Churches of Christ in America.

The Federal Council offered the social gospel its highest platform.[20] At its first session, in 1908, President Frank Mason North delivered a social-gospel address, "The Church and Modern Industry." At the same time the council adopted its famous Social Creed, taken over from the Methodists. In the 'twenties, the council rostrum was open to social-gospel leaders of all varieties for frequent use. Harry Ward, Reinhold Niebuhr, and Kirby Page were associates at one time or another, despite their differences with each other. The council published the *Federal Council Bulletin,* in which the social gospel could be aired, as well as social-gospel books and reports, although these publishing ventures were considerably reduced soon after the war. Shailer Mathews and Bishop McConnell served as council presidents.

The basic units of the council were its commissions, and the first, the Commission on the Church and Social Service, 1909, amounted to the commission for the social gospel. Charles Stelzle came from the Presbyterians' Department of Church and Labor as the first leader. Charles Macfarland became the first full-time secretary in 1911, succeeded by Worth Tippy soon after when Macfarland became secretary to the council as a whole. The original authorization of the commission defined it as a clearing house for information pertinent to the social interests of all the churches; from this rather indefinite sanction there developed the commission's main concerns during the 'twenties—labor relations and industrial relations generally. The commission's research department became a separate Department of Research and Education in 1924, with F. Ernest Johnson as secretary. Johnson was one of the tireless exponents of the passion and was ultimately to write one of the ablest—and the last—defenses of the liberal social gospel, *The Social Gospel Re-examined* of 1940. Through Tippy and Johnson, together with an industrial secretary, James Myers, who joined the research department in 1925, the council maintained a steady schedule of publications and conferences, and promoted discussion of labor, industrial, and social relations through the 'twenties and 'thirties. These commissions were well financed relative to the over-all budget of the council. In 1920 the Social Service Commission received $24,500 of the total budget of $324,000; $11,000 of this went to the research department. In 1924, the commission received $22,000, the newly independent research department $49,000. In 1932, with general retrenchment, the figures were $25,000 and $35,000. Through its *Information Service*, a small, four-page biweekly, the research department channeled social and economic data out to its mainly clerical subscribers, some 5,000 in the mid-1920's.

Since its existence offended many jealous for denominational integrity, the council had a tremendous concern for self-preservation. It also offended those who regarded it as the fruit of liberal theology. It was therefore never given power to enter the life of the churches below the highest levels, and never had continuing contact with ordinary local congregations. The result was to lend it a kind of freedom it could only half exploit, a freedom to support the social gospel but never really to lead it. It was in the council, therefore, that the social gospel often appeared most adjusted to the fact of what the council report of 1919, "The Church and Social Reconstruction," called the "wide and generally conservative membership" of the churches. This membership could be led but not driven, it said, and so prophecy had to be prudent. The enthusiasm of 1919 burned in the council, but there was never any danger that it would follow only visions ahead, forgetful of the flocks behind.

Council policy was a success, so far as survival was concerned. Only two member denominations ever expressed serious ob-

jections to the council's social gospel. The Southern Presbyterians
withdrew in 1912, returned in 1913 upon Charles Macfarland's
explanation of the true aims of the Commission for Social Service,
and withdrew again in 1919. The Lutheran General Synod withdrew in 1919 when it joined with other Lutheran groups to form
the United Lutheran Church, and the new United Lutherans
accepted only "consultative membership" on the recommendation
of its visiting committee, which found the council Calvinistic in
its view of the relations between church and state.[21]

With the exception of the Methodist Federation and the
Episcopal CLID, none of all these homes of the social gospel
allowed freedom for the inner logic to extend itself as it would.
A denominational social-service board was not the place where
a man could sacrifice all to ultimate possibilities. Among individual scholars and teachers within some of the seminaries, as at
Union Theological Seminary, a freer ferment gathered its ad-
herents into something of a community allegiance to the social
passion. Nevertheless, when the social gospel did generate organizations all its own quite beyond the official churches, it is to
be understood that such organizations did not express a self-
conscious and controlling sectarian impulse. The Fellowship for
a Christian Social Order (FCSO) presumed that the churches
were susceptible to its message and, far from organizing as a
body to provide sharper witness to that message, organized in
order to explore it more carefully so that it might be taught more
widely.

First broached in New York City late in 1921, the fellowship
met formally for the first time in Lake Mohonk in New York in
May, 1922.[22] Moving spirits were Sherwood Eddy, international
secretary of the Y.M.C.A., and Kirby Page, then embarking on
his career as full-time social-gospel and pacifist pamphleteer.
Eddy became chairman of the national committee; William A.
Smith, of the Episcopal *Churchman*, vice-chairman; and Page,
executive secretary. National committeemen and members included William Adams Brown of Union, one of the great expositors
of liberal evangelical theology; Charles Reynolds Brown of Yale,
another of the prewar social-gospel leaders; Samuel McCrae

Cavert of the Federal Council; Winifred Chappell, then at the Chicago Training School, later to join Harry Ward in the Methodist Federation; Henry Churchill King of Oberlin; Bishop Francis J. McConnell; Charles Clayton Morrison of the *Christian Century;* A. J. Muste, newly installed head of the Brookwood Labor School; Justin Wroe Nixon of Colgate-Rochester; G. Bromley Oxnam, then at Depauw University; Daniel Poling of the *Christian Herald;* and Harry Ward.

The fellowship acted on a theory dear to liberal educators and psychologists of the period—the theory of group thinking. Isolated individual thinking was inadequate; it was in a group that people, united in their allegiance to general ideals, could come to clear and valid agreement about how to practice them. The fellowship united on the general ideal of a progressive modification of the existing social system toward a system more compatible with Christian life. Propaganda for any particular new system was not intended; rather, through fellowship and group thinking, specific educational and spiritual means for removing definite obstacles to the progress of social fellowship would be studied. The fellowship organized into local conferences with local leaders, held occasional retreats, a regular annual national conference, and, beginning in 1925, a regular summer conference at Olivet, Michigan. At the first Olivet conference, one week was devoted to each of four general topics: economic and industrial relations, international relations, race relations, and family relations. Paul Douglas of the University of Chicago, Sidney Hillman, F. Ernest Johnson of the Federal Council, and Harry Elmer Barnes were among the outside speakers. With Reinhold Niebuhr as chairman, speakers for the industry-economics week in 1926 included Earl D. Howard, formerly head of the labor relations program of Hart, Schaffner, and Marx; Isador Lubin, expert on the coal industry; Harry Laidler of the socialist League for Industrial Democracy; and Gardner Murphy, Washington psychologist. Attendance at the conferences was between 250 and 300.

The fellowship was in fact what it claimed to be—a discussion group. From only the names of clergy listed, it will be apparent that it included representatives of what was to become within a decade a broad spectrum of social ideals. The single significant characteristic of the fellowship was its submergence of such differences in an ethical glow. It did not discuss important tactical and systematic issues, but social-ethical needs in the society. It was not a prophetic community; the social gospel called steadily for prophecy, but prophecy was not its original instinct. Prophecy could be lonely and isolated, and the conviction of the passion was that it possessed an immediately organizing and gregarious word.

There was a drift of principle within the group, however. In 1928 the fellowship voted to dissolve itself within the Fellowship of Reconciliation (FOR). There were at the time about 2,400 members. The Fellowship for a Christian Social Order had begun with its focus upon economics and industry, and had broadened its attention to include war. The FOR had been founded for pacifist witness against war and had broadened its focus to include social questions generally, especially those of class war and industry. When the lines converged, it was the pacifist fellowship that survived.[23] Actually, for all practical purposes, the FCSO had always displayed a pacifist orientation in its emphasis upon educational and spiritual techniques of social change—love did not mean force. The FCSO needed only the extension of the frankly pacifist rationale of the FOR beyond issues of international war alone into a general philosophy of social change for the merger to occur.

The FOR, born of the shock of the First World War, could not have been called in the beginning a social-gospel body.[24] Its founder, Henry T. Hodgkin, was an English Quaker. The pacifism of FOR derived from the historic Quaker tradition—that is, it was sectarian. In 1915, with 4,000 members in England, Hodgkin came to the United States. The first American branch was founded late that year at Garden City, Long Island, among some forty young people touched by Hodgkin's personal witness. In 1917 the FOR offered a kind of communion to several of the ministers who left their pulpits with American entry into the war, some of whom left the ministry altogether for careers in the liberal left of American politics. One of these men was A. J. Muste; another was Norman Thomas, an early executive secretary of the organization. Any precise dating for the organization as a whole would be unwise, but it is safe to say that at some point after 1917 the FOR in America elided from pure sectarian pacifism into a pacifism concerned with political and social tactics. It was to be the work of the leaders of the FOR not to maintain an historic pacifist witness but to introduce pacifism into, and comport pacifism with, the basic problems of politics. So far as its members were conscious of being a vanguard minority, a sectarian flavor did continue to cling to the organization. But as the rationale for this pacifism was its effectiveness as a social technique adapted to every social problem, as the drive of energy was outward, the FOR bespoke a universalizing and churchly morale. For that reason its absorption of the Fellowship for a Christian Social Order in 1928 represented its definite, official emergence as a pure social-gospel agency. The most significant chapter in its history, the debate over "violence" in 1933, turned on a preoccupation of the social passion, class rather than international war. The social gospel was not necessarily pacifist, but pacifism was one of its logical possibilities, and had come close to pervading it when Reinhold Niebuhr brought the social gospel under attack.

The executive secretary following Norman Thomas was Paul Jones, who remained in that post for ten years. Chairman of the national council was A. J. Muste; other secretaries were Devere Allen and John Nevin Sayre. Paul Jones was a member of the Socialist party, and remained so until his death in 1941; in 1940 he ran for governor of Ohio on the Socialist ticket. Muste was head of the Brookwood Labor School in Katonah, New York, teaching the necessity for labor politics. Allen was on the board of directors of the socialist League for Industrial Democracy. Later he became chairman of the executive committee of the League for Independent Political Action, in 1929. The essential complex, among the leaders at least, was pacifism *and* socialism. The FOR included many conservatives, but in the great debate of 1933 a link between pacifism and rigorous social reform was assumed. Kirby Page and Sherwood Eddy further exemplified the

rule, especially after 1930, as well as did Reinhold Niebuhr; all
three were members of the fellowship.

The main organ of the FOR was the magazine *World Tomorrow*, not officially an FOR publication but controlled by its
members. Founded soon after the First World War, its first
editor was Norman Thomas. John Nevin Sayre succeeded him in
1921, with Devere Allen as managing editor. Sayre's regime
marked a self-conscious turn to a definitely religious orientation
in the magazine, which undertook systematic discussions of
social questions of every sort from the standpoint of the FOR
ethic. In 1926 Kirby Page became editor; members of the editorial
council included Samuel McCrae Cavert and Johnson of the
Federal Council and Henry P. Van Dusen of Union. In 1928 a
kind of triumvirate of Page, Allen, and Reinhold Niebuhr headed
the staff. In 1932 another editorial turn was announced: the
magazine was to voice a "radical" position politically. In 1933,
although circulation was at a peak, calls for financial help went
out. Early in 1934 a final announcement by the editors constituted
a landmark: *World Tomorrow* was to be both Christian and
Marxist—Marxist for the timely interpretation of contemporary
history and the goal of a classless society, Christian for timeless
insights into the permanently valid meaning of history.[25] The
road, the editors warned, would be lonely. And it was. The
magazine expired later in 1934. Whether or not its demise was
due to internal tension, the internal tension did exist. The "Christian and Marxist" orientation belonged to the new "realists" of
the new Fellowship of Socialist Christians, in which Reinhold
Niebuhr was the dominant figure. In both theology and politics,
in both the Christianity and the Marxism, there had been in fact
no such team as Niebuhr and Page. The Christian and Marxist
turn would be announced once more, in 1936, with the founding
of *Radical Religion*, by which time both the FOR complex and
the social passion had been split, in both politics and religion.

The denominational agencies were for spreading the gospel.
The two fellowships, FCSO and FOR, were for clarification and
purification of the gospel. Perhaps the most telling organ of the

social gospel, the *Christian Century,* served in both fashions.

In general, the prophets had at least one journal, official or unofficial, available in each denomination, invariably on the liberal side in the theological controversies of the 'twenties. Thus the *Congregationalist,* the *Baptist,* the *Christian Advocates* and *Zion's Herald,* the Episcopal *Churchman* and *Witness,* and others carried social-gospel articles and news from time to time. But for the *Christian Century,* the social gospel was in itself close to being the heart of the total evangel. The journal was founded by the Disciples, and edited by Herbert Willett during the war. The editor who won it eminence was Charles Clayton Morrison. Fulfilling the ecumenical spirit of the original Disciples, Morrison made the *Century* into a nondenominational journal, and by the mid-1920's it ranked as the leading voice of liberal Protestantism. Discussions of theology appeared now and then, but the *Century's* speciality was not critical and systematic. Rather it was unremitting attention to Protestantism's place in the national culture, and in fact to Protestantism as culture and as the national culture. As an editor, Morrison displayed in its frankest, most vigorous form the old morale that conceded nothing as outside the ken of Protestant concern. Politics, industry, international relations, sumptuary morality, education—these and much else were confronted weekly in a direct and specific fashion unknown in the denominational papers. Nothing was evaded. Morrison himself was a regular spokesman of the social gospel. His own personal energies were drawn most fully to the war issue. Personally and through the pages of the *Century,* he helped lead the battle for the Kellogg Peace Pact of 1928. In 1939, 1940, and 1941 he made the *Century* a rallying point for the attack on the Roosevelt foreign policy and helped complete the basic split in apologetics that had come upon the social gospel at large. But effort in any direction to extend Protestantism won space in the journal. Roundly castigating the economic order as un-Christian, often professing to be anticapitalist, the *Century* in its articles offered its 25,000 to 30,000 readers the best coverage of social-gospel problems found in Protestant journalism. In the early 'twenties much of this was due to its editors for social affairs, Alva Taylor of the Disciples, as well as to Morrison. A former Methodist missionary, Paul Hutchinson, became second in command in 1924; Hutchinson, joining the socialist Chicago-Call-to-Action Movement in 1932, saw to it that the sharp political thinking being developed in the 'thirties was not muffled by Morrison's profound involvement in the broad culture-community of the church.

Ably, often enough brilliantly, edited, the *Century* was a voice incomparably more broadcast, though not necessarily more penetrating, than any other social-gospel organ. Aside from the liberal seminaries, there was probably no agency more responsible for keeping the passion vital in the ranks of the ministry. Confident that it spoke for liberal Protestantism as a whole, in many ways its strengths were the strengths of the social gospel, its weaknesses the social gospel's weaknesses as well.

So much for identification of organizations and organs. More important than their particular qualities was their quality in common. They lived on social, and even political and economic, expectations about the culture-community of the churches. The social gospel could not abandon its temple of origin for the purity of separation. It was of the churches. The search for politics would bring this investment of the Word in the culture of the churches under pressure. Once the ties began to break, and some men began to choose for the Word despite the church, the social gospel was in its time of disintegration. The full significance of this investment should appear in this narrative, as it comes to be clear that behind assumptions about the church lay assumptions about the nation. In its last stand, the social gospel would argue that it was justified not only by the character of liberal Protestantism but by the character of America.

In the chapters to follow is the record of efforts to sustain this character. In the realms of capital and labor, strangeness, alienation, and division were overtaking society. The church was estranged from both. Capital had somehow escaped the church; labor had somehow never been won by the church; consequently the church was in danger of losing itself. The problem was how to restore all three into the unity of gospel-based brotherhood.

III

The Faces of Power: Capital

Social-gospel pastors were self-conscious about the business community. They tried deliberately to construct an image that they could use in their thinking. The images they came to work with were not precise. Not until the 'thirties were there important efforts to draw systematically upon theories of ideology and class structure. Yet for the pastors of the 'twenties the picture of business was a power image, part of an emerging tactical sense of the groupings of power in society at large.

Not the product of direct analysis, their image of business drew heavily on the older sense of division, of distance, between the church and centers of power outside the church. Lines of effective communication seemed to have broken down. This points to a distinction to be drawn immediately. The business from which the social-gospel leaders felt divided—the business that they sensed had outrun the old patrols of ethics and moral order —was the business of mass production, of heavy industry, of mass labor: big business. Small business, local business—the business of the independent merchant and entrepreneur—did not preoccupy them. This was a crucial distinction because the social-gospel leaders made nothing of it. That is to say, in their tacit isolation of big business as the real target for prophetic criticism, the churchmen did not distinguish business as ethos. It was the role of Gould, Rockefeller, Morgan, Carnegie, Gary—Protestants all, each in his way—against which the early prophets had spoken. But did the old Protestant spirit of individual enterprise, as sketched by Weber and Tawney, come to purest fulfillment in Carnegie or in the static entrepreneur of Middletown? The prophets preached motives: the social gospel against the gospel of wealth, coöperation versus competition. They preached their psychology of brotherhood as though it bore against the new organizations of industrial power only. Could they imagine, however, that the gospel of wealth, the spirit of competition, and religious individualism did not still burn in the business soul of those middle-class towns, frightened by strikes and monopoly, to which Gladden and Rauschenbusch and the others preached? Perhaps the new captains of industry were not really apostates from the old order but a logical climax of that order. In that case, the uneasiness to which the social gospel gave expression signified a crisis that challenged not only the power of big business but the coherence of the whole middle-class community. The pastors did not want to see it this way. The protests of middle-class Progressivism against monopoly had helped them avoid this more drastic concept of their mission. Avoiding it helped them sustain optimism and faith: if big business alone was the problem, then the ranks of the middle could be hoped to join warmly in the solution.

It was not as though assembling all possible power against big business was to be the social-gospel solution. The situation here was the opposite of what the pastors faced in the new fields of labor: the businessmen were men marked by power, not by helplessness. Their power had set them apart and made them seem inaccessible to the Word. Serious implications, ultimately theological, lurked in this situation. What was human nature that it should be hardened against idealism by power?

Another of the fascinating aspects of Walter Rauschenbusch was his capacity to grasp this situation, propose new sharp answers to it, and ignore the drastic revisions in theology his answers implied. Big business, Rauschenbusch generalized, was the last entrenchment of autocracy. Civilization stood at a turning point where industrial control had to pass from a ruling class to those who manned the industrial machine themselves. How was this to happen? As the next chapter will more fully explain, Rauschenbusch, when arguing tactics, firmly maintained that social-economic interest groups needed separate, organized expression for defense of their interests. The break he made with old social-gospel reliance on the Word alone appeared in his predictions about the role to be played by business in the march to the better society. Not only was business unregenerate, he said, but it would not regenerate itself. He explicitly criticized the prospect of inner reformation: "It is hopeless to expect the business class to espouse [economic fraternalism] as a class. Individuals in the business class will do so, but the class will not. There is no historical precedent for an altruistic self-effacement of a whole class." [1] Considerations of justice and mercy, he insisted, rarely thawed the icy indifference of class-selfishness. Therefore, from this point, he tried to find the interests which might compel industrial reformation from outside.

This was class analysis in a manner that the prophets had earlier avoided. The way of continued avoidance was kept open by Rauschenbusch himself. Businessmen, he said, were not, by and large, as bad as the system. As stewards, they were both more efficient and more honest than stewards of the past—warriors, priests, and aristocrats. The point was that capitalism was not responsible for their virtues. The system generated hardness and callousness, rewarded materialism and narrowness. The system was structurally bad. Some men at least had not yet succumbed to its influence, but they were, he implied, a vanishing remnant. [2] The pastors before Rauschenbusch had been aware of this contradiction, but almost all had preached and predicted inner reformation. This was true despite the radicalism or conservatism of their ultimate ideals. A socialist such as George Herron had expected conversion among the men of wealth just as did Gladden and Peabody. Only an occasional and isolated man like Herbert Casson, at his Labor Church in Lynn, ignored the tactics of preaching to the top. Even Casson, while ignoring it, did not reject it. Nor did Rauschenbusch reject it, but the role he assigned to the idealistic minority of the privileged reflected his instinct for power analysis. It was to be feared, he wrote, that in some final encounter of the classes in the struggle for justice, the class of privilege would institute an "anarchy" of the right, a reactionary coup d'état. In this event, it would be up to the idealistic minority of the privileged to head off, blunt, and subvert their peers. Nonetheless, the real weight behind the drive for justice did not lie with the privileged, but with labor.[3]

Although nominally a question of tactics only, all this put a strain on social-gospel logic, and Rauschenbusch was not to be followed in this hard policy by the pastors of the 'twenties. For them, both optimism and coherence depended upon regarding power as opportunity for strategic conversions and not merely as obstacle. To evangelize and convert power rather than to bring countervailing power against it seemed the essence of strategy. Once converted, power would offer itself freely to control and equalization. Evangelism would in fact draw out something like the "altruistic self-effacement" of a class. The important thing was to get in touch with the new power, and there is no better way to understand the position of the pastors than to examine first the point at which their efforts to overcome the distance meant collision rather than coöperation. The most famous clash proceeded directly from the enthusiasm of 1919—a collision between two goliaths, United States Steel and the Interchurch World Movement. The fact that it was collision rather than compromise testified to social-gospel morale. Yet the Interchurch report on the steel strike of 1919 also exhibited the perspective by which the social gospel saved itself from Rauschenbusch's rigor.

An investigation of the steel strike was authorized in October, 1919, by the Industrial Relations Department of Interchurch, headed by a Methodist minister newly appointed bishop to India, Fred Fisher. The decision to investigate followed a meeting of the National Conference of Interchurch in New York City prompted by Secretary of Labor Wilson, Senator Kenyon, and officials of the American Federation of Labor. The executive committee of Interchurch appropriated $12,000 for the job, and a team of investigators was appointed to work on the scene in Pennsylvania, with Heber Blankenhorn of the Bureau of Industrial Research as chief. Blankenhorn had been a captain in Army Intelligence during the war and a member of General Pershing's staff. The completed report was approved by a committee of seven churchmen on March 30, 1920. Between the time the report received the approval of this committee and the time of its publication, stories circulated that efforts were being made to suppress it. Bishop Francis McConnell was declared to have warned the executive committee of Interchurch that the report would be published whether Interchurch approved or not. The executive committee then handed the report to a subcommittee that included John D. Rockefeller, Jr., Warren Stout of the Brotherhood of Railway Engineers, and Hubert Herring of the Congregational Social Relations Department. After its inspection, the subcommittee recommended publication. On June 28 the executive committee adopted the report, which was published on July 28, 1920.[4]

The Industrial Relations Department of Interchurch intended that the report on United States Steel should be only a beginning, the leadoff for a series of great survey reports on wages, hours, health, and race and human relations in general in American industry. But by the time of publication Interchurch had collapsed. The *Nation,* assuming that the Interchurch movement had staked everything on support from businessmen, took the steel report and the collapse to be related; Interchurch had been scuttled by Judge Gary and his friends.[5] Explanations for the failure of Interchurch cannot be quite so simple; yet the report defined something of the Protestant dilemma, even as it won attention.

The investigation back of the document was professional, using an extensive array of valuable evidence. The ground covered was comprehensive. The report attempted to establish how widespread the twelve-hour day was in fact among the steel workers. It inquired, to a lesser degree, into wage rates and real income among the workers. It endeavored to measure the degree and effect of racial tension in the industry. During the strike the press raised the cry of "Bolshevism"; in 1921 a second report, *Public Opinion and the Steel Strike,* was published, attempting to assess the effect of this cry upon the strike itself, and to assess the role of William Z. Foster in provoking or strengthening it. In this second report, the tactics of the AFL organizers were considered. The attitude of the press and of Pennsylvania public officials and police came under review, as well as the policy of United States Steel officials and their use of labor spies. Developing all this with much detail, the report remains to this day one of the best inquiries into a specific strike situation, a document of considerable interest for American industrial history. It was something in the tradition of the documentary reports of the Progressive era, the reports of Tarbell, Lloyd, Sinclair, Steffens.

It is not germane to our purposes to analyze the data, but to ascertain simply how the churchmen conceived the battle into which the investigation was thrown. With its release, the first report immediately became famous. In the national press, both religious and secular, the attention it received was extensive and for the most part friendly. The railway-brotherhood organ, *Labor,* published most of it in its pages. The *Nation* applauded it. Senator Walsh wanted the report made a public document. The many church papers that commented were almost unanimously in support of the work. The *Wall Street Journal, Industry,* and *Iron Age* were among business papers rising to the defense of United States Steel. One clear effect of the report was to trigger a series of further inquiries into the twelve-hour day. One of them, "The Twelve-Hour Shift in Industry," published in January, 1923, under auspices of the Federation of American Engineering Societies, earned an introduction by President Harding, in which he deplored the practice with his high authority. Soon after publication of the Interchurch report, Judge Gary inspired the American Iron and Steel Institute to sponsor an extended attack on the church investigation and its conclusions; this tome was released in May, 1923. On June 6, a committee representing the Federal Council, the National Catholic Welfare Council, and the Central Commission of American Rabbis released a reply to this attack. On June 25 the Department of Research and Education of the Federal Council issued a special bulletin on the twelve-hour day denouncing the Steel Institute report in more detail. Steel could not hold its position. On July 6, Judge Gary declared that the company had determined to abolish the system, and in its annual report of December 31, 1923, the corporation announced the completion of its changeover to the three-shift day. The twelve-hour day in steel had received the full glare of public attention, and church leaders then and later rightly credited a major share in Gary's backdown to the Interchurch investigation. A battle had been won.[6]

And yet, it was not a battle that pointed very far or very clearly beyond itself. The great Progressive documents were thesis documents, intended to illustrate and buttress a social view. What the report on steel illustrated in the last analysis was the intransigence of one company and its leaders. Elbert Gary and United States Steel had long had a reputation for rock-bound opposition to any new policies in labor relations. In 1919, the Republican party, the Democratic party, the National Chamber of Commerce, and other respectable organizations had endorsed the principle of collective bargaining. Steel disdained such façades; while yielding eventually on the twelve-hour day, Steel emerged from the strike flatly opposed to any unionization, and helped inspire the open-shop campaign of the next two years. It was, as the *Christian Century* noted, a generation behind the times. Not only the churchmen but the public tended to regard Gary as something of a troglodyte. There was a certain fascination inherent in his being, as though he were a kind of prize pagan (Methodist layman though he was) whose conversion, were it possible, would increase the hopes for the Kingdom. During the strike there were efforts to deal with him directly. The Federal Council appointed a delegation to lay its views before him; the delegation called, waited, was received, was heard, and departed. No conversion resulted. Far from disdaining controversy with the churchmen, Gary apparently delighted in the joust, and his technique was an old one. In Boston, a Reverend Victor Bigelow, of Andover, delivered a speech before the Boston Ministers Meeting late in 1920, in which he defended the steel company in every-

thing—its use of labor spies, the twelve-hour shift, all. Gary
ordered the speech printed and gave it national circulation and
Reverend Bigelow a fleeting fame. The word was let fall by company officials directly, and in the Steel Institute report as well,
that members of the Interchurch investigating team were tainted
with Bolshevism, and that some of the church sponsors were
therefore repudiating the report. Bishop McConnell, forced to
emphatic denial, pointed out that church members had helped
write the report. Gary himself, in his speech before the Steel
Institute, issued his own call for a return to the Bible and the
principles of Christianity as the basis for business dealings.[7]

In all this, the potential fruitfulness of the report was restricted. It never made explicit what the prophets claimed in
their logic was the true issue: it did not strike at the "system."
Conspicuously, the issue of unionization and collective bargaining was excluded from the highlight put on the twelve-hour day.
The enormously suggestive data on the ethnic tensions and conflicts within the body of labor, facing any labor policy at all,
were obscured and neglected by the sensational revelations of
company labor spies. That the AFL was inadequate on sheer
technical grounds of internal organization was blurred by the
failure of public press and public authorities to provide a fair,
at least neutral, atmosphere for the conflict. Finally, discussion of
the role of the state was forgotten altogether. Upton Sinclair's
moral in *The Jungle* had been lost in the general public horror
at the secondary scandal of packing-house hygiene. But here,
the report itself represented deflection from basic issues to the
essentially peripheral scandal of the twelve-hour shift and the
stubbornness of one man's will. Attack on the twelve-hour day
was not in itself deflection—that might have been a perfectly appropriate limited battle—but the report betrayed deflection to
the extent that it took itself—and to the extent that it was taken
by the prophets—as an expression of social-gospel power.

Even so, the report might still have suggested a broader moral.
Gary might have symbolized the limit beyond which evangelism
of the mighty could not expect to proceed, and a limit, therefore,
that evangelism would have to take into account. Gary, however,

although not converted, had been forced to yield, ostensibly by the pressure of public opinion, and the moral was drawn that outward conversion at least could be coerced. This was a strange conclusion to the whole affair. The focus of evangelical strategy was upon the will, thoroughly in line with the Protestant tradition, yet, although United States Steel in 1923 conformed more nearly to the standards of the Kingdom than it had in 1920, it would have been extremely difficult to locate and define the conversion of the will that had occurred. There was no real way by which the phenomenon of a Gary could be integrated into the basic social-gospel outlook. Coercion by public opinion was a stopgap, merely a postponement of consideration of forms of coercion less bland than those of moral pressure. By 1932 it could be delayed no longer.

The response given to Gary, however, himself a testimony to evangelical failure, was to highlight examples of evangelical triumph. If Gary symbolized the unconverted, there were those to symbolize the converted. Alva Taylor, social-service secretary of the Disciples and one of the churchmen promoting the report on the steel strike, pointed this out in the title of an exemplary social-gospel article: "Mr. Rockefeller versus Judge Gary." [8]

John D. Rockefeller, Jr., appeared to incarnate a new era of business. Following the strikes and violence at Ludlow, Colorado, in 1914, Rockefeller had inaugurated a shop-committee plan in the Colorado Fuel and Iron Company, which became the model for such plans in more than a thousand corporations, including American Telephone and Telegraph, International Harvester, Armour, and Swift. These shop-committee plans were hailed as a step beyond the old patterns of Christian stewardship, in the direction of industrial democracy—and in Rockefeller's case, the ethical drive was self-conscious. In his book, *The Personal Relation in Industry,* he put himself on record for the higher policy in a manner that Gary would have scorned. Gary jousted with churchmen; Rockefeller consulted them. When F. Ernest Johnson of the Federal Council brought the antiunion policy of the bituminous coal companies in western Pennsylvania to his attention, Rockefeller as a stockholder responded with strong support for a revision in their labor policy. When the council in its investigation of the strike on the Western Maryland Railroad in 1926 found that the chief stockholder, although he was only a minority stockholder, had already opposed the railroad's labor policy, the council nevertheless felt he should have exerted more pressure for his own views. This stockholder was Rockefeller, and again Rockefeller looked to what could be done. For his ultimately successful battle to remove Colonel Robert Stewart (of Teapot Dome fame) from Stewart's post as chairman of the board of Standard Oil of Indiana, Rockefeller received just praise. His name lent strength to the report on the steel strike, and of course Rockefeller was a generous churchman. When the Y.W.C.A. came under attack from businessmen of Pittsburgh and Los Angeles because of its endorsement of the 1919 Social Creed, Rockefeller entered the breach with $500,000 for the Y.W.C.A.'s endangered fund-raising drive. He helped liquidate the debts of Interchurch. He supported the Federal Council.[9]

Thus if Gary was the prize pagan, robust in his defense of the old order, Rockefeller was the prize Christian industrialist, ever prepared to direct his prodigious resources to the battle lines indicated by social idealism. It was perhaps unfortunate that labor trouble should have broken out once again at Colorado Fuel and Iron. The Russell Sage Foundation found the original shop-committee plan of 1914 ineffective in extending any real power to the employees. The United States Commissioner on Industrial Relations declared that the plan was effective only in lulling criticism while retaining absolute power for the company. Certainly Rockefeller had not wanted to deceive and lull. After the 1927 Columbine strikes, he returned to the problem, and this time not only changed the paper policies of the company but shook out the executive force as well. Whatever the actual results would be, Rockefeller exhibited the new will.

He was only the greatest. There were others: Henry Ford, Charles Schwab, Dwight Morrow, George Perkins, W. E. Sweet, each praised from time to time by the idealists. They were—with their shop-committee plans; their public, community, and labor relations programs; their five-dollar days; their eagerness for "arbitration" rather than "conflict"—pointing the way from autocracy to democracy in industry.[10]

They were pointing the way; they did not in themselves constitute the goal. To make the distinction is to make the point that the prophets had not fallen under the enchantment of a more sophisticated form of stewardship. It should be noted that Judge Gary himself had not lacked the sheen of paternalism. Steel had instituted and advertised far and wide its program of workers' benefits; its wage policy had not been particularly bad. But Gary as tempter had been resisted as to a degree was Rockefeller, insofar as the temptation existed to accept his shop committees as final flowers of reform. Bishop McConnell, in his *Christian Principles and Industrial Reconstruction,* displayed an alertness to the temptation that was quite typical: "Capitalists are not as a rule moved by impulses to oppression. Undoubtedly the majority of them mean well by their men . . . But paternalism is an insidious foe to democracy." [11] What Rockefeller displayed was a gratifying willingness to open the industrial area to the idealistic will, but not yet to the fulfillment of that will. The prophets looked for change beyond the patterns of modernized stewardship. What they meant by industrial democracy can be suggested by looking past Rockefeller to a few still more innovating businessmen, in whose direction the churchmen assumed Rockefeller to be moving.

The shop-committee plans of the 'twenties, involving something over two million workers, were concepts by and large of the big corporations. Ranging far beyond these plans were certain industrial "experiments" applied on a smaller scale, almost invariably to one plant under the sponsorship of a single owner. One of these planners was Arthur "Golden Rule" Nash, who owned a textile factory in Cincinnati. Nash had been raised an Adventist, only to leave his church because of what he took to be bigotry. Later ordained as a Disciples preacher, he was censured by that denomination for burying an unbeliever, and once again forsook organized religion. Finally a Universalist preacher took him in hand, and he began to think about a practical experiment

for his religious ethic. Within five years of his purchase, for $60,-
000, of a precarious textile business in Cincinnati, the firm was
able to declare a million-dollar stock dividend. The stock was
divided, one-third to the workers, two-thirds to Nash who, appalled at the prospect of becoming a millionaire, advertised for
immediate ways to give his money away. A forty-hour work-week
was the rule in the plant, with plans for a reduction to thirty-five.
Following the stock dividend, Nash embarked upon a five-year
program for turning the business over to the working force lock,
stock, and barrel. The plant had been the target for an unsuc-
cessful campaign by the Amalgamated Clothing Workers Union
in 1921. In 1925, following doubts and reservations about the
experiment raised by members, the Fellowship for a Christian
Social Order called upon Professor Paul Douglas to investigate
the company's labor policy. Late in that year, Nash called in the
Amalgamated, more without than with the urging of the workers
themselves, to whom he issued a "plea" to accept ACWU affilia-
tion. Nash died in 1927 before the fulfillment of his plans.[12]

Another experiment was that of the Columbia Conserve Company of Indianapolis, a canning enterprise capitalized at $400,000,
with a business of approximately $1,000,000 in 1925 and a labor
force of about one hundred. The sponsor of this experiment, William P. Hapgood, was the son of a well-to-do Midwestern family,
a Harvard graduate, brother of two literary men (one of whom,
Norman, helped man the liberal lines of the 'twenties against the
professional right in his book *Professional Patriots*). Hapgood
liked to deny that he was a Christian, if by that was meant
"churchman." He forswore the church, the creeds, the confes-
sions of faith, the conventional codes of morality; it was in the
ethical and spiritual teaching of Jesus that he found all authority.
From 1917 he launched the company upon a program designed
ultimately to place the business in the hands of the workers and
their elected council. In January, 1925, he began to buy out the
absentee stockholders, the stock to go into a trust fund held by
the workers' council, ownership of the business to pass into
council hands when 51 per cent of the common stock had been
purchased. Through a series of changes, membership on the

council moved toward complete democracy, and the council took power over questions of wages, hours, working conditions, terms of seasonal-work contracts, and the like. The vast majority of the work force qualified for a yearly salary program. Only the council of workers could discharge an employee. Provisions for sickness and old-age pensions were established.[13]

At Wappingers Falls, New York, another experiment was carried out in the Dutchess Bleachery Mill. The chairman of the board of directors was "an earnest Christian layman," Harold A. Hatch. In the Dutchess mill, representatives of both workers and owners constituted a board of management empowered to arbitrate matters of mutual concern, including hours and wages, and representatives of both the working force and the local community sat on the board of directors. A sinking fund maintained to provide 50 per cent of wages to all workers in times of unemployment counted as a first charge on capital. There was no plan for eventual control by the workers. It was from his post as director of industrial relations in this plant that James Myers came to the Federal Council as director of the Industrial Relations Division of the Department of Research and Education.[14]

There were more experiments, some mild and some extreme in intention. One of the latter was the American Cast Iron Pipe Company, headed by John J. Eagen of Atlanta. Eagan was a member of the Federal Council's Commission on Race Relations, and invited the council to appoint a representative to the board of his company. Eagan died in 1924; his will bequeathed the company to its employees. The Dennison Manufacturing Company of Framingham, Massachussetts, supported a program of worker participation in management and a company union shop; the workers, although free to do so, did not choose to affiliate with a trade union. The Henry Dix and Sons Corporation, a New Jersey and New York textile business, was turned over to its workers in 1922 as part of an experiment.[15]

Notices, articles, and chapters on these men and their experiments appeared regularly in the press and publications of the social passion. Nash spoke before ministers' unions and church groups everywhere. Hapgood was a regular speaker at the Olivet conferences of the Fellowship for a Christian Social Order. The fascination was a logical extension of the over-all judgment against the autocracy of the industrial system. Industry was conceived to be susceptible to the same type of democratic constitutionalism as politics—and as the churches themselves. This interest in the actual constitutional structure of industry did not stop with the abstractions of "class," of "labor movement," of "political tactics," but attempted to visualize each man in the concrete conditions of his life—conditions which defined for him the possibilities of personality—and attempted to visualize reform of those conditions in concrete terms. The factory was a logical focus of the social passion because the factory was the critical and possibly the decisive milieu for the newest, latest class within society and would determine the character of the members of that class. From one of the discussions of Hapgood's plant came a clear expression of this:

> The ties of political democracy are more or less remote and its exercise is so occasional as to allow little real experience in its technique, while those of industrial democracy come under the factory roof and are exercised daily with the very tangible tools of technical efficiency.[16]

This comment exhibited a further note: the enthusiasm for industrial democracy drew on deeper roots than those merely of loyalty to political democracy. Political democracy was itself the extension of something more deeply grounded still. The vision of industrial and factory democracy was an unbroken extension of the religious imagination. Man's normative relation to God was free and personal, fortified by attention to the workings of the Holy Spirit, guided and refined by discussion and personal witness in the gathered church, and God was understood as working in all life, including industry and the single factory. Freedom, discussion, personal responsibility, and witness became as essential there as in the church. Freedom and responsibility could be mediated and borne no more by managerial shepherds than by priestly shepherds. In the final culmination of pure social-gospel logic, the factory was to become church.

But if these experiments offered sharper definitions of the ideal, their bearing upon the means was obscure. Speaking of the transfer of the Dix textile firm to its workers, the council's *Information Service* observed:

> It will be valuable to watch the results of this experiment, since its success or failure will tell what can be done in an individual concern. In the nature of the case it throws little light on the next constructive step which must be taken toward the reconstruction of industry as a whole.[17]

A precise definition of why this should be so would have confronted social-gospel thinking with the problem of means in a way it was not yet willing to accept.

The problem of the means would have been the same whether or not these experiments had been successful. Yet there was some instruction in the fact that the two favorite projects should have turned out as they did, for in the end the glamour of both Nash and Hapgood evaporated. Early in the 'thirties, stories began to float about of trouble within the Columbia Conserve plant. A dispute had developed between Hapgood and his veteran workers over the authority to discharge employees; Hapgood was demanding to be released from the terms of the previous agreement. A committee of four was appointed from the contributors to *World Tomorrow:* Sherwood Eddy, Jerome Davis, Paul Douglas, and James Myers. The committee investigated and found Hapgood autocratic. *World Tomorrow* editorialized:

> The collapse of the experiment in industrial democracy at the Columbia Conserve Company is partly the result of a failure of the human spirit, but much more it is a consequence of an inadequate social philosophy and an incorrect social strategy.[18]

The case of Arthur Nash was the opposite. When Nash, under stimulus of the investigation sponsored by the Fellowship for a Christian Social Order, invited in the Amalgamated Clothing Workers, he did not stop there, but proceeded past his own attempts to fulfill the ideal. He went to Montreal in 1926, where he spoke before the convention of the Amalgamated and suggested that the churches unionize their printing houses and other shops. This was more than a somewhat sly if not also telling blow, for he declared further: "The problems of the working people never will be worked out except by class-conscious groups. The forces in opposition to them are so overwhelmingly class-conscious that anyone who did not possess this class-consciousness in behalf of the laborer could not lead him to victory." [19]

Here was the strategy of Rauschenbusch brought forward again. It was not enough, in questions of social idealism, to rely upon conversion of the will; will had to be raised up against will. So long as the celebration of Nashes, Hapgoods, and Eagans, let alone Fords and Rockefellers, was not set in context of a larger strategy independent of converting every man of power into a Rockefeller, a Nash, or an Eagan, the tendency to become entangled in the logic of paternalism, of stewardship, of Tory democracy, remained acute. Although, even in its moderate circles, the social gospel recognized the danger, it faced extreme difficulty in speaking against it, not to make the problem that much more severe. In an editorial of 1926, the *Christian Century* offered another of its frequent and unsystematic bits of realism. The overriding issue for the social gospel, it declared, concerned ". . . the tremendous centralization of wealth and power in the hands of a few irrespective of their personal rectitude." No matter how handled, the editors wrote, power and privilege of themselves were destructive of brotherhood. But, following this impeccable statement of the issue, the *Century* only compounded the old tactics: the men of power were to be converted, not to higher forms of stewardship, but to sacrifice—sacrifice of the power and privilege themselves.[20] They were to efface themselves altruistically as a class.

Efforts to reach the businessmen were made on a wide and regular basis. At the 1919 convention of the Federal Council, the council's Social Service Commission was authorized to sponsor a series of conferences

> . . . in a nation-wide effort to exert the influence of the churches, (a) to induce employers and employees to work out relations of goodwill and cooperation in their industries; and (b) to interpret the Christian spirit and Christian ethic to industrial relations.[21]

The first such conferences were held in Atlanta in May, 1920, under auspices of the local council of churches, with ministers, laymen, and "representative businessmen" participating. Worth Tippy of the commission gave the call of the church and discussed Christian principles applicable to industry. Earl D. Howard, labor relations director of Hart, Schaffner, and Marx, outlined the "practical method of cooperation" in the men's clothing industry. "The discussion which followed each session was animated and the plan of the conference was thoroughly successful."[22] These conferences, in effect a social-gospel version of the revival, made of Tippy, F. E. Johnson, and James Myers twentieth-century circuit-riders. In the next few years they covered the country—Chicago, Cleveland, Wichita, Richmond, New York, Boston, Los Angeles, Seattle. Laymen participating included R. W. Bruere of the Bureau of Industrial Research, Henry Dennison, E. D. Howard, William Leiserson of the Labor Adjustment Board of the Rochester Clothing Industry, Seebohm Rowntree, an English industrialist who sponsored an industrial experiment of his own, and W. F. Ogburn, University of Chicago sociologist. Ministers included Samuel Zane Batten, Samuel Macrae Cavert, A. E. Holt of the Chicago Church Federation, Charles Lathrop, Charles Macfarland, Alva Taylor, and many others. At Chicago, in January, 1926, the largest meeting yet was held, lasting over a month, in coöperation with the Chicago Church Federation. Twenty-five thousand people attended. Five radio addresses were given. William Green of the AFL, Jane Addams, William Hapgood, Hubert Herring, William B. Spofford, and the president of the Illinois AFL gave addresses. In Detroit, in 1926, Reinhold Niebuhr and Ralph C. McAfee, secretary of the Detroit Council of Churches, guided four conferences, gathering local ministers, employers, labor union leaders, and state labor department officials. These conferences continued on into the early 'thirties. Then they slowly died.[23]

Among businessmen, response to all this evangel ran the gamut. If John Eagan or John D. Rockefeller, Jr., represented one extreme, there were many besides Gary at the other. The boycott of the Y.W.C.A. by the Pittsburgh Employers Association in 1919–20

counted only as one of the less subtle cases. Many business organs
found Bolshevism to be infecting the ministry and especially the
Federal Council. In perhaps the majority of instances of articulate
business protest, it happened that the businessman held firm
views upon the correct version of the faith. Judge Gary was one.
John Edgerton of the National Association of Manufacturers was
another. Beginning by denying churchmen any proper voice in
economic affairs, Edgerton proceeded fluently to interpret Jesus
in respect to the affairs of the economy and found Jesus consistent
with Spencer. The NAM issued its own pamphlet, *Industry, Society, and the Church,* which consisted of excerpts from the
writings of Dean Inge. The Baltimore *Manufacturer's Record* felt
that ". . . the world needs more preaching of the Gospel as Paul
preached it." Paul refused to discuss economic, political, and
social questions. The businessmen as a whole tended to be
Pauline. This was shrewd enough; for Rauschenbusch, for the
prophets in general, Paul was something of a stumbling block and
in disrepute. The original endowment of the World's Christian
Fundamentals Association had come from two Los Angeles mil-
lionaires in 1910. The Baptists faced the same alliance in 1920,
when a gift of $1,500,000 came to the Home Missionary Society,
but with stipulations attached as to the creed this money should
help spread. These stipulations, as hardly anyone was surprised
to find, were of the most conservative social and doctrinal order.
In 1925 one hundred Episcopal laymen discovered a conjunction,
in what they deemed the socialistic infection of their clergy, of
unsound economic doctrine and unsound Christian ethic; they
warned the General Convention of the danger. For sophistication,
this was in advance of the approach adopted by the trustees of
the Episcopal Berkeley Divinity School in 1920. Dean W. P. Ladd
of the divinity school had been a member of the Church League
for Industrial Democracy, the Intercollegiate Socialist Society,
and the Committee of 48. The trustees, disturbed by accusations
leveled against the school, agreed that the principles of the CLID
could, if applied, solve social and industrial principles. But:

> In the present state of the public mind and from the standpoint of
> the citizen of the world, whether he calls himself a Christian or not,

we think it unwise . . . for the members of the faculty of the
Berkeley Divinity School to associate themselves with this and other
similar organizations.

This was not fortunate either in rhetoric or philosophy; the
"citizen of the world" was not apt to constitute a figure before
whom the prophets would bow down. An Appleton, Wisconsin,
paper manufacturer, Judson Rosebush, admonished religious
leaders to preach the gospel as Jesus preached it, a cardinal tenet
of which was silence on economic affairs. Rosebush found a grave
miscarriage of exegesis: ". . . misled by that splendid word 'cooperation,' the Methodist church adopted an economic program
which . . . enrolled the great, splendid denomination under the
banner of Sovietism." In a pamphlet entitled "The Revival of Christianity through the Power of Preaching," another businessman,
Manell Sayre, agreed that the church had shrunk into a club for the
upper and middle classes. Sayre's worry over this situation was not
quite that of the prophets, however. Since, he declared, the Christian church had always stood for the principle that man's inner nature required the unimpaired maintenance of private property, it
was of vital importance for humanity that the wage-earning poor be
won once again to Christian loyalty. He called for a new Loyola,
a new Wesley, a new St. Francis, to preach this mission.[24]

In a way, attacks of this sort were less than discouraging for
the social gospel. In an effort to wound Diabolus in his lair, it
was comforting to hear roars of pain as assurance that Diabolus
really did exist; moreover, these roars, obscurantist, uncrafty, and
unwise as they were, made Diabolus seem, if still morally fero-
cious, a little stupid. Where snares and delusion lay were in the
responses of such a transparently sincere Christian businessman as
Roger Babson. Babson, investment counselor, economic oracle,
one of the priests of prosperity—and later, one of the prophets of
the crash—was an active, leading layman in the Congregational
Church. In his books, his apparently incurable innocence blurted
out the fruitfulness of enlightened idealism for cash returns and
the security of investments. Babson was capable of inveighing
against "competition" and the "profit motive" with a cadence un-
cannily similar to that of the critics of the system. He could speak

of the "failure" of the present order. And yet, the basis for his
call upon business support for the churches could hardly have
satisfied the prophetic will: "The religion of the community is
really the bulwark of our investments." The difference in systematic analysis between Babson and the social prophets lay in
what followed their criticisms of the system. The ethical qualities
Babson celebrated were those upon which the ultimate value of
production depended: honesty, industry, thrift, calculation, the
classic virtues of the later Calvinism studied by Weber and
Tawney. The prophets could hardly have denied these virtues;
they assumed them, in fact. But they did not speak of them. They
dwelt on the social virtues, not on the productive virtues. Babson,
in reëmphasizing the old virtues of production, demonstrated
their psychological inadequacy for building the new order. He,
like the prophets, was shocked at the profit motive and the "independence of the economic sphere," but for him the offense was
that these were corruptions of old motives, whereas for the
prophets they were obstacles to the generation of new motives.
For him, the profit motive led the virtues of production into the
degenerate talents of mere speculation and acquisition. This was
an old gospel, not the social gospel. To look on past Babson was
only to peer into slightly more recognizable confusion, the re-
ligion-of-business that had appropriated the most impeccable of
sanctions in its credo that "business is service." [25]

Rarely challenged deeply by it, the men of the social gospel
yet had enormous difficulty in clarifying what was inadequate in
this humanization of the system expressed by Babson, by "business is service," and by prosperity itself. Their basic technique of
resisting the temptation to default was simply to project the ideal
far beyond reach of even the best proponents of the system:

> Someday the Christian spirit will end even the present capitalistic
> domination by the coming of a spiritual, a social, and therefore, an
> industrial democracy . . . someday, neither Nash nor Ford will
> see in Jesus Christ a mender of the rattling mechanism of present-
> day business, but a real revolutionist, whose teachings must ulti-
> mately transform all life. Riches and poverty will both vanish
> when his kingdom conquers all kings and capitalists.[26]

This could only intensify, not solve, the problem of power. Failure of the policy of preaching to the top, as an exclusive, leading, or even simply important tactic, began to be apparent in the 'twenties. As an early exercise in a career devoted to unmasking the realities behind every façade of pretension, Reinhold Niebuhr was applying fact and acid to the legend of Henry Ford as early as 1926. Men of the most moderate temper were soberly discouraged. After many years of preaching on Woodward Avenue in Detroit, Gaius Glenn Atkins judged as follows:

> Realistic laymen were, and have remained, more largely untouched by the whole movement than is generally supposed. I was during all this period the minister of two churches whose congregations included men of status and force in highly industrialized cities. I do not think they shared the official social passion of the communion to which they belonged, knew much or cared much about it. That they knew no more was probably the fault of their minister. But, as far as they did know, their response lacked warmth. The more conservative were politely hostile.[27]

The persistence of and the failure to overcome the distance between religious ideals and the world of big business helped shape social-gospel response to the 'thirties.

IV

The Faces of Power: Labor

The sense of distance between church and big business
was more than matched by the sense of distance between church
and labor. In its efforts to overcome it, social-gospel reaction exhibited a curious mixture of guilt and anxiety, of abstract patron-
age and practical caution. The industrial labor community fell
even more clearly outside the patterns of the old culture. Was it
to be thought of as victim of the new industrial order, or as alien
to the old culture community? Was it to be supported in its
present helplessness or cautioned in anticipation of its future
strength?

As a point of orientation, certain ideas of Paul Tillich can be
useful. Tillich, pastor and professor in exile from Nazism, was one
of the leaders of postwar German religious socialism. Convinced
of the need for a kind of depth analysis of modern culture, he had
sought to correlate the aspirations of modern socialistic labor
movements with ultimate religious insights. With the rise of
Hitler, he came to the United States, to become, at Union Theological Seminary, one of the most powerful spokesmen for a post-
liberal religious approach to culture.

In 1931 he summed up the duty of modern Protestantism in

terms of "The Protestant Principle and the Proletarian Situation." Tillich declared that only by giving up everything inaccessible and irrelevant to the proletarian could the unconditional heart of Protestantism liberate itself for modern use.

> The proletarian situation is not something optional to which attention may or may not be given. It is rather the point at which history itself has posed the question to Protestantism, whether it will identify itself with the traditional forms in which it has been realized, or whether it will accept the challenge which confronts it in the situation of the proletarian masses and that calls in question a large part of its present-day life and thought. . . . The Protestant judgment becomes concrete, actual and urgent in its application to the class situation of today. . . .[1]

Like Karl Barth, leader of European neo-orthodoxy, Tillich had made the postwar decade the occasion for protesting the identification of religion with modern culture in any of its guises. The absolute could never be identified with the historical, the temporal, the relative, the finite. Tillich protested particularly against those identities between man and God claimed by the culture-Protestantism of nineteenth-century liberalism. Unlike Barth, however, Tillich found in the historical conditions that provoked this protest the content of the protest itself. Barth had been a religious socialist before the war. After the war, which inspired his prophetic resignation from liberalism, he resigned from politics also. He appeared to have withdrawn from history. His religion constituted a timeless word that could never be claimed for temporal purposes. On the other hand, Tillich insisted that protest and politics had to be combined. Against a culture claiming to be closed, religiously sanctioned, self-sufficient, the Protestant principle demanded that politics reopen culture to freedom. The Protestant principle was a principle of judgment, but it was first and always a concrete judgment, seeking out the actual situations where pretensions to closed, self-sufficient meaning flourished, and seeking out also, thereby, the practical, workable lines along which judgment could be expressed.

When Tillich insisted that Protestantism must make sense of

and for the proletarian, he was endeavoring to fuse into one gesture responses to the whole range of modern Protestant anxiety—individual, cultural, political, philosophical, and theological. In America, the accumulation of nerve for such a response waited upon an American tragedy. It was not until the 'thirties that self-consciousness was sufficient for the problems to become clear. By then, both Barth and Tillich were known. American rejection, by and large, of Barth expressed a measure of American Protestant conviction that immediate American conditions, political, economic, and cultural, still offered good ground for religious truth. Could there be a choice for Tillich, however? Could the old identification of religion with culture be broken by support of labor? Where this was attempted, the social gospel began to disintegrate, above all under the attacks of Reinhold Niebuhr, who did for a few crucial years follow the course proposed by Tillich.

In the 'twenties there were no clear lines of division; all choices were obscure, complicated, indecisive. In those years the social gospel remained idealism at that last stage in which fusion of principle and culture could still be assumed as a source of strength. Its concern with labor displayed, therefore, all the expected complexity and inner tensions. At one point the church community exhibited a defensive reaction, at another its concern was more guilty than defensive. Where the guilt came out, sometimes men asked simply that the old community be extended to include labor, and sometimes they rejected the terms of the old community in the name of labor. Where they rejected, they might demand a new fusion of principle and culture, or they might undertake to reject all fusions alike. None of this was clear-cut. Rarely were such distinctions self-consciously drawn. It is as important here to convey the flux and blurring of patterns as to bring out and sharpen the patterns.

The flux derived first of all from the fact that labor was felt to be outside, and even against, the church. There was no feeling, after all, that the business masters individually were not in the church. Judge Gary was a practicing Methodist. The alienation of business was one of principle; the businessmen accepted no adequate Christian discipline, and the church was going to have to struggle to avoid passive, pious acquiescence in their hegemony. Labor, on the other hand, it was believed, was not in the church at all. Here was alienation in terms of community. This alienation could be thought of as one not only of community, but also of principle. Consequently, a forsaken labor community would have to be converted to the ideals of the church. On the other hand, it could be the church that was lost, having fallen captive to class ideals; in that case the church would have to be converted.

Programs for "labor churches" displayed the shades of feeling here, especially the program of the Methodists. Postwar Methodism had extensive plans for labor evangelism. The sum of $6,-632,800 of its enormous Centenary Fund was to go for churches for industrial workers, many of them in the area of the steel strike in Pennsylvania, including McKeesport, Connellsville, Braddock, and Monessen. Some Methodists clarified their reasons for support of this program:

> The need for insurance against Bolshevism, as the Centenary program for Americanization has so aptly been termed, was never more strikingly demonstrated than on September 22, when twenty-four great labor unions . . . inaugurated their long-pending strike against the United States Steel Corporation . . . The five pivotal churches . . . will play a great part in the modification of the danger from polyglot masses of industrial workers.[2]

The *Christian Advocate* filled in some of the cultural coloring of this strategy still more frankly, praising the "anthracite mission" ". . . where Protestant Christianity in its endeavor to nourish the spiritual life of the people comes into collision with the superstition and intense bigotry which the Slavs have brought with them out of centuries of priestly intolerance."[3] The *Advocate* was not a social-gospel paper in its own right, but its pages were open often enough to the slogans and demands of the social gospel. The editor, James Joy, spoke from time to time for profit-sharing, collective bargaining, and shop committees. In fact, the sense of this insurance policy against Bolshevism could be under-

stood only as part of a larger policy, expressed well by Methodist
Bishop Mouzon:

> Labor in America must be Christianized . . . there is no place on
> the soil of America to transplant the anti-Christian socialism of
> Europe. Whoever develops class-hatred among men is an enemy
> of Jesus Christ . . . And again, capital in America must be Chris-
> tianized . . . Capital, proud, self-conscious, selfish, indifferent to
> the rights of men, unconscious of its power, is utterly un-American
> and utterly un-Christian.[4]

Here was the double alienation perfectly expressed, written with
absolute self-confidence in the righteousness and power of the
church community standing "between" capital and labor. Here
there was no notion that the church was culturally classbound;
labor's alienation implied no deficiencies in the church; the
solution for alienation lay wholly in the conversion of labor. This
was not a peculiarly Methodist spirit. Methodists simply gave
it, as they gave most of the nuances of the social passion, the
sharpest, least hesitant voice.[5]

Labor churches of an opposite sort were few. Herbert Casson's
church in Lynn, established in 1894, was not an imitated model.
There were indeed to be famous churches; the most outstanding
in the 'twenties was the Labor Temple of New York City, founded
by Charles Stelzle in 1910, later directed by Edmund Chaffee.[6]
But the Labor Temple escaped the original problem by forsaking any recognizable Protestant character, to become a kind
of lower or lower-middle-class variation upon the religion of
community service and humanism typified in the church of
John Haynes Holmes. Remaining closer to the original idea was
the Grace Community Labor Church founded in Denver, directed
first by George Lackland, then by Aaron A. Heist. Methodist in
origin, turned nonsectarian, Grace Community held both official
and unofficial relations with organized labor, housed a labor college, and sponsored an open forum. Even so, it finessed the basic
problem as had the Labor Temple.[7]

At both poles, in number and success, the fruits were sparse.[8]
The paucity in each instance followed from the same difficulty.

The tactic of anthracite missions called for unusual subtlety and long-range imagination. The really massive defense measures of Protestantism in the 'twenties were measures not of evangelism, but of rejection of the alien, as in fundamentalism and the Klan. Where instincts to identify with labor flourished, it was much easier for the idealist to leave the ministry altogether and adopt the cause of labor as the faith, rather than linger in the ambiguity of labor temples. What the social gospel retained, then, was an uneasy feeling that the Protestant church community was on the whole class-bound, without sharp ideas of what to do about it.

Certainly one thing that had to be done was to establish direct communication across the distance. The churchmen made themselves hopeful of labor's response. Labor leaders themselves were frequently asked what they thought of the situation, and a general formula emerged, pleasing to the pastors both as justification for their attack on the classbound attitude of the church and as support for their hopes to overcome it. Jesus was a laboring man; he had belonged to the ranks of labor as a carpenter and had stayed there even as preacher; but in the churches

> . . . the real Jesus has been let go. . . . If the workers had the same faith in the Church that they have in the Bible, there would not be half enough churches in the country to hold them . . . The vast majority of workers speak of Jesus Christ and the Church as two separate entities, because they believe in Christ and his teachings, yet find little of the spirit of the Brotherhood of Man in actual practice in the Church of today. . . .[9]

Thus, although there was something to be said for the indictment of "A Bourgeois Church in a Proletarian World," this was too harsh a way of looking at things. It was not really a proletarian world in which the proletarians sustained loyalty to simple, uncorrupted Christian ideals. Nor was the church truly bourgeois as long as it might save itself by throwing off its corruption and liberating the ideals in which it did fundamentally believe.[10]

This tendency to solve problems of tactics by dissolving them in good will appeared rather consistently in the labor-relations program of the Federal Council. In the fervor of 1919, the Council had taken the labor-church tack, recommending in its 1919 report, "The Church and Social Reconstruction," the creation of "hundreds of powerful, highly socialized and democratically organized churches in working class neighborhoods and industrial centers." [11] No such program emerged. The council's plans cooled from missionary forms to diplomatic. Annual meetings with the American Federation of Labor, annual Labor Sunday Messages, and strike reports became its service to labor. Each year, wherever the AFL was holding its annual convention, the council secretaries, primarily James Myers, encouraged local churches to invite union leaders to address an evening service or some church club. Thus in Atlanta in 1925, nine AFL officials occupied pulpits. In Los Angeles in 1927, under the direction of Edwin P. Ryland, who was the local church delegate to the Central Labor Council and a frequent strike mediator, a highly successful exchange took place, and it was affirmed that Jesus, a worker in the building trades, might well have been an AFL man Himself. John P. Frey, of the Metal Trades Workers, spoke before the New Orleans Ministerial Union in 1928: "There has been nothing more encouraging to the labor movement in the last fifteen or twenty years than the interest of church groups, and their intelligent studies of labor problems. . . ." Eighteen New Orleans churches observed the day. These were all displays of high diplomacy, occasions of ceremony at which each representative found opportunity to affirm a flawless ideal solidarity. AFL leaders displayed an impeccable talent for such meetings. Speaking before the Northern Baptists in 1926, William Green found only the deepest natural harmony between church and labor: "They are both of the people. Their membership is drawn from the masses of the people. Both are idealistic in character and are founded upon the innermost feelings of the heart and mind . . . Both organizations are seeking to find a solution of social and industrial problems." Little more could have been asked from the AFL executive committee than its statement of 1923: "[The labor movement] has always taught that the material is essential to something higher, and that the inspiration of our movement has its deepest springs in something above and beyond the material." [12]

Little, it might have been thought, could happen to mar diplomacy where the forms of diplomacy were so well understood. But, the fact that diplomacy had ultimately to do with power and not only with sentiments would not be denied. Early in the summer of 1926, James Myers of the Federal Council submitted a list of prospective labor speakers to the executive secretary of the Detroit Council of Churches, in preparation for the October convention of the AFL. On September 13, eighteen of Detroit's two hundred Protestant ministers met together to plan for the affair. Reinhold Niebuhr, chairman of the Industrial Relations Commission of the Detroit Council, reported a general interest. Five ministers asked for labor speakers, others asked for their denominational social-service secretaries. The Y.M.C.A. had already invited William Green to speak as the climax of the occasion.

In Detroit, a city of open-shop convictions, employers had by then suggested that ministers devote their September sermons to "educational work in the pulpits," as an offset to the October convention. Early in September, the Detroit *Saturday Night* published a cartoon depicting a laboring man in the pulpit clutching a stink bomb. The Building Trades Association circularized its membership with recommendations that word be conveyed by members to their ministers that the proposed October "love feast" was unsuited to the established order of Detroit. On September 27, the *Detroiter* published an open letter to Detroit churchmen from the Board of Commerce, suggesting that the planned exchange of pulpits really amounted to a scheme for making Detroit into a closed-shop town. The letter dwelt upon the un-American as well as un-Detroit character of the proposed labor speakers, including William Green.

Of the five ministers who had intended to invite labor speakers, three were overruled by their church boards. Reinhold Niebuhr, of Bethel Evangelical, and Augustus P. Record, of First Unitarian, held to their plans. But it was the action taken by the Y.M.C.A. that held all attention. The Y.M.C.A. was at this time engaged in a $5,000,000 fund-raising drive. Among its pledges it counted $1,500,000 from Henry Ford, a nonunion enterpriser; $500,000 from Fisher Bodies, a nonunion enterprise; and $300,000 from S. S. Kresge, a nonunion enterprise. The president of the board of directors of the "Y" was Mr. C. B. Van Dusen, who was also head of the Detroit Kresge's. Van Dusen discovered in September that there was reason for concern over the success of the fund drive. The Y.M.C.A. withdrew its invitation to William Green.[13]

It was not at all clear, in the flurry of accusation, recrimination, and soul-searching that followed, that Protestantism or even Detroit Protestantism had suffered a defeat. Indignation stormed on the floor of the AFL convention on October 6 and 7. Nonetheless, James Myers of the council invited Green to a meeting Sunday afternoon, October 10, in the Congregational Church of Gaius Glenn Atkins, and at that meeting, with Lynn Harold Hough presiding, Green, Alva Taylor, Worth Tippy, and Niebuhr carried through the original plan of the exchanges. In the end, there were eight labor speakers in Protestant pulpits, more than had been originally scheduled, as well as social-service men from various denominational headquarters. On October 28, the executive committee of the Detroit Council of Churches, in a resolution drafted by Hough, accused the Building Trades Association, the *Detroiter*, and all others inciting the controversy of being guilty of improper intimidation of the church. All in all, counterattacking smartly, the social-gospel and liberal ministers of Detroit had avoided surrender. There had been humiliation, however, and in the upshot the serenity of the diplomacy with high labor circles was discounted—and discounted in the eyes of both sides. Any shift toward labor in the power center of the church would not occur without turmoil. In the estimate he wrote in 1932 of the indifference of the men of power, Atkins was undoubtedly not forgetful of the 1926 convention. That convention undoubtedly advanced the education of Reinhold Niebuhr.

The annual Labor Sunday Messages were written by the Federal Council staff. To be used as texts for sermons, placed in the hands of parishioners or used in discussion groups, reprinted in church papers, these messages were distributed by the tens of thousands. The 1920 message declared flatly: "Our industrial life has been built on wrong and un-Christian foundations." Antagonism between employer and worker, unemployment, poor wages, all marked the system. Competition and the profit motive infested its spirit. In efforts at reform there could be no question of violence; only extremists turned to violence. But service, the golden rule in the factory, a fair share to labor of increased productivity, had to find their place. Specifically, the church insisted upon labor's right to collective bargaining. The authors of the message felt that when both the two major political parties and such an organization as the National Association of Manufacturers accepted collective bargaining in principle, business had no valid grounds for failing to accept it in practice. The message of 1923 pointed out a fault of organized labor; sometimes it failed to take into account the needs of the entire community: ". . . the new economic advantage which with the turn of the business tide has come to labor enhances the stewardship for which it must give an accounting." Labor's proper tactic in pursuing its rights was to appeal to public opinion. By that route the twelve-hour day had been abolished in steel. Two years later, in a survey of shop-committee and employee representation plans, and applauding William Green's announcement of labor's new desire for coöperation, the message concluded that the future lay with a displacement of the "less scientific method of conflict" by the "technique of coöperation." Since, however, the future was yet to come, a "Christian technique of conflict in areas within which there is frank divergence of interest" would have to carry things through. In 1926, the message noted with satisfaction the rise to labor leadership of men of large personal capacity and social vision, men with a sense of social responsibility and insight matching that of the new leaders in industry. The 1929 Labor Sunday observance set a record, with mass meetings coast to coast and 40,000 copies of the message mailed out. In 1930, the message focused upon problems raised by the expanding productive capacity of the machine.[14]

In an editorial of 1927, the *Baptist*, whose editor, V. M. McGuire, was to run for political office in Chicago in 1932 on the Socialist ticket, condemned these Labor Sunday Messages sharply. They were becoming, the *Baptist* observed, more politic, less prophetic, year by year. Their "softness and evasiveness" was because of an effort to make the most of a growing humanization of industrial ideals found among businessmen, but the editor of the *Baptist* was not satisfied with that.[15] In effect, the *Baptist* was complaining of the pull exerted upon the council by its own constitutional position within the churches, identical with the pull exerted upon the churches by their social position within the nation, as fatal to free and fair exercise of prophetic judgment. The Labor Sunday Messages, like the AFL exchanges, had become exercises in diplomacy. They adjusted their generalizations to the sensibilities of everybody between the extremes. The 1920 message had contained strong words, and in the council's *Information Service* early in 1921, other strong words had been found, in direct support of labor union aggressiveness:

> . . . many of our labor organizations are developing new powers of initiative and constructive intelligence, are abandoning their old policy of mere dickering for better terms of employment and are grappling with the problems of industry itself . . . as radicalism becomes absorbed in the regular labor movements it gains a constructive quality.[16]

But this early postwar encouragement for a definite, rather rigorous labor strategy dissolved. Agents of the church as a whole, the spokesmen of the council let their sense of the church's position between two outside forces draw the messages back into line; their balanced admonitions were rationed out with a merely rhetorical equality, without concern for the inequalities of power.

The council's strike reports were something else, however, for strikes pinpointed the problem of labor in a way that conventions and high-level diplomacy did not. Study of strikes offered a chance to focus ideas about the position of labor in the march toward justice. From the beginning, the pastors had rather shied from this chance. Struck by their sudden recognition of a new class of men in need, the early prophets were stunned by sudden realization of the danger to the old, stable, and right order of things represented by these men. It was a measure of Gladden's imagination that despite the impact of the great strikes of the 'seventies, 'eighties, and 'nineties, he could think about them with sufficient detachment to realize that they were more than "disturbances," they were also symptoms. Even more: he saw in the strikes not only symptoms of disease, but also suggestions of cure. Gladden did not try to sanctify the labor movement; it had not occurred to him even to speculate upon it as the dynamic to which all other agents of justice would be but allies. Nevertheless, he did not stultify himself in demands for eradication of symptoms before the disease had had fair analysis and fair treatment. He believed that labor had a destined field of action. He did not apply to industrial leadership in its strength and to unorganized labor in its weakness the impartial tests of "motive" and "purpose" without recognizing that the difference between strength and weakness bore upon the problem of tactics for pursuing the ideal.[17] This was strictly a function of Gladden's slightly more sensitive political imagination. It had little to do with the liberalism of his ideals. Men to both his right and left, in terms of the end they envisioned, failed equally to rise to the issue. Thus, in Francis Greenwood Peabody's *Jesus Christ and the Social Question*, the chapter on the industrial order was a classic demonstration of how to veil the scene of going industrial conflict behind the abstractions of the ideal. Change, Peabody insisted, depended wholly upon an increase in righteousness, particularly among the powerful; religious men could not support tactics that did not directly imitate the ideal, that did not, in other words, refuse all coercion.[18] On the other hand, men like George Herron and those who followed Bellamy were just as far as Peabody from taking Gladden's first steps in tactics. They had penetrated no further than Peabody in imaginative grasp of the facts of the changing order. They were simply more appalled than Peabody, not more radical, and therefore projected a more fixed, final, and frozen vision of the ends. Bellamy's utopia stood beyond a transitional apocalyptic nightmare that he barely tried to politicalize. This was natural. It was because he had the nightmare that he had the utopian vision; but what man, reading Bellamy, knew what anyone's role was to be while waiting for the year 2000?

There were men who went beyond Gladden: Casson of the

Lynn labor church, Joseph Cook in Boston to an extent, W. D. P.
Bliss of the Society of Christian Socialists, and Father J. O. S.
Huntington. But it was Rauschenbush who stood foremost, and
although Rauschenbusch was hailed for many things, what stamps
him most sharply in retrospect is his estimate of tactics, the
first clear, concrete estimate in the annals of the social passion.
The negative side of his tactical analysis has been touched upon
already: "Every social class in history has used whatever weapons
it had—sword, law, ostracism or clerical anathema—to strike at
any other class that endangered its income." Altruistic self-
effacement of a class could not be expected. This did not mean,
however, that Rauschenbusch had overcome the instinctive social-
gospel reaction to the turmoil in the industrial scene: "Strikes are
war, and 'war is hell' . . . If our industrial organization cannot
evolve some saner method of reconciling conflicting interests than
twenty-four thousand strikes and lockouts in twenty years, it
will be a confession of social impotence and moral bankruptcy." [19]
Here was tension, but in facing his problem, Rauschenbusch did
not immediately appeal to the utopian principles of the end for
guidance concerning the means. He held to his field of inquiry,
and by so doing occupied ground that was to cost half the labor
of Reinhold Niebuhr and the realists of the 'thirties to reoccupy
against the semipacifism of the late 'twenties. As for Gladden, so
for Rauschenbusch the existence of strikes and of classes was not
only symptom of disease, symbol of evil, but hint at the cure,
a sign to the route for overcoming the evil.

> Truth is mighty. But for a definite historical victory a given truth
> must depend on the class which makes that truth its own and fights
> for it. . . . the idealists alone have never carried through any great
> social change. In vain they dash their fair ideas against the solid
> granite of human selfishness.[20]

It is well to transcribe the views of Rauschenbusch on this
point in precise detail, for he was speaking, in almost identical
words, the language summoned by Niebuhr in Niebuhr's attack
upon the moralist. Rauschenbusch did not back away from the
final issue over which the social gospel broke: he did not shirk

facing the pacifist. It was to the interest of all sides, he wrote, that the process of social change be evolutionary and not catastrophic.

> On the other hand, the Christian idealists must not make the mis-take of trying to hold the working class down to the use of moral suasion only, or be repelled when they hear the brute note of selfishness and anger . . . All that we as Christian men can do is to ease the struggle and hasten the victory of the right by giving faith and hope to those who are down, and quickening the sense of justice with those who are in power, so that they will not harden their hearts and hold Israel in bondage, but will "let the people go." [21]

This was clear enough. In the end, Rauschenbusch could not help insisting that the role of the idealists was crucial after all, but he set their role firmly in context. They were the hope for peaceful and rational change, they were the hope for a new order not maimed and embittered at birth, but they were not the central dynamic for change and a new order. The central dynamic lay with those for whom the ideal was entangled with bread and butter. These bread-and-butter crusaders could be helped to bear the ideal—often enough the ideal had to be set upon their shoulders in the first place—but they alone were the ones who could bear it to historical victory.

The immediate postwar years seemed to signal renewal, on a broader, more bitter front, of the very literal social struggle Rauschenbusch had seen and felt, and which he had thought inevitable. Those years were marked by a rash of strikes, product of possibly the most confused period in American labor history. Labor had made gains during the war. The railroad men had won the eight-hour day in 1916. Labor-management coöperation during the war led a good many labor leaders to feel that organized labor had emerged as an accepted partner of the industrial community. AFL rolls soared to more than four million. Wages rose, not wholly in pace with prices, but nevertheless in a manner quite unknown since the Civil War. The harmony ended quickly. Wage-cutting began within a year of the armistice. The AFL suffered three punishing blows in a row:

loss of the steel strike, the deflationary crash and unemployment of 1920–21, and the open-shop drive. Membership fell well below three million within three years of war's end. The AFL in reflex forsook whatever tentative interest in industrial unionization the steel-strike effort had displayed, and retired to the cultivation of its privileged position within the community of labor as a whole. The obstacles to further unionization were severe, in any case. Large numbers of the labor force were men from the last waves of prewar immigration—masses of men huddling together in the factory towns of Pennsylvania, Ohio, Michigan, with whom labor organizers could hardly communicate. They were unaware of the principles and chances of civil liberties, and ready, often enough, to endure company police as they had endured authority in the Habsburg empire. Southern Negroes imported into the Northern war plants had stayed north, available as breaker-boys, twelve-hour workers, and strike-breakers. Two large industries, bituminous coal and textiles, were in a state of chronic instability. And into what would have been enough confusion in the early years, the Palmer parties injected a hysteria for which the actions of a dying I.W.W. provided some minimum excuse.

In this situation, no one of the resolutions of the Federal Council or of the denominations in national convention, and no one of the innumerable resolutions of district or city church groups and federations, approved use of the strike for any reason, whether as economic or political tactic.[22] The strike was a violation of the method of coöperation, one of the "less scientific techniques of conflict." Yet by and large the strike was not condemned in the 'twenties as it had been so often before. "Understanding" rather than condemnation had been the intention of the report on the steel strike. There were to be no such ambitious investigations under church auspices in the following years, but a policy of reports on a much smaller scale, already cautiously begun by the Federal Council, was carried on. The Social Service Commission issued a pamphlet on the 1919 Lawrence textile strike. After a study of the coal strike of 1920 by Worth Tippy, the commission issued a bulletin surveying the perpetually beset bituminous industry and, together with the National Catholic Welfare

Council, sponsored publication of an independent scholarly study. In Denver the violent transportation strike of 1920 inspired a group of laity and churchmen to invite a joint Federal Council–NCWC investigation, which was published in October, 1921. In 1926 the ministerial associations of Cumberland and Hagerstown, Maryland, requested an investigation of the Western Maryland railroad strike; by then, the work had been taken over by the council's Department of Research and Education. In the Passaic strike of 1926, the largest textile strike of the times, the local ministerial association drew back from a council offer to investigate, but the council went in nevertheless, upon urging from various denominational social-service boards. During the recrudescence of trouble in Rockefeller's Colorado Fuel and Iron Company, the ministerial associations of several Colorado towns asked the council in. A dispute over company-benefit-association plans in an Indianapolis textile firm was investigated in 1927. Still further coal trouble called forth a report in 1928, and a report on the textile situation in Marion, North Carolina, appeared in 1929.[23]

These reports went out primarily to ministers and were for the use of ministers. They were at once efforts to convert the ministry itself to an understanding of labor and supplies of technical intelligence for their use as idealists. They expressed the social gospel's postwar demand for scientific resources, and gave something of an amateur's familiarity with the fields of society to which the abstract creeds, resolutions, and ideals were supposed to apply. The reports hinged on the premise that an informed public opinion would be a wiser and more just public opinion. Whereas formerly, in the absence of facts, the general public reacted solely to the disorder and violence of strikes, which in turn were always held to the account of the strikers without consideration of the causes in terms of justice, now, more enlightened, the public would be less frightened. Eminent authorities had already sanctioned such church efforts to fill this vacuum in public knowledge. Albion W. Small of the University of Chicago, one of the generation of sociologists still rooted directly in the evangelical ethic, proposed a permanent Interchurch

Survey Commission to investigate class conflict generally and to circulate reports on its findings, both as a work good in itself and as a means for the church to win labor. R. H. Tawney, speaking from English experience, sketched and recommended a permanent department for research and education.[24] Plainly, of course, the council's reports were not up to these high recommendations. Its investigations did not begin to provide a coherent picture of industrial labor relations in general, if only because the principle of decorum observed in waiting for an invitation by local church forces provided an arbitrary selection of cases, and the industries concerned most frequently tended to be exceptional in context of the larger issues (as was U. S. Steel, although for opposite reasons). But these reports emphasized an important feature of the industrial scene—the lack of some regularized agency or means for getting the facts that underlay the strife. The impetus here was the same one that had led hospitals, schools, and settlements to be founded by evangelical energy and to take their place among nonecclesiastical "secular" organizations of the society. The ultimate agency to which the council looked for taking up this work on its proper scale was the federal government, to which it issued appeals for inquiry into the coal industry and into textiles on occasion of the Passaic and Marion strikes.

In this way, these reports were of more than a little symbolic, although of no scientific, significance, and the churchmen liked to feel that they amounted to a kind of witnessing to the faith, a testimony to the seriousness with which the social translation of the faith was conceived. The point was that the testimony was offered to labor. The steel report proved most advantageous here, as the editor of *Zion's Herald* once found:

> On Sunday of last week we spoke before a group of radical working men, and at the close of the address an attack was made from the floor on the Christian church as the creature of capitalism. In reply we simply told the story of the steel strike and the Interchurch report. Those facts immediately turned the tide and the whole audience broke out in hearty applause at such evidence of the church's interest in the worker.[25]

Why should men sharpen their ideas when audiences cheer those they have? Did the strike reports, however, represent positive advocacy of a labor program? This was another question, and one which the editor of *Zion's Herald* obscured for his readers because he obscured it in his own mind. Paul Blanshard, a member of the League for Industrial Democracy and former minister himself, put the issue:

> We recognize that the neutral attitude is advisable in investigating industrial facts, but the attitude should not continue after the facts have been disclosed. We feel that the church should be just as militant in its opposition to industrial ills as it was in the fight against negro slavery or the saloon. Why play safe? Jesus didn't.[26]

The reports of the council did not display this militancy. An important goal of the social-gospel program was to achieve neutrality, to transcend class captivity. The council issued a bulletin sharply criticizing the open-shop drive of 1921; [27] otherwise there were no occasions when combat was joined on specific issues on the industrial front. The drastic injunction of 1922 against the railroad shopmen provoked no comments on injunctions in general nor were clear views on unionization derived from the strike reports.

Strikes did call out displays of militancy, however, for some men had let logic lead them well beyond prudence, beyond the security limits of the culture-church. If the church as neutral and impartial judge was classically expressed by the steel strike report, the classic case of the social gospel in passionate advocacy was found in the Lawrence textile strike of that same year. At Lawrence, social-gospel idealism broke free of its origins, became autonomous, no longer shackled by its attachment to older order.

The basic story of the Lawrence strike can be summarized quickly. Thirty thousand textile workers facing a wage cut struck on February 3, 1919, led by AFL United Textile Workers organizers. The UTW wished to accept the wage cut, after proportionate reduction in hours was offered. The workers objected, the UTW withdrew, and the workers were left with only a provisional, poorly experienced strike committee to lead them, manned for the most part by immigrants. Onto this scene came three young ministers, A. J. Muste, Harold Rotzel, and Cedric Long. Under their leadership, primarily that of Muste, the strikers held out until, in June, 1919, they received a wage boost, a cut in hours from fifty-four to forty-eight, and recognition as the Amalgamated Textile Workers Union.

The resolution of the three ministers was to have significance for social-gospel history generally. Carried out in days when the atmosphere hung heavy with fears of Bolshevism, anarchism, and revolution—the Seattle general strike of 1919 and the great strike in Winnipeg providing fodder for the fearful—and taking place, moreover, on the scene of the exploits of Giovanitti, Carlo Tresca, and Gurley Flynn only seven years before, the Lawrence strike was made for violence. Machine guns were shipped to the police. The violence came, but it was police violence alone. Muste, Rotzel, and Long were pacifists who organized a policy of non-resistance that, when the violence struck, made painfully and conspicuously clear from which direction it had emanated. Muste and Long were beaten by the police and jailed at one point in the strike. There appears to be little doubt that their style of leadership was the decisive factor in the whole affair.[28]

Muste was an ordained minister, raised in the Dutch Reformed Church, trained at Union, then pastor of a Newtonville, Massachusetts, Congregational Church, from which he resigned in 1917 in conscientious objection to the war. He had left the Dutch Reformed because of difficulties about creed. After Lawrence, in 1919, he attended upon the Utica textile strike in company with Paul Blanshard, who was also initiated into the local jails. Muste went on to more strike experience at Paterson and Passaic, New Jersey. In 1921, he became head of the Brookwood Labor College at Katonah, New York, which was inspired and endowed by still another former minister, William Fincke. Brookwood taught to its handfuls of labor men coming in each term the concepts of a labor movement devoted to more than wages and hours, devoted to larger causes, primarily those preached by social-gospel churchmen, and to the ultimate cause of literal industrial democracy. Muste wanted all labor organized, he wanted a labor party, and he wanted a program transcending enlightened capitalism. He was a Socialist party member from before the war; by the early 'thirties he was to find the Socialist party too conservative, and in the Conference for Progressive Labor Action he steered the haunted line between the Socialists and the Communists. Muste's interest always fixed on the means, however—a dedicated labor movement—and the Lawrence strike was his port of entry into a life directed to that movement. The theological scruples that drove him out of the Dutch Reformed Church had ended, Muste believed, his church career. Actually, they had not; he had had his church in Newtonville. But the break with the ministry and the going, visible church was easy: the sum of the evangel had become ethical, and there was nothing except Jesus' way of life, equally the Tolstoyan or Gandhian way of life. The future lay in labor, and labor became the whole field of concern; in effect it became both potentially and actively the church itself.[29]

Harold Rotzel, an ordained Methodist, had also resigned his church in 1917. After Lawrence, he took to raising chickens. He identified with the labor movement, but he was also a pacifist, and the fearful inner tension of this dual commitment perhaps fitted a man poorly to do more than serve as witness. Rotzel formulated his tension: "I am still determined to take the position of a conscientious objector in the labor movement, if the issue of a violent class war is ever clearly drawn, but I hope that this time may never come." [30] The stigmata of the true radical pacifist were in this statement: suspension of potential contradictions between the radical and the pacifist poles in a simple, abstract "hope," and the actual priority of the pacifist commitment if choice had to be made.

Cedric Long too did not return to the ministry, but entered the coöperative movement, to become head of the Co-operative League of America.[31]

The passionate advocacy at Lawrence made for breakup in synthesis and released the social gospel from the church. There were other instances of resignation from the ministry during the period of the social gospel: in addition to Muste, Rotzel, and Long, there was Paul Blanshard; there was Fincke; there was Albert Coyle, who became editor of a labor paper; there was the most famous of all, Norman Thomas. There was to be Howard Williams, who became executive head of the League for Independent Political Action. There were to be Francis Henson and Homer Martin, entering the educational and political action divisions of the AFL and the CIO in the 'thirties. Of course, in some instances this dispersion expressed nothing more than correction of personal errors in choice of calling. In other instances it expressed a deeper logic; this was true of Muste, who will be studied further in the course of this book.

It was one of the aims of the prophets to pour a stream of evangelized laity into the labor movement and the coöperative movement, but that they intended the labor movement as itself a religion is another question, one that this book, concerned not with the flow of converts to the social gospel but with the style and content of social-gospel preaching, will answer from the testimony of the ministers themselves. For most of them, there was some equivalence between separation of the social gospel from the church, and separation of the "social" from the "gospel." For Muste, Rotzel, and Long, the church appeared unfit and unwilling to lead or even take part in the program necessary were the ideals seriously to be pursued. Whether more because it was classbound or more because it labored under a burden of code and creed irrelevant to modern issues, the church was a needless hindrance to those who were serious. But this constituted a violation of inner social-gospel unity, for in that unity the church was necessary, first, and partly unconsciously, as culture-community, but further as symbol of the fact that the social gospel was not a complete gospel, and was false gospel when mistaken as complete. The vectors here will be traced further, and Muste will be one of the guides. All that need be grasped now is the heavy charge at the labor pole, a charge that could split men off from the church.

Splitting off was not a necessary result, of course. There were other instances of immediate personal engagement that did not end in resignation from the church. A minister sat on the General Strike Commission in Seattle in 1919. Men like Andrew Phillips and Theodore Miner in Pennsylvania were acquainted with state troopers taking down the names of churchgoers at the doors. In New York, Charles Webber opened his Church of All Nations to strikers during a dispute in the paper-box industry in 1926. A. A. Heist had opened his Grace Community Church in Denver to strike meetings during the Colorado Fuel and Iron strike. Examples mounted in the 'thirties. Harlan County in Kentucky introduced Union Seminary students to the local jails as revolutionaries. At Paterson, New Jersey, two of the pickets arrested in the silk strike were Episcopal clergymen, one of whom, Bradford Young, took on organizing duties at the Brooklyn Edison Company late in 1931. A Brooklyn Presbyterian minister, David Cory, and Episcopal Elliott White were both manhandled in the Brooklyn Edison trouble, together with several Union Seminary students. In Springfield, Illinois, the Springfield local of Socialists appointed Reverend Douglas Anderson chairman of the Midwest Striking Miners Relief Fund in 1932. A Church Emergency Relief Committee, with headquarters in New York, collected funds for the Danville, Virginia, millworkers on strike in 1930. Christ Church in Philadelphia, where Cameron Hall was pastor, was used by the International Ladies Garment Workers Union on strike in 1930. In Allentown, Pennsylvania, in 1932, a Reformed Church pastor, W. D. Mathias, was instrumental in getting a Federal Council investigation into the textile strike, in helping organize the Church Emergency Relief Committee, and soon after in forming a local labor college.[32]

The calculated reasons that might have been working in any given case of such involvement will have to be made out further; but at the heart of all of it there pulsed the same thing found in the council's milder, less direct, less personal efforts—a desire to witness, to testify, approaching in some instances the sacramental. William B. Spofford, secretary of the CLID, caught something of the spirit, especially the spirit of the early 'thirties, in his declaration that those few Christians who realized that the

classbound culture-church was not going to help much in bringing in the new order could best serve their ideals by lending
themselves to the workers, suffering police clubs and militia
bullets at their sides.[33] While this was a little melodramatic,
even for the times, it caught the combination of sacrificial and
sacramental. These gestures of solidarity were deliberate efforts
to dignify areas of life left untended by the static and closed
church-as-culture. There was a priestly element in these prophetic
gestures; many high-church Episcopal clergy suggested it. Here,
too, even where the emotion was fed back into the church with
an extra loyalty, as it was by the high-church followers and the
seminary students of that generation, the strain on social-gospel
unity mounted.

The spectrum between diplomacy and sacrifice had its exponents at all points. Some of the shades can be exemplified by
completing the story of ministers at Lawrence. Muste, Rotzel, and
Long were not alone. The Massachusetts Congregation of
Churches sent the dean of the Yale Divinity School, Charles R.
Brown, to the scene to write a report. It was on the model of the
council's strike reports, basically sympathetic to the strikers,
although somewhat out of touch with the immediate situation
in which the action had occurred. Carefully balanced admonitions
were dispensed to both sides. The Reverend Victor Bigelow of
Andover, who was soon to deliver the speech reprinted and distributed by Judge Gary, voted against the report; otherwise,
Dean Brown's work was unanimously accepted. Two years later,
Brown, in his book *Social Rebuilders*, speculated upon Moses as
the first great labor leader; he observed how Moses had originally
and mistakenly begun with reliance upon personal violence.
Brown correspondingly recommended a season of reflection in the
land of Midian for the leaders of the IWW.[34]

A fifth outside minister had appeared at Lawrence. Bill Simpson, 1915 graduate of Union Theological Seminary, had abandoned his first church (but not the ministry) for a mission of
peripatetic poverty, preaching at street corners across the country,
wherever there was call. There were calls to student groups, to
summer conferences, to retreats. There was a call to Lawrence,

as there was to be a call to Passaic. Simpson lent a sacramental presence to Lawrence, but he was beyond the reaches of the social gospel. In literal poverty—work shoes, work pants, open-necked shirt, personally tending acreage in New Jersey as a base —and literally peripatetic—traveling only by foot and hitch-hiking—he could be taken best for what he did not inspire: the social passion was not the pathos of Assisi.[35]

The pastors in the Massachusetts Federation of Churches at one point in the Lawerence strike made an offer to mediate; the owners declined.

The Protestant ministers in Lawrence followed a policy of hands off. Their own parishioners were involved only indirectly. A majority of the strikers were Catholic; the leading Catholic priest in Lawrence was hostile to the strike.

At Lawrence all the pastors committed were from the outside and there was no matching commitment from ministers in the town. Passaic in 1926 repeated the pattern, by and large.[36] With the strike under way, George H. Talbot, pastor of First Presbyterian and president of the local ministerial association, wanted the ministers to mediate. He worked toward this end with Theodore Andrews of St. George's Episcopal, with the pastor of Passaic First Methodist, and with the secretary of the local Y.M.C.A. Andrews spoke strongly for the workers in the name of a "revolutionary Christianity." Before the churchmen could swing into action, however, the issue of outside, "red" leadership was raised, and Andrews alone refused to give it top priority. All the other churchmen backed away. At this juncture, the Federal Council offered assistance in the person of James Myers, and was refused. The council went in, nonetheless, supported by James McDowell, Hubert Herring, and Charles Lathrop of the Presbyterian, Congregational, and Episcopal social-service departments, as well as by Inquiry, the Methodist Federation of Social Service, and the New Jersey social-service department. The annual conference of Methodists at Newark spoke sympathetically of the workers' demands, but commended the AFL for its battle against outside leadership. Muste, Norman Thomas, Bill Simpson, Myers, and representatives of the Methodist Federation and the

CLID all visited the town. In the Danville and Marion textile strikes, the pattern was repeated with particular sharpness.

This was not invariably the pattern. During the Colorado strikes of 1927–28, the Colorado Methodist ministers as a group spoke out strongly against the coal companies' refusal to deal with the AFL and against violations of civil liberties; Heist's Denver church provided a focus. At the New Bedford strike of 1928, the secretary of the local church council, John M. Trout, denounced the proposed wage cut, the council as a whole made the strike its leading concern, and there was considerable pulpit support for the workers.[37]

Yet by and large, the pattern was that of Passaic with Andrews, of Allentown with Mathias, of all those instances where only one or two of the local pastors adopted the strike on their doorstep as an embodiment of the issues of the passion, while most of the "concern" came from outside. Very often Protestant concern *had* to come from outside; if the pattern reflected the will of the ordinary pastors, it also betrayed the inaccessibility of the proletarian situation. Passaic dramatized this more emphatically than Lawrence. Action did occur in Passaic, culminating in a formal resolution calling for a Congressional hearing, a resolution signed by churches and religious bodies among others. The names attached to this resolution constituted in themselves an education for Protestant churchmen—Daily Slovak American, Katolicky sokol, Slovak Catholic sokol, Slovak Evangelical Union of America, Petofi Workingmen's Sick Benefit Society, Polish Democratic Club, Russian-American Citizen Club, St. Vladimir Russian Orthodox Society, St. George's Episcopal Church, Marie S.S. dei miracoli Italian Catholic Church, Ascension Ukrainian Church, St. Anton Hungarian Club. The *Christian Century* commented upon this resolution: "Here is the church, intervening at last in an industrial situation which has compelled the attention of the nation. But what church?" [38]

The alienation was truly severe, but whether these responses were lyric or political, cautious or sacrificial, they greeted labor's efforts to strengthen itself. It was generally accepted that there would be a labor movement and that it had a role to play, even though the role was hopelessly vague. One idea was common to the cautious and the sacrificial alike: labor should fight for more than itself. A mere bread-and-butter labor movement, demanding nothing more than a fuller share of the fruits of the system, would not change the system and was not enough. The implications of this insistence, however, were free-floating. Some men drew directly upon the principles of the Kingdom for their criticism of bread-and-butter policy, bypassing all thoughts on the tactics required for limited ends. William Smith of *The Churchman* wrote that "labor has introduced no Christian principles into the industrial conflict. . . . Ownership is still the goal of covetous eyes." [39] Demanding of labor immediate imitation of ideal principles, Smith was able to restrict his social-gospel energy to its oldest form, preaching alone. But in Rauschenbusch, the same demand had stood in broader context. Bread-and-butter motives often served as an originating driving-power for the justice-bearing class, but: "As long as the working class simply attempts to better its condition somewhat and to secure a recognized standing for its class organization, it stands on the basis of the present capitalistic organization of society." [40] As for the concrete program that Rauschenbusch thought labor should make its own, he offered clear judgments. It was the program of Socialism, not just "socialism" or even "Christian socialism," but the Socialism of the Socialist party—purged, of course, of its nonessential European excesses. Such a political context was necessary to prevent the "higher mission" demands upon labor from resulting in indifference, if not opposition, to the labor action actually going on.

Any such clear orientation as Rauschenbusch's was not available in the 'twenties. One of the casualties of enthusiasm was the coherence of the left. Political orientation of any sort was faint. This was why the response of the prophets to industrial strife partook of immediacy. It was clear, in the face of costly, often embittered, and frequently inconclusive industrial encounters, that there had to be some other way. Shop-committee plans, high-level diplomacy, and public pressure appeared to be immediate answers at a time when no better ones were offered.

Even in this period, though, there were hints of a kind of passive vision of an articulated, self-conscious labor program. The "experiments" in social order that fascinated the social-gospel mind included not only the factory laboratories of Nash and Hapgood, but much vaster tryouts on a national scale. Russia was one. The British Labour party, its experiment still in blueprint only but nevertheless developed far beyond ideal abstractions, was another. More must be said of both. An admiring envy for what the British Labour party represented as a fusion of ideal, explicitly religious imperatives and a practical, labor-based program, was found in churchmen of all shades of enthusiasm. Without drawing any practical inferences, nevertheless with transparent longing, the moderate William Adams Brown compared American church-labor relationships to the British. Bishop McConnell, criticizing American socialism for its doctrinaire rigidity, lauded the British Labour party for its large human view of things, beyond the pale of narrowly economic obsessions. G. Bromley Oxnam took the British labor movement for a new missionary endeavor, a genuine extension of the teachings of Jesus. In 1924 in a brilliant article, one of the early masterpieces of a mind sensitive to the problem of tactics, Reinhold Niebuhr analyzed the great tactical, political strength the British Labour party drew from its amalgam of economic doctrine with cultural inheritance rooted in religion. Harry Ward, who gave the Labour party forty pages in *The New Social Order,* was another matter, since to him it was not rigorous, deep, or prophetic enough.[41]

This interest expressed a certain readiness and willingness and expectation. The disappointment of this expectation should count as half the story of the social gospel in the 'twenties. There was labor, but no real labor movement.

Early in 1927, the *Christian Century,* reviewing the strike at Passaic, observed that the strike counted as a defeat for AFL leadership: the English, Irish, and Scottish old-line masters had had to be forced to take into the citadel Slavs and south Europeans with leaders of their own. From then on, the AFL was called in the pages of the *Century* a snare and a delusion. "The American Federation of Labor has become quite as orthodox as the church."

The editors offered a climactic definition of what labor's mission should be:

> Organized labor has won practically every gain made by labor since the industrial revolution began. Its aim should be, of itself, to bring about a social revolution equal in its gain for humanity to that brought by the industrial revolution. That thing it cannot do unless it challenges the whole regime of capitalism by offering, as steps in social progress, a program of fraternal cooperation without the dogmas of Marx, an application of the principles of democracy to industrial organization, a ringing challenge to laissez-faire and the whole system that rests on profits first, and a contribution to an era of world peace wrought out on the basis of humanity first. This it cannot do by becoming orthodox, socially respectable, bureaucratic, and a mere factor in a capitalistic society. Capitalism is only a phase in social progress; it is no more permanent than was feudalism. The rise of the third estate put an end to feudalism; the rise of the fourth estate should profoundly modify capitalism by inaugurating an era of industrial democracy, and cooperative leadership in this direction belongs to labor.[42]

AFL leadership did not measure up. The strike reports had told the story: failure at Lawrence, at Passaic, in Colorado, in steel, failure in imagination, failure in will. And when the voice of Matthew Woll, sponsored indiscriminately by the AFL and the National Civil Federation, poured poison over such an accredited agent of the passion as Sherwood Eddy—not to mention A. J. Muste at the Brookwood labor school—ethical was added to technical evidence of failure. Men like Ward of the Methodist Federation and Spofford of the CLID had of course been criticizing the AFL throughout the decade, but the *Century's* criticism was more crucial. Ward was measuring the AFL against the standards of the ideal future, but the *Century* felt the greater failure to be its paltriness in the present.[43]

An active labor movement was the missing half of the work of the prophets in the 'twenties. Without it, everything was off center. With it, the evangelization and humanization of business leadership would have carried implications true to social-gospel idealism. The shop-committee plans and the industrial experiments would have had the context they required.[44] The ideal of the church as a "neutral" in industrial conflict would have made the sense the prophets ideally intended. But confronted by this vacuum, not only the program but the logic of the prophets inevitably suffered, free-floating, without definite reference, provoking that impatience with "mere" words, resolutions, and creeds heard increasingly through the decade. A labor movement was needed from which the logic could rebound, by which it could find substance and orientation, to which it could refer its distinctions in moral and social theory. An idea of the cost inflicted on theory by this vacuum could be gathered from the anxiety of the prophets over the problem of class. Men of all shades were troubled by it, and one of the reasons was that it concealed two meanings not distinguished in practice. There was class defined strictly by external differences of economic and social power, and there was class defined by an internal, self-conscious sense of division. Roughly, all the prophets were anxious about the second. Roughly, it was the history of the social gospel gradually to seek out the roots of the second in the first. But the second—"class-consciousness"—was a terrible problem in itself, for it violated the principles of the ideal, it violated brotherhood.[45] The obvious, uncomplicated response was to preach to those who nursed class antagonism, a class-transcending brotherhood and good will. It was difficult ever to believe this was not the heart and center of tactics, for what was its opposite? Worth Tippy defined it in answer to the rhetorical question, "Shall employers and workers fight or coöperate?" "The Christian looks upon class struggle as upon war, to be resorted to only in extremity, when there is no other recourse. . . ."[46] No such extremity, he observed, existed in the United States. In the same rhetorical fashion, the *Christian Century* asked in 1925, "Can a Radical be a Christian?"

> Unable to trust in the efficacy of any appeal to our moral nature [these radicals] see no way of reforming human society except by pitting the self-interest of the exploited against the self-interest of the exploiters and permitting a war to the knife to divide the issue between them. If the creed of this sort of radical is true the prospects for human society are dismal indeed.[47]

What was the way out here? Perhaps some shades and degrees between fighting and coöperation might have been considered. Perhaps the shades and degrees within the portmanteau word "class" might have been thought of; perhaps the easy identification of "self-interest versus self-interest" with "war to the knife" might have been discarded as too easy. But these distinctions would not have been compelling had they been made; there was no rich field of experience to give them substance, no area in which they could have been honed out, checked, and unified. An aggressive AFL, a CIO, a National Labor Relations Board —not to mention a Taft-Hartley Act—did not exist, and thus there was formless threat and counterthreat, punctuated by outbreaks of raw will confronting raw will. In a shapeless present, the dangers of a hypothetical future class-war seemed to have reality. Categories remained unrefined, the image of labor and of labor tactics obscure and confused. It was notable that the only escape from this situation involved a tour de force: Muste solved all problems by adopting dogmatic pacifism to accompany his radicalism, with the two bound together by, as Harold Rotzel said, a "hope" that they would never conflict. Tours de force aside, for lack of a field of experience in which to test their ideas, the prophets could only drift, in both theory and works, until a whole new field of experience, one of convulsion and crisis, after 1929, redefined their problems for them.

This is not to deny that the broader logic of the social gospel tended to intensify the vacuum in which the prophets moved. The day was to come when some of these distinctions, between one kind of class-struggle and another, one kind of coercion and another, were quite literally and formally debated in the Fellowship of Reconciliation. One thing was to appear in that debate in late 1933; such distinctions could not be drawn without making basic changes in the deepest religious logic of the social gospel as a whole. Such distinctions could certainly no longer be thought of as direct inferences from the ethics of Jesus. The imitation of Jesus, that is, inner conversion of the ego, provided no instructions on how to translate ethics into tactics. The 'twenties had certainly displayed a steady dilution of the absolute ethic in practice in any case, without the concomitant revisions in theory that were eventually to prove necessary. The disjunction was seen perfectly in the two passages quoted from the *Christian Century,* the one its attack on radicals in 1925, the other its attack on the AFL in 1928. The time difference meant nothing; the theme of 1925 persisted. The difference was one of reference; the passage of 1925 had none, or else had one only with respect to a hypothetical future enslaved to a hypothetical radicalism. In the passage of 1928, the reference was concrete. In the first, therefore, the appeal was to the pure strategy of reliance upon conversion of the moral nature, but in the second the appeal was essentially to a plan for using class interest to serve universal interest.

This was Rauschenbusch's realism echoed, but the AFL fell so far short of being plausible as the bearer of the ideal, in both its weakness and its lack of idealism, that the *Century* felt little temptation to give up its undefined absolutes. The same was true of Harry Ward, incessant in his search for the true bearers, and equally frustrated.[48] How, from the cleavages of or through the dynamics of a class society, could a classless society be born? One result of the vacuum and frustration of the 'twenties was that most of the social-gospel leaders could continue to cling to their view that anything less than some kind of conjunction between power and righteousness—for Ward, an absolute conjunction, identical with history itself—was unacceptable. No one was faced with a class politics in which he might see the manifest shortcomings of all social groups, and yet be forced to see as well the effectiveness, at least provisional and partial, of even selfish, shortsighted, bread-and-butter politics in ameliorating and possibly eliminating some woes of the system. No one was forced to see that justice did not necessarily have to wait on righteousness.

V

The Faces of Power: the Church

Capital and labor were problems for the church; to the deepest, most serious, and most stubborn thought of the social-gospel prophets the result was that the church became a problem for itself. Emergence of awareness of these "others"—capital and labor—provoked revisions in awareness of the self. The social gospel induced a new stage in Protestant self-consciousness, the ultimate form of which was to be theological.

Here is one description of the kind of church many of the prophets fervently felt social-gospel logic demanded:

> . . . the New Testament Church was *fighting something* . . . in the life of the early Church we find an exhilaration of spirit, and intensity of fellowship, a moral energy that we can still feel in the New Testament like the throbbing of a great dynamo . . . The sequence of events to which this paper has striven to draw attention has never failed in Christian history. Wherever there has been a battle against the great exploiting powers of injustice which measure men in terms of profits, which use them as a means and not as an end, there has always inevitably followed such an enrichment of life and an intense reality of spiritual experience that has not appeared at any other time . . . If the church at large today could only believe that,

it would throw itself recklessly and with a genuinely careless rapture into a struggle for a Christian social order and a deadly conflict with all that impedes it, no matter how respectable, or how hallowed by tradition.[1]

This *esprit* of the early church was a touchstone frequently utilized in the social-gospel canon. Those early believers of the first-century fellowship, with their common meals, their high morale, their knitted unity maintained against a world in decline, showed what the spirit of Jesus in men could mean. They were men of a certain sort: dregs and fringes, outcasts and seers, above all men of the urban wilderness, slaves, the lower-middle, the workers themselves. In men of this sort the Word had found true lodging—not in respectable worshippers of the status quo.

And although Constantine, with pomp and power, merged in unholy wedlock the church and state, arousing ecclesiasticism, dogmatism, and pride, and although even reform was no sure help, for reformation could easily mean the exchange merely of one dogmatism and pretension for another, yet the tradition of prophecy had not been suffocated. Its first clear reëmergence in the West was to be dated from the twelfth century. From then on, rising up, falling back, but perpetually generated anew, witnesses passed on the passion: Franciscans, Waldenses, Taborites, Lollards, Anabaptists, Levellers, Diggers, many more whose cries were lost, whose names were forgotten. Their spirit was always that of brotherhood in Jesus, and this brotherhood always meant brotherhood in this life for all men on earth. One of the most persistent themes of Christian history stood thus reinvoked: the cry for radical purity, the desire to purge away the complicating stifling accretions of theology and mere culture and mere tradition dividing men from one another, the thirst for radical simplification around a passion to imitate the absolute.[2]

Plainly there was an eagerness in the social gospel to preach the Word to all quarters; the eagerness to preach, however, seemed greater than the quarters' desire to receive. Clearly there were difficulties in planting the Word in capital and hardships in sowing among labor. But one audience at least could be thought prepared to receive—the church itself, the congregations of the churches themselves. Here the faces were familiar, memories common, rhetoric inherited, intentions appreciated. And yet was this not the middle-class church, the church classbound and separated if not alienated from labor? Was this church to throb with moral energy, glow in fellowship, set out in battle against the great exploiting powers of injustice?

The answer was "yes." "Yes" in that mass program for evangelization projected by Interchurch in 1919 and "yes" in the Federal Council's report on industrial reconstruction. The idea that the social evangel was a matter for sectarian action alone hardly appeared. The Word was prophetic, but the courage to prophesy drew on a reservoir in the society itself:

> Religious people in the United States have the power to change the public attitude . . . They have enormous resources at their disposal. There are over forty million communicants of the various churches. These persons ask the supremacy of Jesus' way of life and are at least nominally committed to his leadership. Many of them are troubled over the strife and misery of this day and are increasingly sensitive to the evils of modern industry. For the most part their intentions are good. They will do the right thing.[3]

To be able to count upon a marching force of forty million was to be able to cast all problems on the crest of an all-engulfing triumphant wave. Or even twenty million. Or ten. By 1940 Kirby Page was measuring the success of his evangel in terms of the thousands, not the tens of thousands or the millions. But in the 1920's men preached the evangel as though there were saving majorities, if not already assembled, waiting simply to be activated.

Filled with this sense of strength, the social-gospel churchmen read the social spectrum not as capital–bourgeois–labor, or as upper–middle–lower, but as capital–church–labor. The fusion of social-gospel principle with the community of the middle classes was what they meant by "church." The problems of alienation, disorder, and injustice that they confronted were after all found clustering at the two poles outside the church: capital and labor.

A great social continuum lay between, where the problems did not obtain and where men were free therefore to meet those problems in terms of principle. The idea of the neutrality of the church in the disputes of the social order hinged to this view. Uncommitted but sympathetic, neutral but not indifferent, the church had the power for decisive intervention. Charles Clayton Morrison put it this way: "The church is the one institution that, being in a large measure concerned in the controversy, has at the same time the power and the motive to influence both parties to better understanding. There is no other organization either interested or competent to the same extent." [4] Morrison always had the courage of his abstractions: to the campaign of 1932 he contributed a call for a "Disinterested Party," consisting of those millions of citizens outside and above the stakes of politics, who had only to organize to coerce the old-line parties from their corruption, partisanship, and power politics. The pastors rated the power of public opinion so high because they equated it with the power of this vast church-community. Public opinion as target for the social evangel dominated the methods of men like Kirby Page and Francis McConnell. In many ways it preoccupied the professional educators among the prophets, such as George Coe, the outstanding theorist of religious education, chief follower of John Dewey in his field, who spoke of the "public mind" and of "changing the public mind-set" as the center of tactics for social change.[5] This public, this church, these millions were quite literally the theologically more-or-less liberal, suburban, small-city, small-town, and even rural, millions of Protestantism, in the East and especially in the Midwest. This was the culture-community to bear social-gospel principles.

There was hidden prudence here, of course; wherever neutrality was urged without some conspicuous agonizing over the "captivity" of the church, suspicion asked whether behind the slogans of love, justice, and new order, the good old order did not remain as a higher priority. But the image of the church came to much more than this. There was not much prudence in Harry Ward, yet Ward as much as anyone found, at the beginning of the 'twenties, the conjunction of culture and principle. "Which Way Will Methodism Go?" he asked in 1921.

> The people called Methodists are now largely of the middle class. There is a sprinkling of industrial wage earners and a small representation of finance. The bulk of the strength is rural and small-town. This section has long had an economic grievance against the financial world and its control of credit, transportation and distribution. The small business man, the salaried and professional people who make up the most of our city membership, are fast finding out that the present economic arrangements are pinching them and their children as they have long been squeezing the industrial wage-earner. Therefore the economic interest of our constituency is likely to incline them in the direction of applying the principles of the gospel to the economic situation without stint or limit, as long ago the same conjunction of economic interest and religious idealism met in the prophets of Israel.[6]

This conjunction of ideal and interest was precisely the formula by which Rauschenbusch had singled out the labor movement as primary candidate to bear the ideal. Ward and Rauschenbusch differed little on this, however. For Rauschenbusch, also, the church was enlisted into the historical march on the new order. For him, the middle-class communities incarnated the type-virtues of the new order; they were the virtues of liberal evangelical Protestantism, and he expected the Protestant community to spread them. Labor was the necessary army for a breakthrough on the industrial front, socialism the necessary economy for industry, but the virtues served remained the same. Ward, reciprocally, called upon labor too to bear justice; we have noted his castigation of the simple bread-and-butter unionism of the AFL. Ward was to drive on in his search for tactics far beyond any point Rauschenbusch anticipated or would have sanctioned; but for both men, the visible church, the community of the congregations, was understood to be a majority for the ideal. Labor rightly would have to act for its interests, but, rightly construed, its interests were those already incarnate in the Protestant town.

In other words, there were none for whom the new evangel was a mighty Word such as to shatter the vessel of the church. No one debated the chance that the new evangel might cleave the church; no one, debating the evangel, tried to judge or choose— for the new Word and attendant shattering of the vessel, for the vessel against the Word, or for a softening of the Word to accommodate the vessel. Everyone assumed the resources of the old religious culture lying at hand for the new social order. The nerve for this was rooted in a deep history. Memory kept alive the church of the past, which had struck at slavery, at debtors' prisons, at drink, had founded the schools, the hospitals, the colleges, the settlements, and of course the missions over the world. All were still flourishing, however much their true origins were forgotten. There had always been a reservoir of energy flowing into the society, and although these efforts had been directed to limited ends, ends within the system, there was nothing to suggest that energy was lacking for wrestle with the system itself. As Rauschenbusch pointed out, what was new was not the energy but the vision of what it could attain. Rauschenbusch himself knew, absolutely, the tradition upon which he relied: the Lutherans, he noted, especially Missouri Synod, had been holding back; Catholicism would be, as it had always been, an obstacle around which carefully to steer; the resources he counted on flowed directly from the Puritan Revolution.[7]

This was the long memory; there was a shorter memory. These were Rauschenbusch's words in 1912:

> Were you ever converted to God? Do you remember the change in your attitude to all the world? Is not this new life which is running through our people the same great change on a national scale? This is religion's energy, rising from the depth of that infinite spiritual life in which we all live and move and have our being. This is God.[8]

As Rauschenbusch saw it, the heritage of religious democracy from Protestantism, and of political democracy from the Enlightenment, had depended upon the middle classes. The next extension of democracy into the economic sphere depended upon labor. In the politics of the Progressive era, he found justification for the hope that the old democracy and the new would not clash or remain apart, but would, in some fashion, fuse. The fusion was a religious chemistry. The politics of Progressivism; Populists singing the Lord's Prayer to open their conventions; Henry George and his followers speaking with religious cadences; the Wilsonian program flying openly ethical banners: these were the forms of the gospel ethics in politics. Tentative, incomplete, the forms nonetheless proved the persistence in American society of its basic ethical drive. Middle-class and agrarian ferment among those feeling the pinch of the system, fearing to be further squeezed, needed little to be transformed into classless fervor. Just as with Rauschenbusch, Ward's remarkable portrait of the Methodists drew on his memories of Progressive days—of the Methodists in Ohio, Chicago, Oak Park, whom he had known before the war. Progressivism was not the ideal, but it proved that ethical majorities could be organized. Implicitly, Progressivism was Protestant. Therefore the new social order was for the sake of protecting and nourishing the church, as much as the church was intended as a means toward and agent for the new social order. As Rauschenbusch put it:

> . . . the Church has the greatest possible interest in a just and even distribution of wealth. The best community for church support at present is a comfortable middle class neighborhood. A social system which would make moderate wealth approximately universal would be the best soil for robust churches.[9]

The accuracy of this image of the church community, as at once model society and potential majority for the new society, was another question. How sharply, for instance, did the social-gospel liberals see into the actual class structure of the Protestant communities? In 1921, inspired by Federal Council churchmen, the Institute of Social and Religious Research was founded to "bring the methods of social science to bear on religious and socio-religious problems." [10] An orgy of fact-finding followed. The income and expenditure of churches; the training of ministers; membership rolls; country, town, and city variations; church schools—all received statistical exploration. Yet little if any of the data opened up any of the areas important to the social passion. The book of Paul Douglass and Edmund Brunner, *The Protestant Church as a Social Institution,* summarizing the vast research, admirable for what it supplied, offered nothing directly systematic on the status of Protestantism vis-à-vis labor, capital, or politics. When, however, here and there, other studies were made in the 'twenties, they hinted that the image of a monolithic, comfortable, idealistic, bourgeois Protestantism needed considerable shading, at a minimum. In ninety-six churches in Chicago, A. E. Holt found that the unskilled labor group did indeed provide less than half its share to the congregations. But the business group also provided less than its share; skilled labor provided a higher proportion than business. The telling oversupplies were provided by the clerical occupations and professional people. But over all, labor groups numbered more than 35 per cent of total membership.[11]

Moreover, some of the "natural" labor churches of Protestantism were not only invisible to the liberal leaders, but also were closed to them and to the social gospel. These were churches in industrial villages, in New England, in Pennsylvania coal country, in Southern mill country. Many of the pastors in these churches had been, and very often remained, millhands or miners. They were not even aware of the social gospel as such; they had no contact with the centers of denominational organization and with the colleges and seminaries where the liberal prophets taught and were trained. A high proportion of their churches depended upon "the company" for a lease, for the pastor's salary, for maintenance funds, for, in other words, existence itself, and the influence of the company upon the pulpit was usually direct.[12]

Studies made in the 1940's suggested further shadings. Following the categories of "upper," "middle," and "lower," Protestantism displayed a clear upper and middle orientation: 56 per cent of membership fell there in the South, 71 per cent outside the South. Episcopalians, Presbyterians, and Congregationalists showed the highest upper-middle quality. Both the Baptists and Lutherans carried over 50 per cent in the lower. Lutherans held the highest proportion of urban manual workers. But here again, the areas outside an image of the monolithic middle also fell outside the social and theological orbit of the passion.[13]

Such hints suggest that the social gospel had not sensitized the feel of liberal leaders for the actual fabric of the Protestant community. Protestantism perhaps both included more of a labor constituency than the prophets recognized and was further from communication with it than they realized.

More drastic evidence against the image of the saving and savable church might have been seen in the fundamentalist controversies. Few things perhaps were more remarkable than the silence with which the prophets responded to this catastrophic revelation of the true limits of religious liberalism. They had not written off the fundamentalist community. Ward's Methodists of 1921, pinched and squeezed by the system, included it. Page's forty million included it. Rauschenbusch had not discounted it. The possibility that fundamentalism testified to social, economic, and cultural interests that bypassed or swamped social-gospel interests was simply never taken up or explored. The liberal prophets were silent—that is, they were not provoked to despair —because as liberals they could assume the gradual dissolution of fundamentalism under the influence of reason and education. But the question remained: would Protestant leaders of the liberal church, whether devoted to the social gospel or not, ever come to grips with this challenge to their own picture of the position of Protestantism in the society?

But then, was there not at least the liberal church? By the end of the 'twenties, Harry Ward's mood had turned to somber indignation at a somnolence which was plainly that of the liberal church. What does one find, he asked? Great obsession with the machinery of ecclesiasticism, infinite tinkering with technique in education, in psychiatry, in counseling—such things absorbed the leaders. Money went into mortgages to pay for Methodist-Gothic cathedrals, cults of liturgy, mysticism, and ritual fascinated denominations that had once been plain.[14] The first stage of Reinhold Niebuhr's deliberate abandonment of the social-gospel synthesis, in the late 'twenties, took form as an attack on the liberal church. In *Does Civilization Need Religion?* Niebuhr recalled an ideal of asceticism and ethical purity, which he believed the liberal church had forgotten in its endless questioning of whether the cosmos was friendly, rather than of whether society was friendly, and by its endless self-congratulation over the harmonization of science with Christianity, rather than the harmonization of classes. In 1930, Halford Luccock published *Jesus and the American Mind*, just as though the response to his fervid call upon the church for sacrificial enthusiasm had provoked an equal and opposite despair: the American mind, Luccock cried fiercely, had been given over to money and the cult of success, and the Puritan ethic itself had degenerated to the point of baptizing the surrender. In a few years, Luccock would be writing a tough-minded survey of the social scene from a new socialist perspective, in the course of which he wholly denied the capacity of the church to play even the new, negative, minimum role, then assigned to it by the liberal prophets, of serving as bulwark against a fascist right.

The prophets had only the liberal church, which was not as large as they thought, and now it seemed not as available for the work of idealism as they had hoped. Devoting its energy to its suburban cathedrals, elaborating its freedom and leisure in private spiritual adventure, liberal Protestantism was trying out the fruits of the old Puritan ethic, fruits that the old ethic itself had not known how to enjoy. Protestants were learning how to spend and consume, having produced and saved as Calvin and Wesley had urged. They were beginning to elaborate the "American way of life" that the industrial system had made possible. Sophistication was of more urgency than justice, for in the "normalcy" of the 'twenties there were no serious threats to security from injustice. Voices on the left were hardly audible, while on the right the new voices of coöperation and the religion of business-as-service steadily overbore rumblings of the old monopoly steamroller. All old problems would be solved in an endless summer of expanding prosperity. The humanist mysticism upon which the liberal church had embarked represented above all the idealism of people at ease, beginning after long subjection to discipline and prudential rigor to indulge themselves.

There were profound and worthy hungers behind such indulgence, often enough as men began to sense the possibilities for experimentation and expansion in their own lives. The social gospel had nothing to say to, no provision for, no means to resist or imagination to harness, such hungers. It preached discipline and denial too much like that from which the liberal congregations were escaping. Perhaps the most poignant of the many forms of isolation from which the prophets suffered was their isolation from the real excitement of the decade. This excitement was so often unpolitical, apparently purely literary or esthetic or moral, that it seemed irrelevant. Along with that, it was often wounding. Such satirists as H. L. Mencken and Sinclair Lewis, such new moralists as Judge Ben Lindsay and the enthusiasts for Freud, were usually taking aim at the evangelical and fundamentalist communities, but liberal Protestants were by no means unscathed. More widely and subtly, the whole spirit of the Lost Generation and the Jazz Age, at once passionate and disillusioned, seemed simply to have forsaken the landmarks of the past, whether liberal or orthodox, progressive or conservative. Protestantism had never been more profoundly out of touch with the cultural vanguards, and the social gospel served in no way as a bridge for reconciliation. This meant that it was committed still more narrowly to politics, even as politics grew more frustrating; it remained unable to enter the broader fields of the culture and perhaps find instruction there. In this incapacity it shared the position of the Protestant community as a whole, closed in upon by a society rapidly taking form as a popular culture unprecedented in our history, far beyond the patterns of the nineteenth-century harmony that the social gospel had first wished to protect and extend.

VI

The Nonpolitics of Hope

Seeking closer and more stable relations with capital and labor, the social-gospel pastors were going beyond mere proclamations of the ideal, into the realm of means. They were becoming political, in the larger sense of the word. They had many inhibitions to overcome in their search, as, seeking both righteousness and power in the same agent, they found it difficult to accept compromises, partial measures, short-run expediences. This was to be seen more explicitly in their judgments upon politics in the narrow, more conventional sense, the politics of parties and state action.

Protestant leaders of all theological persuasions, of all the major denominations, engaged in politics on at least one major issue during the 'twenties—the defense of Prohibition. With heavy church support, the Anti-Saloon League endorsed candidates and mounted active campaigns. The Methodists established their Board of Temperance, Prohibition and Public Morals across the street from the Capitol in Washington, as an active lobby and information center. In face of criticism and protests, Methodist bishops bluntly announced they would be troubled by no questions of propriety involving separation between church and state.

On the front of international relations also, although it drew no more than a small fraction of the energy poured into Prohibition, church leaders went directly to political leaders and the government. They supported the League, the Kellogg Pact, the Washington and London conferences, opposed Japanese exclusion, intervention in Mexico, military missions in Latin America, the War Department's "educational" campaign in the schools, and the proposed cruiser program of 1927. Of special interest to the social gospel, the peace front was of interest to the liberal church at large, and this larger church plainly felt no guilt at intervening in political decisions of the society. Political action and interest, in short, had in them nothing strange for the churches in the 'twenties.

In seeking the politics of the social gospel, though, there is no cohesive story to tell such as that of the peace front or the Prohibition crusade. Peace-front action in the 'twenties depended upon specific occasions; it always came as a "yes" or "no" reaction to a clear-cut proposal of political policy already formulated by politicians. No such political action was possible for the social gospel: there were no occasions. Setting aside the outlines for over-all, programmatic change glimmering through such documents as *The Church and Industrial Reconstruction,* if the social creed alone be scanned, only two articles, as issues in national policy, had anything like active political life in the 'twenties—the one on liquor traffic, the other on child labor. Protestant support appeared for the Child Labor Amendment, but it did not serve as a major rallying point. Beyond this, there was nothing. Despite all platonic support, collective bargaining did not appear on the schedule of politicial debate; public works, minimum wages, maximum hours, were not up for decision, nor were shop councils, profit-sharing, and democratic control of industry. Whatever the pieties of political platforms on any of these matters, none had become articles of political discipline; consequently there was never an issue on which the social-gospel citizen might decide "yes" or "no." [1]

The social gospel devoted itself to advertising and sanctifying these issues *as* issues; it devoted itself to education. This could be said to have been its politics, but this would not be saying enough. In a sense, just as the ideal business leadership did not exist, and as the ideal labor movement did not exist, and as the ideal church did not exist, so too the ideal politics did not exist. But more can be seen than frustration with the Republican and Democratic parties. The social gospel had a difficult time simply comprehending politics as a method or technique or process, quite beyond its incidental embodiment in the two parties, and social-gospel thoughts on method and means and technique are most sharply to be seen where social-gospel thinkers hardly confessed it was indeed of means and method they were thinking.

A short sketch of the political reasoning of the *Christian Century* exhibits the controlling instincts of the broad social-gospel middle. Recall that the *Century* was not a family organ, devoted to private news; its subject was Protestantism in the world, and its editors spoke out without hesitation on any topic, often enough loudly, without circumspection, naming names, and without petty cares to make this day's voice harmonize with the last. Its editors were the keenest and most persistent of political observers.

After the party conventions of 1920, the editors adopted a line that became standard: by comparison with 1912, the two great parties had reverted to materialism. "It is a difficult position for the men and women who have political ideals and find themselves shut in by the leaders of all parties, and compelled to approve the formal commonplaces of partisanship or remain silent." [2] In practice, of course, this meant support for the Republican party, together with a kind of platonic good will for the occasional leaders of liberal ferment. Two editorials appearing in 1925, within four months of one another, revealed the tension here. The first spoke of Coolidge's inaugural the previous March:

> [It had been] as near being a national sacrament as any political event in the remembrance of our generation . . . [There was] something almost high-priestly in the way he lifted the whole nation up to God in an eloquent and understanding commitment of himself and the state to high sovereignty. No statesman in our history has

uttered words of moral interpretation which surpass those with which the President closed his inaugural address.

The other saluted Senator La Follette following his death:

> The status of democracy is not reassuring today, particularly in America . . . There are few men in Washington who inspire confidence . . . Moral issues are not wanting, but they do not arouse the public conscience. Political problems beset us but they do not fertilize our minds. Nothing seems to lift us out of our stupor . . . We could not well afford to lose La Follette. We needed his fine zeal for social justice and his undaunted courage.[3]

Nothing had happened in the four months between. These two statements were parts of the same mental organization, parts of a field of feelings rather than contradictions within a system. Coolidge was not in fact a hero for the *Century*. The tax policy of his treasury secretary, his armaments policy, his Mexican policy, the *Century* found less than ideal. That "the business of America is business" the *Century* did not believe. Coolidge's 1927 Thanksgiving proclamation provoked as bitter, biting an editorial excoriation of the American ethos of the 'twenties as could be found in liberal literature.[4] But the panegyric was as genuine as the lament. The key word in each of these texts was the infinitive "to lift." The *Century* asked its politics to rise above politics, to lift itself and to lift all; it asked politics to transcend interest, to take as its materials high character and high vision alone.

Wholly in this spirit, the tribute to La Follette did reflect the dim outlines of what many of the prophets were prepared to accept. *Information Service* formulated the prospect raised by the 1924 campaign:

> . . . indications are that if the movement develops coherence and integrity[,] a party somewhat similar to the British Labor Party will be formed with the Socialist Party undertaking to play the same part in it that the Independent Labor Party . . . plays in the British labor movement.[5]

The *Century* did not adopt the La Follette campaign, nor was it adopted by any significant group of the prophets. But like the

editors of *Information Service*, so Morrison and his colleagues on
the *Century* foresaw realignment of the parties, dividing avowed
conservatives from avowed liberals, and found the prospect good.[6]
By 1928, realignment lagging, political frustration began to drive
some of the prophets, determined upon political energy, into third-
party action. For most, however, this move was not possible, and the
logic of the *Century* in 1928 provided an explicit measure of the
displacement of the social gospel by the interests of the culture-
community in which it tried to breed. In slow stages betraying inner
torment the editors spent the year working themselves up to their
predestined endorsement of Herbert Hoover. They were not sure of
Hoover on the Kellogg Pact; they were not sure of him on Latin
America; they were wary of his views on labor; all in all, they took
Al Smith to be the better man. But Smith had chosen the leading
issue: Prohibition; and on Prohibition the *Century* would go for
Sahara.[7]

This was easy. It was also easy for the *Century* to discount
liberal hopes that the Democratic party led by Smith could be
remade to a liberal pattern. Apology throve elaborate, however,
at the choice, not against Al Smith and the Democratic party, but
against Norman Thomas and the Socialist party. Morrison deliberately concentrated his objections to supporting the Socialist
party on the level of tactics and not of ideology. The *Century*, he
wrote, remained liberal; it still believed in the long-range issues
of economic and social reconstruction for which the Thomas
candidacy stood. But long-range issues were not the only issues;
there were important issues to be decided in the immediate
campaign: Prohibition, Catholicism, world peace. Those who
felt the weight of these issues would be Hoover men.

This argument derived from an analysis Morrison had published a month earlier, of proper and improper church intervention in politics. He began by declaring that the church already
was in politics: "It has a right to be in politics. Always and everywhere it has been in politics." This did not mean, however, that
a church party should be formed. It did not mean the church
should claim authority over the state; it did not mean that ecclesiastical coercion should be exerted upon the state. Nor did it

mean that the churches should be speaking out on each and every issue, that the church should always have a "line": "The church has no testimony to bear on the technique of farm relief, or the tariff, or government ownership of water power, or a score of other problems which disturb the electorate." How, then, did the church decide what, where, and when its participation in politics should be? [8]

The answer was of peculiar simplicity: it should not decide. If there was still a *decision* to be made about intervention, the time had not yet arrived for intervention. In natural order, the political issue and the character of the church should coalesce; response to the political issue should arise painlessly and flawlessly from the church's living creed. Thus the two issues for the Protestant church in 1928 were those of Catholicism [9] and Prohibition, for the living creed indicated clear positions on both. Someday, a conviction that war was a sin would be an article in that living creed also. Someday, a conviction that the economic order of poverty and plenty constituted a sin would be part of that living creed. When they were, the church could, should, and would act upon them in politics. Meanwhile, its political action should remain within the limits of the living creed as it then existed.

Such politics displayed the social gospel once more cut to the perspectives and interests of the culture-community of the church. Morrison in the last analysis had no political advice for those Protestants whose living creed did comprehend the issues of economic justice. He could not advise sectarian action. Much more important here than the problem of propriety and tactics— whether a Protestant spokesman might lobby in Washington or claim to speak for the church unless he had a polled, statistical majority of the congregations behind him—was the question of what effect it had upon Protestant leadership to think constantly in representative terms. This was Morrison's problem, and the answer he gave in 1932 summed up the culture-church's view of itself. Once again he denounced both the major parties; and again he rejected ideological third-party action. In their place, he proposed his "Disinterested Party," enlisted from the millions of citizens who held no stake in the selfish scrambling of the major parties, who believed in the principles of a better social order, and who could, organizing together, bring pressure to bear upon the professional politicians, forcing them to follow the dictates of disinterestedness or to lose their political positions. Right politics was the intervention of righteousness.[10]

Thus, the social gospel was caught coming and going, between its own conception of righteous politics and the previous interests of the culture-community. This trap did not appear to be serious, because politics did not have, to the social-gospel mind, any truly distinct and important role. For one thing, the liberal leaders had given little direct thought to the role of the state, either in the pursuit of justice or in the new social order itself. They criticized "mere" state socialism, whatever the rigor of their ideals. Thus Bishop McConnell, speaking out of an avowed common-sense libertarian inheritance, said: "Nothing in human experience suggests that any central body of Society will be wise enough to tell how the resources of the larger social groups shall be expended."[11] Harry Ward doubted that state ownership of industries and control over the economy guaranteed the true democracy he sought; if it was perhaps a program for transition, it was not the model for the new order.[12] Ward came to believe in the absolute wisdom of a central body, but not, as shall be seen, through any new appreciation of the order of politics. The prophets wanted not simply to contain industrial disorder and social conflict, an aim that might have focused on the role of the state; they wanted to provide for the Christianization of men. Industrial democracy was understood in terms of adjustment not only in the relations between capital and labor, but also within the direct, detailed, personal environment of each man. It meant the factory as church. E. E. Kresge, a Reformed Church minister of Allentown, Pennsylvania, in his sketch of the industrial organization of the future, summed up the whole vision nicely:

> The managers and superintendents of local industries might be elected as we now elect our public school teachers—the people electing a Board of Directors, and the Board of Directors electing the superintendents and managers. Each community would attend to its own local industries, while the state and federal government would attend to the basic industries which concern the welfare of

all the citizens of the commonwealth, and upon which all local industries depend.[13]

This was the theory behind the industrial experiments. The focus lodged where the change in will, in inner character, could be directly obtained and exercised. If the state was to participate in the Christianization of the social order, it would participate more as a consequence of its own Christianization than as an instrument of the Christianization of the society. The new ground rules it would police would have been established previously by the democratization of the spirit of industrial leaders and of labor.

To generalize upon this: democracy meant a state of being even more than a process; it referred to a type of character more than to a pattern of outward relationships. It meant a type of man. Politics was not seen as in its nature a realm of power, nor political democracy as a particular arrangement or distribution of power. There was no suggestion that political democracy represented not a hermetic "area," as Rauschenbusch set forth, either converted or unconverted to the ideal, but a way of adjusting interests and doing the society's business. It was precisely the same situation with respect to the democratization of God. The undemocratic God of Calvin, the autocratic God of absolute sovereignty, had to yield to the Friend and Companion, to comport with the inner democratization of men. But the relationship between the two, democratic God and democratic man, was vague.

In short, so long as they could feel a sufficient—or potentially sufficient—majority for righteousness available in the church, and so long as politics did not, on the level of tactics, figure as critical, the prophets were not forced to reflect that the ideal politics they demanded was contrary to the permanent nature of politics, and was perhaps not politics at all. Once more, Bishop McConnell, famous for his tactical realism as statesman within the church, illustrated the point when he was confronted with the actual character of politics in the world.

> So, again, with the temptation to use political means for the sake of advancing spiritual ends. It is, of course, possible to use political means without bowing down and worshipping the devil; but there

is inevitably so much keeping company with the devil that the fineness of saintly manner is lost.[14]

But society's need for political method was unremitting. Decisions were always pressing to be made. If the saint abstained, the devil would make them.

In the campaign of 1928, a telling handful of Protestant ministers, leaders of the social gospel, supported Norman Thomas. McConnell was among them. Late in the year, after the election, a group of liberals including these social-gospel ministers organized the League for Independent Political Action (LIPA). Members of the LIPA included John Dewey, Paul H. Douglas, Norman Thomas, Oswald Garrison Villard, James Weldon Johnson, Harry W. Laidler, Robert Morss Lovett, W. E. B. Dubois, Sherwood Eddy, Devere Allen, A. J. Muste, Reinhold Niebuhr, and Kirby Page. The first secretary of the LIPA was Howard Y. Williams. Williams had been pastor of the St. Paul People's Congregational Church, and had already embarked upon politics in the most direct fashion: in 1926 he had run for mayor of St. Paul on the ticket of the labor-progressive political association of that city.[15] Although it included many Socialists and eventually endorsed Thomas in 1932, the rationale behind the league was not so much a desire to witness to socialism as a desire to be political. The difference was a real one. There was semi-Socialist political potential in social-gospel ranks in the 'twenties, but it had not precipitated out, partly because the Socialist party was not "available."

To return to Rauschenbusch once more: despite his pleasure, in 1912, at the political atmosphere, Rauschenbusch had passed explicit verdict on the two major parties. Both had fooled their worker constituencies; both represented merely capitalist interests. Rauschenbusch spoke for the Socialist party.[16] His choice was prophecy and certainly not a representative act, yet it was not untrue to social-gospel vectors. In 1912, the Socialist party had good promise, to the minds of serious men, of becoming a permanent and major political agent on the American scene. It seemed able and willing to draw upon long-standing reservoirs of political sentiment filled by the Populist West and by anti-monopoly, liberal middle-class circles in the East. It appeared a potential beneficiary of new political audiences in the industrial towns and immigrant enclaves of the Eastern cities. In Eugene Debs, a highly flavorful, winning leader, a kind of Hoosier Marxism promised both fundamental ideological realism and native American pragmatism.

But the party lost respectability with its stand on the war. The platonic admiration of prewar liberals drained off with the respectability; most of the party's leading intellectuals were lost. The prophets who opposed the war—Norman Thomas, A. J. Muste, Harold Rotzel, John Haynes Holmes, and others—and who in the same motion embraced socialism, chose only semi-political, educational agencies, such as the League for Industrial Democracy and Brookwood Labor College, devoting themselves to socialist education and not to socialist politics. Disrepute and disruption over the war might not have been enough, but there was more. In 1912, 12 per cent of the Socialist party membership was enrolled in its foreign-language associations; by 1919 the foreign-language associations provided 53 per cent. The party's center of power had shifted to New York. The Communist schisms had taken place by the elections of 1920, and the effect was not purification, but degeneration, of the left into an ideological rough-house, with all hands competing for the banner of orthodoxy. At the 1920 convention of the Socialist party, some considerable effort by Victor Berger and August Claessens was required to defeat a resolution announcing that the churches were agents of the rich and regulated souls in the interests of the rich. None of this was environment for Protestant churchmen.[17]

And then deeper than all this, social-gospel leaders could not have hearkened easily to third-party politics in the 'twenties, no matter how ideologically pure, for they had believed in their own majority. The Socialist party was now a sect; the social gospel thought in terms of a church—a church it wished to bring up to ideological sectarian purity, but that it wished to remain a majority. For the *Century* and the Federal Council, this was to remain so always.

The ultimate thrust of social-gospel logic was sectarian, however. The sectarianism remained buried in the 'twenties, because the sect assumed a stubbornness and inertia about the world that the prophets could not and would not yet believe. More important, there was no "disguised sect" to provide a home for the righteous, separating them from the compromises of the world while hiding from them the fact of their isolation. The Socialist party had been such a disguised sect in 1912; its politics were those of ultimate ends, yet men could believe it would soon collect its majorities for legislation of those ends. The LIPA also had some of this character of the disguised sect. In practical politics men work in terms of a "pragmatic future," a future in which someone can accept responsibility for the results of a given policy or decision, as a political leader accepts it for his term of office. At best, politicians who have to make decisions can perhaps be instructed by a somewhat longer "visible future," for which rough predictions can be made as grounds on which to sketch the outlines of responsible longer-range policy. The prophets thought in terms of an "ideal future," however, the ultimate achievement of the new social order, and defined an acceptable politics as that politics alone appropriate to the ideal future. The LIPA was a new organization for the celebration of the ideal future. As sectarian politics, it offered haven to the idealist, who knew politics was the ultimate test of his idealism, and who was no longer able to tolerate the short-range cultural commitments of the church-community to the Republican party.

Nevertheless, this was a critical moment in the history of the social gospel. It represented the first deliberate departure from a "representative" role, from the investment in short-range, cultural calculations such as Morrison defended. It represented also a definitive commitment to politics, where calculations in terms of power were basic. Thereby, also, it represented contact with those "others" implied in McConnell's evangelical recoil from politics—those not of saintly manner, who might upon familiarity turn out not to be diabolic, but who would remain indeed "other," not possessing identical interests with and not to be assimilated into a universalization of the saints. This was a moment, in other words, when the social gospel could begin to become a weapon of reformatory and critical power for Protestantism, the travail of a new self-consciousness, released from prudential and defensive commitments. It was a moment when its true destiny, of criticizing rather than extending the culture-religion of Protestant liberalism, was anticipated.

VII

The New Man

The preceding chapters have narrated a tale of frustration. There was no ideal business leadership; the ideal labor movement failed to appear; the church rested complacent and passive in its middle ground. Because of these failures, politics naturally remained in the wrong hands, unavailable to righteous majorities. Still, hope for ideal business, ideal labor, ideal church, and ideal politics could persist, for behind the vision of a new social order lay a vision of ideal individual order. Behind the politics lay a psychology. The social gospel, preaching a new community, preached a new man in the conviction that man was of such a nature that he could become ideal. Not until this most basic of all grounds for hope came under fire would political frustrations begin to shake the hopes of the heart.

This chapter will be concerned not so much with how the new man was to come to birth as with his character. Rauschenbusch can be looked to once more for a beginning. So far as the nature of human nature was concerned, Rauschenbusch again had exhibited a realism that liberals were later to be accused universally of having lacked. Many did lack it. But Rauschenbusch defended a doctrine that liberalism had generally been eager to mute, that of original sin. Original sin, he observed, was one of the few tenets of the old individualistic religion that pointed toward a solidaristic, social view of the Christian task. One of the major efforts of his *Theology for the Social Gospel* was to follow this clue and socialize the old doctrine. Sin became organized in institutions and social systems, perpetuating itself through the spiritual authority of society over its members. The old evangelical religion, too much preoccupied with the soul of the isolated individual, had not trained people to see the spiritual entities beyond themselves. Following Schleiermacher, Rauschenbusch pointed to the sinfulness that precedes all acts of sin, provoked in every individual by the sinful acts and conditions of others around him. The particular form taken by sin in the individual was simply a function of the form it took in his social group.[1]

Twenty-odd years later, Reinhold Niebuhr also would be speaking of a sinfulness that precedes all acts of sin, but in a precisely opposite fashion. Niebuhr would be speaking with a "vertical" reference, of a relationship between man and God, of a relationship given in every moment, without a history. Rauschenbusch spoke with a "horizontal" reference, of a relationship between man and man. Horizontal, this sinful relationship therefore had a history, was subject to changes, to fluctuations, and thus to elimination.

Three examples of Rauschenbusch's attention to sin in his two earlier books illustrate three perspectives upon the problem of elimination. "In urging the social duty of love," he wrote in 1907, "Christianity encounters the natural selfishness of human nature."[2] What was this natural selfishness? It was a quality not of the man, but of the baby. Every baby was egoistic and followed the instinct of self-preservation. "But this is not a hostile force." It was necessary for existence. Oddly, here the individual was inspected independent of that kingdom of superpersonal forces discovered by the social gospel. In any event, was this individual substance amenable to the hope for the Kingdom? Yes. In adolescence, Rauschenbusch wrote, powerful instincts for devotion, service, and sacrifice appear, which are as natural as egoism. The task for Christianity was to reinforce them. The dominance of

this natural goodness and gregariousness of human nature depended upon patterns of society to evoke, extend, and reward
them.[3] It was thus not necessary to deny evil instincts in men;
it was necessary only to insist that such instincts need not determine behavior. They could be sublimated and transcended.

Rauschenbusch wrote further: "Approximate equality is the
only enduring foundation of political democracy. The sense of
equality is the only basis for Christian morality. Healthful human
relations seem to run only on horizontal lines." [4] A development
of the last sentence would have led the liberal logic into severe
difficulties. To imply that something in human nature should be
tempted away from morality by inequality as such was serious
testimony against the "natural" goodness of that nature. On this
basis, the Kingdom might have seemed more a necessity than a
possibility, a concession to the sinfulness of man rather than a
vision of his potentialities.

The statement was completed, however, with the words: "Consequently true love always seeks to create a level." True love, that
is, could precede equality. It was this true love that inspired the
ideal of equality in the first place. But how could it get into human
nature, prior to equality? How could it survive, once implanted?
On this, Rauschenbusch had only pure religious answers. The
origin of this true love was clear enough: it was revealed by Jesus
Christ. The basis of its persistence in the face of inequality was
clear enough: those bore it who believed in Jesus Christ. The
idealists to whom Rauschenbusch addressed his realism on capital
and labor were those already committed to Him, in personal,
evangelic faith.

Unfortunately, none of this was as clear as it seemed. How
was it that the spiritual authority of sinful society, preceding all
acts of sin, failed to corrupt the faithful? Again, we are referred
to Rauschenbusch's picture of the culture-community of sincere
believers, the church of middle-class Protestantism, somehow untouched by the social issues he confronted. But this sociological
assumption about the church was rooted in deeper evangelical assumptions that carried Rauschenbusch's whole social gospel. For

some men at least, there was some kind of salvation prior to the Christianization of society. Of what service was the Christianization of society to them, if they were already saved? This: it would allow them to live without the stresses, strains, compromises, and torments they would be forced to undergo in a non-Christian society offering no fusion of their motives and those upon which the system depended. Rauschenbusch, in other words, wished to "add on" the social gospel to the evangelical personal gospel. The content of this prior personal salvation was therefore critical. In the *Theology*, Rauschenbusch offered still another analysis of sin. There were, he wrote, three stages of sin: sensuousness, selfishness, godlessness. Sensuousness was sin against the higher self; selfishness was sin against the good of men; godlessness was sin against the universal good.[5] The social gospel sought to repair the inadequate views of the old evangelical faith with respect to the second. With the first, "sensuousness," Rauschenbusch revealed that when he contemplated the prior self, the self prior to society, the salvation prior to the social gospel, he retained the contents of salvation standard in the old individualistic evangel: discipline of the flesh, with the ultimate fruit of self-control capable of supporting the standard virtues of the middle-class church-community: thrift, industry, honesty, love for the immediate neighbor, charity for the poor, piety within the church. This prior salvation worked in terms of an implicit flesh-spirit, lower-higher dualism in human nature, which would be part of the work of Niebuhr to reject.

This conception of salvation reveals what Rauschenbusch did not do. He did not define personal salvation in any terms drawing from his social gospel. He did not draw his sense of personal salvation from contemplation of the relations between self and society. He had no guarantees that the old salvation from sensuousness, even when protected by a Christianized social order, was adapted to the maintenance of a personal center of meaning for the individual. Ultimately, Rauschenbusch failed to defend a center of religious meaning prior to, in some sense independent of, social salvation, from invasion by society and the political. He failed to defend it because he believed the flow of force would all be in the other direction, from the centers of prior salvation outward.

He believed this so much that he felt able to claim for his mission of Christianizing the social order all the authority of the old evangelical claim that Christianization of the individual was possible. The act of making this claim pointed toward an equation of Christianization of the social order with Christianization of the soul. This was to leave the individual, with his inner unity and composure, his sense of meaning and integrity, exposed to politics. Was not this Rauschenbusch's own sense of the perils of the times? An un-Christian system was drawing men not simply from a social gospel, but from any gospel at all.

The process by which old evangelical salvation could come to be equated with social salvation—by which religion could come to be displaced by politics—Rauschenbusch himself often displayed. In his interpretation of the teachings of Jesus, for instance, where he stated the views of liberal scholarship with special sharpness, he attacked the emphasis being laid by various European scholars upon ascetic and eschatological elements in Jesus' thought. Jesus was not, Rauschenbusch insisted, in His best teaching pointing beyond history. If, he declared in 1917, the war "purges our intellects of capitalistic and upper-class iniquities, we shall no longer damn these sayings as eschatological, but shall exhibit them as anticipations of the fraternal ethics of democracy and prophecies of social common sense." [6] This was a firm step toward identifying Jesus Christ, as the final resource for belief, with social ethics and common sense. It was also to identify Him with reason. Rauschenbusch went so far as to say that Jesus, unlike His contemporaries and the men of some sixteen or seventeen hundred years following, had understood the essence of modern social science. The same thing happened in Rauschenbusch's appropriation of Christian vocabulary for describing the social-gospel goal. Part iii of *Christianizing the Social Order* was entitled "Our Semi-Christian Social Order." Christianizing the social order, Rauschenbusch wrote, meant squaring it with the ethical convictions of Jesus. The social order was *semi*-Christian because only certain sectors of it were so squared. These were, first and most of all, the family and the church; the schools ranked next; and finally, politics. These were not ideal constructs. Rauschenbusch was going on empirical observations. He was referring to a long historic change in the family, from the patriarchal, despotic, exploitative family of the past, relying on force, selfish in its relationships, to the modern family, democratic in its life, solicitous of personality. Political life was a newly saved sinner; this was the book of 1912. The economic order remained beyond the pale. Large-scale industry continued to generate conflicts and evoke the instincts against which Christianity struggled.

But did Rauschenbusch truly mean that the "salvation" of the economic order was equivalent to "salvation" in its Christian sense? It was at once clear that he did not and that he advanced the confusion. The terms "Christian social order," "ethic of Jesus," and "Kingdom" meant more than he meant by them here. If—improbably—they referred to typical family life among Christians, they could not have referred equally to politics. The ethic Rauschenbusch was proposing for the new social order was in fact a rationalistic equalitarianism. In a discussion of the European coöperatives, he pointed to their one-man–one-vote principle: "Here, I think, we have the difference between saved and unsaved organizations. The one class is under the law of Christ, the other under the law of mammon. The one is democratic, the other autocratic." [7] But the family could hardly have been characterized as a one-man–one-vote organization. Certainly the law of Christ here was not that law of Christ he knew from the evangelical faith. A severe inner disintegration in vocabulary was taking place. Translated to the field of society, the vocabulary lost touch with basic tensions in the evangelical heritage. The way was left open to that drift by which the content of salvation tended to become the values of social life.

Rauschenbusch had not opened the way himself. It had been opened with the captivity of the sanctified life to that comfortable middle-class neighborhood and its variations he himself admired. But to admire it in the vocabulary of Christian salvation was to expose its members to every disturbance in the social order as a disturbance of the soul. This dependence of the soul on system was not radical so long as it was contained in tradition, with its realized complexities, tensions, and compromises. But for the social gospel, not only traditions but imagined futures had to share the realm of meaning. How far could identification of salvation with social issues carry toward investing the most universal visions with evangelical sanction?

Later social-gospel attempts to assimilate personal with social gospel followed this fault-line in Rauschenbusch's thought.

> It is of the very essence of Christianity as a way of life that it cannot be attained by individuals acting alone. Christian virtues are social virtues . . . One gets on Christian ground the moment he sees the world, rather than his own soul, as the subject of redemption. He will attain his own salvation as a product of his own redemptive effort.[8]

In the tract containing this statement, in 1922, F. E. Johnson of the Federal Council was endeavoring to demonstrate that the social gospel was not a "substitute" for the old gospel of individual experience. But he observed it must be remembered that the subject for redemption was the "personality," not the "individual." It was false to polarize and separate the personal and the social gospel, for the personality was itself social, the sum of social relationships.

> Now at length emerges the true relationship between the individual and the social elements in religion. We have seen how difficult it is to maintain individual character and worth without social support. We have seen how life itself in its "personal" aspect is socially conditioned and can attain a higher moral status only by the transformation of those relationships in which active life consists. It now appears that the very content of redemption is social . . . The redeemed life has been redeemed by a new purpose that is in harmony with the Kingdom—not merely by having individual sins forgiven. Religion is individual, therefore, in that it demands the devotion of the individual will, but it is social in that its purpose has to do with the redemption of the world—this present world— by introducing a more spiritual social order.[9]

This doctrine of the personality was Johnson's doctrine of the self, and he left little field to the self as individuality. Certainly Jesus would not have neglected any aspect of the self in His teaching, and, Johnson said, that teaching was summed up in "personality."

Strategy followed: the personality could not be saved except socially, therefore the personality was to be socialized. Better: the individual was to be socialized.[10] Perhaps the majority of the words of the prophets were directed to this end. This was in effect the implied thrust of Rauschenbusch's work—to engender in the individual a sense of his dependence upon society. To evoke this sense of dependence was the prophets' equivalent to the sense of dependence upon God preached by individualistic evangelical theology.

The systematic elaboration of this program was offered by the leaders of religious education. The ablest exponent of the progressive theories, George Albert Coe, a student of John Dewey, published his most noted work, *A Social Theory of Religious Education,* in the same year Rauschenbusch published the *Theology.* Coe was at Union Theological Seminary until 1922, when he went to Columbia Teachers College. He had presented his ideas of liberal psychology first in 1900, with *The Spiritual Life,* and developed them further in *The Psychology of Religion* in 1916. *Education in Religion and Morals,* 1904, was his early effort to set the implications of the new psychology for religious pedagogy. In *A Social Theory*—dedicated, we might note, to Harry Ward—Coe integrated the new theories with the social gospel.

These were theories of American pragmatism. In place of Kantian categories of the understanding, there was substituted a genetic analysis of the mind as a functional instrument displaying growth and phases of development. In place of postulated moral biases or unchanging inner drives, there was substituted a concept of needs and energies, highly plastic, functioning as a complex, subject to an evolutionary development. The sociology followed. The ideas, ideals, and truths conceived by the individual were functional; the area of function in which they were created and in which they operated was interpersonal life. In those various societies in which the individual functioned, his

creeds were tested, accepted, rejected. In the process of acceptance and rejection, habits and convictions were formed; such
habits and convictions constituted the personality or the self.

Human nature, in other words, was pure potentiality. Presumably the forms it could take were infinite. Coe, like Dewey and all
the American pragmatists, took this to be a morally positive fact.
This was pure faith, often enough uninspected, quite outside the
field of the theory, but the progressives always accepted it. Here
was that plasticity firing the imagination of Rauschenbusch trans-
posed from society to the self itself.

In *A Social Theory* Coe underwrote the assumption, or leap of
faith, that plasticity somehow in itself carried positive moral
meaning, with two ideas nominally part of the theory of pragmatism, but actually outside it. He found, among the instincts of
original human nature, one of both special significance and special
strength: the "parental" instinct, functioning not only between
parent and child, but between adult and adult as well as between
child and child. In a generalization similar to those by which
Rauschenbusch and, later, Kirby Page swept away fifteen centuries of Christian history as apostasy, he identified Christianity
with this inherent force: "Whatever be the case with other religions, the Christian religion, which finds the whole meaning
and destiny of man in divine fatherhood and human brotherhood,
is the flowering of a particular instinct that is active from infancy
onward." [11] But this was in fact untenable; the parental instinct
was being dissolved by the pragmatic psychology, which was
moving on to eliminate all notions of underived, "original" instincts in human nature, in favor of the concept of a more or less
totally undifferentiated center of energy, all differentiated expression of which—habits, motives, instincts—was a product of experience. There was nothing inherent; all depended upon history.
Coe abandoned the "good" parental instinct in his 1928 book,
The Motives of Men, making thereby that much clearer the fact
that the plasticity as such was his inspiration. [12]

His second line of support was the more important. It
amounted to a social-psychological rendition of the social-gospel
faith. It deserves unmediated presentation.

The possibility of success in educating for democracy lies in the fact, first of all, that in our selfishness we are not at one with ourselves, but are stirred to unselfishness also by instinct, and by the habits and institutions that have arisen therefrom, and second, that selfishness and brotherliness do not have equal capacity for organizing themselves. Love of one another produces a degree of cooperation, which is the massing of human energy, that is impossible to greed, licentiousness, and the lust of power. Selfishness tends to disorganization and ineffectiveness in the long run. Temporary equilibrium may be attained in some cases by balancing the selfish interest of one person against that of another, but permanent stability is not attained in this way. Have we not learned the lesson that the massing of individual self-interest into a group selfishness is the way of class struggles within a nation, and of wars without? Massed selfishness tends thus to be anarchic, and to pull itself down in the ruin of its competitors. But love builds and destroys not. Unwise love may destroy, but it is the unwisdom, not the love, that is responsible. What the friends of democracy have to do is to put administrative experience and scientific analysis into the service of the brotherly purpose, and to train children in the resulting concepts and methods as well as in the love motive.[13]

The themes contained here were repeated hynotically in social-gospel literature. First: the problem of the inner unification and integrity of the self was a problem of morality. The poles of the personality were summed up in selfishness and unselfishness. This gave up Rauschenbusch's intention to preserve an area or an aspect of the self transcending society and social ideals. His intention, exhibited in carrying over the sin of sensuousness, he had not been able to make good if only because, in sensuousness, he had himself calculated the "prior" self only in moral terms.

Second: group selfishness was the projection of individual selfishness. The morality of the group could be inferred from the morality of its members. Group psychology, as a separate sort of analysis, hardly existed. It could not be seen that the sum of individual good neighbors might be found to issue in a union of good neighbors for war on another union of good neighbors. This was basic social-gospel sociology: there was no real sociology. The family way of life provided the model for community, class, factory, nation, family of nations. The social bonds typical of the small organic group were to be expanded to the large group and society universally.

Third: unselfishness promised permanent, total equilibrium. There was no temporizing with anything less than a vision of the final end, lasting and universal. The wish was for completion, the wish of a middle haunted by thoughts of society given over to struggles between capital and labor.

Fourth: the true variable in the history of social morality was the reason and wisdom of scientific social science. The triumph of morality awaited its sway.

If it was not Dewey who provided the theoretical grounding for the infinite plasticity of human nature, and therefore its potential apotheosis in. coöperation, it was biology or anthropology. Harry Ward drew upon Prince Kropotkin, Fabre, Drummond, and a dozen others.[14] The institutional economists, the organicist philosophers, the new historians—all were witnesses on the stand. Kirby Page mentioned Benjamin Kidd; more directly, he drew upon a true-to-life social laboratory: "The experience of war-time should convince us beyond doubt that SELF-SACRIFICE IS JUST AS NATURAL AS ANY OTHER OF MAN'S INSTINCTS AND UNDER APPROPRIATE CIRCUMSTANCES IS ABSOLUTELY SUPREME IN THE AVERAGE PERSON." [15] Discovery of this guiding fact was the work of scientific reason, and scientific reason was the key to the new order. "There is every reason to believe," the Federal Council officers wrote in 1928, "that science can now adopt social ideas as specifications of a great task to be accomplished for humanity and proceed by the scientific method to assist in evolving a new industrial order which shall be increasingly characterized by righteousness and peace." [16]

A clear and exhilarating break with the psychology of orthodoxy and liberal individualism, this vision of the plasticity and potentiality of human nature explains why the social gospel was not forced to turn to some proof, peculiar to itself, of the "goodness" of human nature. The question of the "goodness" of human nature had been settled by liberalism, and even, in many ways, by evangelical orthodoxy long before. Sinless sanctification for the individual had long been within the range of standard hopes for the evangelical. When the neo-orthodox of the 'thirties rose against the political-social illusions of the moralists, they would eventually be forced to attack this older perfectionism as well. The older liberal individualism had simply drawn limits where sanctity ended. It had drawn the line of laissez faire; it had drawn the line at certain works and vocations; it had drawn the line at certain agencies of regeneration. The social gospel erased such lines.

Rauschenbusch was the last man able to profit from the expansion of vision without severe reciprocal effects. In his inability to register systematically the difference between the rationalistic equalitarianism of the new social order and the regenerated life of the individual, he had left the way open for a massive reversal of the logic, by which standards appropriate to the new economy were fed back into the individual. George Coe was spelling out this reversal in 1917, with reference to the family. The area of supreme significance in the educational process, he wrote, lay here: "It is the fundamentals of social justice that are at stake in the child's experience in his father's family."[17] The central significance of the family in social-gospel logic was standard, but Coe brought out the possibility Rauschenbusch had passed by. It was not as though the family did in actual practice inevitably provide the organizing model for larger groups or generate the character fitting its members to reform society, nor as though the family was in actual fact a "socialized" or "Christianized" area, as Rauschenbusch had suggested. The family itself might need Christian reorganization. This was actually truer to Rauschenbusch's sociology of capitalism than Rauschenbusch's own picture of "areas," for was not the industrial area more than a peripheral, pagan late addition to the society, which had grown up somehow while the Christian moralist was not watching? Was it not itself a new, psychologically organizing force for other areas? Coe, it is true, did not propose his Christian reorganization of the family in 1917 because he found the family ravaged by capitalism, as he later believed; he did it on the basis of the logic of socialization itself. In *The Motives of Men* and *Educating for Citizenship* (1932), he did analyze the malign influence cast by the industrial ethic upon the individual and his small-group life. The analysis led him to reduce considerably his estimate of what the schools—and, by implication, the family and the church— could achieve, since they also were captive to the system. But the reorganization he demanded in 1917 was more striking just because it displayed the thrust of the logic on its own vector, breaking through all prudential limits.

Coe feared that the family would provide the individual a security and inner composure closing him to the further socialization required for the "democracy of God." Such an individual might be indifferent to the tasks of democracy. Therefore he redefined the family ideal. "The unity of the family cannot be made perfect until family consciousness is fused with a wider social consciousness, particularly through participation by all members of the family in remedial and constructive social enterprises." [18] It was not enough that the family should be democratic in its inner life; it should not have an interior consciousness of its own at all. The implication bore directly on the social-gospel ideal: "There is simply no possibility of fulfilling love in a narrow circle except by treating the circle as a section of the total social sphere. The exclusive family is the self-undermining family." [19] Coe listed ways the family must avoid exclusiveness:

> Every Christian church and every Christian family may be expected
> to identify themselves, as a matter that involves their own life or
> death, with such movements as these: To abolish child labor; To
> shorten the hours of labor . . . To increase the income of most
> families; to forestall unemployment . . . To improve housing condi-
> tions. . . .[20]

The list continued through duties for political action. The family was to be politicalized. The personality, the self, was to be politicalized.

The church, the family, the self, were to be reformed according to the canons of political action; their interior consciousness, their sense of significance, security, unity, and freedom were to be submitted to the abstractions of political idealism and of rationalistic, world-reforming social science.

The security of the soul was being entrusted to politics.

How could logic have been allowed to run free to this point? Even in total abstraction, such a vision of the self would appear to be one of chilling nakedness, of ultimate exposure. Three definite elements in the prophets' world serve to make this comprehensible; we have seen them already. First, the world around them was that mixture of ideal and real social life that they called the church. The real church itself, that further mixture of the saved and the unsaved, ranked easily as the most living range of their experience. The society in terms of which they wished to socialize the individual was just this ideal society of the church-community of the middle, winsome and warm and personal. The middle would chasten, harmonize, and absorb capital and labor, conflict would end within its body, society would become church, and it was therefore safe to urge each man to become universal, to leave him exposed to the whole.

Second, the politics visualized by the prophets also bore a warm and winsome character. The prophets did not feel their hands being forced by politics; they thought of politics only as forced by their own hands. It would be taken from the grasp of mere politicians pursuing nothing but private, personal greed and ambition, and be given over to sanctified leaders equipped with love and wisdom. Nor had the state been taken into social-gospel thought as a major political agent for centralized action in the society, with its concomitant abstraction and impersonality. Politics did not, that is, appear as the invasion of power into principle, the invasion of the collective into the personal.

Third, this new soul appeared to be, after all, but the old soul writ large, the old soul sanctified in the evangelical faith. It was not the social gospel that had dissolved Calvinism. The liberal individualists had been preaching the perfected life, in God, in Jesus Christ, in history, and in society, long before. The social gospel had only to amend and supplement older definitions of perfection.

In short, the socialized soul, exposed to society, was able to presume historical fair weather, neither too hot nor too cold.

The chapter to follow describes the two forms of absolute politics that lurked in this peculiar moment. Reason, preached by Harry Ward, drove on toward final purification and universalization of the vision of the ends. Love, preached by Kirby Page, intensified and purified the doctrine of the socialized self as a political means. In both, nemesis had begun to overtake the logicians. These extreme evolutions of the passion rested more on anxiety than on hope, provoked by the psychology sketched in this chapter. The self had been left exposed, whatever the weather, and the totalitarianism of Ward on the one hand, the pacifism of Page on the other, were both efforts to reshelter it, as the historical weather began to seem to them, both men of sensitivity, to be turning bitter.

VIII

Two Routes to Security

Forty-five years old at the end of the First World War, Harry Ward had already entered the first rank of the prophets. His work had been concentrated within his own denomination, the Methodists. He had written social-gospel study texts for Methodist Sunday schools. He had taught at Boston University's theological school. He had helped found the Federation for Social Service and had become its leader. As noted, he once thought of the body of Methodists tactically, as a group in whom interests as well as idealism worked in the channels of the better social order. By 1919 Ward was at Union Theological Seminary, where he remained until 1944.

The year 1919 marked something of a shift, when Ward was really launched on his career as the "stormy petrel of Methodism," for it marked his first notable identification with secular social-action groups, which eventually made him the most active clerical participant in secular organizations of any of the prophets. This did not lead him to give up his professional church orientation. Ward had opposed the war and joined the People's Council in doing so, a step more drastic than any taken by Norman Thomas, A. J. Muste, or other clerical pacifists. But whereas Thomas left the ministry to become chief of the socialist League for Industrial Democracy, and whereas Muste left for labor education at Brookwood, Ward did not leave. When he became head of the American Civil Liberties Union (ACLU), he remained in the ministry. The difference was important: Ward always argued the one-to-one correlation: for him, the ACLU was a natural extension of the passion, and not a new departure.

His troubles within the church began with the January-February, 1919, issue of the *Social Service Bulletin*. It was an issue devoted to Russia. The introductory sentences read: "The aim of the Bolsheviks is clearly the creation of a state composed entirely of producers and controlled by producers. This is manifestly a Scriptural aim." Within a few weeks, church leaders, church papers, and church boards, not to mention outside parties, had taken sides. The internal politics of any Protestant denomination were complex, of the Methodists especially so. In this instance, the line of attack ran through the Sunday-School syndicate. The editors' section of the syndicate voted to cancel Ward's contributions to the lesson series and to destroy the plates of his books. The *Christian Advocate* approved and helped lead the fight. Ministers in Pittsburgh, Denver, and Chicago, among others, protested the editors' action; explaining that they did not necessarily approve of the *Bulletin's* discussion of Bolshevism, they did support Ward's books as good books. Bishop McConnell, president of the federation, and George Coe, a member, gave Ward militant support. Coe declared that the syndicate publishers were angry at Ward for having agitated the matter of labor conditions in the Methodist Book Concern. Eventually, the books disappeared from the Sunday school lists. In addition, a test was made of the constitutional workings of the Social Service Federation. A poll revealed that the general council of the federation had not been canvassed on running an issue on Russia; that had been Ward's decision alone; indeterminate agreement was reached by the executive committee that further discussions of Bolshevism in the *Bulletin* would be restricted.[1]

The tempest was unsatisfactory. Ward's own position was that

Russia was an experiment. It was to be observed, its unacceptable features rejected, its legitimate challenge to idealism accepted. The attack upon him was indiscriminate and obscured this approach. But the defense too was not, in the end, discriminating. Fixing on the right of the federation to sponsor whatever inquiry it wished, freely and openly, ideas about Russia itself were not sharpened. What Ward said about Russia in *The New Social Order*, published later in the year, was clear enough. First, its program remained on paper; verdicts would have to wait on practice. Second, it was clear that the theory of dictatorship by the proletariat was foreign to the West. Ward said: "It is conceivable that the Soviet program might mean advance for Russia, but delay and disaster for a nation with more democratic political development." [2] In all this, it is important to a grasp of Ward's development to appreciate that at this point, 1919, he had no dogmatic quarrels with the social gospel. He, like the prophets in general, deplored class conflict, and like the others advertised the social gospel as a means for avoiding it. In his consciousness of the "conjunctions of economic pressure and idealistic impulse," he displayed more power-realism than did most of the prophets, but his problem in this period was not so much tactics as it was the celebration of the ideal.

In 1922, the convention of the underground Communist party was raided by FBI agents in Bridgman, Michigan. As head of the Civil Liberties Union, Ward defended the rights of the Communist leaders. Another uproar within the Methodist church followed; General Conference in 1924 was called upon to censure him for his actions, but refused. In 1926 the federation fell under attack for its Evanston Conference, where Ward was alleged to be in contact with radical journalists who wanted to present the conference as a rally for left-wing politics. Certain federation members were connected with the Communist party campaign in 1932, and in 1936 the most concerted effort of all to deprive the federation of its role as agent of the church was organized.[3] By this time, Ward had driven his own thinking on to its conclusion; from 1933 his position was rigid. But the essence of this thinking had not been and was not to be doctrinaire Marxism; it remained a religious vision, mystical, rationalistic, universal, of the Kingdom.

As Ward saw the modern era, humanity was coming to consciousness of itself. It was striving to shape itself into an organic unity. The movement of the common life now was aimless and blind, but vision was growing. It was as though there was at the heart of Being itself an ache and longing to come to self-determination. The modern era was determined by this effort of humanity to make conscious choice of the ends for its associated life. This was a religious ideal, and the history of religion was identical with the history of this consciousness. "This concept of a religious fellowship as wide and as lasting as the universe has been a slow historic growth." [4] For Ward, there was in the simple fact of ferment in the common life, in "the upthrust of the dark millions," a promise not only pertinent to but the heart of the vision of the Kingdom. Here was a kind of social-gospel version of the "radical liberalism" of the Chicago school of theology, the theology of immanence cast as radical humanism. The test of the ideal would be settled "by the appeal to the facts and tendencies of social evolution; there is no going behind or beyond that court." [5] Since Ward was first of all a man of the social gospel, and not first of all a radical liberal (theologically speaking), he equated without stress this immanent spirit of humanity with the teachings of Jesus.

The American Civil Liberties Union acted to guarantee ferment its freedom, as did the American Committee for Justice to China. Ward visited China on a world tour in the 'twenties. Writing that the situation was confused, problematic, inscrutable, he nevertheless cabled from Shanghai for funds in aid of—what? [6] The ferment itself, almost in its pure abstraction, without specifications. Unlike the semi-social-gospel peace groups, which in their world-mindedness were primarily concerned with the negative goal of saving America from foreign entanglements and therefore organized "hands-off" committees, Ward scoured the world for positive causes and wished to lend a hand.

Ferment needed channels. In itself undifferentiated, it needed blueprints. *The New Social Order,* devoted in its first half to celebration of the basic energy, in its second half was given over to assessments of existing programs. All were found wanting: the British Labour party, the new Soviet Russian experiment, the League of Nations, the Socialist party in America, independent labor parties in America, the labor movement in America. Each lacked the rigor of the absolute. The discussion could hardly have been less tactical. The situation seemed to Ward so clear that preoccupation with interim stages of social organization was dallying. His reaction to collective bargaining was to invalidate it as incommensurate with the final stage of social evolution.

In the fervor of his imaginings, Ward did not resolve the tensions in theory characterizing social-gospel thought. He solved them in the old way, by dissolving them in a vision of the absolute. Two problems may be mentioned: the problem of "sin" and the role of "science." Ward did not attempt to wash out sin, to wash out, that is, all that resistance to fellowship rooted in more than ignorance alone. As he put it:

> The spirit of the capitalist order is far older than the capitalist system. It has deep roots in human nature and a long course of development in human history. Its abandonment is no small matter. It involves the substitution of the spirit of cooperative service for the spirit of strife and conquest, and the choosing of the promotion of the common welfare of humanity as the end of life instead of the pursuit of wealth and power.[7]

In this remarkable passage, a secret was given away: "capitalism" was not really the issue. Here the nonsociological core of social-gospel sociology stood revealed, particularly significant in Ward, who excoriated capitalism in the sociological sense far more persistently than the other postwar prophets. His sociological anticapitalism was uncompromising, yet he no less than the others rested in the end upon a pure abstract revivalism, independent of definite social conditions. It was not only capitalism that was to be ended, but a spirit "far older."

Ward gave the bearing of science upon social salvation one of its sharpest statements after Rauschenbusch. The role of scientific

insight in his philosophy of history was essential; the frustrations
of the movement of life toward self-consciousness and self-mastery
followed from the failures of self-consciousness, which were
failures in knowledge. But he was contradictory, like Rauschenbusch, about the actual present state of scientific sociological
learning. At one point:

> The science of society is still in its infancy and its central task is to
> clearly outline and analyze the fundamental principles of human as-
> sociation that they may then be applied to the increasing activities
> of mankind. This is the great adventure of tomorrow.

But at another point:

> . . . the advent of political democracy and the industrial revolu-
> tion made inevitable the final overthrow of the class system by exalt-
> ing the principle of brotherhood and supplying both the technical
> capacity and the power of mass organization which makes possible
> its realization in daily living.[8]

There was no real indecision here however; rather, there was a
need to believe science was ready. Thus, just as his sense of the
shortcomings in the British Labour party, the Socialist party, and
Russia never led him to think of a politics adapted to shortcomings, in the same way no sense of the ignorance still regnant
in sociology ever led him to think of a politics adapted to ignorance. His criteria for politics were that it should possess both the
righteousness and the science necessary without tarrying.

Ignorance existed truly at only one point; where was the conjunction of righteous science with the power necessary to exercise
it?

The formula to which Ward finally came was this: the leadership of ferment by men of absolute vision. The leadership was
to be direct—the men of absolute vision were to be political
leaders. Ultimately, Ward concluded that the logic by which
ferment would present to these men the opportunity for enforc-
ing their vision was Marxist.

He came to these positions only out of the typical social-gospel
analysis of the power-groups of the society. In 1919 it would have

been impossible to distinguish his position here from that of the authors of "The Church and Industrial Reconstruction," or from that found in the dozens of articles and tracts of the time, all infused with the sense of the saving majority. We have caught his expectations of the Methodists. His early view of the middle classes was, if anything, more optimistic than the norm. "Its pioneer spirit ought to put it in the vanguard of those seeking a new world. Its ideals are those around which a new order will crystallize, whether it follows or forsakes them." [9] He also had the typical anxieties about labor: would it seek power and freedom for itself alone or for all? His answer, like most of the answers, held back from the advanced position of Rauschenbusch: it all depended, he wrote, upon the strong. "The strong are called to sacrifice . . . Will the educated idealists of the middle class sacrifice anything for the development of the working class?" [10] Labor was not, that is, decisive. For Ward, there were too many sources of ferment and protest against capitalism for that: farmers, the Midwestern towns and villages, unspecified but large groups of the middle, all qualified as well as labor as bearers of the idea.

In this, he exhibited the instincts of the Progressive, in whom social idealism was fortified by the haunting specter of a show-down struggle between industrial capital and industrial labor, with the middle caught between. But as the 'twenties wore on, Ward could not follow the course common among disappointed Progressives, moderating and surrendering the idealism as the specter dissolved in prosperity. The anxieties of Progressivism had inspired him to embrace the utopian vision, and this vision generated its own anxieties. In one direction, consequently, his recourse was to continue to insist upon the material failure of capitalism, to insist upon the continuing potentiality of ferment rising out of economic need. In the final year of prosperity, his estimate of the American scene drew more upon the interior demands of his own thought than upon the facts before him— although the facts were in no necessary contradiction to his estimate: America was beginning to duplicate the extremes of luxury and poverty in Europe; agriculture foundered; labor lagged further and further behind in the race of consumption. [11]

And in another direction, he merely hibernated. It was increasingly impossible to talk of self-generating saving majorities to bear the idea to victory. Actually, Ward never had argued that the discipline and science necessary to organize ferment emerged from the experience of the fermenting classes themselves. In fact, to him it had seemed an advantage that the vision of the absolute should be sustained apart from the struggles of fermenting interest groups. It was an advantage, for instance, that Bible scholarship had rendered knowledge of the absolute ideal "objective." [12] The new order could come into being only animated by the spirit of sacrifice; it was therefore well that its bearers could not possibly be thought committed to the interests of any class. The new order required science; it was well, therefore, that its bearers possess scientific detachment. Thus the importance of the "educated idealists" of the middle class, rather than the middle class itself, became clearer.

The two most influential men of the time, Ward wrote in a fascinating article of 1925, were Lenin and Gandhi. In the bare simplicity, the sacrificial passion, of both lives the masses instinctively recognized absolute disinterest. Both men were supremely self-confident; they *knew,* and in their knowledge they acted; they were scientists of society. And who were Lenin and Gandhi? Both were educated idealists rising out of the middle classes. The year following, Ward discovered General Feng in China, another man of disinterest—and a Methodist from the missionary school in Shanghai, a Chinese version of the bourgeois idealist.[13] Here were examples of the critical conjunction—righteousness, science, and power united; here the idea lived already served by hands ready to shape ferment and make the ideal universal.

In General Feng's leadership, obscure and pathetic if not comic, Ward's will to believe might be measured. For America in the 'twenties, these particular points of conjunction were not instructive. Neither Lenin nor Gandhi could be said to have been responsible for the fact that their societies had been jockeyed into precisely that plastic moment offering the hand of idealistic disinterest free play. No intelligible tactics for America could be drawn from their examples. All the American idealist could do was wait.

But to wait, while nursing ideas about what such men might achieve, was to drive the vision on to completion. In the early 'thirties, American ferment appeared to be unloosed again, the prophets were realerted at all stations, and Ward was ready with his climactic ideal.

For Kirby Page, also, the social passion was everything. He had no other commitments within the church. An ordained minister, his work did not center in a parish, preaching ministry, nor did he man denominational or interdenominational machinery or teach in the seminaries. He manned the social-gospel organizations themselves. Besides serving as a secretary in the Fellowship of Reconciliation, he served as secretary of the executive committee of the Fellowship for a Christian Social Order. From 1926, he served as chief editor of the *World Tomorrow*. A conference-goer in the old tradition, he appeared at Olivet, at Silver Bay, at Lake Mohonk. Foremost, from his home in New Jersey and offices in New York, he posted the pamphlets and articles that made him the tractarian of the social gospel. From 1921, his books and pamphlets sold more than a million copies. Page was twenty-eight years old at the close of the war. He had served as a secretary in the Y.M.C.A. with British troops in 1916, with American troops in 1917. He returned home a pacifist. Taking the pulpit of Ridgwood Church of Christ in Brooklyn in 1918, he resigned in 1921 to devote himself to the speaking, writing, and fellowship that were his full-time duties between the wars.

His first concern was war and peace, but parallel to his labors for peace, Page evangelized for a better social order. For the Federal Council, he edited the problem-discussions volume, *Christianity and Economic Problems*, in 1922, and published his own small book, *Incentives in Modern Life*, the same year. To the "Christianity and Industry" series of tracts, he also supplied "Collective Bargaining," "Industrial Facts," and "The United States Steel Corporation." As editor of the *World Tomorrow*, his

attention roamed as far as the scope of the social gospel. There
was no particular integration of the two sides of his evangel, no
field of logic uniting the action for peace and the action for
justice in, say, a Marxist or semi-Marxist analysis of capitalism.
This was not to appear among the prophets until late in the
'thirties. In Page's pamphlet, "War: Its Causes, Consequences and
Cure," national economic systems were not listed among the
causes; in his "twenty-two point program for patriots" of 1931,
the only point touching upon economic affairs was his call for
reduction in tariffs. This absence of economic analysis followed
from the instincts of the social gospel, to appeal directly to the
psychology of the persons involved in each concrete situation;
each "danger zone" was assessed independently, and for each the
therapy was direct, a change in spirit.[14]

But, to repeat, war was his first concern. War had not been
a preoccupation of the social gospel in its first generations. It
had not figured in the picture of forces rising to menace the old
culture-community. The tradition of peace societies within the
church was older than the social gospel; that older tradition of
specific and limited reform that had included abolition and
temperance was self-consciously transcended by the prophets in
their sociology. It was through men like Page that war did enter
the minds of the prophets, through men like Page that self-
conscious pacifism entered their debates, demanding attention
not only for the politics of peace, but for the politics of justice
and the new order as well.

What Page had seen in Europe in 1916 and 1917 was the
"kingdom of evil." He was wounded by what he saw, the wound
was absolute, and for it he proposed an absolute therapy—the
literal, unyielding imitation of Jesus. His career was devoted, first,
to preventing the evil from ever rising again, and second, to
preparing Christians to resist if and when it did reëmerge. Half
the story of his politics rested in the fact that the difference
between the two goals was always obscured. In his first short
book, *The Sword or the Cross*, the first words read: "Struggles
between nations and struggles between classes we shall surely
have during the coming decades. All indications point to further

wars between nations." [15] Here was, clearly promised, discussion of a program for maintaining absolute witness in face of the evil realities of the world. But the last words of the book read otherwise:

> To increase the number of men and women in all lands who will refuse absolutely to sanction the use of any unchristian weapon, who will follow without compromise the teaching and example of Jesus Christ, and who will seek diligently by every possible means to spread abroad in the lives of individuals and of nations the spirit of Jesus, this is the only sure way to abolish war.[16]

The tug of the pragmatic hope was stronger; by 1925 it was controlling. "For the first time in human history, it is now within our power to adopt certain practical measures which, if adopted, will remove the probability, although not the possibility, of another great war." [17]

Page threw himself into pressing the practical measures. The target was public opinion. "Lack of information is the chief reason why the citizens of the United States are not demanding a more vigorous and far-sighted foreign policy." [18] Human nature did not require changing; the reservoir of will and morality was full; it needed only to be enlightened. The first tracts therefore were filled with the statistics of enlightenment and disillusionment: casualty figures and financial costs, secret treaties and the machinations of their authors, colonial exploitation and Allied profiteers, the myth of war guilt and the myth of a democratic British Empire. All proved the pragmatic and moral futility of the crusade that had been fought under the banner of Wilsonian idealism. It must not happen again. The practical measures followed: American membership in League and World Court, American support for the outlawing of war, abandonment of all military and political imperialism in Latin America and Asia, freedom for the Philippines, reduction and if necessary cancellation of war debts both Allied and German, reduction of tariffs, disarmament led by America. Page never suggested that any of these measures ranked as cure-alls. His estimate of the outlawing movement, culminating in the Kellogg Pact, judiciously and accurately emphasized the inadequacy of a focus upon juridical, rather than political or economic, action as a self-sufficient strategy. He pointed at the weaknesses of the League and the manifest difficulties under which that body labored. But these were measures that, Page believed, America could take; they were better taken than not taken, and they were measures, therefore, that pacifists could advocate as steps on the road to abolition of war.[19]

Clearly, in these measures the logic of pacifism was linked with a logic for America. Not only Christians but the nation should be prepared to resist the kingdom of evil if and when it reappeared. Pacifists in the 'twenties as in the 'thirties denied that they were isolationists. They advocated nonimperialistic internationalism. They opposed the disillusioned isolationists who wished America to stay home armed on all coasts, and the imperialist isolationists aspiring to American empire in a Latin America closed and armed against the irrelevant conflicts of Europe. Neither isolation nor empire was the way. Independence for the Philippines, nonintervention in Latin America, and cancellation of the war debts would at once improve America's claim to just character and at the same time withdraw her from entanglements in the world pattern of injustice. So there was defense in depth: abolish war; disentangle America; disentangle pacifists.[20]

The last was the crux of the matter. These practical measures might have been pressed by any one of the peace leaders in the church at large. But for Page, there was more—the ultimate logic of pacifism itself. Pacifism prepared for ultimate as well as proximate challenges, and although foreign affairs in the 'twenties were not designed to bring it out, Page felt driven to supply such preparation. What should the Christian have done in Belgium in 1914? This was the critical question for a pacifist catechism. What should he have done, that is, if he had really wished to follow the true teachings of Jesus Christ? He should have maintained an attitude of unfaltering good will; he should not have taken up arms. "Would such a course have stopped the Germans? . . . Almost certainly not." But: "The method of armed resistance resulted in the death of 26 million people and well-nigh wrecked a continent. Could the method of active good will have possibly been a more ghastly failure?" [21] This was not the whole problem, however, for certainly no one would have found it satisfactory to have left Belgium in the hands of its conquerors. So, another question: ". . . how could aggressive good will have freed the soil of German invaders?" The response: "By convincing the German people that they had no reason to fear invasion of their own land, and thereby depriving the militarists of their support and driving them out of control of the government . . . If the fears of the German people could have been removed by acts of good will on the part of the surrounding peoples, I believe they would have refused to support the armed occupation of Belgian or French soil, but would have driven the militarists from power and ended the military occupation." [22]

This went very far, but, still pragmatic and prudential, the argument had not yet come to bedrock. The obvious weakness in this review of tactics for Belgian Christians in 1914 was the assumption of mass pacifist action. Page was arguing that a national policy of pacifism would have been effective, but perhaps his pragmatics would not have applied if one Belgian alone, or only a handful, had met the Germans with aggressive good will. In the forty-eighth of his fifty-question catechism, Page forced himself to face this question: what good would conscientious objection accomplish if only a small percentage of citizens undertook it? "The chief value . . . is the example set. . . . It is out of similar action by small groups throughout human history that great social reforms have arisen. What good did it do for the early disciples to die in the arena . . . ? What good did it do for Savonarola and Huss to die for their convictions?" [23]

With this, Page was being forced outside the old social gospel. The social gospel was not pitched to the sociology of small-group sectarian action; it was able to afford its hopes, its social theory, its ethical Jesus, and its religion in general, only so long as it kept its confidence that something like majorities or at least sufficient and strategic resources of power for social change were available. Page's position at this point was a concession in the direction of preserving the absolute within the soul of the idealist at the expense of social effectiveness. But even this was not quite yet the bedrock; his justification for isolated pacifist witness still remained pragmatic. The small group would eventually become a large group. Only through a transition of clearly unconscious elisions did Page come to the final point: "Every follower of Jesus is under obligations to obey the will of God regardless of where it leads and what it costs. . . ." [24] Regardless!

The difficulty Page experienced in confessing this hidden, final, nonpragmatic, nonpolitical sanction testified to his social-gospel idealism. He never really felt himself in a position where he found it necessary to declare that now, here, at this particular juncture of politics and history, men must obey the will of God even though their obedience would not affect the situation in an ideal manner. He always argued the political value of pacifism. It was in *Jesus or Christianity* (1929), one of the significant books of the last days of the unreconstructed social gospel, that Page too dismissed 1,600 years of Christian history as corruption, because in all that time Christianity had not followed the politics of love. Intelligent good will, efficient sacrificial love: this was the sum and substance of Christianity. No implications were to be drawn from the fact that, through 1,600 years, it had been something else. Christianity was not, Page was saying, perhaps a reconciliation with history, a reconciliation of man with himself. It was a blueprint to which man and history were to be conformed.

Page of course had already been exposed, in 1916 and 1917, in a most bitter fashion, to historical storms not so directly felt by the majority of the pastors. His pacifism was the posture of a soul fortifying itself, suffused with its memory of battlefields, never free—for all its trust in public opinion, its proclaimed faith in the saving majority of the church, in the responsiveness of human nature to love—from apprehension of battlefields ahead that could invade and ravage the soul once more. Pure love was the only final protection, the only final security, and even though Page argued it as politics, he would cling to it when its politics crumbled. Pacifism was to be the storm cellar of the social gospel. [25]

In the 'thirties, none of the prophets could escape the storms. Would they all follow out these lines of logic to the end? Of course not. Both Page and Ward were carrying their passion beyond the secure limits of the culture-community of the church. The council, the *Century,* a clear majority of the social-gospel ministers, would remain domesticated within this disciplining, restraining, prudential context. But if we glance once again at a man whose life was practicality, who himself deprecated utopian visions, who proposed neither pacifism nor scientific social leadership as patterns for politics, we find the same essential vision of salvation held in the heart. Francis McConnell's multiple career was all of a piece. His very duties in the church, as Methodist Bishop of Denver, Pittsburgh, and New York, as president of the Federal Council, kept him intimate with the absurdities of extremism, but nevertheless aware that change was a social possibility. The personalistic philosophy that he expounded and expanded from the model of his mentor, Borden Parker Bowne, was a theological version of common sense—pluralistic, open-ended, hag-ridden by neither first principles nor final values. As a prophet, he presided, he did not dictate. He wished to keep the process open, the life moving on—and not for the sake of closing it over at some ultimate moment, but for its own sake. Yet perhaps there was no difference between the incarnation of common sense and the incarnation of absolute love or absolute reason, for what did the politics of common sense look like when internalized? These were McConnell's words:

> In the language of the fashionable psychology, the subconscious self would be so transformed that even the impulses would of themselves move in the direction of social helpfulness. We would be delivered from that practice of repressive self-discipline which makes the subconsciousness a dark cellar out of which all manner of wild impulses are trying to burst, and would have instead a practice of control leading out of the inner recesses intense spiritual forces "domesticated" into the system of activities around us.[26]

It was this central religious vision of total sanctification that Ward and Page were defending, its prodigious extremity that encouraged the extremity of their politics.

IX

The Meaning of Jesus

In a book published in 1929, *The Twilight of Christianity*, Harry Elmer Barnes singled out social-gospel pastors for special praise. Barnes was a popularizer and polemicist of the New History, the New Reason, the New Social Science, proposing a common-sense scientific reconstruction of everything. His book was devoted to annihilation of the last remnants of super-naturalist, nonscientific religion. Barnes was not antireligious; he was "cordial to any type of secular religion devoted to the cause of making this life here on earth more pleasant and worth-while." The social gospel, he said, was so devoting itself. Barnes lauded Kirby Page, Harry Ward, Sherwood Eddy, Jerome Davis, Reinhold Niebuhr, and Francis McConnell for their efforts. But why, he asked in exasperation, did these six men, and others like them, insist upon importing Jesus, His ethics, and His alleged teachings into their discussions of social affairs? Why did Page base his peace politics upon the teachings of Jesus, "which in this field are more than usually fragmentary and contradictory"? Why did Eddy try to justify his brave struggle for social justice

on the ground that it conforms to the teachings of Jesus, who could no more have carried on an intelligent conversation on social and economic problems with Sidney Webb, Paul Douglas or Thorstein Veblen than he could have interpreted the most abstruse formulae of Einstein. . . . The uncertain, vague and contradictory notions of a very obscure religious teacher in a long past stage of civilization

were no basis for social science, any more than for physical science or natural science. The Jesus stereotype had to be laid to rest.[1]

Barnes expressed a feeling not uncommon among intellectuals of the 'twenties, for many of whom Christianity was what it had been for the *philosophes* of the eighteenth century, a baggage of useless tradition. Let religion become, as John Dewey was to say in *A Common Faith*, devotion to the noblest ideals of humanity at large. More than this, however, Barnes was striking at a vulnerable point in the social gospel itself. In the hands of radically liberal seminarians, theology was becoming a celebration of emergent process, of the "ongoing" continuities of Western culture, and, more specifically still, of American culture. God was that spirit in process, or that structure, or that ground, out of which value emerged. Ultimately indebted to twin genii of the nineteenth century, Hegel and Darwin, this theology was presented as a natural, reasonable extension of the Christian imagination. Old conundrums of theology remained, but the new theology drew their sting. Thus, in face of the fact that not all processes worked for the emergence of value, and that not all emergents were good, the new theologians debated whether God was "limited" or not, as had theologians before them. But the debate was not compelling, since even a limited God was that portion of process destined to prevail over all. This idealistic-naturalistic theology merged without stress into pure humanism, where all the attention bore on the human participation in process, and the "quest" appeared as the object of religious concern, "questing" as religion itself.[2]

The story of the National Conference on a Christian Way of Life was a perfect exemplification of these currents. "Inquiry," as the conference soon was called, was set afoot by the Federal Council early in 1922: "The purpose of this undertaking is to promote the serious study and full discussion of industrial, racial and international problems in the light of the spirit and teaching of Jesus." A national committee, headed by William Adams Brown and including Sherwood Eddy, Kirby Page, Harry Ward, and Justin Wroe Nixon, drew up plans. By 1923 an expanded membership of Inquiry, including educators, social workers, and other laymen, came to regard the method of the inquiry as more important than eventual findings. It was the process, the quest, that was the essence. Rather than beginning with some explicitly recognizable Christian authority, the group preferred—as Herbert Croly of the *New Republic* put it—to look at life itself for its possibilities, to see if it might, if lived warmly, inquisitively, and loyally, imply a religious or (even) a Christian fulfillment. Some of the churchmen left; others stayed; but the "Christian" in the original name vanished.[3]

By all the logic of the social gospel, this was a natural fate. Religion was to be social, democratic, and scientific. Jesus had understood and meant this, according to the prophets; but it was not necessary to be convinced by Jesus' teachings to be convinced this was true. After establishing the liberal-social content of Jesus' teachings, social-gospel polemics then dismissed the teaching of all that sweep of Christian experience since Jesus, essentially by emphasizing the sociological ground of all theology. Thus, Hellenistic culture explained mystical doctrines of Trinity and Christology; feudal social patterns explained doctrines of the Atonement. But Jesus, they argued, remained untouched by sociology, a fixed and eternal figure pointing unambiguously to the patterns to which democratic religion now aspired. As Rauschenbusch had argued on the issue of eschatology, Jesus had to be claimed to have had modern views in His own time. In the succinct summary of another scholar: "The 'Kingdom of God,' we may believe, was a democratic conception in the mind of Jesus, but it has been largely an autocratic conception from his day to ours." [4]

Nevertheless, Barnes' question missed the point, if only because he took the logic for the spirit. The point was that the prophets, in their social science, in their politics, in their efforts to convert the system, were implementing something older than their social science and, indeed, than their social gospel. They were implementing the ideal of entire sanctification, of complete personal union with Jesus Christ, of—in a word—perfectionism. The stream had come down from the pre-Civil War generations of the evangelical revivals, and not a single one of all the leading prophets did not show himself within that heritage.

Evangelical perfectionism had always centered on Jesus, and the reasons for this were not dismissed, as Barnes would have liked, in concepts of "cultural lag." What was sanctification, what was perfection? Essentially, unification of the will, eradication of inner contradiction, completion of the personality, stabilization, an end in a final self to the self's process of creating the self. Such a vision required special representation. An image of absolute being, beyond becoming, it required the absolute symbol. Sectarian in its original impulse, the circumstances of the flourishing of American perfectionism were also circumstances allowing to perfectionism life in the relative world. In its original impulse, perfectionism fed upon inexplicable tensions between expectation and reality, between the individual and his social world, and it continued to do so in the 'twenties. A particular sort of world, the imbalances of an open society, stimulated the hope and sharpened the anxiety for balance, stability, and security within. But always, just because it was an open society, once the balance and sanctity within had been established by conversion, the idea of action took hold. The saint was drawn outward, back into the broader society, feeding sanctification into reform, trying to resolve the original outward imbalance that had helped inspire the perfectionist gathering in the first place, or else, as was more usual, trying to prevent any future imbalances altogether. This was the logic of the sect-as-church, and Barnes missed the heart of it. The perfecting moment, the moment of withdrawal into union with the absolute, controlled the return, seeking union with history.[5]

American history had offered vast opportunity for such logic to seem plausible to large numbers of people. Puritans had anticipated it in the seventeenth century, in concepts of an American Israel. Nineteenth-century reform persistently justified itself as a kind of final infusion of holiness into the body social, bringing it up to divine specifications. The Civil War itself, as later the First World War, was assimilated into the logic as a kind of climactic crusade. The imagery with which Bryan and Theodore Roosevelt explained Populism and Progressivism was not decorative, but religiously compelling. In the twentieth century, hypostatization of an "American Way of Life" showed the tradition still vigorous.

But unlike the earlier tradition, the social gospel could not implement the logic without socialization of the idea of personality, which was to say, socialization of the idea of perfection, and Barnes would have been shrewd to have made a small adjustment in his complaint. He might have asked not why Page and Ward and Eddy and the others accepted Jesus, but why Thorstein Veblen, Sidney Webb, and others should have to. The prophets could not, in terms of social-gospel logic, have shown that the social scientists were not advancing salvation quite apart from whether or not they themselves testified to Jesus. But dangers lay here, beyond Barnes' question. To abandon the symbol of perfection as Barnes wished was to lose a critical power the perfectionist ideal had had and in fact still had. By its measure, anything and anyone could be judged short of the ideal. Without that measure, the danger was that of prophecy disappearing into utilitarian idealism without a murmur. This was the fate of Inquiry and the leading hazard of religious liberalism.

This was not, however, the vastest danger. The greatest tragedy of all would be for prophecy to disappear into utilitarian idealism *without* abandoning the perfectionist symbol—to sanctify the utilitarian and lose the meaning of sanctity. This was precisely what the social-gospel pastors often felt the middle-class church of individualistic piety had already done. But they were threatened by the same thing in their own conception of their goal, and in the decade ahead, they were to be faced by the temptations of a utilitarianism more adequate to the task of stabilizing the system than the politics of business and prosperity. Through the 'twenties they had searched and waited without success, but the 'twenties had had no New Deal. The greatest irony of the 'thirties was to be that the resistance of conservative Protestant congregations to the program of reform helped keep many of the pastors from identifying the social gospel with the New Deal.

On the other hand, this was to have the effect of turning many of the pastors directly into sectarian politics, offering more righteousness but less hope than the New Deal; this split would be fatal.

Only a successful attack upon the central concept of the prophetic synthesis, that of the sanctified, perfected life, could release prophecy from its pathos. Such an attack would be release, by releasing politics and the system from total responsibility for the personality, and by releasing personality from its deepening dependence upon the system. As far as official exegetical basis for the social gospel went, ground was already crumbling. In 1928, for instance, in *Jesus on Social Institutions*, Shailer Mathews recanted on his earlier views that Jesus taught a historical fulfillment of a new religious society, conceding that this was not precisely what Jesus had meant by the term "Kingdom of God." Mathews still argued that Jesus' ethics constituted a program for the new social order, but American scholars generally were having to face the insistence of European scholarship upon the eschatological elements in Jesus' thought more seriously than had Rauschenbusch. The socially adaptable, scientifically organizable, perfecting and sanctifying ethical teachings, at once the possession of Jesus and the possibilities of human nature, took on a harsher, more ascetic, possibly inimitable cast. It would always remain possible in the 'thirties to claim that those teachings were "relevant" to personality and to the structures and manners of society and politics; but possibly the relevance was that of an eternal criticism, eternally disrupting the stabilities and completed sanctities of life, both inner and outer, guaranteeing that history remain always open.[6]

Really to draw the lessons of social-gospel experience, then, would be more than to criticize its politics and social vision. It would be to criticize the type of man who had dreamed its politics in the first place, the sanctified man, the good man, the moral man who would moralize immoral society.

X

The Politics of Urgency

In the last months of 1932 and the early months of 1933, the *Moody Bible Institute Monthly* interpreted the troubles of that time as heralding the last days—premonitions of eschaton, the crisis preparing for the millennium for which men had only to wait. In the same months, the *Social Service Bulletin* of the Methodist Federation for Social Service, concluding that the crisis was absolute, announced its commitment to the creation of the new social order that must arise from capitalistic disintegration, a new order for which men had only to act. The two declarations were equal and opposite reactions to the same cause. An extreme example of articulate fundamentalism, the *Moody Monthly* took the depression to verify and justify its own faith. It proclaimed what it had always proclaimed before—that this world was not for salvation, that its course was fixed and out of men's hands, and that before it gave way to the Kingdom it would get worse. Organ of the extreme prophet of the social gospel, the federation *Bulletin* had always understood that, within capitalism, nemesis was being prepared. It responded by proclaiming even more strongly that society was meant for salvation, that the life of false kingdoms must shatter, and that men had only to identify themselves with destiny to break through into the new world.

When, very soon, it seemed that the slide into annihilation had decelerated, at least for a time, each of these prophecies underwent necessary adjustment. The last days still lay ahead, although possibly not in the immediate future. The new social order still waited, but possibly capitalism could yet summon to itself the power of the state for an interregnum of fascism.

The depression constituted, for the men of the social gospel, a massive challenge to the integrity and moral rationale of American society. The similarity in the responses of the *Moody Monthly* and the federation *Bulletin* reflected a fact common to both: neither felt the integrity of its religious witness entangled in that society; for both, the ultimate center of meaning stood fixed, in the one instance beyond history, in the other beyond capitalism.

But between these extremes of professional millenarian fundamentalism and professional millenarian radicalism, Protestantism as a whole did stand entangled in the crisis, socially, financially, ethically, and also theologically. It was perhaps unfortunate that the pattern of entanglement was so often ironically symbolized. In Pittsburgh, a new East Liberty Presbyterian church, projected to soar above its thirteen-story skyscraper neighbor, began to arise by the endowment of Andrew W. Mellon. It was to be the most beautiful parish church in America, and "there will also be a place where any poor person may be temporarily cared for." But the entanglement could also evoke pure charity. In Chicago, for instance, the Baptist church of Johnston Myers, being slowly abandoned by the migration of its parishioners to the green suburbs, dispensed something more than half a million meals to some tens of thousands of men through dark months of the depression. Finally, entanglement could mean the simple harassment of all men, trying to maintain solvency: Methodism had expanded its indebtedness from $19,000,000 in 1921 to $67,000,000 in 1930; in 1932, the committees, boards, and commissions at General Conference submitted to a panic of budgetary anxiety and retreat; on the last day, in haste, without attention, resolutions were voted to display the social conscience of the church.[1]

As a moral phenomenon, the depression might have demonstrated a basic Augustinian principle that the fortunes of history were distributed without discrimination between the good and the evil. Confronted with such a principle, the liberal idealist might have been driven to leap immediately onto the Barthian rock, the rock around which history swirled, from the boat in which he had been endeavoring to navigate history. But the social passion of the 'thirties was to remain in the boat, its schisms the disputes of navigators. The storms in America were not so great as storms could be; the American will to ride the torrent was old and deep. The problem for one party, consequently, was to make sense of harsh historical events within a philosophy of optimism, for the other to preserve the will for navigation and social action under guidance of a philosophy more pessimistic.

Within months after the economic decline began, early in 1930, the concrete phenomena of unemployment and physical want drew first attention. Unemployment had been visible to the prophets from 1920 on. In fact, unemployment had been taken as a chronic phenomenon, part of the evidence for the technical inability of the system to provide for its own, and the administrative committee of the Federal Council had endorsed, early in 1929, long-range planning of public-works and workmen's-compensation laws in the states. However, the unemployment from 1930 was more than injustice for a few; it was a disease of the whole, cancerous, immediately threatening. One focus of the social gospel was defined, as the depression advanced, by concentration upon relieving unemployment as such. In the church at large, money drives, odd-job plans, make-work projects, and direct charity typified action everywhere, of which Johnston Myers' church was only an extreme example. This was the spirit of charity, in both senses of the word, neither special to nor denied by the social gospel, and, in its inadequacy, testimony to the need for something, in the moral sense, less, in the social sense, more. The Federal Council led the way in calls for a federal public-works program and unemployment insurance. In January, 1931, the council joined with the social-service boards of the National Catholic Welfare Council and the Central Committee of American Rabbis to sponsor in Washington the conference on Permanent Preventives of Unemployment. The general committee included Bishop McConnell, Jerome Davis, Alva Taylor, Bishop Scarlett, and Reinhold Niebuhr; one of the speakers was Harry Ward. For a second joint conference, early in 1932, the necessity for broad-gauged action was affirmed: ". . . it is now time that the engineering principle of planning which has been so successfully introduced into industrial factories should be extended to the control of entire industries and of industry in general." It was noted that ". . . suggestions made by Mr. Gerard Swope are . . . a welcome indication." [2]

The demands of the council remained safely within the system. They represented generalization of the strategy of missions to businessmen. Not that this was to accept whatever the established powers desired by way of a plan; businessmen were still called upon to act in the name of the ideal, as the Social Service Commission explained in 1932:

> . . . if our individual system of ownership and control of property is to continue, those who hold economic privileges must adopt a new attitude of intelligent social concern based on a long view of their own and their neighbor's interests . . . Up to the present time there is no adequate answer to those who contend that privileged classes do not surrender their privileges until they are taken from them. It remains to be demonstrated whether social conscience and social intelligence can together bring about our economic salvation. [3]

But from 1930 on, regular pronouncements from enlightened business leaders—Swope and Owen D. Young in particular—had been appearing. Under an administration headed by the man who had preached industrial rationalization as the very apotheosis of capitalism, and had himself—as Secretary of Commerce—more than any other man pressed it forward, the leading American proponents of the idea that irrational structure lay at the heart of all ills were speaking from within and for the established powers.

The pull that the idea exerted was strongest at the two poles of the passion: just as for the council, so for the Methodist Federation *Bulletin*, "planning" loomed as central to all else. The *Bulletin*, however, insisted that capitalism could not plan. [4] Ward had already offered his vision of the rationalized society, in terms capitalism obviously could not meet. But the council refused to ask "Who shall plan?" It was without strategy, or rather, its strategy presumed that those who had the power would be those to plan. Justin Wroe Nixon, pastor-professor in one of the classic paternalistic communities of the country, Rochester, New York, thought this way in 1930, arguing that "we live in an age when for good or for ill the business class occupies the most strategic position as far as effecting changes in our culture are concerned." [5] In Chicago, where unemployment was early and acute, the Chicago Church Federation, not known for conservatism, expressed the same view. "We have the capitalistic system with us and it gives evidence of being fairly permanent. Any effective amelioration, any immediately helpful remedies, must be sought within the system." [6]

In the same way, the other, weighty "representative" voice of the social gospel, the *Christian Century*, also asked in 1931, "When Will America Begin to Plan?" The *Century* found the time ripe for an evangelism preaching voluntary liquidation of the competitive order for a planned economy ensuring the goods of life to all, and concluded: "What is needed is a moral awakening among those now in control of the industrial machine." [7] The controlling level of the *Century's* response to the crisis situation could be seen in the cycles through which it ran: apprehension as each winter approached, detailed and foreboding description of danger during the winter itself, then a slackening away. It was this immediacy of need which instructed the *Century's* political choice in 1932, once Morrison had satisfied his idealism by proposing the disinterested party. Abandoning the criteria by which it had endorsed Hoover in 1928, the *Century* fixed upon the need for some measure of present relief as the guiding issue. Roosevelt appeared no less conservative than the President, so no choice could be made on that score. And Hoover was the abler man. There were no illusions about the President's social philosophy, but "Mr. Hoover, if elected, will surely be driven by events from his doctrinaire *laissez-faire* position before many months have passed. The automatic processes of the capitalistic system will not reabsorb the ten million unemployed." [8] Therefore, Hoover again.

In this focus upon planning, one of the constituent elements of the social gospel tended to precipitate out. The Federal Council and the *Century* refused to embark upon some leap of politics that might imply a risk to good order. This was not based on a hidden devotion to business interests and leadership *per se*. The council was soon to issue statements supporting the New Deal, deploring the "coercive" aspect of the National Recovery Administration but subscribing to its principle of agreement and coordination in place of competition. The case of the *Century* was more complex. Even while supporting Hoover, it did not disavow its "anticapitalism." Later supporting governmental action and the leadership of the New Deal, it criticized the New Deal program as too conservative.[9] But the *Century* refused to endorse third-party ideological politics. This failure to ask who shall plan, and the failure to face the bearing of this question for the value and fruits of the plan itself, was rooted not so much in some implicit captivity to the established powers, as in a deeper, more profound captivity to the continuity of American life, characterized—as the council and the *Century* saw it—by the great central community of the middle-class church.

This essentially reflexive imagination was displayed very clearly in J. W. Nixon, who, as noted in his book of 1930, keyed hope for a better society to the vision of businessmen. In that book, the possibility that a new social group had or even might have pretensions to leadership went unnoticed.

> We have little sympathy with those who are constantly bemoaning the fact that they are living in a civilization where the business class is dominant. We greatly prefer living in this civilization to living in one dominated by either a hereditary aristocracy or a priesthood. The quest of business men for power is no more ardent than similar quests in history on the part of nobles and ecclesiastics.[10]

By 1940 other leaders were also available, and Nixon readily accepted them. Alongside Owen D. Young appeared Sidney Hillman. Nixon commenced to speak for a mixed economy. "We begin with an inherited economic system of competitive private enterprise. We have to develop a co-operative or communal system which will help to keep private enterprise in balance." [11] This line of development paralleled that of the council and the *Century*.

Whether this reflexive position ever developed anything like an effective analysis of the power to achieve, and the means for maintaining, mixed economy, and whether in this position anything like a fertile interplay developed between the interests of politics and of religion, are questions to be discussed later when the answers have had some time to emerge.

The idealism of the social gospel had begun, in the 'twenties, to break free of its domestication and to develop autonomous power. When provoked by a fear that the system was not only, by the ideal canons of the logic, unjust, but incompetent even in its own terms, unable to guarantee stability, idealism spoke in more definite, political ways.

The socialist and semisocialist resolves passed in the early 'thirties are not to be taken as representative. Perhaps the most accurate judgment would be that these resolutions represented the sentiments of those who voted them when they were voted. Nevertheless, there had been no such resolves before. Methodists led all the rest. The bishops, meeting in Philadelphia late in 1930, began to open the way; they spoke strongly of the visible distress; without presuming to judge ways and means to relieve distress, they insisted that if new principles of justice were needed, they should be invoked. The Central German Conference in Ohio, in October, 1931, attacked capitalism roundly, calling it "social Jacobism"—referring, as an evangelical assemblage, to Jacob, not to Jacobins—although not suggesting socialism by name or program. The Southern California and Pittsburgh conferences went as far in 1932.[12] Ferment boiled over in New York East. In 1932, unanimous endorsement of social ownership of the principal means of production and distribution was announced. Unfortunately, this was the kind of performance that had made church resolutions questionable. Describing the actual proceedings of the conference, one of the pastors, C. N. Hogle of Babylon, New York, wrote that "the eastern Methodists in general and the New

York East conference in particular have not gone socialist. They have only adopted another report." The report had been written by "a pair of nice young fellows," no one had wanted to argue, there had been no discussion, the report had simply been moved, seconded, and passed. Another correspondent denied the implications of this comment, but there were certain statistics: of fifty-five ministers testifying to their willingness to lead in drastic reform to prevent future depressions—out of ninety-five at the conference—only twenty-six had specified socialism as the means.[13] In any event, in 1933 New York East, while supporting social control of basic industries, voted down social ownership by a small majority. In 1934, the ministers voted through a straightforward socialist resolution. Meanwhile, Detroit had spoken strongly, New England in 1934 declared that productive and distributive industries should be public services involving public ownership, and Pittsburgh announced that "the only alternative to the present system is one in which social ownership and control is gradually and widely inaugurated and developed. . . ."[14] That all these were Methodist resolutions testified to the leadership Methodism had developed among the social-gospel pastors, but more especially to the unusual character, freedom, and autonomy of district Methodist conferences. At General Conference in 1932, where laymen were important and where responsibility for financial affairs centered, the perfunctory resolves had no socialist tinge whatever.

Other socialist resolutions were heard. The New York district of the Evangelical Synod, in Buffalo in 1931, announced the disintegration of capitalism, called for a third party, and spoke for increasing public ownership of utilities, resources, and industries. The thirty-five directors of Methodist religious education, meeting at Garrett Institute in 1932, pointed to the "essential bankruptcy of the present industrial capitalistic regime" as a fact to be assimilated into their work. George Coe generalized that "democracy and capitalism do not go together." Meeting on call of the Ohio Council of Churches, the ministers of Ohio, indicting capitalist individualism, profiteering, and competition, witnessed in effect to the necessity for socialism. The Commission of Christian Associations, uniting the student divisions of the Y.M.C.A. and the Y.W.C.A., issued a pamphlet in 1931 entitled "Toward a New Economic Society," in which a new political party to press socialist programs was demanded: the national press gave it space, the national officers of the "Y" were flooded with protests and announced that the pamphlet did not represent the views of the organization.[15]

No denomination in official convention subscribed to any resolves remotely socialistic. Such conventions brought together not only all wings of the clergy, but clergy and leading laymen not commonly sympathetic to the social gospel. For a measure of socialist sentiment within the clergy, the record of official, or semiofficial, and institutional expression could not be enough. A poll taken by the *World Tomorrow* early in 1934 offered a clearer picture.[16] Questionnaires were sent out to 100,000 clergymen; 20,870 replied. Following an assay of views on such specific issues as income and inheritance taxes, national labor unions, and the banking system, preferences between capitalism and "a coöperative commonwealth" were polled. For capitalism: 5 per cent. As a definition of alternatives, the choice between capitalism and "a coöperative commonwealth" was in itself the social-gospel mind at work. Since "coöperative commonwealth" counted as synonym for the Kingdom, even the 5 per cent for capitalism was a little surprising. Then, however, those who voted for the coöperative commonwealth were asked to choose, from among "drastically reformed capitalism," socialism, fascism, and communism, the system best suited as means toward the coöperative commonwealth. The over-all percentage for socialism came to 28 per cent, and by denominations, 34 per cent of the Methodists, 33 per cent of the Congregationalists and the Evangelicals, 32 per cent of the Reformed, 30 per cent of the Disciples, 24 per cent of the Episcopalians, 22 per cent of the Baptists, 19 per cent of the Presbyterians, and 12 per cent of the Lutherans. The proportion of socialist choices among clergymen in cities over 90,000 ran somewhat higher than for the nation at large; in Detroit, Denver, Chicago, Los Angeles, New York, and Seattle the proportion ran close to 50 per cent. The editors wrote: "Among all the trades, occupations, and professions in the country, few can produce as high a percentage of Socialists as can the ministry."

The greatest, and probably the most revealing, difference between denominations did not appear in these choices, but rather in the percentage of replies received in the first place. Baptists and Lutherans returned the fewest: 9 per cent and 14 per cent, compared to the over-all average of 21 per cent. Of the major denominations, Baptists—with their thousands of Southern clergy —and Lutherans—with their rigorous views on the separation of the spheres proper to church and state—remained least involved. The Methodists, with a return of 28 per cent, were most interested in the poll, and with them the Evangelicals, the Congregationalists, and the Reformed. The poll of course could not therefore have been taken as a poll. What it indicated was, at most, that some 21,000 clergymen had found it worthwhile to check their views on social questions, and that of these, considerable numbers were for various advanced social policies. With 6,000 of the 21,000 identifying themselves as such, it seemed likely that 6,000 and perhaps a few more of the nation's clergy were socialists in outlook. This was not many. Yet, evidence that the cutting edge of the social passion had become socialistic was manifest. In the roster of those who attested for socialism, the leaders of the passion appeared well-nigh unanimous. Bishop McConnell, Reinhold Niebuhr, Sherwood Eddy, Paul Hutchinson, John C. Bennett, Edmund Chaffee, Ernest Fremont Tittle, Halford Luccock, Dan Brummit, and George Lackland were on record, among others. The list would include Kirby Page. Harry Ward considered the Socialist party too mild.

Another straw in the wind had appeared shortly before the elections in 1932. Polling the membership of the Fellowship of Reconciliation, the *World Tomorrow* received some 1,700 ballots from 8,000 mailed out. Hoover drew 20.4 per cent; Roosevelt drew 2.9 per cent; Foster drew 1.6 per cent; and Norman Thomas drew 75.1 per cent.[17] With all reservations made upon the inferential value of such figures, it still was clear that within the Protestant pastorate the scanty band of prophecy had grown to something of a genuine minority. Perhaps one in four Northern urban Protestant churches was likely to be led by a man for whom social change was an accepted ideal, sometimes vivid, often socialist. In Northern seminaries the proportion was apt to be higher.

Here and there, sentiment mounted to organization. In Chicago in April, 1932, a group of ministers, most of them Methodist, most of them members of the Social Service Federation, held a Call to Action Conference. Its outgrowth was the Christian Social Action Movement. In its *Leaders Handbook*, seven tests for a political program were laid down, and a clear conclusion drawn:

> At the present time most of us believe that the declaration of prin-
> ciples and the economic aims of the Socialist Party of America most
> nearly coincide with these principles. The burden of proof would
> seem to rest upon the individual Christian, who desires a Christian
> order, to justify failure to support the party devoted to such ends.[18]

The apologia offered for this political program followed the standard social-gospel lines of the 'twenties: the highest aim of religion was moral; the ultimate moral criterion involved pro- vision of opportunity for the highest possible fulfillment of per- sonality; the religious individualism of Protestantism—derived from the Reformation—had helped dissolve the solidarity of secular life, political, economic, and social, and must be over- come. Most of the members were from the Chicago area, among them Dan Brummit of the *Northwestern Christian Advocate*, Paul Hutchinson, Blaine Kirkpatrick, Owen Geer, and Gilbert Cox as chairman. Kirby Page, Theodore Miner from Pennsylvania, and Paul Arthur Schilpp from California were among the mem- bers. Conceiving itself a tactical organization, this Chicago group hoped to stimulate similar bands of Christian leaders elsewhere. The sense of the times was acute among them: emergency educa- tional methods were urged: "FOMENT DISCONTENT . . . Each pastor should do more than comfort his people; he should increase their consciousness of existing wrongs and deliberately foment and increase the discontent of people with the intolerable conditions now existing."[19] The movement did not flourish. By

1936, Geer and Kirkpatrick were under fire at Methodist General Conference.

The climactic expression of the socialist response came in New York with the formation, late in 1930, of the Fellowship of Socialist Christians (FSC). Crystallizing among ministers of the Conference of Younger Churchmen, numbering in early 1932 around one hundred, this group was devoted from the beginning to a socialist translation of Christian principles, with definite loyalty to the Socialist party. It was first of all a religious fellowship: the name chosen had not been "Fellowship of Christian Socialists." From the beginning, Reinhold Niebuhr was the dominant figure. Buell Gallagher served as chairman of the executive committee in the early days, with Roswell P. Barnes, John C. Bennett of Auburn Theological Seminary, and Frank T. Wilson of the Student Christian Movement on the committee. Francis Henson, an Episcopalian, of Columbia and the Y.M.C.A., and Edmund Chaffee were also early leaders. After formal organization in 1934, a rigid personal discipline was introduced, including a tax laid upon members mounting stiffly on income over $1,400, the receipts to be distributed for purposes pertinent to the organization. After the discipline was inaugurated, five hundred members remained. A system of groups of twelve was developed for discussion of problems in theory and tactics for Christian social action. There were no illusions about winning over the churches. The fellowship hoped rather, by revealing deeper aspects in Christianity, to bring at least some few Christians to commit themselves "to the disinherited who are fated to be the champions and the heralds of a new society." FSC members along with the pacifist socialists had an outlet through the *World Tomorrow* until its collapse in 1934. A quarterly, *Radical Religion,* was founded as the regular organ of the group in 1936.[20]

Following by three years the disappearance of the Fellowship for a Christian Social Order within the Fellowship of Reconciliation, the appearance of the Fellowship of Socialist Christians marked the beginnings of a Protestant social realism self-consciously opposed to liberalism and thereby, in its next stage, to the social-gospel synthesis. The political and social thought it struggled to express became the anvil on which the new theology was hammered out. With Niebuhr as its leading figure, the fellowship through all its later transformations was to display its two fronts—political and religious—as the double edges of a single sword.

What was the rationale behind this socialism of 1930 to 1934? To a large extent, it was a desire to affirm steadfastness in the face of challenge. The fantasies of the ideal were called to prove themselves in the concrete. The Socialist party offered something that had been lacking in the social gospel, a definite rallying point for its converts of the middle and, more precisely, for the pastors themselves. The evangelized businessman could always have found specific work at hand for implementing the ideal as could the leader of labor. The ministers fulfilled their own pledges of commitment in the Socialist party, and could advertise the Socialist party as a channel for the commitment of all those idealists of the middle who could not easily pour themselves out any other way. This depended in part upon the emergence of the Socialist party as a living option, which it had not been in the decade before.

For one thing, Prohibition had been removed from the political arena, for all but the most implacable followers of wan hope. No Protestant idealism of any persuasion could have failed to take that issue into account, so long as "wet Democracy" figured as a major force opposed to a clearly "dry Republicanism." Some of the Protestant leaders indeed continued even in 1932 to give allegiance to the GOP as guardian of the noble experiment, despite all evidence that the Republican politicians were intent upon getting out from under an incubus. If one of the grand old men of the social gospel, Charles Sheldon of Topeka, listed his preference for socialism in the *World Tomorrow* poll, he had nevertheless voted Republican in 1932 on the great issue. And if *Zion's Herald* had spread its pages to social-gospel rhetoric for fifteen years, 1932 found those pages still devoted to endless efforts at honoring the President with leadership of the cause he so obviously wished to abandon. The chairman of the Chicago Call to Action group, Owen Geer, protested the repeal plank in the Socialist platform of 1932 as a needless waste of thousands of votes.

Perhaps the most spectacular case of trying to ride two horses to the bitter end was that of Clarence Howells, director of the Reconciliation Trips into the exotic neighborhoods of New York. Howells demanded that his party be both dry and radical; the Republicans were neither; the Democrats were neither; the Socialists were wet. Howells announced that he was voting for Foster and Ford. But for most social-gospel ministers, the final, open desertion of the Anti-Saloon League by the Republican party meant not such last-ditch logic, but simple freedom to vote by standards of the passion alone.[21]

Then, the Socialist party had come to offer itself as a reasonable choice for the idealist of glowing but not ideological character. Its days as a self-justifying society of purists intent upon the intricacies of doctrine faded as opportunity for strength seemed to arise. The shift was marked by the appearance of Norman Thomas as leader. Former Presbyterian minister, in his rhetoric and personality an embodiment of the virtues honored by the social gospel, and a figure apparently of more than sectarian appeal, Thomas was the ideal candidate. His Socialist party did not propose doctrinaire insults to religion; it did not propose revolutionary melodramatics or materialistic denials of the importance of the spiritual energy of dedicated men; it did propose basic social transformation. Allegiance to the Socialist party, therefore, was an ideal way of pledging the good faith of idealism faced by the challenge of crisis.

More than this, however, there was desire for political action in itself. Behind the League for Independent Political Action in 1928 had worked the hope of its leaders that, from the reservoir of the old American progressive tradition, together with the new interests of labor, a new third party might be drawn, which would become a major party. Norman Thomas was a member of both the Socialist party and the LIPA. LIPA liberals, led by John Dewey, urged Senator Norris of Nebraska to take up the role La

Follette had played in 1924. A broad and basic reconstitution of
the political public, on lines dictated not by abstract ideology
but by tension already present in the old public, was the hope.
Failing to win Norris for another progressive-labor crusade, the
LIPA endorsed Thomas in 1932, and in 1933 the editors of
the *World Tomorrow* urged the absorption of the LIPA into the
Socialist party, rejecting the continued call of the LIPA for a new
party.[22] That this was not singly out of ideological loyalty was
apparent in Reinhold Niebuhr's insistence that the question of
whether the Socialist party or some new party would organize
the forces for economic justice was pragmatic. Niebuhr had
registered his own demand for politics as such in 1930. He had
rejected, on the one hand, the "economic action" of the AFL,
and, on the other hand, the revolutionary action of the communists, which, he said, served only to sate the perfectionism of
romantics or to slake a despair for which in America there was
no need. The proper course was responsible politics in between.
He admitted the difficulties facing third-party action; the overwhelming importance of the Presidency in the American constitutional system, for instance, led the impatient political public to
abandon third parties after one try. Nevertheless, without a new
party, the intelligent political action that alone could bring about
changes in economic relations essential for justice was impossible.
The duty of years of patient effort rested on those who understood this fact.[23]

Political pragmatics and the principled anxieties of disguised
sectarians both entered the Socialist party. Such a heady mixture
was bound to be fissiparous. Early in 1934 a group within the
party organized as the Revolutionary Policy Committee (RPC),
protesting the failure of the Socialist party to exploit the field of
labor unrest. Its chairman was J. B. Mathews, one of the secretaries of the FOR; its executive secretary was Francis Henson,
fusing high-church Episcopalianism with Marx. The RPC, holding the Communist party too dogmatically revolutionary, considered the leadership of Norman Thomas and the militant
liberals too mild, too devoted to evangelizing the idealists. Both
Kirby Page and Niebuhr castigated the RPC and its "Appeal" of

1934 as no better than the Communist party itself, this appeal going in fact beyond the manifesto issued by the Communists upon their withdrawal from the Socialist party in 1919. One of the issues here was violence. The Socialist party itself, in a season of unremitting internal uproar, had moved to the left by the time of its 1934 convention in Detroit, but this was a move defined in terms of the ends; the 1934 declaration of principles was written by an FOR pacifist, Devere Allen.[24]

The issue troubling RPC leaders reflected a final aspect of the social-passion response to the crisis. Not only was its attention to labor renewed, but now, to labor as a power group, the attention was sharper than it had been in the 'twenties. Organization of the unemployed attracted pastors from coast to coast. In many if not in most instances, these Unemployed Citizens' Leagues or Organized Unemployed were nonpolitical, devoted to self-help and immediate survival. Often clerical sympathy was no more than further expression of that concern for labor of the 'twenties which had not been tied to politics. The Federal Council's commissions on unemployment were their largest form. But in the 'twenties there had also been the Emergency Committee for Strikers' Relief, founded by Norman Thomas and the American Civil Liberties Union in 1926, which drew Niebuhr, McConnell, Howard Melish, Paul Hutchinson, Charles Gilkey, Clarence Howells, Edmund Chaffee, and Paul Jones, among others, as sponsors. The Emergency Committee continued its work, and a Church Emergency Committee for the Relief of Textile Strikers was founded in the early 'thirties, including Alva Taylor, Worth Tippy, James Myers, William Spofford, Hubert Herring, Charles Webber, Russell Bowie, and Jerome Davis as sponsors. These two groups did not concentrate strictly on unemployment; they displayed the semisocialist drive behind the new concern for labor. In Washington, organization of the unemployed led to a United Producers League, which took on local political power, supporting federal relief, public works, increased income taxes, and public ownership of utilities and natural monopolies. The Central Methodist Church of Tacoma served as headquarters. In Chicago intensive efforts were carried on through a Workers Committee on Unemployment. The church of Theodore C. Hume served as meeting place; W. B. Waltmire was a moving spirit in the work; Paul Hutchinson, A. E. Holt, and U. M. McGuire, editor of the *Baptist,* participated. The Chicago Workers Committee joined with the National Federation of Unemployed Workers Leagues, intended to provide structure for the unfocused political energy of the unemployed. A Chicago social-settlement director, a graduate of Union Theological Seminary, Karl Borders served as president of the Chicago group until, in an election in 1933, Communists succeeded in infiltrating the executive body. Borders then departed. Bishop McConnell, indefatigable sponsor, lent his name to the New York center.[25]

The Revolutionary Policy Committee's appeal within the Socialist party pointed in the direction of A. J. Muste's Conference for Progressive Labor Action (CPLA), and Muste gave the labor tactic of the passion its sharpest statement in these years. If there was ever a flaming leader, if there was ever a man who sought to translate the passion into reality with his own action and his own will, it was Muste. An earlier chapter has noted that Muste left his walk-up flat on Appleton Street in Boston for the streets and police clubs of Lawrence, for Brookwood Labor College at Katonah, for the sallies into Utica, Passaic, and the Paterson general strike of 1931. Muste had written, while still chairman of the national council of the Fellowship of Reconciliation in 1929, his answer to the dilemma between pacifism and social reconstruction that his companion-in-nonarms at Lawrence, Harold Rotzel, had left suspended in hope. "The basic fact is," he wrote, "that the economic, social, political order in which we live was built up largely by violence, is now being extended by violence, and is maintained only by violence!" No one could counsel abstention from violence unless he was identified in spirit with the victims of the system built on violence. But even then:

> In a world built on violence one must be a revolutionary before one can be a pacifist: in such a world, a non-revolutionary pacifist is a contradiction in terms, a monstrosity . . . Things being as they are, it is fairly certain that if a group of workers goes on strike for better conditions, other methods having failed, they will commit some

acts of violence and coercion . . . Shall the pacifist who has identified himself with labor's cause therefore seek to dissuade the workers
from going on strike? . . . My own answer is an emphatic negative,
because I am convinced that in these cases the alternative of sub-
mission is by far the greater evil . . . in general the amount of
"red" terrorism in history is a bagatelle compared to the "white"
terrorism of reactionaries.[26]

Late in 1929 Muste led in organizing the Conference for Progressive Labor Action. The CPLA was directed toward the abolition
of capitalism and the institution of a planned economic order; it
was committed to parliamentary action in politics, but emphasized economic organization and economic struggle. The power
of a Morris Hillquit in the Socialist party, Muste believed, proved
that it was not truly a party of the left; Communist party policy
was actually counter-revolutionary, its tactic of dual unionism
serving to break up, not enhance, mass labor strength. The CPLA
was another middle way. It challenged John L. Lewis' United
Mine Workers, worked in the Southern Industrial League and
the Progressive Farmers League in the Carolinas, and sent men
into strikes in Paterson, Brooklyn, and elsewhere. In 1932 it
turned its main efforts to organization of the unemployed—in
Seattle, Youngstown, Pittsburgh, Philadelphia, and Allentown.[27]
    Whether the "economic" tactics of the CPLA proved to be
built on shifting sands among the unemployed, whether the thrust
of urgency drove beyond its confines, in any case there was
farther to go. The dialectic of 1929 had not been rigid; provision
had been left for new action in new circumstances: ". . . one
must be a revolutionary *before* one can be a pacifist. . . ." Late
in 1933, at the Pittsburgh convention of the CPLA, a group of
men acting as a Provisional Organizing Committee instituted the
American Workers party; Muste was chairman, J. B. S. Hardaman
vice-chairman, and Louis Budenz secretary. Next year Muste
was on the front lines again, at the prolonged and bitter strike in
the Electric Auto-Lite plant in Toledo, in full-fledged revolutionary guise. The tension had been broken. The pacifism in the
strategy would be resumed at the end of strategy.[28]
    The great story of Muste was that in the end he did not remain

a victim of strategy. The American Workers party fused with the Trotskyites in 1934 as the Workers party. Soon, guided by the wisdom of the revolutionary leader himself, the Trotskyites sought to infiltrate—reinfiltrate—the Socialist party. There were fissions. Louis Budenz went to the Communists, Muste left the Workers party altogether and went to Paris for a period of calm. In 1936 he returned to the Fellowship of Reconciliation, testifying to a reconversion to the way of love from the Leninist-Trotskyist way of violence. This book shall take him up again in this last stage, as he offered love in the face of the greatest violence of all, world war.[29]

In the National Religion and Labor Foundation, more stable expression was given to this continuing and sharpened attention to labor. Jerome Davis of Yale Divinity School had long had the ambition to found such an organization. He, together with Harry Ward and others, had made a start toward collecting $20,000 for it when, in the crash of 1929, the funds were wiped out. In 1932 he decided to proceed without outside money. One secretary, Francis Henson, was paid by Davis himself, another, George Douglas, served without pay. Willard Uphaus took over as executive secretary in 1933 and remained until after the outbreak of the Korean war, when he resigned under pressure, his opposition to the Korean war and U.S. policy generally being thought detrimental to the organization. Early sponsors included Francis McConnell, Reinhold Niebuhr, A. J. Muste, Allen Knight Chalmers, Robert Whitaker, and Ernest Fremont Tittle. The foundation, beginning its days full in the season of crisis, was announced to stand "for the interest of prophetic religion in building a workers' world." "Unalterably" opposed to capitalism, it proposed "to help the workers by hand and brain to take control of our economic life by organizing as workers, consumers and citizens." "Locals" in theological seminaries, fraternal delegates to labor union meetings, active lobbying for labor legislation, traveling economic seminars, all appeared on the program. In 1938, W. B. Waltmire of Humboldt Park Methodist Church in Chicago took over as chairman of a local Religion and Labor Fellowship, intended as the first of many. Charles F. Maclennon, an Ohio Presbyterian, assumed the directorship of a Religion and Labor Center in Cleveland, intended to repeat the success of the Labor Temple in New York.[30]

In the crisis situation, anxiety flowed into everything, and the anxiety in every case flowed from a threatened disruption of society as a carrier of value and meaning. This was an atmosphere for the disintegration of synthesis. Thus, the conservative component emerged more distinctly in the council and the *Century* while the utopian component emerged among the socialists. Both were efforts to deal with the same threat. The ultimate disintegration would be that of the religious sanction itself. This would be Reinhold Niebuhr's story. His work would be highlighted by its contrast with the final efforts of some of the prophets to maintain the old synthesis in its purity. These prophets must be taken in context now, before Niebuhr. Ward on the one hand offered his climactic vision of the ultimate ends, Page struggled to maintain the absolute means; Niebuhr could accept neither.

XI

The Final Form of the Absolute

In Harry Ward the link between anxiety and total politics became absolute. The pages of the Methodist Federation *Bulletin* began to reflect total crisis and breakdown late in 1930 and early in 1931, earlier, by and large, than was the case at the other watching-posts of the passion. From then on, filled with the doings of liberal and radical groups in coal town and mill town, in local church and district conference, in labor action group and political action group—and in China, Mexico, Europe as well as in America, for the image was world-embracing—the four small pages conveyed a vision of protest, ferment, and action, here, there, and everywhere, which had somehow to come to coherent expression. In 1932 the *Bulletin* devoted issues to canvassing programs to harness the times: planners from Swope to Stalin; unemployment relief schemes from Hoover to the Communist party, U.S.A.; labor action from the AFL to the Communist Trade Union Unity League. News of Protestant efforts from everywhere suggested to the *Bulletin*'s readers that they regard the ferment as religious.

Late in 1932 the *Bulletin* began issuing special appeals for financial aid; to the uncertainty of survival for capitalism was added uncertainty for its own. A net of $1,169 was received; only a gift of $1,500 from a fund established in memory of a Methodist pastor brightened a darkening future. In November, 1933, its budget reduced from $7,000 to $4,000, the *Bulletin* announced its determination to justify its continued existence by playing a definite vital role in the struggle between the old and the new world. "This new year for us is one in which a page of history has been turned . . . We have definitely entered the period of state capitalism . . . To realize where this leads one must understand that state capitalism and economic Fascism are synonymous." The new strategy followed: "Keep as many of the middle class as possible from going Fascist." Federation members had pulpits, Sunday school classes, high school and college classrooms, secretarial jobs, editorships; they should speak out. The Federation was preparing four-page *Crisis Leaflets* to be distributed: "They can be used the way earlier Methodists used their tracts." In a series of issues running through 1934 and into 1935, the *Bulletin* analyzed the New Deal as a program for bolstering capitalism through state power.

Here and there the sense of crisis provoked pleas for "thorough and thorough," for absolute action, always to be heard at every juncture where society seems to threaten to crumble into mob. Representative of no wing of the prophets at all, the following words—from an ordained minister, federation member Robert Whitaker of California—suggest one style of the heresies into which social-gospel logic could lapse, the hysteric projection of will and apocalyptic expectation.

> The fact is I have come to realize that the period of general economic education has mainly passed now. The emergency ripens so fast that the issue of the hour is how we are going to react to the crisis. It is no longer a question of the need of a revolution; the question is as to the method of bringing the revolution to pass . . . To this conclusion I have very definitely come: that there is little hope of making any considerable change in the psychology of the masses except as the sequence of radical social action outside of respectable ranks; that the work of revolt will have to be carried through in two sections, the first of these, the long suffering and no longer quiescent

disinherited and unemployed who will respond to their desperation rather than to any well digested education; the second, a trained and disciplined group who will know how to function in a Lenin-leadership when the hour of opportunity comes. Consequently our concern is to build the understanding leadership for the crisis from those who need no longer the milk of infantile adaptations to their timidities and polite prejudices but are ready to talk business and digest the strong meat of direct revolutionary preparation.[1]

But—although Kirby Page and the pacifist prophets thought otherwise—the critical element in Harry Ward's own reaction to the early 'thirties was not a move toward Lenin-leadership and violence. Actually, Ward had already talked of disciplined leadership to fill the gap left by the failure of the middle-class church and saving majorities. On the other hand, he had deprecated the idea of violence; nor did he promote the idea that violence was called for in 1932. He remained antipacifist, but it was not his antipacifism that distinguished him. Rather, it was his climactic appeal to a model of total righteousness and total power. Ward exhibited the extreme logic of opposing the sorry present with an ideal future; tactics were secondary.

As chairman of the American League Against War and Fascism, succeeding J. B. Mathews in 1934, Ward emerged as the leading clerical defender of the United Front through the years ahead. He took, without much attention to democratic processes, the Methodist Federation into the league as a constituent member. A rhetorical question in the *Bulletin,* following a discussion of communism, suggested the apology for common action: "Is there any reason why religious radicals should not cooperate for these objectives?"[2] The objectives were the essence, and communists had a thoroughgoing notion of objectives. Ward regarded the Socialist party as too conservative to warrant his joining. The *Bulletin*'s other editor, Winifred Chappell, worked for Foster and Ford in 1932.[3]

The "friends of the Soviet Union" were relatively few, even in the early 'thirties, but they were conspicuous in certain echelons of the American intelligentsia, especially the literary intelligentsia. As indicated, Ward was almost alone as a leading American clerical friend. He was, for instance, the only clerical sponsor of the American Society for Cultural Relations with Russia. But Ward was more than just a friend. He had spent a year in Russia, in 1931–32, inspecting the new society with his own eyes, and the circuit-riding of 1933 and 1934 began to carry new messages: "What We Can Learn from the Soviet Union," "The Soviet's Challenge to Religion." Behind the united front lay the symbol of Russia. In Ward's case, the symbol drew out from the social-gospel logic assumptions and anxieties that the logic had ignored. The subject of this chapter, then, is not Russia or even the symbol of Russia, but why Russia could be seen as symbol.

In his ideas about Russia, Sherwood Eddy, who, unlike Ward, rejected the united front, also rejected Russia as an absolute, and refused to take his American pragmatics from Communist directives. Those ideas will help emphasize this perspective by offering a kind of control. Before dissecting Ward's final utopianism, therefore, it is valuable to analyze Eddy's wrestle with Russia.

In 1931 Eddy published, following his visit to Europe in 1930, *The Challenge of Russia*. At the end of his official career as Asia secretary for the Y.M.C.A., Eddy, sixty years old, was one of the great missionary generation preceding the First World War. He had logged his fifteen years in India, his travels and teaching in China, and his ecumenical visits to Europe. In the 'twenties he had led a troupe of educators and ministers to Europe every summer, and had already gone into Russia in 1923, 1925, and 1929, as well as twice, in 1911 and 1912, before the revolution. A member of the Fellowship for a Christian Social Order, he had collaborated with Kirby Page, twenty years his junior, in the "Christianity and Industry" series as well as other works, with some yet to come, preaching the redemption of society. In *The Challenge of Russia* and his later *Russia Today* (1934), he celebrated the story of a society in process of self-conscious self-construction. At the heart of this society lay a new will, directing all its parts, infusing all its parts with a single social passion. Its aim was to liberate the higher aspects of human nature. "They do not plan first to change human nature, but the social situation, so that a whole network of healthy motives can enable both the individual and society to function more effectively than the old capitalist profit motives which had commercialized and debased almost all human relations." [4]

The two books surveyed the techniques of this will in operation —in agriculture, industry, education, law, religion, treatment of criminals. All this was the good side of the Russian experiment, and Eddy generalized it in terms straight out of the social gospel: "The Soviets are learning that the family circle may be widened for the toiler to include his country, his class and the workers of the world. . . ." [5]

But there was a bad side to Russia also:

> Communist ethics demands the subjection of the individual to the well-being of the proletariat . . . It derives its sanction from the absolute social control of the Party majority. Its goal is social welfare. The individual personality is not yet differentiated, valued, freed, or assured of development. Collectivism suppresses individuality save as the individual is a unit in conformity and submission to the social whole. The individual is lost in the mass.[6]

Thus, Russia was fulfilling a great ideal at the price of another great ideal.

This other ideal was the heritage of the West:

> In Western ethics the *ideal* is the fullest development of every human personality through the cooperative effort of the community, ever-widening in intent to the creation of a world-wide brotherhood . . . the first and chief emphasis has been placed upon the individual, not upon the community.[7]

In each, therefore, there was a good side and a bad side. Somehow the two approaches stood in the relation of thesis and antithesis; synthesis would be the better world:

> Someday the Russian East may rise above the narrow confines of class war, and the West of selfish profit, to the service and building of a common humanity. In the meantime we doubtless err in being too individualistic and they too exclusively social in their emphasis. We are building a richer, fuller human personality and they a juster social order. Each has something to learn from the other.[8]

Here was convenient, easy symbolization of an age-old problem. But there was a peculiarity buried in this dialectic of Eddy's. Russia was actually fulfilling its own ideal; against Russia he charged its neglect of another ideal. The West only posited an ideal; in actual practice, it was not fulfilling even that. "We are paralyzed by natural selfishness in an individualistic, competitive, class economic system which develops personality only in the favored few at the cost of others. . . ." [9] Pages and paragraphs were devoted to describing the suffocation of the ideal of personality in the capitalist jungle of inequality, injustice, and strife. The West, in short, was not fulfilling either ideal.

The problem in Eddy's analysis was this: how, if it was corrupted, ignored, and subverted, could the ideal of the Western thesis count in favor of the West at all? The fact was that Eddy's feeling for the resources and values available in the West came to him only negatively; whenever he confronted the Russian scene, his mind flooded with realization that something was missing. His own shorthand for it was, plain and simple, individual liberty. In one paragraph of the two books, his own vision of the good society forced itself through:

> We do not mean by a complete society . . . a drab, dead level [of] life. . . . Rather, we mean a humanity which tolerates and includes political opponents and all enemies in the dialectic process occasioned by a healthy conflict of ideas, parties, and minorities, all of which will make their contribution to the final synthesis and symphony of life. [10]

It was a vision of the open society. Society was not to be the good man universalized. The socialized individual was not to be the universalized individual. The unity of large-group life was not to be the unity of small-group life expanded.

In this reaction to Russia, Eddy displayed the libertarian values he had assumed, uninspected and unstated, in the social-gospel notion of the Kingdom. But the fact that those values had been left to be assumed, without assimilation into the social logic, left him half-blind. He could recognize them when he found them absent; he could not support them when he turned back to the West. Consequently, what he really charged against the West was not its failure to fulfill its own ideal, but its failure to serve "personality" in its pure social-gospel sense, flawlessly consistent with abstract "brotherhood," emptied of the inherited libertarian richness. As a consequence, he could never formulate the negative "challenge of Russia" implied in his analysis. This was the challenge—actually, the warning—that social justice and harmony might not necessarily serve personality. What, after all, did the example of Russia offer the West? It suggested no route by which the West could move from its corruptions toward the "synthesis." It suggested only that the route of social justice, planning, and harmony was not, whatever its virtues, guaranteed to lead to the ideal goal. Of course, there was no such synthesis as that of America and Russia; Eddy was playing the old game of setting up an abstract system as the basis for criticism of an existing system. Universal, abstract constructs of a new social order were self-defeating; a new social order for the West, for America, already had its origins, resources, and forms in the West, in America, and not in the first century, nor in Russia, nor in heaven.

These difficulties could not have chilled the fascination Eddy felt, for it drew upon depths also quite beyond the range of the avowed interests of the social passion. The fascination was rather nicely measured in Eddy's estimates of Russia's own chances for realizing the synthesis. These estimates were violently contradictory, the fascination simply transcending without facing the contradiction. First, the *Challenge* ended in a pious hope:

> Russia . . . is changing more rapidly than any country in the world. The vast work of education, not only in schools, but in cooperatives, trade unions, youth organizations and local self-government, will have an almost inevitable democratic trend in ever-widening circles. No tyranny can permanently maintain itself even in Moscow.[11]

Such hope was pious because Eddy himself had forestalled it eighty-five pages before. It would be hard to imagine a more drastic rift:

Once again, history repeats itself in the indefinite continuity of a dictatorship. It postulates its future millennium . . . where the state itself will "wither away" and men will do right from force of habit and early training in a favorable environment. But practically, within the limits of human experience, that time never comes . . . Actually a dictatorship which was theoretically "temporary," must not only be indefinitely extended but ever tightened and rendered more complete. It is true that the new environment created by the communist system largely eliminates the dangerous motivation of personal greed . . . but it begets a lust for power and a contempt for liberty and for individual personality that may prove as prolific a root of evil as the love of money.[12]

How Eddy could leave himself hanging in this obvious tension becomes clear only when it is seen that for him Russia symbolized more than justice, more than brotherhood, more than a new social ethic in life. It symbolized Meaning in life:

> We of the West have witnessed a philosophic decadence and disintegration. Where feudalism once united the world, capitalism has divided it up by the competitive anarchy of a loose individualism. Not organized society but the insecure individual is now the unit, where every man is for himself.[13]

On the other hand:

> Russia has achieved what has hitherto been known only at rare periods in history, the experience of almost a whole people living under a unified philosophy of life. All life is focussed in a central purpose. It is directed to a single high end and energized by such powerful and growing motivation that life seems to have supreme significance.[14]

Here it was. Here was the deepest ache and the deepest anxiety of a declining laissez-faire world. The trouble with the West was not that there was no justice; rather, there was no belief. The enchantment was gone. Eddy's last sentence could be taken as the secret desire of the social gospel; he was making of the Russian plan something like an equivalent to the theological doctrine of God the Creator: here eternal significance rooted, and he knew that men needed to feel themselves linked with the source of eternal significance. Eddy himself was a man who had access to eternal significance in the old evangelical fashion, the fashion that had allowed a laissez-faire world to believe in itself before its own economic thrusts broke its own harmonies. But he understood in a general way the economic and social reasons for the fading of enchantment and belief in the laissez-faire world, and he understood that economic and social changes would be required if belief was to be restored. So he was fascinated by Russia, where economic and social changes were themselves the content of belief. He did not succumb to the fascination. His rejection of the Russian model was explicit: its evils were ". . . so serious, so enduring and so of the essence of Communism itself that they would make it quite impossible for me ever to accept it." With the experience of the New Deal before him, as the 'thirties wore on, he revised upward his estimate of the resources of meaning and liberty available in the United States, both as good in themselves and as resources for justice. Nonetheless, his purely intuitive reasons for not succumbing still left the logic open to devastation, the economic and social reform of laissez faire open to the internal hemorrhage of the old liberties, the empty personality, haunted by meaninglessness, open to invasion by the American Way of Life.[15]

Where fascination, for Eddy, meant the confusion, for Ward it meant the fall, of an angel. Ward also had already gone to Russia, in 1924, "to see whether the New Economic Policy meant a return to capitalism." During his visit of 1931–32, he asked whether, with the Five-Year Plan, "the building of socialism was developing incentives which promised more for the continuing of human society than those which are manifestly failing in the capitalist world." [16] *In Place of Profit* (1933) was the report he filed of that investigation.

In this book, Ward discovered at last the route and the agents by which ideal vision could be fulfilled. Even more critically, he was able to drive ideal vision on to its final illumination. The link between the two was not accidental. Like Eddy's books, *In Place of Profit* sketched out how men worthy to be citizens of a new social order were being produced. The techniques, trials,

triumphs, and tribulations of the leaders in their labor to mold
the new man filled the whole long volume. "It is doubtful if there
has ever in history been such an organized conscious attempt as
this to change the customs and habits of a people, certainly not
since the great days of the Roman Church." [17] The motivation of
the new man was to be social-gospel motivation, the final goal,
democracy.

> . . . the directing group becomes less and less the inner circle of
> the Party and more and more the whole number of activists through-
> out the population. This process accelerates as a classless society ap-
> proaches . . . When the number of activists . . . has reached the
> maximum that is possible . . . then the power they will have in
> their hands will be as near to self-control by the whole of society as
> it is possible to come.[18]

The secret of this great work was an open one: a logic to history
existed, the key to this logic had been discovered, and the key
properly rested in the hands of its discoverers. Dialectical materialism clarified the opportunities history offered, and dialectical
materialism understood how to grasp those opportunities. It was
a philosophy of action. "It continually demands change and provides a method for moving life from one plane to another . . .
It calls for a continual series of action-thought-action, constantly
breaking and uniting these opposites to achieve new forms of
human living." [19] Those were mistaken who thought the laboring
classes or the dark millions could hold the key themselves to
create the new order; this was for the philosophers. "The Communists desire a classless society. They conclude by historic
analysis that it can only be realized by the working force. Hence
they help them to power for this purpose, not merely to give them
the victory over the capitalists." [20]

The origins of these philosophers, these leaders, these men of
the "inner circle of the Party," these righteous technicians, were
wrapped in some obscurity, in, almost, the holy haze of the classic
myth of origins. But no cause for worry hinged here, for the
righteousness was certain. "The values that are now relied upon
are those that led the older revolutionary leaders to revolt and
those who were of bourgeois origin to separate themselves from

their class." [21] In the last analysis, leaders and values both were themselves products of history and could therefore be trusted: "The appearance of leaders of revolt among the class in power is recognized by all students of the nature and history of revolutions as the sign of the disintegration of a social order. Dialectical materialists go further and explain how it leads to the formation of the new order." [22]

It would hardly be wise to look long for Ward's answers to the classic conundrums clustering around the role of history in Marxist theory. Whether, for instance, the science of dialectical materialism itself was a product of social disintegration, whether it was the only possible interpretation of disintegration, whether its truth was visible only to the eye of some mysterious previously generated righteousness, whether in fact righteousness might not be defined *by* dialectical materialism rather than *be* the discoverer of dialectical materialism—these questions remained obscure. It did not really matter. The enlightened righteousness and the enlightened means were united in the same agents, and that was all that was needed. It was not the fact that these agents were the Communist party, in all its historic familiarity to us today, that must evoke wonder. Ward's usual designation, "the Party," was enough. By "Party" he meant cadres of holy men.

> A comparison . . . is that which likens the Communist Party to the Jesuit Order in the days when it was the power behind every throne in Europe. Communist organization is more like that of a religious order than a political party, also they both seek larger ends than the politicians. The Jesuits tortured and burned people for the good of their souls, the Communists ask them to live meagerly and discipline them in "Isolated Communities" for the sake of a nobler society on earth. They both use the state to protect their own organization as the Communists did when they banished Trotsky. The essential difference is that the Jesuits used the state to protect a religion and enhance the powers of a church while the Communists use it to enhance a social ideal.[23]

The vision was profoundly unpolitical: "power" as such was a signal for no reflections at all. If there was a class, a group, a sect, a church, a party, or a man in whom righteousness and science united, then to add power was to complete a proper trinity. All power to the proletariat; all power to the Soviets; all power to the party and to the inner circle of the party. All power to the sacrificial leader: "Practically unconscious of himself as an individual, [Lenin] was absolutely sure of the ideas he had absorbed and the method he was using, confident that nature and history were behind him." [24]

Ward had solved his problem, and since he had solved it, his feelings were strong enough to allow him to dissolve the doubts Eddy had raised.

There remains the question of whether the Party . . . will not . . . become an end in itself. History is full of cases in which a priesthood guarding a sacred truth has become the ruling power and finally more mighty than the truth itself, which it has then corrupted and destroyed.[25]

He raised the doubt; but then, with wonderful ease, he found the answer to lie in recognition of the doubt:

The Communist leaders recognize this danger and try to avert it by continually recruiting from the masses. But they rely more on teaching the masses to think and act according to the dialectical method, for that will make the Party ultimately unnecessary. In the Communist society where people will be sufficiently intelligent to choose wisely and socially minded enough to act for the commonweal, its leadership will not be needed. Stalin recognizes this . . .[26]

The leaders, recognizing human nature, would triumph over human nature.

Eddy had not been able to set liberty and social harmony in right and coherent relation, but he had at least remembered liberty. Ward did not. Why he did not, we can hardly say, except to recognize that the anxiety leading to Eddy's fascination with the image of Russia in the first place was in Ward's case conclusive. He made the same appeal to the category of meaning: ". . . the significance of the Plan is that it gives the masses that which our liberals are so afraid of, that which life has not had since the break up of the Middle Ages—a central purpose." [27] Searching for analogies for this galvanization of all men through

central purpose, Ward recurred to the evil that was the result
even more than the cause of the emptiness of the West:

> The whole constructive task of building socialism is dramatized as
> a great war. The party member is told that he must fulfill in the
> factory the duties of a rank-and-file soldier . . . So [the worker]
> is enlisted in shock and storm brigades, in the light cavalry for in-
> dustrial or agricultural emergencies, or in the cultural army.[28]

In the moral equivalent to war, men would find the meaning that
war provided so disastrously.

Ward here, like Eddy, was driving an ethical rhetoric into
metaphysics. In terms of social psychology, the need for which
he was seeking nostrum was *anomie*. One thing was certain. The
insecurity, the lack of significance, the *anomie*, testified to so
openly by Eddy and Ward, did flow from the disintegration of
social harmonies left to the play of a laissez-faire world, and this
meant that new forms of order and control were required. But
this did not mean increase of any kind of order and control anywhere. The disintegration of those old harmonies flowed at least
partly from the fact that control and rationalization had already
intervened partly, in certain areas among certain groups. Judge
Gary's United States Steel was an example of heightened order
in its limited sphere, which acted to heighten disorder and
anomie in wider spheres. The conflicts of modern times were between highly rationalized fractions of a society for which there
was no over-all rationalization. If the metaphysical anxieties of
the West rooted in these conflicts, then rationalization had to be
pushed further. In the United States, touched least acutely by the
crisis, the responses were nevertheless along this line. Mildly in
the New Deal, less mildly in those centers of enlightened leadership to the business right, still less mildly to the democratic-
socialist left, and with rigor among such "exposed" intellectuals
as the few literary fellow-travelers and the few religious leaders
such as Ward, planning and rationalization were pressed as the
key.

But central, systematic, more and more universal planning was
not only the means to overcome anxiety. It also lay at the heart

of anxiety, not merely in its imposition of routine and abstraction upon the variety and particularity of human energy, but in its infinite extension of the demand upon the will to choose and to be infinitely responsible. To plan universally meant to have assumed universal responsibility. The will took up responsibility for the "laws" of harmony, whether "natural" or "divine." Since the purpose of planning was to overcome anxiety, the purpose of the new social order came ultimately to include closing off the will against all anxieties at once by a final rationalization, which would leap once and for all beyond all further demands for self-consciousness, decision, and change. This was the logic of society-as-its-own-evangelist, the reversal of the logic of the early social gospel. The personality would be scoured of its private and unconscious deviations, so that it could both contribute to and take within itself the whole. In its heroism, in its passion for universal freedom from all but itself, the will left nothing untransmuted:

> But of course the effective controls of the socialist state are exerted to direct expenditures into certain desired channels from the standpoint of present productive necessity and in the end will have to direct it also toward the achievement of health and well-being. Socialist society cannot afford to have its citizens over-eating or buying unnecessarily. There are scientific standards for consumption as well as for production and sooner or later they will be established and observed.[29]

Why should a dialectical diet not fall within the scope of central purpose?

With consummate loyalty to the implications, Ward spelled out the final resolution of anxiety:

> The person is treated as a living cell in a growing social organism. It is the socialised individual who appears. This is what the students mean when they say, "We want people to have their own hobbies, but we don't want them to do things as separate individuals. We want them to follow their tastes and interests in groups." They have no interest in the problem of the personality . . . it is certain that when the Communist view of man's relation to the cosmos appears it will interpret the universe in social, not personal, terms. . . .[30]

There was precision in the nemesis. Ward, like the other prophets, had begun by celebrating personality. Infinitely worthful personality demanded brotherhood. Ultimate extension of brotherhood through ultimate extension of the rational will ended in the ultimate annihilation of self-consciousness, of personality. Man's pretension to be God ended in his destruction as man.

Ward continued on through the 'thirties as chairman of the League Against War and Fascism. He denied that the league was controlled by communists; there were churchmen who joined the league with the same understanding, but who left, declaring Ward wrong.[31] In any event, he remained, following a course few men did. Very soon, the league—its name changed to the League for Peace and Democracy—shifted attention from domestic to international affairs. The difficulties for orthodox dialectical interpretation of the international scene, in trying to define the proper course for a capitalist democracy, were considerable. In 1937–38, Ward and the league opposed arms increases and conscription, but demanded embargo on Japan and Italy, then upon Germany. Following Munich, Ward announced that the pretensions of Britain and France to be democracies had been exposed, but at the same time he called for economic noncoöperation to halt the fascist powers. It was an obscure period, none of the dialecticians explaining how economic noncoöperation was an adequate policy without some dealings with the bogus democracies.[32] The Hitler-Stalin pact of August, 1939, produced a strange rhetorical alliance with some of Ward's erstwhile opponents, the pacifists and neutralists, as he asked, in the November, 1939, *Social Questions Bulletin:* "What are the war aims of the allies? . . . Can Hitler and Hitlerism be stopped by war? Will the victory of the allies produce anything better than it did at Versailles with all its consequences?" The pact, however, proved too much, not for Ward, but for the Methodist Federation. By a vote of nineteen to two, the executive committee of the federation called, late in 1939, for an embargo on Japan—and upon Soviet Russia as well.[33] The dialectical route was proving too tortuous, and at last Ward was not allowed to lead the way unquestioned. In 1940, the membership came to a sad decision.

Three points of view divided them: all-out aid to Britain short of war; absolute noninvolvement; and economic aid covered by rigorous safeguards. They could not agree on anything except that the federation should not try to take a stand; it should ignore the problem altogether and dismiss its members to express themselves individually as they would.[34]

Early in 1940, resigning his post with the American Civil Liberties Union, Ward, 68 years old, went to Mexico for six months on doctor's orders. The League for Peace and Democracy disbanded; at a testimonial dinner, before an audience of five hundred, Ward attacked President Roosevelt, Father Coughlin, and the movement to aid Finland. Recuperation in Mexico might have offered escape from a hard season, but Ward returned and was soon inquiring, in the *Bulletin,* why the defense program had to be so large. In early June, 1941, at a Mother's Day peace parade in Cleveland, he analyzed how the war was developing into a "new streamlined Anglo-American imperialism." But history's surprises had to be acknowledged, including the surprise of Hitler's invasion of Russia. Early in the fall, rather shockingly, Ward asked if, the new situation being what it was, the federation ought not review its decision to take no stand on the war. Hastily he answered himself: No; the original grounds of difference remained. This was to say, not quite all the original grounds; but for the pacifist members of the federation, June 22 had changed nothing. They had been neutral *before* August, 1939 [35] and the Russo-German Pact. Their logic was not geographical.

Ward was the burning mystic, the pure mystic, in whom the logic of absolute vision burned away all but itself. The rest of the prophets of the social gospel, less logical, remained men of their origins and environment, full of that hardly avowed, assumed, almost instinctive inheritance called "church," never articulated in the passional logic. The logic itself exposed the inheritance to attrition. This was so, not in the insistence that individuals are actually social beings rather than isolate and self-sufficient monads, but in the sociology of the logic. The values and the social relationships that defined the individual personality in its highest worth were to be given quantitative universality throughout the society. Society could become the family. Nothing in the logic prevented the reasoning from reversing itself. Personality became defined in terms of those relationships that could be organized, legislated, universalized, submitted to the plans of abstract technical social science. The reversal had already begun in Rauschenbusch. It appeared in Page. It appeared in Coe. It was not absent from the pronouncements of the council and the exhortations of the *Century*. It left Eddy's ideology disrupted. Ward carried it to the end. There was a kind of retribution, a reversal of roles, by which family, congregation, school, hobby-group—and diet—submitted to the *Gleichschaltung* of central purpose.

Somehow, there had to be systematic provision for the possibility that in imagination, in taste, in eccentricity, in invention, men were more lyric and various and extreme than could be cultivated by anything but the most extemporized, provisional management, by anything but a politics limited to the pragmatic future. In the next stage of the social passion, these limits upon central purpose would be implied in reservations upon the capacities of both human reason and human love. How could such reservations be incorporated into politics? They might paralyze all social reform and thus invite further massive crises of breakdown, which in their turn would provoke still more pretentious responses of total anxiety and total politics. This would be the new problem for prophecy, unknown to the social gospel. The shorthand is not perfect, but in a sense, Marx had been added to Mammon as the enemy. The fact that Marx was a false answer to Mammon did not mean Mammon was any the better or any less threatening. Nothing had been solved; much had been complicated.

XII

The Meaning of Violence

Ward's response to the season of crisis, his climactic utopian vision, fulfilled one thrust of general social-gospel logic. There was nothing in it of itself perverse, scandalous, or unique in terms of that logic. Ward stood almost alone, not because of the extremity of his logic, but because he had chosen the wrong bearers of the logic. Yet this was not the point for which he was attacked. Not the argument that historical incarnation of utopia could never occur; not the argument that, whether such incarnation could occur, certainly Soviet Russia was not it; not—most symptomatic of all—the argument that any utopia as such, in itself in the first place, was an evil and not a good ideal—none of these were marshalled seriously against him in the circles of the social gospel. The group that included most of the prophets at this time, and of which Ward could not, because of his views, have been a member, was the Fellowship of Reconciliation, but Ward and the FOR were not divided on the issue of utopia. Rather, now, and with climactic fulfillment of another thrust of the general logic, the old, the ancient, the classic problem of the means was isolated for final decision, and to greater ultimate effect than the tacit banishment of Harry Ward.

The great FOR task of the early 'thirties was to draw what the pacifist leadership took to be a line to their left. In the general shift to the left in those years, the prophets were testifying to the seriousness of their idealism, and a temptation at the heart of all seriousness emerged to harass them: to be serious meant to be willing to do something, to be willing to do more than before, to be willing, in short, to do almost anything in the name of seriousness. And *anything* could come to mean violent things. It was on the issue of how to draw the line against violence that the FOR suffered schism late in 1933.

The leader of those most anxious that the line be drawn was Kirby Page, and Page thought of Ward as proof of the necessity for drawing it. The line between violence and nonviolence was critical. But Ward, to repeat, was not a member of the FOR. The opposition to Page within the FOR came from men who did not follow Ward in his celebration of the Russian experiment. It came from men with whom, in fact, so far as immediate practical political choices were concerned, Page agreed. For Page, Ward represented a false absolute, but the debate within the FOR came finally to involve whether there could be a domestication of the absolute in politics at all, and whether, therefore, the sanctions of Christianity could be claimed for any politics.

Absorbing the Fellowship for a Christian Social Order in 1928, the FOR had become the leading society of liberal Christian idealists in the early 'thirties, its preoccupations extending across the board of social-gospel interests. Signs of faction and dissent began to appear in debates in 1932, provoked by proposals to apply boycotts to the Japanese opening their campaign in Manchuria.[1] Through the next year, the argument mounted, coming to climax in December, 1933, but the climax did not turn on the Japanese in Manchuria or on international war; rather it turned on the class struggle. The continuity of the debate from early 1932 to late 1933 marked the final definitive emergence of pacifism as an issue for the social gospel as such, as an issue, that is, for domestic American politics. Page's class pacifism of 1933 was unified with his war pacifism of the 'twenties, and its fullest meaning will finally be traced in the renewed war pacifism of 1940.

Late in 1933, the executive committee of the FOR mailed out a questionnaire soliciting members' opinions on the degree of coercion in the class struggle to which members and secretaries of the FOR might go while remaining loyal to the principles of the fellowship.[2] Of the four secretaries—John Nevin Sayre, Charles Webber, Howard Kester, and J. B. Mathews—the views of Webber, Kester, and Mathews had been called to trial. The questionnaire, the executive committee hoped, would suggest whether to retain or dismiss the three men. Six alternatives were offered under Section II of the questionnaire, and they made up the heart of the poll. The 1,089 replies were distributed as follows:

> . . . in seeking for "a social order which will suffer no individual or group to be exploited for the profit or pleasure of another" . . . the members and secretaries should go so far as to:—
> 1. Proclaim the ideal . . . through methods of love, moral suasion and education, but refuse to identify themselves with either . . . class . . .
> Agreeing: 229.
> 2. Identify themselves . . . and protest against the use of violence by the police, militia and under-privileged . . . distribute relief to workers striking . . . ; attempt peacefully to maintain civil liberties . . . but without the use of any form of coercion.
> Agreeing: 210.
> 3. Assist in organizing workers into unions and in leading them in strikes . . . and if need be in a nonviolent general strike; assist in organizing the workers into a political party which will use non-violent measures . . . dissociating themselves from any group that used armed violence . . .
> Agreeing: 192.
> 4. In case the legal owners of essential industries resort to armed force . . . refuse to use violence against them but offer to serve the workers . . . in . . . nonviolent ways.
> Agreeing: 333.
> 5. In the situation described in No. 4 consent to the use of armed force if necessary to secure the advantage of the workers, but regretfully and only while the necessity for it continues.
> Agreeing: 106.

6. In anticipation of general class warfare, assist in the arming of workers . . . ; when war is fully joined, urge workers to acts of violence and participate with them . . .
Agreeing: 19.

Two of the secretaries, Kester and Mathews, voted for position 5, and were dismissed by the council, by a vote of 18 to 12. The debate that followed, intense, at times acrimonious, personal, and bitter, defined the impasse of a broad center party of the social gospel. The center position of the FOR, items 3 and 4, represented the all-out pacifist attempt to come to terms with the problems of power while still clinging to the rock of the absolute. The first striking fact about the poll was the assumption on the part of the committee drawing it up—Reinhold Niebuhr, Edmund Chaffee, Webber, and Arthur Swift—that the question of identification with labor was settled; position 1 represented only the minority unreconciled to the fellowship's expansion of focus in the first place.

In the years 1931, 1932, and 1933, social-gospel leaders had come to regard the phenomenon of class-consciousness as something to be accepted and somehow made use of, rather than as something to be first of all deplored, fought, and even denied. John C. Bennett, at Auburn Seminary and active in the Fellowship of Socialist Christians, argued that class-consciousness was in fact a necessity; without it, labor would not build the effective unions essential to the pursuit of justice. To be neutral in the class struggle, he argued, was equivalent to standing neutral in the struggle for justice itself. Devere Allen of the *World Tomorrow* urged this same necessity for class struggle, concretely as a labor movement led by socialists. Allen helped carry the Socialist party to its most revolutionary posture—theoretically—in Detroit in 1934, still, be it noted, as a pacifist. And as Kirby Page saw it, the class-consciousness of the workers had been imposed upon them by the prior class-consciousness of the businessmen, and was necessary.[3]

The attitude left behind by this clear assimilation of class strategy was still being voiced by those who had voted for position 1. Dwight Bradley voiced it, protesting a discussion by Francis Henson, an FOR member, of the question, "Must we have revolution?"[4] Henson had insisted upon the need for a distinctly socialistic leadership, accepting the class struggle as a fact; his ideas ran somewhat to the dramatic, as he called upon prophetic local religious fellowships to spawn a body of professional revolutionists such as Lenin called for. If they were not precisely those envisaged by Robert Whitaker in the pages of the Methodist Federation *Bulletin,* they were something like them. A member of the abortive Revolutionary Policy Committee within the Socialist party, Henson thought of the call for revolutionary leaders as equivalent to the call for foreign missionaries in days gone by. He was not defending violence; he did not necessarily expect violence. He thought the breakthrough into the new order might take anywhere from twenty-five to a hundred years, and he did not want means used that might too seriously corrupt the ends.

But Bradley, a Newton, Massachusetts, clergyman, rejected even this view; it was, he insisted, incompatible with the principles of Jesus.[5] Niebuhr and Henson, Bradley said, accused their associates of a lack of realism, but they were the ones who truly lacked realism, in their effort to combine Marx and Jesus, to bind the method of class warfare and coercion with the Christian method of group coöperation and good will. Liberal Christianity accepted the standards of Jesus, wished to apply them to real conditions, and could not give them over to the causes of war, whether international or class in nature.

Bradley was not arguing the issue on which Kester and Mathews were dismissed. Whatever Marx had said, Bennett, Allen, Page, and the expositors of position 4 did not agree that class struggle meant class warfare. Class-consciousness did not mean class hate. Coercion did not mean violent coercion. Here at last the distinctions denied the consciousness of the 'twenties were being hammered out, and it was between these distinctions that a major party of the fellowship, and particularly Kirby Page, threaded their way.

In our sketch of Page's devotion to the causes of world peace and pacifism, we saw that his disavowal of war rested principally on a conviction of the pragmatic uselessness of war for any purpose. His pacifism he conceived first of all as an effective guide for political prevention of war. These pragmatic calculations depended implicitly to a major, if not determining, extent upon the favorable power situation of America. Also, veiled and often totally buried, there was an appeal to the teachings of Jesus as the ultimate sanction for pacifist politics, and it was at the juncture of this final absolute sanction and the pragmatic sanction that obscurity gathered, for here the pragmatic political meaning of pacifism was jeopardized. An absolute sanction demanded pacifism in every instance, that is, prior to the pragmatics. Page's solution was to insist that there were no cases causing contradiction, although in his attempt to meet the classic catechetical problem of Belgium in 1914, his "case" splayed out beyond any pragmatic future into unspecified hope, and pacifism had to be justified finally, "regardless" of where it led and what it cost. The pragmatic sanction burned away.

But these catechetical problems were problems of theory, of hypothetical ultimates. When the FOR metamorphosed temporarily in the early 'thirties into a society primarily concerned with socialism, Page found himself in a new situation. The pragmatic context for class pacifism in America was more definite and real than the context for the war pacifism of the 'twenties. The demands upon responsible ethics were sharper and clearer. In the season leading up to the poll, Page, in articles entitled "Is Coercion Ever Justifiable?" "Is Coercion Compatible with Religion?" and "A Socialist Program of Deliverance," laid down the pacifist line for the new situation.[6] He justified coercion when exercised "in the family spirit." But violent coercion, the coercion of class war, was unnecessary; the basic fact militating against it was that it was, in America, tactically, pragmatically absurd. It could not possibly succeed; it would call forth reprisals that would put an end to radical activity for decades ahead. Nonviolent action, on the other hand, returning to the struggle time and again, could hope for success. In his books of the middle 'thirties —*Individualism and Socialism* (1933) and *Must We Go to War?*

(1937)—Page repeated and extended his proofs of the foolishness of violent action in America.

The most sensational result of the FOR debate was the resignation of Reinhold Niebuhr. Niebuhr published his explanation in the *Christian Century*.

> Modern capitalism breeds injustice of the disproportions of economic power which it tolerates and upon which it is based. We expect no basic economic justice without a destruction of the present disproportions of power and we do not expect the latter without a social struggle. Once we have accepted the fact of the reality of the social struggle we do not feel that we can stop where the middle portion of the fellowship has stopped. We are unable to stop there because we can find no stable absolute in the shifting situation of the social struggle where everything must be finally decided in pragmatic terms.[7]

Niebuhr was speaking from position 5. Did he therefore anticipate an hour of decision when violence would be the gauge? It would have made no difference for the issue in question whether he did or not, however, for the two positions, 4 and 5, were not designed to test political expectations, but to test principles of political choice. They were the only two choices that proposed different responses to the same situation. Page's choice of 4 was also to be understood as good whether he did or did not foresee an hour of violent decision. The two men had registered a difference in principle.

The clarity of the division in principle nevertheless was obscured by the fact that this hypothetical situation was an actual issue in the pragmatic calculations of the times. It was obscured by Ward's adoption of a rigid rhetoric of united front orthodoxy; it was obscured by Niebuhr's prolonged pragmatic uncertainty; it was obscured by Page's continued use of the hidden absolute, now more disguised than ever.

Ward's rejection of pacifism did not derive from any belief in a strategy of insurrection, but rather from his conviction that the political right would use weapons that would have to be met in kind. The point here, a classic issue in Marxist ideology, remained wrapped in mists. Just what would happen in the hour of decision? Conceivably, if a skillful exercise of violence by the "reds" could overthrow the "whites," might not original violence be justified? Marxists never explained why not. Instead, the accepted logic was to justify a reflexive violence forced upon the reds by antidemocratic whites attempting to overturn a peaceful democratic victory previously achieved by the reds. Ward was conventional here. His difficulties arose in trying to fit this picture to the American scene. In the book in which he offered his fullest strategic analysis of American conditions, *Democracy and Social Change* (1940), he noted that Marx, in his portrayal of the class line-up, was usually portraying a situation at the climax of capitalist disintegration, at the hour of decision itself.[8] Ward was unable to read back out of this logic of the climax an interim strategy adequate to the facts of the situation before the climax. Driven by his vision of what might follow the climactic hour, he always spoke as though that hour were imminent; and yet he knew the class situation prescribed by Marx did not exist. Knowing it, still the tempting idea of an hour of decision numbed his feel for the immediate political scene. The New Deal—from the Marxist point of view—obviously was postponing rather than hurrying on the hour of decision, and Ward therefore was unable to see the New Deal except as it resembled the fascist threat of the counterrevolutionaries. This was inconsistent with his own recognition of the power of the New Deal to draw the teeth of some of the extreme, truly proto-fascist groups of the middle 'thirties. He suffered from the old problem of the eschatology of Jesus all over again. Ward, like the members of the Communist party, was the literal believer, rigid in expectation of the Coming. And he carried over the old evangelical haste, also, which had always struck to save this soul, now, here, instantly, and which had nerved the social gospel, as in 1919, to speak of saving the world "in this generation."

Niebuhr, on the other hand, in 1932, 1933, and 1934, exhibited an at times morbid sensitivity to some of the most delicate nuances of what might be opening up on the political stage. In his own practicing political choices, he was for several years indistinguishable from Page. Both had been members of the LIPA. Niebuhr had, just as Page, warned against preoccupation with what had happened in Russia in 1917 as pure fantasy for America. In 1933, he had sharply rejected revolution as "unthinkable." It could mean nothing but disruption of the whole fabric of society and years of strife to follow.[9] Soon after the debate in the FOR, he and Page were both among those who rejected the Revolutionary Policy Committee. In reply to a *Christian Century* criticism of his "dogmatic" expectation of violence, he wrote:

> . . . I am not at all interested in predicting or insisting that social change must come by violence . . . If one could count on the wisest possible statesmanship on the part of both the retreating and the advancing social group such a contest might be as much without violence as was, for instance, the Spanish revolution.[10]

The illustration was unfortunate; the Spanish fascists did not provide its measure until 1936, however, and by then the debate was closed.

Nevertheless, Niebuhr's views in that time remained inscrutable. He rejected the démarche of the RPC; yet, in his reply to its manifesto, he declared:

> If [the RPC] would say that it believes that the final social struggle will involve at least the temporary abrogation of democracy and that the only question is whether Fascists or Socialists will make use of the dictatorship which emerges from the destruction of democracy, I would agree with [it].[11]

Where the RPC betrayed its lack of realism, he felt, was in its debates about a dictatorship of the proletariat in a country without an authentic proletariat.

This reply to the RPC followed Niebuhr's answer to the *Century,* and it might have been thought that his mood had darkened in the meantime. Actually, his mood had fluctuated by the month. Niebuhr had written other strong words earlier, late in 1933, *before* his reply to the *Century.*

> The longer democratic methods of arbitration hold out the more will society be spared unnecessary conflict and chaos. It may be prophesied with almost dogmatic certainty that they will not hold

out to the final crisis because it would be contrary to nature if an old governing group capitulated without exhausting every resource at its disposal to maintain itself . . . in the hour of crisis both [groups] will probably use the same weapons. For the weapons of physical combat are finally available. . . .[12]

Finally, in justifying his resignation from the FOR, he declared: "I share, roughly speaking, the political position of Mr. Mathews." [13] This of course was not true. Mathews had no political position; he was an adventurer, into and out of the RPC within months of the FOR debate, into and out of the League Against War and Fascism, and on his way toward serving as star witness before the Dies Committee in 1938. Despite his unfortunate choice of an ally, however, Niebuhr was making his point in the debate: violence could not be categorically ruled out as a means. He who did rule it out would, at the hour of crisis, be lost.

The ambiguities at this juncture of Niebuhr's thinking were products, however, not only of his judgments of the power scene, but also of the fact that this was the period of emergence for his new departure in religion. Almost certainly, an extrapragmatic, "dogmatic" interest did lead him to posit an "hour of crisis." Niebuhr needed a sharp line of at least theoretical division between his politics and social-gospel politics to match the sharp line between neo-orthodoxy and the liberal religion of the social gospel. The evidence for the failure of liberal religion was political evidence, and Niebuhr sought to sharpen the lessons of this evidence. His dispute with the *Century* illustrated his problem. Morrison did not argue for an absolute moral distinction between violent and nonviolent coercion, for Morrison did not claim to be a pacifist. But Morrison did seize upon any pragmatic admission that nonviolence *might* see the politics of justice through to success to reëmbrace the political psychology Niebuhr was combating:

> Mr. Niebuhr, in demonstrating the inevitability of violent class con-
> flict, by pointing out the psychological and ethical effects of power,
> opens up the possibility of the exact opposite. For he puts upon
> the lips of the prophets of God a gospel of love which the prophets
> have never preached before! Until they have preached it, until

they have once made the heavens ring with it, it is too soon to deliver ourselves over to the pessimism of a gospel of violence.[14]

Let, Morrison cried, a hundred prophets of reality preach this realism to the men of power! As an admission that the prophets had never understood that power was the question, this cry was devastating, more devastating than Morrison intended, and more devastating than was wholly fair to the prophets themselves, but the admission gave Niebuhr his problem. How could he prove his case without stretching the facts of the crisis? His "almost dogmatic certainty" of the hour of crisis in 1933 amounted to such stretching, for he had previously insisted that there were "unique elements" in America "which may postpone the ultimate crisis until the end of the century." [15] Even this, although it provided a comfortable margin of error, amounted to stretching, for such long-range predictions were essentially incompatible with Niebuhr's emerging religious outlook, in which man's capacity for such masterful predictions was deprecated. Niebuhr made no real use of his prediction politically. What instruction was there for 1933 in the line-up of forces in the year 2000? But he was tempted to such predictions in his need for a sharp line of division between himself and the religious liberals.

Kirby Page, finally, argued the futility of revolutionary violence in America, and with complete pragmatic plausibility. The trouble was that his arguments did not catch his true opponents in the FOR. They caught only those like Ward, and more cleanly those like Robert Whitaker and A. J. Muste, who wished to act as though the hour of decision had already arrived. Once again, the extrapragmatic ground for his choice in the debate had to be smoked out. Niebuhr was driving against the distinctions between class consciousness and class hatred, class struggle and class war, nonviolent coercion and violent coercion, not as meaningless, but as invalid when taken to be absolute ethical distinctions.[16] By the light of the FOR center, position 4 was a religious politics based on the ethic of Jesus, and position 5 was not. The fellowship had amended none of the creed with which it had explained its war pacifism during the First World War. Page was still claiming a direct religious sanction for his politics. Niebuhr, as Page paraphrased him, claimed that "nothing is clearer than that pure religious idealism must issue in a policy of nonresistance which makes no claims to be socially efficacious." [17] Page denied this. He was still fighting for the social-gospel synthesis. Moving beyond the politics of pure persuasion, positions 1 and 2, he agreed that persuasion was not enough. But in nonviolent coercion he believed he had a formula combining practicality with pure religious sanction. This fusion of the pragmatic with the gospel apology Niebuhr had set himself to break, and the crux now was the apology. In practice Niebuhr himself spoke for nonviolent coercion. But he also spoke against the tie between religion and politics in the FOR. Instead of synthesis or fusion, he found tension, the tension from which sprang his neo-orthodoxy. His line of attack on the FOR middle, in other words, was not from the side of politics alone. It came from both sides, simultaneously, from both politics and religion, in eagerness that both be liberated from the confusions they had caused each other.

As it happened, a purely religious attack on the FOR was delivered at the time with a force and a purity not later to be surpassed. H. Richard Niebuhr, Reinhold Niebuhr's brother, had never been a man of the social gospel. At the same time, he had never been a man of the old gospel, individualistic in piety, resentful of the idea that patterns of society and world had something to do with the soul. Instead, he was interested in rescuing religion from captivity to its culture, more than in rescuing middle-class culture from itself. For him, religion had to be rescued from the social-gospel synthesis, because restoration of Christian vitality and freedom was the whole issue. This was not true of Reinhold Niebuhr, for whom restoration of political vitality was of simultaneous importance, and it was due to this difference that Richard Niebuhr could state the religious attack on the FOR more directly in 1933. He stated it in strong, precise words.[18] Richard Niebuhr believed that the FOR, and nonviolence, did not represent true Christian pacifism, but rather humane, humanistic moral idealism. He believed the FOR middle was inconsistent with itself in ruling violent coercion from the repertory of means by which the goals of moral idealism might be pursued; he believed that a true Christian pacifism was needed.

With his brother's protest against identification of the gospel with pragmatic moral idealism, Reinhold Niebuhr agreed. But he could not have agreed with what he took to be the political bearing of Richard Niebuhr's protest. It was too "pure." A politically incompetent religion was not to be followed by a politically irrelevant religion.

The two Niebuhrs had divided already on a political issue— policy toward Japan in Manchuria.[19] Richard Niebuhr had advocated "meaningful inactivity," Reinhold Niebuhr "meaningful activity," more precisely, economic pressure. Where Richard Niebuhr attacked the FOR from one side only, Reinhold Niebuhr attacked it from both sides at once, breaking the old fusion, reorganizing the two principles that could not, according to Richard Niebuhr, be made parts of one whole, into some new kind of whole compromising the integrity of neither.

All this Page and his fellows resisted. They had moved far enough in assimilating the facts of the political world to be able to claim pragmatic adequacy for their position, while yet they could claim the old special ethical and religious sanction for their politics, against overt utilitarians. The domestic political history of the United States in the 'thirties favored this final effort to save the old fusion. The liberal pacifists were slowly driven into surrender, nevertheless. Page remained a socialist as well as a pacifist, and the political history of the 'thirties gradually deflated socialist expectations. In his defense of pacifism against the revolutionaries, Page came to abandon one of the old fortresses of the social-gospel spirit: he no longer argued the certainty of success. His argument became negative.

In laying foundations strong enough to sustain arguments in favor of peaceable methods of revolution, it is not necessary to prove that success is inevitable or even highly probable. It is sufficient to demonstrate the *relative* advantages of this strategy in contrast to revolution through civil war. The fact that the odds are heavily against victory in the effort to transform capitalism through non-warlike means does not invalidate this procedure, since the barriers to triumph through violent seizure of power are far higher.[20]

Thus did Page back into his final resting place, the sect. Here the method appeared to have lost some of its efficacy, and the practicality of Jesus was fading. The prophets had not before been accustomed to finding the odds heavily against them.

Of course his retreat was relatively painless. Page was not forced to make it against all instincts. The social scene in 1937 was less desperate, less threatening, than it had been in 1932 and 1933. It was possible for men to begin suggesting that perhaps the transformation of capitalism was not equivalent to a gospel task after all. Elsewhere, however, politics had begun to stalk the pacifists in their utilitarian outposts more seriously, and there sharper retreats were required. As the war drew on, and as the FOR leaders improvised policies of more and more obvious desperation, the bedrock rationale of the pacifist ethos at last began to come clear. There was a Jesus way of life, "no matter what," there should be loyalty to the Way of the Cross, no matter what. True believers should hold to the ideal in every instance, in any case.[21] We shall inspect the politics that pacifism offered from 1939 to 1941, in an effort to perpetuate its claim to responsibility. By then, however, Page himself had retreated too far into the sectarian fortress to be able to lead in pressing that politics. Leadership in this awful task required a man who had already abandoned pacifism because of its practical weakness, only to return to it haunted by his efforts to pursue the absolute with violence. This was to be A. J. Muste. In studying Muste, we shall try to touch, in order to feel its tension, the nerve of this final pacifist version of the social gospel. It was an effort to save the individual soul from the ravages of politicalization.

By then, however, Muste, the pacifists, and the liberal leaders of the social gospel generally, moderates and socialists alike, all had a far more formidable opponent than any they had faced in their struggles with the old gospel, with Mammon, or with Marx.

XIII

Reinhold Niebuhr: Political Morality

In 1915 Reinhold Niebuhr came as a young man of twenty-three from Yale Divinity School to the small church of eighteen families, Bethel Evangelical in Detroit, where he was to remain throughout his parish pastorate. He testified that he both entered and departed from the parish ministry with reluctance.[1] His church flourished, but it was not in the flourishing that hung the fruits so much as in the pastoral experience. A sense for the religious resources of the ordinary, unpretentious layman, transcending those proffered by official shepherds, pervaded the pages of his reflections over these years. The essence of the experience lay in the essential ambiguity, the ultimately dubious quality of the ministry itself—that "professionalization" of the "good" man.[2] It is a little difficult to see that this ministry helped provide the analytic abstractions of his later thought with much of their living pulse or much of their concrete texture, but it is possible to imagine that it helped sustain Niebuhr's lifelong insistence that the ultimate reaches and fruits of religion are beyond the domestication of society.

Destined to develop the most mordant criticism of the captivity of the churches to their own success, he himself could leave for

Union Theological Seminary in 1928 with a career as a successful minister behind him. Niebuhr himself flourished in the larger church and civic life of Detroit: member and chairman of the mayor's Commission on Interracial Relations, member of the Industrial Relations Commission of the Detroit Council of Churches. The important fact was that it was Detroit. The organizing symbolic power of the city for Niebuhr's career, while not necessary, yet was central. Detroit was laboratory. There, society as reduced to "a mass of individuals, held together by a productive process," was coming true. In the Ford factories, rationalization of the work force, and consequent depersonalization of the workman, came true. The entanglement of efficiency and autocracy in industry, of social power and social intransigence in the holding classes, of social comfort and insensitivity in the middle, and of social disintegration and helplessness in the working force, were receiving diagrammatic expression.[3]

In this time, also, Niebuhr's participation in the church life of the nation was begun, to flourish until, well before he left for Union, he had become a leader of Protestantism. His circuits were very much social-gospel circuits. A leader in the Fellowship for a Christian Social Order, member of the Fellowship of Reconciliation, a member of the executive committee of the Federal Council and representative for the Evangelical Synod in the council's administrative committee, a frequent speaker at student conferences and at colleges—perhaps that above all, prolific author of articles in religious and secular journals, contributing editor for the *Christian Century* and the *World Tomorrow,* he repeated the pattern of energy and tireless evangelism of the prophets as a whole.[4]

In an early, youthful statement in 1916, Niebuhr made use of the form of discussion that was to stamp his thought throughout his career, that of not logical, but social, historical, psychological antinomies, between which he discerned a living dialectical play. The duty of thought, while illuminating the antinomy, was to conform to it, not to polarize it into static contradictions nor to relax it into some prudent mean. The particular antinomy of 1916 anticipated a famous theme. The moral man of 1916 was the man of individual conscience, immoral society the nation at war. Here the dialectic was simple, one-sided, and wholly tragic. The war was a story of "The Nation's Crime Against the Individual." Individual conscience had outgrown that of the nation and the race. "The crime of the nation against the individual is, not that it demands his sacrifices against his will, but that it claims a life of eternal significance for ends that have no eternal value." [5] Modern war, originating simply in commercial rivalry, entailed no eternal ends.

Nevertheless, with American entrance, Niebuhr supported the war. In a statement a decade later, he characterized himself as having succumbed to the war enthusiasm, forgetful of pacifism; as having identified a form of civilization with the Kingdom of God; as having believed in an easy reconciliation of Christian ethics with political necessities of the day.[6] One among the many expressions of Protestant repentance for the record of the churches in the war, this *mea culpa* might safely be taken more as analysis of the general experience of liberal churchmen and rather less as Niebuhr's specific experience. Yet, however much reservation, doubt, and disturbance not typical of a preacher "presenting arms" the *Notebook* entries for 1917, 1918, and 1919 revealed, Niebuhr was distinctly among the liberal war supporters and not apart from them. It was a function of the age of illusionment.[7]

The war "made me a child of the age of disillusionment." [8] In a *Notebook* entry for 1919 Wilson already appeared as a man being made play of by a sly Clemenceau and a shrewd Lloyd George, with the significant comment: "Wilson is a typical son of the manse. He believes too much in words." [9] With the first appearance of documented study of wartime diplomacy, the reaction was sharper. "Gradually the whole horrible truth about the war is being revealed . . . How can we ever again believe anything when we compare the solemn pretensions of statesmen with the cynically conceived secret treaties?" And Niebuhr concluded with a comment that provides a measure for the development of a modern American mind: "Here was simply a tremendous contest for power. . . ." [10] But while this specific disillusionment was common to the postwar generation of Protestant liberalism, and acted sometimes to put the idea of iron, if not the iron itself, into Protestant liberal souls, for Niebuhr it meant a logic, set in motion, that kept his thinking uncrystallized, in systematic flux, throughout the decade ahead. The critical lesson of the war lay in the church's acquiescence to the claim of eternal significance for ends that had no eternal value. "The war convinced me that religion can be effective only if it resists the embraces of civilization." [11] The war had cast everything but the personality of Jesus into relativity; that—a spiritual and moral ideal of absolute and transcendent nature—remained.

An explicit, often vivid sense of the transcending character of religious values: this was a pole in Niebuhr's thought. To forget it would be to misconstrue the over-all pattern of that thought. Religion, as he saw it in that time, did have resources to offer society. These were the resources celebrated by the social gospel, the resources of ideal vision. With its high evaluation of human personality, religion inspired a social imagination in men that could never rest content with any particular social achievement, and nerved them to follow it.

> The facts of human nature are sufficiently complex to validate almost any hypothesis which may be projected into them. Therefore the assumptions upon which we assay our social contacts are all important . . . A vital religion not only prompts men to venture the assumption that human beings are essentially trustworthy and lovable, but it endows them with the courage and inclination to maintain their hypothesis when immediate facts contradict it until fuller facts are brought in to verify it.[12]

This distinction between "immediate" and "fuller" facts led Niebuhr at times to appear to relax what he avowed was a tension; insisting that this religious faith was a foolishness and absurdity, he could declare also that reality did after all slowly approach the ideals implicit in it—including the ideal implicit in human character, that of ethical freedom.[13] But emphasis upon the tension, not upon the approaching identity, characterized his outlook. The Gospel principle of love was not pragmatic; it was in real conflict with the common-sense morality of social life; it was a true foolishness. Niebuhr tightened the tension by pointing to St. Francis as the supreme follower of Christ—St. Francis, who had not been a social worker or politician.[14] The 'twenties were marked by a restless, yet steady, consideration of this dimension —restless because its implications for effective social action were ambiguous, steady because no doubt attached to its reality and value. The vividness and to some degree the poignance with which Niebuhr dealt with this dilemma in the 'twenties tended to disappear into abstraction as his thought moved into, first, the political realism, and second, the theological revisions of the 'thirties, but it remained an absolutely essential structure for that thought.

From the tension there emerged the distinction between moral man and immoral society. The article of 1916 had already displayed it. In 1927, in warnings he addressed to pacifists, Niebuhr posited the selfish, unmoral group as a historical given. In the year following, still before the storm, the theme deepened: "All human groups are essentially predatory and tend to hold desperately to their privileges against the pressure of the under-privileged who demand a fairer share of the blessings." [15] In the fashion of the social gospel at its theoretical best, Niebuhr's attack upon the Ford factories drove not simply against Ford's politics and hypocrisies on wages and hours, but against the Ford factory as a place unfit for human life. Even at its economic best, modern industry could remain destructive of human values. Its sin was double: automatic process compounding autocratic management. The Christianization of America would not be economic and legal redemption alone, or for proletarians alone, but redemption for all men from their status as functions in a social process.[16] This emphasis dominated Niebuhr's first book, *Does Civilization Need Religion?* and reappeared in his analysis of both capitalism and collectivism in the *Reflections on the End of an Era*. The whole modern world, as it appeared in *Does Civilization Need Religion?* threatened man with reduction to machine-life: a depersonalized society was building up within a depersonalized universe. These were twin threats, and Niebuhr considered that intellectuals were particularly susceptible to the ravages of scientific determinism and depersonalization. But science was not truly the threat, for eventually science would be forced to abandon its makeshift, amateur determinism for a metaphysics that would not be deterministically imprisoning.[17] The real threat was that carried by industrial civilization.

In answering "yes" to the question, "Does civilization need religion?" Niebuhr attacked the church community in a fashion sharper than was common in the social gospel. Liberal religion —the religion of America and of the comfortable classes of the West in general—did not have an answer to the main threat to human values. As between the two threats, liberal religion had chosen to challenge the impersonal universe rather than the impersonal civilization. Although even on the field of its choice liberalism was not winning its battle—since its science was not modern enough—its real error lay in the choice itself. Liberal religion was blind to the cruelties of modern society. Niebuhr explained this blindness by using the group analysis that anticipated his use of Marx as a guide to political realism: modern religion had failed to generate socially redemptive powers because it was captive to the classes that did not feel the cruelties and hence did not feel the need for social redemption. It appealed to the theological simplicity of Jesus rather than to His ethical rigor.[18]

In the face of such a church, and more generally, given "the paradox of religion . . . that it serves the world best when it maintains its high disdain for the world's values," [19] the strategy Niebuhr proposed for religious idealists was an intensified expression of that departure we have seen among others also in the late 'twenties, their abandonment of the basic social-gospel hope that the church could lead in social redemption. Too enmeshed with the interests of society, the church would command neither the insight nor the courage required. But it could serve as a recruiting ground. The movement for redemption would be, as such movements always had been, a minority movement, but many would come to it from the church. Certainly, it should be a layman's movement. Its interest should lie in rebuilding the social order rather than in rebuilding religious institutions. These minority laymen would live by an old religious mode adapted to modern times.

> The new asceticism must produce spiritualized technicians who will continue to conquer and exploit nature in the interest of human welfare, but who will regard their task as a social service and scorn to take a larger share of the returns of industry than is justified by reasonable and carefully scrutinized needs.[20]

These "religio-moral" forces, Niebuhr wrote, must combine the "wisdom of serpents" with the "guilelessness of doves" if they would aid in the moral regeneration of society. He speculated that this task of moral regeneration might be too difficult for the immediate future and that, meanwhile, the strategy should be the "largest possible measure of immediate detachment."

> If religion cannot transform society, it must find its social function in criticizing present realities from some ideal perspective and in presenting the ideal without corruption, so that it may sharpen the conscience and strengthen the faith of each generation.[21]

Whether the asceticism of the spiritualized technicians was a form of high disdain or not, whether, in other words, this asceticism was the ultimate form of religious witness, could not be told from Niebuhr's words. The ambiguity was one of the early instances in which he wavered in judging the gravity of a situation, tempted both to pessimism and to action. In any case, for Niebuhr the church community was not one pole of tension; tension ran through the body of the church itself.

Niebuhr's direct and persistent attention to politics in the 'twenties fell within the context of this concern for the fate of ultimate values in a civilization peculiarly threatening to them. This meant that he was guided by the basic conviction that fundamental change in the system was necessary; but he had no clear line of strategy to urge for bringing change to pass. He was capable of voicing an emphasis upon pure technique in the same fashion as the educators, the secretaries of the Federal Council, Ward, and the majority of the prophets:

> . . . it seems that the world needs light even more than good-will and love, and enlightenment even more than regeneration . . . The

emotional and volitional element in morality has been a fairly constant factor in history, and progress has come by development of
the rational which fashioned new engines to utilize the hitherto dissipated powers of man's moral purpose.[22]

Technique was not to mean a new-model stewardship; yet, like
these others, Niebuhr too could stress the will and insight of the
privileged as the key: "The hope of an ethical civilization rests
not upon the possibility of making power completely ethical but
upon the possibility of creating enough intelligence and conscience among the holders of power to make a gradual equalization of power possible." [23] Its suggestion that ethics demanded
equality echoed Rauschenbusch. Despite its concern for power,
however, it was not the "political morality" of *Moral Man and
Immoral Society*, according to which the reduction of power
could come only through a power opposed. Class consciousness
appeared as a challenge to be met and overcome, not as a means:
". . . the church can justify its opposition to the class consciousness of the proletarian movement only if it is willing to make
an appeal and to make a successful appeal to the holding classes
to save the industrial proletariat without regard to selfish interests." [24] In fact, while his attack upon "liberalism" had already
begun, Niebuhr took the technique of pitting self-interest against
self-interest as itself a liberal technique.

Of the active political agencies in the West, the British Labour
party caught his attention as exemplary. On the one hand, it
profited from the social ideals of the church, which in England
had not been inundated by individualistic Puritanism. On the
other hand, it refused to adopt a Marxist stance, hence did not
alienate the middle classes as did German social democracy, for
instance. But Niebuhr could not press for British Labour party
strategy in the United States. There was no adequate labor force
in the field; the AFL lacked resources, energy, and imagination.
As early as 1927, Niebuhr mentioned Sidney Hillman as an example of the leaders needed if labor's recourse was not to be
outright radicalism, but, he observed, the prospects in 1927 for
such leadership were slight.[25]

Here, too, there was wavering. The lack of focus in Niebuhr's political outlook in this period derived from his oscillation between a moderate confidence in the fruits to be won from preaching and a pessimistic foreboding that preaching—mere words—went for naught. Thus, he found proof of the incompetence of the American mind and conscience faced by industrial civilization in the celebration of Henry Ford as an exponent of humane industrial strategy, and yet he appeared to feel, along with most of the prophets, that a reservoir of idealism already existed in the culture, which could be tapped for social action if only the middle classes could be freed of their illusions, if only the idealism could be broken loose from captivity. Its captivity to individualism and puritanism, to nationalism and laissez-faire optimism, to ideology subtly identifying the universal range of idealism with the particular comforts of the ideologists, all drew his liberating attacks. Then, once again, the pessimism would be invoked with unqualified rigor:

> History will have to come to the aid of the gospel before America can be Christianized, and bitter experience must teach the nation that the way of privilege and pride and power is not the way of life. For us, as for the time of Amos, the day of the Lord must be darkness, and not light, and things must become worse before they can be better.[26]

A flat, total reversal of the character set upon history by the social gospel. The difficulty with this judgment, delivered in 1925, was that the idealist would find it almost impossible to act as though it were true, and until history did come to the aid of the gospel, Niebuhr himself did not act upon it.

In 1939 Niebuhr said of *Does Civilization Need Religion?*:

> I wrote a book, my first, in 1927 which when now consulted is proved to contain almost all the theological windmills against which today I tilt my sword. These windmills must have tumbled shortly thereafter for every succeeding volume expresses a more and more explicit revolt against what is usually known as liberal culture.[27]

Actually, the book was full of anticipations of later themes, and Niebuhr of course had aimed it as an attack upon liberalism. He had presented things in tension—the individual and society, religion and culture—and had elucidated the tension, especially between religion and culture, through an analysis of groups, a method he was always to use. The book was not in customary liberal style, and its guiding theme, the location of ultimate religious values high above assimilation by any culture, was not liberal.

The broadest sense in which the book did remain liberal was its picture of religion as morality. The pressures that forced out the first suggestions of non- or trans-moral values in religion were slow and intricate in operation. They did not appear in *Moral Man*. But if religious values remained the values of morality— in the narrow, social sense of the relationship of man to man— Niebuhr had already driven his formulation of them to the point where he could later speak of them as "impossible" ideals, relevant to society but unrealizable. Religion would then have to become something more.

The frustrations of social idealism which he analyzed were also in the liberal manner. One was the weakness and failure of reason. In a chapter with the significant title "Social Complexity and Ethical Impotence," Niebuhr interpreted Protestant individualism and laissez-faire sociology, not so much as ideological apologies for the going order, as ideological surrenders to the growing intricacy of commercial and industrial relations. There was in fact a "cultural lag." He also spoke of "nature" as a source of frustration. Nature included "instincts" leading men to prefer immediate to ultimate values, "a stubborn inertia in every type of reality which offers resistance to each new step in creation," and even death, the final resistance. "Nature" foreshadowed an explicit "nature-spirit" dualism in *Reflections on the End of an Era*, where the liberal portrait of human nature had still not wholly given way.[28]

That "complexity" and "nature" frustrated social idealism could hardly be denied. That frustration was compounded by the prudential dilutions of idealism in comfortable churches could also hardly be denied. But at this stage these frustrations were unorganized; they obscured rather than illuminated what Niebuhr was trying to get at. Clearly, he had a will to press against liberal optimism. He wished to call the instrumentalists from their breathless worship of the infinite plasticity of man and society to a realization that plasticity as such was a morally neutral fact. Man could become devil as well as angel. Little could be gained in this direction by pointing out bad instincts alongside good instincts, or by emphasizing the complexity of society as against enthusiasts who believed social science made all things simple.

Niebuhr's liberalism would begin finally to crumble only once he began to insist that utopia was frustrated not by accidental, temporary, and contemporary factors, but by permanent factors. The fascination and the difficulties of his early attacks upon liberalism were due to the fact that his sense of the permanent basis of frustration was liberated in him by a crisis that was in truth only temporary. In his book of 1927, one passage alone anticipated the neo-orthodox psychology: "It is man's sublime and tragic fate that he must find happiness in the search for infinitude amidst the flux of time and he can therefore never accept the portion of mortality for himself with equanimity." [29]

Under pressure, social-gospel politics moved in one of two directions, toward sectarian myth or toward expedient compromise. The sectarians—like the pacifist Page and the revolutionary Ward—managed to protect some of the critical quality of their idealism, but at the expense of relevance. The others—like the *Christian Century* and the Federal Council—worked closer to relevant realities, but with the loss of the cutting-power of their religious word.

In the early 'thirties Niebuhr above all others sought to break out of such dilemmas. His mind was already set to follow out a new economy, in which religion and politics would stand in new relationship. Neither would serve as cloak for the other. His mind was always turned toward facts that had to be done justice, the hidden facts, the hidden truth, truth that challenged, more than toward facts and truths that confirmed. The war had been the first fact, Detroit the second. The depression was the third.

Niebuhr was "ready" for the depression. That is, he was prepared to receive it as a shattering blow, not only to the old system, but also to all old hopes. As early as 1931, only twelve

years after the enthusiasm of 1919, he had his formula: "The real
fact about our civilization is that it is flirting with disaster." [30]

A melodramatic formula, Niebuhr was never able, nor did he
wish, to prove it by the facts of the American scene alone.
Actually, for him the depression was a European experience as
well. Then, and for the next ten years, he far more than any other
American Protestant leader tried to do justice to the total scene
of the West, and in Europe more than America he found the
immediate evidence of disaster. Thus, in contrast to Harry Ward,
Niebuhr drew lessons from Germany. Germany, he wrote in
1932, was "A Prophecy of Western Civilization." If Germany
escaped communism, so might the West; communism might be
isolated while the West pursued slower means.[31] Germany's actual
fate sharpened his sense of danger later, and at no point in the
'thirties did the agony of Europe appear to allow relaxation.

Yet Europe could not be translated directly into American
terms. At the very time, early in 1931, when Niebuhr was speaking of disaster, he was also writing that the United States had
decades, perhaps, during which to avert a crisis such as Germany
faced. It was true, he agreed, that the men of great power would
never divest themselves of their power voluntarily, but they were
few, and Americans, largely middle-class, taught by schools and
churches devoted to democracy, could yet reorganize society on
the basis of a better ethic. This was to be one of Niebuhr's
persisting problems: how far could America's relative strength in
the crisis be conceded without feeding illusions? Within eighteen
months, he was contemplating the possibility that American
middle-class culture, at its zenith in 1929, would be in full decay
by 1950. This kind of oscillation continued, as has been seen, to
mark his thinking during the debate on violence in the FOR.
In *Reflections on the End of an Era,* published in 1934, he
explicitly denied that differences in America were of the type, or
enough, to exempt her from the general perils of the industrial
West.[32]

In any case, the spirit of the new formula dominated, and
disaster provided a context for politics radically unlike that of
the social gospel. This context was given by history, it was not

a construct of idealism. It pointed to a minimum and not to a maximum achievement; it did not allow any man politics that recoiled from the materials at hand.

Moral Man and Immoral Society, the most important book in the history of the social passion, drew upon the crisis. It was a second edge, a sharpening of the political, realistic edge of the same sword that *Does Civilization Need Religion?* had sharpened on its religious side. Niebuhr's attack in 1927 was intended to free religion, his attack in *Moral Man* in 1932 was intended to free politics, both from utilitarian compromise.[33] The most crucial compromisers were those Niebuhr called "the moralists, both religious and secular," good men whose problem was power. They were to remain Niebuhr's favorite chosen audience from then on.

The basic thesis of *Moral Man* was simple: if good men wished to help create a better world, they would have to support methods they themselves might not, as good men, otherwise choose. Politics could not be pursued effectively now as though the better world was already in existence. Niebuhr argued inductively. In two central chapters, using the group-analysis method he had already adopted in the 'twenties, he examined the moral behavior of two types of groups—nations and privileged classes. Neither, he found, could be expected to transcend their interests, and neither, in pursuing their own interests, could be expected to contribute to a new order. In the chapter following, therefore, a third group was examined, the proletariat. The proletariat held a basic potential power, the interests of which did gear into the chances for a new order. This was the basic structure of realism: that social morality was a morality of group interests, that the first consideration for strategy was a calculation of power, that the heart of strategy was to oppose power to power.

Along with this realism about the means, *Moral Man* insisted upon realism about the ends. The goal appropriate to politics was not embodiment of the high ideals of religion. It was justice. Justice was not love; it was equality of one sort or another—an exterior, objective relationship rather than the interior, subjective state of love. In Niebuhr's reading, the origin of justice as an ideal was a little obscure. He could not find it in the

teachings of Jesus, because Jesus taught the sacrificial love of the
Kingdom, not a new social order. At times, he indicated that the
vision of justice was a product of reason. It did crop up in
religion itself, however, as the millennial hope most vividly
expressed in the left wing of the Reformation. Finally, he indicated
that it derived from the life of the proletarians themselves, both
as a reaction against the inequalities from which proletarians
suffered and as a celebration of the rigorous equality in their own
ranks.[34]

The title of the last chapter of *Moral Man,* "The Conflict
Between Individual and Social Morality," like the title of the
book itself, suggested what was eventually to prove the most
fundamental line of modern attack upon liberalism. Justice was
the climax of social morality, the goal of politics. Love, on the
other hand, could be approximated only between individuals. An
unjust society could frustrate love and indeed chill it at birth,
and love could therefore demand justice. But justice did not
guarantee love. Social morality did not exhaust individual
morality. It was not in politics, not in solving their social problems,
that men understood the nature of human nature and fulfilled
their lives.

Justice did remain a more relevant standard for politics than
love, however. Like love, it was always able to suggest higher
possibilities in any given situation. It could never be exhausted
as a source of criticism and inspiration. At the same time, unlike
love, it presupposed the competition of life with life. It presupposed both permanent and fortuitous recalcitrances of man
and nature. Pursuit of equality did not demand that conflict be
dissolved and all men socialized, for what was pursued was not
an end to conflict, but equality in the conflict. Justice did not
require inner revolutions in seeking its outer ones.[35]

With this, Niebuhr's departure from the social gospel was clear.
In the broad center of the social gospel, allied to the church
culture, idealism was actually a corruption of the true gospel of
love, and this corruption was not realistic, only prudent, leading
to a politics both too weak and too conservative for the times.
The strategy of preaching to the top had no sanction either, not

because it had no value, but because it fed on illusions about the nature of power. Paths like those of Page and Ward—the absolute means and the absolute ends—were shut off. It was not that Page's nonviolence was useless, but that it could be justified only on pragmatic grounds, not as a religious absolute. As for Ward, the utopian myth ended in confusion all around, sanctioning fanatic means out of touch with realities, and an ideal society swallowing up the individual.

What then was the proper route? By 1928, Niebuhr was already into third-party activity in the League for Independent Political Action. In 1932 he supported the Socialist party, and continued to do so during the decade. From the middle 'thirties he consistently supported the idea of a new mass party, "educated" by the Socialist party. The reasons for this course were complex, gathering up most of the frustrations and contradictions haunting any effort to attack liberalism on American soil. For the present we can deal with the simplest of them. Realism required something more than a liberal analysis of society, and this Niebuhr found in class analysis, in which the economic faults of the old system were linked to its injustices, the two together pointing unmistakably to the proper political response. "Mass production requires mass consumption; and capitalism is unable to provide mass consumption. From this basic ill of modern society all other defects seem to spring." [36] The role of the Socialist party was to teach and work toward solution to this illness of the times.

> The building of [a mass American labor] movement is just begun or hardly begun. In fact, it is so much in the stage of infancy that exact specifications for the strategy of the day of revolution belong in the category of romantic day-dreaming. It is the business of socialists to prove to the workers that nothing but the social ownership of the means of production can heal the sickness of society, and that the attainment of this goal will be something more than a picnic or a parliamentary debate. Beyond that, it is not necessary to go. [37]

This was something more than the old liberal instinct that, contemplating a world of brotherhood and industrial democracy, could call itself socialist. It was that old instinct in part, certainly, but educated now by a formal sociology of realism, that of Marx.

Marxist socialism had always seemed alien, at least in their understanding of it, to the social-gospel pastors. They had objected to Marxist sanction for violence, to Marxist animus against religion, to Marxist materialism, and to Marxist assignment of an exclusive role in social redemption to the proletariat. Rauschenbusch had expected that socialism in America would take on a "post-Marxist" character, not dogmatically pacifist but not assuming violence as an inevitability. He objected to Marxist antireligiousness; he believed it derived from the experience of European socialism with Roman Catholicism and Protestant state churches. Religion in America—Calvinist, evangelical, liberal, separated from the state, ethical to its marrow—would oppose no such obstacles to socialism as had conservative, official European Christianity. Strictures against Marxist violence continued into the 'thirties. They appeared in Matthew Spinka's *Christianity Confronts Communism* and in E. Stanley Jones' *Christ's Alternative to Communism*. Violence was one of the "negative" factors in Sherwood Eddy's picture of Russia; the evil of violence helped nerve the last phase of A. J. Muste's pilgrimage, his reëntry into the Fellowship of Reconciliation. All this proceeded without notice of those passages in the Marxist canon contemplating peaceful revolution in England and America, and certainly without comprehension of Marxist discussions of violence. The objection to "materialism" was even looser. It was entangled in the vocabulary by which the social-gospel pastors tended to equate the acquisitive spirit or the capitalistic spirit with material greed, a confusion that could hardly be cleared away until sin was relocated in spirit itself, and until the equation of spirit and the spiritual with goodness and idealism was broken. It also confused Marxist materialism with materialistic psychologies, wherein the "higher" motives of men were explained by "reducing" them to biologically based drives. Spinka, Jones, Eddy, and others carried these confusions into the 'thirties as well.[38]

On the other hand, such a non-Marxist as F. E. Johnson of the

Federal Council could see that Marxist materialism was not the materialism against which the churches inveighed.[39] This situation need not be dwelt upon. These were objections to a popular image of Marxism; they never pretended to a systematic or critical understanding of "what Marx really meant." Such an understanding had not been necessary, for the pastors had felt neither in need of nor in fear of Marxism as a political movement. What the pastors hoped to domesticate, when they called it socialism, was not Marxism, for Marxism was a power-political method as well as a vision of coöperative democratic ends. Their socialism was to be a gradual extension of traditional democratic practice into industry, borne by forces already equipped with a philosophy, peacefully, on the spur of idealism and religion, and through class collaboration.

The rejection of this vague socialistic hope for something sharper was symbolized by the organization of the Fellowship of Socialist Christians, and the fellowship stressed one doctrine above all, the role of the proletariat. This doctrine offered Niebuhr a resolution of Rauschenbusch's fear that labor as a class would rise no higher than a bread-and-butter movement. The proper ideal, justice, had in the workers a group more or less automatically prepared to bear it. All perspectives of every class in society, Niebuhr agreed, were relative, but because the proletarians, being disinherited, stood more completely outside modern society than other men, their perspective was relatively purer than others. In the proletariat were fused both the self-interest required to carry any ideal to victory, and the particular ideal, equality, that was both the highest practical norm for politics timelessly and the timely prescription for the specific sickness and crisis of the West.

In *Reflections on the End of an Era,* Niebuhr spoke repeatedly of the "inevitability" of the rule of the workers.[40] That rule was in "the logic of history," and with it, the anarchies and catastrophes of the West would be over. This notion remained somewhere in his thinking throughout the 'thirties. He never tried to substantiate this "inevitability" of proletarian rule by any sort of systematic empiric inquiry. This was not the point, for the attractions in Marxism for Niebuhr did not root primarily in political realism. They were attractions of another order.

For one thing, Marxist celebration of the proletariat tapped that guilt to be found in the social gospel itself, the guilt at the failure of the church community, liberal society, and Christianity generally to make a place for the workers of modern industrial culture.[41] Such guilt had sent pastors onto picket lines in Passaic, Paterson, Utica, Lawrence, as it continued to lead them in the 'thirties, in Toledo, in Flint, at the Republic Steel plant in Chicago, at the mills of the South. Seen through this guilt, Marxist radicalism could appear a secularized version of the worker and peasant discontent expressed in the apocalyptic sects—especially those Anabaptists, Taborites, Fifth Monarchy Men precious to the best of the Protestant tradition.

Such guilt, concentrated in Marxist doctrine, blended into a larger theme as well, of great significance for Niebuhr's emerging theology and philosophy of history. God chooses, he came to say in *The Nature and Destiny of Man*, "the things which are not, to bring to nought things that are." [42] The disinherited would inherit the earth. The strong, through the very implacable assertion of their strength, prepared their own fall; the weak, through their very purification in weakness, were prepared as the agents of the wider order. Here political myth meshed with religious philosophy; in the 'thirties, trying to argue his political and religious realism simultaneously, trying to prove the cogency of one in terms of the other, Niebuhr could not but have found the conjunction tempting. The appeal of the political myth was, that is, extrapragmatic; but only much later would Niebuhr be able to abandon such myths and argue his religious philosophy independently.[43]

Finally, Marxism generally was able to make sense of catastrophe. The Marxist view of the course of history, Niebuhr said, was

> . . . more able to affirm the moral meaning in contemporary chaos than orthodox history, since the latter tends to regard all history as unredeemed and unredeemable chaos. It is superior to liberal Christianity because Christian liberalism is spiritually dependent

upon bourgeois liberalism and is completely lost when its neat evolutionary progress toward an ethical historical goal is suddenly engulfed in a social catastrophe.[44]

Of all the failures of the liberal mind, this was easily the most conspicuous. To the First World War Rauschenbusch had been able to offer nothing but a free-floating imperative. "God is in history," he had written, and then, reflecting the beginning of disturbance in himself, went on: "Where others see blind forces working dumb agony, we must see moral will working toward redemption and education." [45] What was Harry Ward's grim search for totally righteous, totally wise total power but the effort to continue to see? And what, on the other hand, was Kirby Page's pacifism but an effort to see, in a kind of desperate tour de force by which the soul, its fate committed to politics, and in a season of apprehension, projected its own image as the world? Short of such extremities, liberalism was forced to become parochial. In 1940, F. E. Johnson of the council, unwilling to accept sectarian desperation, insisted simply that orderly process was "more normative" than catastrophic, and that the "crisis theology" would pass with the crisis; it was more a European than an American affair anyway.[46] Johnson, that is, found no norms either in the times or in the world outside the United States. There had hardly been a book written by a social-gospel pastor of which it could not have been said that, while perhaps adequate to those situations where politics had not carried close to conflict, it had nothing to say where politics had. Marxism carried the great prestige that it sought to give meaning and coherence to an era of storm and struggle without forsaking hopes for a more ethical social order.

The economic problem of consumption, the role of the proletariat, and the problem of crisis then all came together, fused in Marxism, to emphasize that realism meant separation from the politics of the moralists. After the 1932 campaign, Niebuhr became even more involved with Socialist party affairs, eagerly attending upon the confusions of the Detroit convention of 1934. Until 1936 he, along with the other younger "militants" who had wrested control from the old guard of the 'twenties, was optimistic about the future of the Socialist party itself.[47] Then, that future darkening, he was optimistic about the chances for some new alignment, with the socialists the intellectual core of a new mass party. The outlines of this party were not clear. In 1937, Niebuhr found it pleasing that the smaller parties of the left seemed willing to coöperate in a new organization, but of course they obviously could not constitute a new mass organization in themselves. The key to a mass party was labor, and the key to labor was the CIO. Niebuhr was watchfully hopeful, but soon it appeared that the CIO was planning political action entirely in union hands, offering radical and liberal groups no choice but absorption and uncritical support of labor candidates. The crisis came in New York, where labor leaders undertook to free themselves from the Democratic party by organizing the American Labor party, without satisfactory participation for socialists. Once the American Labor party appeared, the New York vote for the Socialist party collapsed, and the death knell was ringing. The Socialist party would have to resign itself to the role of a socialistic educational force within labor ranks. If socialism was to come, a farmer-labor party, "gradually schooled by necessities," would have to be its instrument.[48]

All this was an effort to follow out the basic strategical duties laid upon the realistic idealist by the analysis in *Moral Man* and *Reflections on the End of an Era,* and even more important, the polemical duties laid upon the realistic theologian, intent upon convicting liberal religion of its errors. The difficulties were immense. The disruption of an already battered Socialist party by the American Labor party testified to the morale of uninstructed, unenlightened trade-unionism. But Niebuhr did not give up the third-party hope easily. In 1940, "a genuine farmer-labor party of national scope" still belonged "to the inevitabilities of American politics. It may come in four years and it may not come until eight years hence." [49] Niebuhr was calling for a third-party movement once again in 1944.

Not until he helped organize Americans for Democratic Action (ADA) did Niebuhr abandon this controlling hope. With the

ADA, in the postwar years, he accepted the established two-party system, never to resume his nearly twenty years of agitation on the fringe. Not until then could he allow his sense of disaster to seek something other than direct, literal political expression. Even then, however, Niebuhr was not accepting the mainstream of liberal politics. The virtues in the American political system, which he was then able to see, he explained in terms of "conservatism" in the classic sense of Burke, for which he found a classic religious basis in the realism of Augustine.[50] There was never to be a return to the utilitarian middle, confusing religion and politics; the illusions of liberalism still remained to be attacked.

This ultimate result reëmphasizes the point that, in following the Socialist party and using categories drawn from Marxism, Niebuhr was doing more than simply responding to prospects of disaster that "the moralists, both religious and secular," refused to see. He was also trying to justify his way of seeing the facts in the first place. This new way, this new perspective, was not simply political, but religious. Behind what could have been thought to be the simplicity of his political loyalties there had been the utmost complication, the result of Niebuhr's emergence as the religious, as well as the political, exponent of realism.

XIV

Reinhold Niebuhr: Religion and Politics

Social-gospel pastors tried to give positive political and economic content to religious ideas. Niebuhr's thought, on the other hand, was "a gradual theological elaboration of what was at first merely socio-ethical criticism." [1] He was unable to ground his "timely" analysis of the crisis of the West except in "timeless" theological categories. Among the neo-orthodox, religious ideas were "critical"; they were not intended to have unambiguous positive political content, but rather to provide a context for politics.

The remarkable conclusion to a book of social, political, and economic analysis was the last chapter of *Reflections on the End of an Era,* entitled simply "The Assurance of Grace." One of the earlier American followers of Karl Barth, E. C. Homrighausen, at the time pastor of an Indianapolis Reformed church, had already praised *Moral Man and Immoral Society* as the herald of a truly theological approach to social strategy. Homrighausen had himself raised his voice against the social-gospel synthesis; his praise was an example of the first shocks of recognition among the rising neo-orthodox.[2] But "grace" in the *Reflections* was the first positive theology. That had not appeared in *Moral Man*, where Niebuhr had been preoccupied with the integrity of politics and reluctant to jeopardize that integrity. In the *Reflections*, however, he was ready. He gave the sense of crisis a final turn, positing a thoroughly tragic view of the West, and it was out of such pressure that the new theology extruded.[3]

The grace that Rauschenbusch understood, of God and Jesus Christ in history, was not the grace of the *Reflections*. The grace to which Niebuhr was pointing carried no positive guarantees for politics, for society, or for history. It was not a resource that, supplementing the virtue and intelligence of men, guaranteed the Kingdom. It was a resource that consoled men for the fact that the Kingdom was an impossibility in history. Even more, this resource could allay the anxiety of men so that they need not compound the tragedies inevitable in history by insisting upon perfection in history.

This was obviously a resource needed only by those men who felt within themselves a thirst and an ache for the Kingdom in the first place. But the social gospel had been more than an effort to induce such a thirst; it had also reflected the fact that modern history engendered such a thirst in men, willy-nilly. This was one of Niebuhr's important insights about modern times.

> . . . the tendencies of an industrial era are in a definite direction. They tend to aggravate the injustices from which men have perennially suffered; and they tend to unite the whole of humanity in a system of economic interdependence. They make us more conscious of the relations of human communities to each other, than of the relations of individuals within their communities. They obsess us therefore with the brutal aspects of man's collective behavior. They, furthermore, cumulate the evil consequences of these brutalities so rapidly that we feel under a tremendous urgency to solve our social problems before it is too late. As a generation we are therefore bound to feel harassed as well as disillusioned.[4]

History itself was politicalizing the soul. People were being emptied of themselves, given over to the abstractions of social organization.

It was appropriate that grace, a saving power, should be the first clear form of Niebuhr's theology and that it should appear as climax to a volume of political inquiry. It was a decisive break with the social-gospel synthesis, opening a way for the soul to save itself beyond the necessities of society and politics.

If this was the first clear theological break, it was not a line Niebuhr went on to exploit. As soon as he began his "theological elaboration," he also had to begin his defense of its political relevance. Grace was especially vulnerable to the criticism that it allowed escape from political problems altogether, a retreat from timely issues into timeless security, indifferent to history. With the gradual emergence of a whole generation of neo-orthodox spokesmen, Niebuhr was to be criticized for his continuing reluctance to expound such more positive aspects of his theology as grace, those of its elements offering sustenance, direction, and security, and not only criticism. But Niebuhr was directing his theology against illusions in the conviction that those illusions were at the heart of the contemporary crisis. Until the crisis was understood and met, any potential "positive" meaning of neo-orthodoxy could not be clarified, could not, perhaps, even be known.

In this Niebuhr was not, originally, alone. The new theologians as a group began in criticism, and, moreover, in socio-ethical criticism. In the fall of 1933, in the *Christian Century*, John C. Bennett, a Congregationalist, one of the generation of younger theologians coming to maturity in the 'thirties, registered his discontent in an article entitled "After Liberalism—What?" Somewhat more than a year later, Walter Horton of Oberlin, crediting Bennett's article as his inspiration, published *Realistic Theology*, a title expressing the spirit of the attack and naming the discipline to which the attackers were called. Realistic: to be tough-minded about society, about politics, about history, about man. Theology: to set the search for new meaning and realism in the fullest possible context.[5] Not long before, a group of Protestant leaders, most of them stationed in seminaries and universities, most of them in their thirties and forties, had met in

New York City for two days of discussion and debate on pre-circulated papers diagnosing and prescribing for contemporary Protestant thinking. Twice each year, meeting for two days each time, the members of this Theological Discussion Group continued their inquiry through the 'thirties. The organizing hand had been primarily that of Henry Van Dusen of Union Seminary. Members included Bennett, Samuel McCrae Cavert, Robert Calhoun of Yale, Horton, John Mackay of Princeton, Reinhold Niebuhr, Richard Niebuhr, Wilhelm Pauck from Germany, Paul Tillich, and some two dozen others.[6] The appearance of the Theological Discussion Group at the height of social-gospel convulsion, the dominance in its membership of leaders of the social passion generally, confirmed the meaning of *Moral Man and Immoral Society:* the new reformation of Protestantism in America was to be nerved by politics.

The major focus in the realism of this period was critical, and Niebuhr summarized it succinctly in 1939, looking back over the years he had devoted to the attack on liberalism. What was liberalism? "I should say primarily 'faith in man.'"[7] Bennett had pointed the same way in his article of 1933, and Horton had agreed. Agreeing, he uttered the word that the vocabularies of hope and expectation had been sedulous to ignore: "I believe that the basic human difficulty *is* that perversion of the will, that betrayal of divine trust, which is called sin."[8] Men began to speak of "orthodox" Christianity once more, for its insight into this basic human quality.

It took some time for this revival of the ancient doctrine of original sin to crystallize into definitely religious form. With Niebuhr, the process was fulfilled in his masterwork, *The Nature and Destiny of Man*. There, in the opening pages, he provided the basic form of his description of human nature.

> The obvious fact is that man is a child of nature, subject to its vicissitudes, compelled by its necessities, driven by its impulses, and confined within the brevity of the years which nature permits its varied organic forms, allowing them some, but not too much, latitude. The other less obvious fact is that man is a spirit who stands outside of nature, life, himself, his reason and the world.[9]

This was definition in terms of situation, in terms of a system of coördinates—nature and spirit, finite and infinite, time and eternity, necessity and freedom. It was a "religious" definition, for by it man's need for religion was explained. "This essential homelessness of the human spirit is the ground of all religion; for the self which stands outside itself and the world cannot find the meaning of life in itself or the world." [10] Sin was explicable in terms of man's existence in this situation. ". . . man, being both free and bound, both limited and limitless, is anxious. Anxiety is the inevitable concomitant of the paradox of freedom and finiteness in which man is involved. Anxiety is the internal precondition of sin." [11] The fundamental form of sin was the effort to deny the reality of man's situation, that is to say, the claim to have overcome it.

To liberals of the 'thirties—as well as since—there was to be much that was baffling in neo-orthodoxy, but little more affronting than its persistent preaching "against" human nature. The real problem throughout the debate was how sin related to time, to history—more precisely, to politics. The whole meaning of neo-orthodoxy rested here, and most of the difficulties Niebuhr had in arguing his theology clustered here. The best way to begin, in illumination of this problem, is to follow the stages by which Niebuhr's discussion of human nature emerged from socio-ethical criticism into theology, how *Moral Man and Immoral Society* led to *The Nature and Destiny of Man*.

His discussion in *The Nature and Destiny of Man* examined the nature of man in the sense of "each" man. Sin pertained to each individual man (and not only to the individual, but to each act of the individual). The argument was not "individualistic," although it did not draw on evidence in social, political, collective behavior. The book was a treatise in philosophy and theology, not in social psychology.

The argument had begun in social psychology, however. In *Moral Man*, Niebuhr used induction, appealing to observed facts of class and national behavior that showed a higher level of moral life in intimate, organic relations than in the larger group life of classes and nations. The bare fact of the discrepancy was not the

issue; argument joined between those who differed as to the
reasons for the discrepancy. Some clear explanation was necessary. In *Moral Man*, Niebuhr's explanations remained unsettled.
He deepened, but he did not actually go beyond, ideas he had
already used in *Does Civilization Need Religion?* five years before. Again he seemed to find the "complexity" of society the
source of its immorality, complexity making for the "bafflement"
of love and reason. Again he observed that, while men obviously
displayed gregarious, "social" behavior as well as egotistic,
selfish behavior, reason simply added power to both, purifying
neither. And, again, he found no clue in the mere plasticity of
human nature.[12] The portrait in *Moral Man* was the liberal
portrait crumbled, but not yet painted over. Without denying
the power of reason, or the importance of altruistic impulses and
human malleability, Niebuhr rejected the optimistic implications
the social-gospel pastors had drawn from them. At this point he
had no principle to justify his rejection, however. Neo-orthodox
reasoning appeared only here and there in *Moral Man*, submerged, as in *Does Civilization Need Religion?*, in the unorganized induction. It appeared when Niebuhr touched upon
human self-consciousness:

> Self-consciousness means the recognition of finiteness within in-
> finity . . . In all vital self-consciousness there is a note of protest
> against this finiteness . . . [Man's] protest against finiteness makes
> the universal character of his imperial dreams inevitable. In his
> sanest moments he sees his life fulfilled as an organic part of a har-
> monious whole. But he has few sane moments; for he is governed
> more by imagination than by reason and imagination is compounded
> of mind and impulse.[13]

Reflections on the End of an Era exhibited Niebuhr's last effort
to hang his discussion of human nature on a straightforward
"higher-lower" dualism. Here he defined "nature" as the impulse
to universalize the ego even to the point of destroying or en-
slaving all competing forms of life, while defining "spirit" as the
impulse to subject the ego to the universal even to the point of
absorption or self-annihilation. The book's final chapters on grace

followed partly from the impossibility of acting in the world of history in terms of pure spirit. But this nature-spirit dualism was obscure in its heart. If there was such a thing as "pure nature," as distinguished from "pure spirit," it was apparently the "will-to-live." But Niebuhr himself observed that the will-to-live was not an impulse to universalize the ego. That impulse appeared only when the will-to-live was mixed with self-consciousness and reason, and was transmuted into the will-to-power, into the impulse of imperialism: ". . . the imperialistic force in life is not pure nature because imperialism arises only when natural impulses are directed and organized by mind." [14] Reason, however, was not the cause or the inspiration of this imperialism. Another element in the situation somewhere transmuted natural impulses into imperialism, and the *Reflections* did not illuminate it.

This illumination was the achievement of *An Interpretation of Christian Ethics*. In this work Niebuhr first really argued the doctrine of original sin, and in this work the focus of his discussion moved from the collective behavior of man to the nature of man as such. "Men must strive to realize their individual ideals in their common life," he had written in *Moral Man*, "but they will learn in the end that society remains man's great fulfillment and his great frustration." [15] With *Christian Ethics*, the dualism of individual and society was demoted, to simply one among several expressions of a more profound dualism, that of the existence and the essence, the nature and destiny, of man. Man was man's great fulfillment and his great frustration. The shift here was equivalent to a shift from the social-gospel emphasis upon man's relation with his fellow men to an emphasis upon man's relation to God. The analysis had left the social-psychological for the metaphysical and religious. Sin was rebellion against God; it was the pretension of man in his finitude to being absolute. "This explanation of the matter . . . emphasizes the spiritual, rather than the natural, character of human evil. . . ." [16] Sin was rooted not in nature, nor in the "conjunction" of nature and spirit, but in spirit itself. The crucial nature of this shift in perspective was given a clear reading through the concept of anxiety: sin was inevitable. What the orthodox doctrine of original sin was trying to indicate in its myth of the fall of man was sin as "an inevitable fact of human existence, the inevitability of which is given by the nature of man's spirituality. It is true in every moment of existence, but it has no history." [17]

Herewith Niebuhr had his explanation for the immorality of society. In imperialism, the purest concrete expression of sin, men mix "the finite with the eternal and claim for themselves, their nation, their culture, or their class the center of existence." [18] Rooting in the anxiety inherent in the human situation, imperialism was by definition the sin of the "righteous," for imperialism always promulgated its own virtues as apology. It was not a function of the weakness of reason; it was not a function of some antisocial natural impulses. Reason and impulse were both mixed into the thrust of imperialism, but imperialism might increase and flourish with the strength of reason and the goodness of impulse, as well as not. The immorality of society followed, not from the negative qualities and incapacities of men, but from the positive attractions society offered them in their human predicament:

> It is possible for individuals to be saved from this sinful pretension, not by achieving an absolute perspective upon life, but by their recognition of their inability to do so. Individuals may be saved by repentance, which is the gateway to grace . . . But the collective life of mankind promises no such hope of salvation, for the very reason that it offers men the very symbols of pseudo-universality which tempt them to glorify and worship themselves as God.[19]

Thus, in the complexities of society men did not meet the bafflement of their reason so much as the quenching of their anxiety. With a positive eagerness, they fled from themselves and the limitations they could see all too easily in themselves into the myths and illusions of limitlessness offered by society. They, as men, could not be the center of existence, but it, the fortress of their collective security, might be.

In light of such a situation, the basic formula for political morality issued in *Moral Man* now struck deeper. Power was required to restrain power, in order to prevent the rule of religious, not merely political, absolutism.

As soon as sin began to be discussed, some uneasiness was provoked, even among critics of liberalism, that the doctrine might engulf analysis of specific social evils. Walter Horton, in his chastened book of 1934, affirming the profundity of the orthodox insight, nevertheless simultaneously insisted that orthodoxy had not known how to control its insight: ". . . it laid such stress upon sin in general, as a universal human condition, that it failed to grapple realistically with the cause of particular sins." [20] Orthodoxy had failed to recognize that social justice had a place among the things "necessary for salvation." John C. Bennett, similarly, in a book of 1935, *Social Salvation,* pointed out how theologians had disastrously oversimplified the problems of social evil by calling them all sin—as Marxists called them all capitalism and sociologists all complexity or cultural lag. Bennett, therefore, numbered sin as only one of many roots of social evil: cultural lag, complexity, antisocial instincts, capitalism—all had their part. In *Christian Realism* (1941), where he undertook to assimilate the full religious doctrine of sin, Bennett remained intent that it not be used to dampen social action and hopes. "I believe that the liberal optimists of the past generation and the theologians who deduce their view of human possibilities from a dogma of original sin which goes beyond the evidence are both wrong." [21]

What was the relationship of the doctrine of sin to responsible social and political action? This was the problem Niebuhr had given himself, and it was not answered simply in the insights of *An Interpretation of Christian Ethics.* At times he came close to what Horton and Bennett feared, swallowing up every proximate explanation of injustice in one ultimate explanation: ". . . all evil in human life is derived from an effort to transmute finite values into infinites, to seek infinite power and infinite wealth and infinite gratification of desire." "There are no forms of historical reality which do not contain this sinful admixture." [22] Yet he did not intend to substitute original sin for inertia or nature or capitalism or complexity, or any other "horizontal" explanations

of social injustice. Sin was a kind of field of force in which all
human life proceeded, not one among other causes, but, no matter
how ambiguous the logic, a different dimension. There were no
phenomena that could be isolated strictly as products of original
sin, as distinguished from other phenomena isolated as products
of complexity or capitalism or bad instincts. Sin was a religious
category which in itself did not deny explanations of social evils
drawing upon the sciences. It was a limiting concept, preventing
such explanations from pretending to be exhaustively, totally
sufficient. Classic doctrine was not to replace politics.

Niebuhr's intentions here needed no proof beyond his own
vigorous political activity. Nevertheless, he had to make it formally clear that neo-orthodoxy did not mean withdrawal from
politics, and this he endeavored to do in his criticism of Karl
Barth. This criticism was sometimes a little wooden, a little me-
chanical, for there were few American Barthians in view. American liberals were pointing to Barthianism, however, as proof of
the dangers of orthodoxy, and so Niebuhr took position.

He was a little time taking it. Barth did not appear on the
American scene as more than rumbling and rumor until the late
'twenties. Niebuhr reviewed his first book in translation, *The
Word of God and the Word of Man*, late in 1928.[23] His criticisms
without exception were all to be found empty within a few years.

Barth, Niebuhr said in 1928, was "not even above describing
the ethics of the sermon on the mount as the definition of the
ultimate ethical ideal which man can never reach." Just seven
years later, in *Christian Ethics*, Niebuhr himself was speaking of
love as the "impossible" pinnacle of ethics. Barth, he said in
1928, "in order to escape the relativism of a theology which is
based upon and corrected by biology, psychology, social science,
philosophy and every other field of knowledge," put forth a
theology "which has no other way of authenticating itself except
by the fact that it meets a human need. This is a sorry victory.
Relativism may be defeated but at the price of a new and more
terrifying subjectivism." Just such an extrication of theology from
dependence upon the sciences was part of the meaning of *The
Nature and Destiny of Man*; just such an analysis of religion in

light of the human need inherent in the human situation constituted Niebuhr's own procedure from the time of *Christian
Ethics.* "We can," Niebuhr said in 1928, "escape relativity and
uncertainty only by piling experience upon experience, checking
hypothesis against hypothesis, correcting error by considering
new perspectives, and finally by letting the experience of the
race qualify the individual's experience of God." Such a broad,
social concept of evidence he never discarded, certainly, but
from 1934 on, Niebuhr drew more and more explicitly on a kind
of individual analysis, concluding eventually that the ultimate
evidence for neo-orthodoxy could only be found in the self. There
was no "finally" in the testimony of the race.

Thus, by the early 'thirties, Niebuhr was arguing in opposite
fashion, charging that Barthianism was *not* meeting men's needs
in the life they actually lived. A return to issues transcending
time and history, Barthianism also, he said, tragically abandoned
the issues of time and history. Niebuhr continued to show some
indecision in this criticism, for he was hitting Barthians rather
than Barthianism. Barth himself refused to be smoked out on the
application of his theology to social problems. It was Friedrich
Gogarten who, applying the theology, was moving further toward
the right, to the point of reaction and fascism. It was Emil Brunner who, applying the theology, and even as an avowed enemy
of capitalism, had helplessly been able to find no sanctions for
a realistic politics for social change. Brunner was able to support
nothing more than a defensive politics, holding the social dikes
against disorder, breakdown, and convulsion. Niebuhr himself
hinted at the necessity for some sort of distinction between
Barthians and Barthianism, by prefacing criticism with the un-
expanded comment that a "modified" social radicalism was in
fact compatible with Barthianism.[24]

The hint was not pursued. In his Gifford lectures in Edinburgh,
Niebuhr attacked Barthian theology once more. Barth de-
preciated the human and human needs in his static polarization
of man and God. Barth imperiled the moral relativities of history
in his exclusive emphasis upon the religious fact of the sinfulness
of all men. In his pretense to describe God as person and never-

theless as "wholly other," Barth merely suppressed his real reasoning, which was to derive the concept of personality from human life—the only source from which it was possible to derive it. Speaking only of the Kingdom, or eternity, above history, Barth plunged history itself into meaninglessness, and lost the Biblical concept of the Kingdom at the end of history. In his denial of any "point of contact" between man and God, except the point that God, for inscrutable reasons, deigned to supply in one single special revelation, Barth rendered meaningless the idea of man as made in the image of God.[25] In all this, Niebuhr adopted an attitude toward Barth similar to that adopted by Niebuhr's own liberal critics toward himself.

As noted previously, Barth had once been a Christian in politics. In the years before the First World War he had been active in the Swiss religious socialism inspired by pastors Kutter and Ragaz. Like Niebuhr, except that it happened some sixteen or seventeen years earlier, Barth had known his season of crisis. The war credits voted by the German Social Democrats in 1914 were an analogue to the crash on Wall Street in 1929—except that the one was much more painful, for Barth had expected much from the Social Democrats, Niebuhr little from unreconstructed capitalism. Elmer Homrighausen, in a reply to one of Niebuhr's criticisms of Barth, insisted upon the importance of this background. The Barthian revolt, he declared, followed from and was based upon the social problem. Barth, said Homrighausen, was a real alternative in America.[26]

It was exceedingly doubtful that Homrighausen could have carried his point. Homrighausen took it that Barth was demanding a shift from the strategy of saving the world through political programs—socialism, syndicalism, reformed capitalism, whatever —to the strategy of reconstructing the human will. This was also the tenor of Richard Niebuhr's criticism of the social gospel, although Richard Niebuhr refused to speak as a Barthian on the ground that Barthianism did not include the vital elements in the American religious tradition.[27] All this, however, looked remarkably like a return to the old social-gospel debate over environmentalism—whether men were to be saved directly or indirectly, through preaching or through nurture. It could not have been to the point for Reinhold Niebuhr. Niebuhr's position forswore the debate over environmentalism completely: politics was not intended to save souls and could not be pursued as though it were.

Niebuhr, on the other hand, never took it upon himself imaginatively to enter into Barth's polemical position in Europe in light of Barth's own religious-socialist past. Instead, he tended to criticize Barth almost wholly from a kind of "timeless" perspective. If the Barthians would leave their studies and go out to act, he wrote, their pessimism would not be so great, for vigorous moral activity created its own sense of expectation. As it was, they were trying to escape the "nicely calculated less and more" perpetually necessary in history and politics. This ignored two possibilities. First, Barthianism might have been, given the historical situation, a "nicely calculated less." Second, vigorous moral activity might, on "timely" considerations, have been thought the source of simply more illusions compounding the troubles of an end of an era. To some extent, this was precisely the view of Paul Tillich. Reinhold Niebuhr did not, in other words, ever really close his argument that Barthianism, in and of itself, as a theology, decreed dangerous strategy.

Some of his difficulty was due to the American scene. Where a man like Barth might find all political alternatives hopeless in Europe, in America he might still feel political hope. Attentive to Europe, Niebuhr himself once likened the European situation to that of the Flood, against which Christians could do nothing but collect those treasures they could and go onto their ark.[28] But he could not imaginatively identify with such a situation, despite his attention, and in rejecting Barthianism, he tended to mix timely with timeless criticism, without nicely calculating the less and the more for Europe on the one hand and America on the other.

In his criticism he did nonetheless reject the idea that neo-orthodoxy allowed politics to be dismissed on principle as religiously irrelevant. Religious fulfillment in God, "beyond" history, at the "end," was nothing more or less than the fulfillment of all meaning and value created and brought to fragmentary, contradictory expression in history. In this historical task, politics remained essential.

This criticism of Barth registered Niebuhr's commitment to politics, but Barthians and orthodoxy were not his important opponents in the 'thirties. Niebuhr's essential aim was, not to keep religion and politics from flying apart, but to break up their fusion. His ideal opponents were those for whom politics had taken on religious dimensions, those who had succumbed to symbols of pseudo-universality proffered by society and politics, and among these there was one plain case.

As Karl Marx had observed, the beginning of all criticism is the criticism of religion, and in criticizing Marxism Niebuhr clarified his theology much more than in criticizing Barth. Marxism was politics in its most imperial form, religion. At the same time, this criticism revealed the razor's edge Niebuhr had to try to walk. As we have seen, he found in Marx strong assistance for his criticism of the liberal moralists, and yet, as early as his earliest use of Marx, he had objections to bring to the Marxist mythology, to everything in Marxism that had a religious, and not simply a political, charge. In *Moral Man*, sweeping the boards of all utopianism, conservative, liberal or radical, he actually directed his sharpest words explicitly to the Marxists:

> The hope that the internal enemies will all be destroyed and that the new society will create only men who will be in perfect accord with the collective will of society, and will not seek personal advantage in the social process, is romantic in its interpretation of the possibilities of human nature and in its mystical glorification of the anticipated automatic mutuality in the communist society . . . Lenin, the brutal realist, when dealing with the realities of today . . . turns sentimentalist when envisaging the possibilities of tomorrow.[29]

Before this sort of criticism could be grounded, Niebuhr's neo-orthodoxy had to emerge. Without it, this insight was as free-floating and unsystematic as Sherwood Eddy's recoil from totalitarianism. Partly because he did not have such ground, Niebuhr found himself entangled in the most contorted, and rather desperate, logic of his career. In the last chapters of *Moral Man* he addressed himself to the question of what chance the proletariat really had to win justice. They had no chance, he said, through revolutionary socialism. They had almost no chance through parliamentary socialism. In other words, justice itself—let alone utopia—was an illusory goal. Yet, a gradual, parliamentary approximation of justice was possible. Even this was not possible, however, without the illusion that full justice was possible, for without such an illusion labor would lose heart. "The abandonment of the eschatological element in socialism means the sacrifice of its religious fervor and the consequent loss of motive power." [30] Therefore, Niebuhr concluded, in magnificent obscurantism, let the illusion be maintained.

Such an answer, similar to George Sorel's prescription of revolutionary myth, was impossible, and Niebuhr soon abandoned it. His deepest reasons were religious, but by 1933 he had abandoned it also on pragmatic political grounds. Clearly, he argued, any successful labor movement, in the United States at least, would need allies from among farmers, professional people, and small-business people. The "fanatic vehemence" generated among proletarians by their illusions of victory would frighten off such allies and thus be self-defeating. Even if proletarians were to win, the harshness of their unaided struggle would lead them to be brutal in victory, thus compromising the justice they had sought.[31]

This sort of pragmatic objection simply exposed the intolerable difficulties in trying to apply Marxist categories, not only on the American scene, but for idealists anywhere. Marxist prophecy of the increasing alienation and degradation of labor, making of this alienation precisely the basis for proletarian victory, asked the idealist indefinitely to suspend his own moral feelings. Anyone who believed that the justice possible here and now was the justice to fight for, as distinguished from some final justice hovering in the ideal future, could find no comfort in it. Niebuhr did not try to follow such Marxist logic in his politics; his eagerness for a new party and for a labor movement was hardly directed at worsening the lot of labor. An active labor movement, plus labor action to win short-range economic gains, would, it is true, be likely to compromise the inner, "subjective," disinterested quality of labor's perspective. But the rise of labor within, not against, the system might go far to allay the basic economic sickness of the system, and thus to allay the crisis, and do so, moreover, without that monopolization of power that was in itself an evil by the standards of realistic ethics. By the late 'thirties, Niebuhr still saw labor as the key to strategy, but quite without those subjective overtones of religious character that had helped attract him to Marxism in the first place.

By the end of the decade, the pages of *Radical Religion* were carrying empiric, inductive criticism, drawn mainly from the American scene, that crumbled even the form of such problems. It was noticed that the technological advance of the industrial system was narrowing, not broadening, the proletarian base. A kind of "new" technological and tertiary middle class was being spawned instead; individual farming was being strengthened, not weakened; labor interests grew less, not more homogeneous; the "natural" political ineptitude of agrarians and small enterprisers seemed to be dissolving; separation of management from ownership opened possibilities for economy-wide planning short of expropriation; the power of the state to enter the economy not as a committee of the ruling class, but rather as something of a stabilizer and fair-rules enforcer, was being demonstrated. Such facts of immediate observation spelled the end of any recognizable use of Marxism for strategical political guidance.[32]

Accordingly, the coherence of Marxist catastrophism grew ambiguous also, as the 'thirties wore on. The need for a philosophy equipped to maintain meaning in the face of catastrophe increased as the threat of war increased, but Marxist meaning was hinged to its increasingly inadequate account of the class struggle. Marxist canon itself, of course, had been extended to explain war, but these explanations seemed increasingly dogmatic and merely deductive, especially from American perspectives, if Harry Ward was any example. More than this, no matter how well Marxism might or might not explain modern wars, it became increasingly evident that it could offer no guarantees at all of what would issue from war, especially in the United States. By 1940, therefore, Niebuhr's criticism of a liberal ethic that could only be engulfed in catastrophe was doubled and trebled, but it could no longer be Marxist criticism in any sense. The stake he saw in the war was the survival of Western democracy, however incomplete, however sick; democratic processes held priority over any logic of how socialism might be plucked from hours of chaos.

With respect to all these facets of Marxism, Niebuhr thus had narrowly pragmatic ground on which to reject it. But it was not such strictly pragmatic ground that supported his deepest assault. His decisive criticism of Marxism bore against its specifically religious character, its eschatology, and here his criticism of modern politics culminated, for here he found its very idealism wrong. Once again the evil he ferreted out was utopianism. It was not only that the Marxist utopia inspired fanatic vehemence; it lived on the illusion that justice as such would guarantee human value.

He made this criticism specific in *Reflections on the End of an Era.* In *Does Civilization Need Religion?* he had already stressed the depersonalization wrought by the economic system. In *Moral Man,* his attention bore wholly upon the economic injustices of the system, and in the *Reflections,* he organized his discussion even more sharply in terms of problems of injustice and mass consumption. But in the *Reflections* he also returned to the older theme and analyzed bourgeois civilization in terms of personality. A critical paradox appeared: the outstanding achievement of bourgeois civilization was its discovery and affirmation of the individual, but this affirmation had come to work to the submergence of the individual. Sprung loose from the old controls of hierarchy, tradition, status, family, craft, community, the individual had been sprung loose so far that he was in danger of falling into the mass, of losing his individuality in the crowd. Mechanistic and rationalistic culture disintegrated organic bonds and threatened new, more political, more abstract ones. The individual was being politicalized. The question then arose: was an answer to the economic inequalities and anarchy of capitalism necessarily an answer to the depersonalization of capitalism? No.

> There are indications that communism will substitute a mechanistic collectivism for the mechanistic individualism of a bourgeois civilization . . . In this, as in some other respects, communism is too much the child of capitalism and lives too much by a precise negation of the vices of the latter to bring real peace and happiness to mankind.[33]

In fact, the communist response deepened the evil, for communism sought consciously to rationalize what bourgeois culture had rationalized only unconsciously and indirectly and, often enough, to its regret once done. That is, communist rationalization, as we have seen Ward preach it, was not so much extension of control over those economic-political areas left in conflict by capitalism, as it was a reverse penetration of every last center of organic life remaining—the community, the craft, the family, diet, hobbies, the full range of the personality. It was a fulfillment of, not a protest against, politicalization: ". . . communism reveals itself to be the victim and not the nemesis of a capitalistic civilization, destined not to correct the weaknesses of a bourgeois culture but to develop them to the last impossible and absurd consistency." [34]

More will be said of this level of analysis. Niebuhr himself did not pursue it, although it opened the way for resolution of the leading problems with which he was always to wrestle. Such resolution was approached more closely in the work of Paul Tillich, whose relation to Niebuhr will be discussed. Niebuhr, intent upon the timely problems of capitalistic breakdown, was not willing to risk the dilution of his political realism by a criticism of Marx that might seem to draw on standards too far removed, too "timeless" for immediate use. But this one sharp sociological criticism of communism demonstrated the controlling level of his rejection of Marx.

As a political religion, Marxism demonstrated that the crisis of Western politics was a crisis of religion, and that the crisis of both religion and politics was identical with the fact that politics had become religion. Men's sense that the world was a realm of meaning and coherence was at stake in politics. The doctrine of God as Creator was at stake. The situation had come about following bourgeois identification of religion with history. Political religion, seeking to meet the breakdowns of laissez-faire harmony, was simply a more drastic form of the liberal synthesis—the abstractions to which men submitted themselves simply a little more emptied of individuality, men's personal resources of security and significance simply a little more at the mercy of more nearly universal policies. There was in truth no politics that alone could meet the situation in the West, however realistic, however balanced. Until the magic circle was broken and religion was seen to point at least beyond politics and the power of rational social efficiency, if not "beyond history," the storm and struggle would not come to an end before they grew worse, political religions would continue to precipitate out of a culture that knew religion only as projection and completion of human perfections: ". . . it will be necessary for our generation to return to the faith of prophetic Christianity to solve its problems." [35]

Calling, in *Moral Man*, for politics adapted to the times, Niebuhr thus ended by calling for religion adapted to the times and to all times. Did he in fact, however, establish that prophetic neo-orthodoxy had "timely" significance? In *Reflections on the End of an Era*, he had hesitated. "When the hard realities of history have once again dissipated the utopian dreams of the present the emphasis of classical religion upon the experience of grace will find its way back again into the moral and religious life of the race." [36] Did he then, insisting that "our generation" could not solve its problems without a return to prophetic Christianity, consign that generation simply to "hard realities," as necessary preparation for such a return?

To a very large extent, he did: it was part of his realism. It would not do to "believe too much in words . . . the vicissitudes of history . . . determine the time and season when illusions wax and wane. . . ." [37] So far as the chances that realistic religion would be understood at the end of an era were concerned: "A Christian-prophetic interpretation of life is at a disadvantage in periods when the total dimensions of life are obscured by specific perils and immediate possibilities." [38]

What, then, did prophetic religion mean at the end of an era but the extrication of a few from their illusions? The most Niebuhr was able to say in the mid-'thirties was that it is always possible at least to discover the fallacies behind the illusions and "thus to guard against them even when their time was ripe." It was just such a guard, such a moderation, that he invoked in rejecting, after his momentary tour de force in *Moral Man*, the "illusion" that might inspire the workers. Certainly "the moralists, both religious and secular," no matter how few they might be, might be diverted from adding to the illusions of an era in which politics was being divinized—without, of course, throwing them into the apolitical despair of orthodoxy. Otherwise, apparently, "hard realities" were required to educate the times.

This element in Niebuhr was perhaps the deepest testimony to his will to face facts. He cannot be understood as though he invented neo-orthodoxy as the solution to the problem of the times. He could not fall back into the classic liberal argument, that "if only" men would believe, all would be well. Of course, if neo-orthodoxy were to become the faith of all men, it would be the way out from the disastrous alternatives Niebuhr saw in Western history; but so would liberalism, if all men believed. Niebuhr, however, appreciated that there were timely obstacles to belief. Not calculated "study," but "the pressure of world events" had inspired his religious turn, along with his political turn.[39] Not clean, logical, unbroken lines of positive argument, but the broken, often incomplete lines of "the gradual exclusion of alternative beliefs" made up the plot. Neo-orthodoxy was what was left after faith in social science, in liberalism, in Marxism (as well as in apolitical orthodoxy, conservatism, etc.) was excluded.

The Christian mind that Niebuhr found in St. Paul, Augustine, Luther, Kierkegaard, was a thing of extremes, unified, but unified only at high tension, a mind that sought to face and embrace the extreme before it sought unity, because the extreme had already come upon it and no unity but false unity could be gained by ignoring it. It was a mind that knew violence and catastrophe, personal and political, not as mistakes, not as cultural lag, not as the work of peculiarly bad and selfish men, but as real experience, experience that, bound into the existence of the self, therefore had to be given ultimate meaning.

The political experiences of the West were such existential experiences for Niebuhr, and neo-orthodoxy was the philosophy by which they took on meaning for the self. But the political world Niebuhr accepted as his own was vast; no other American Protestant leader was as attentive to Europe. The themes of struggle and catastrophe, of fanaticism to the right and fanaticism to the left, of utopians demanding the politicalization of the heart, were hardly too lurid for the portrait of European man.

Were they appropriate for America?

To this persistent problem of the American intellectual, of how to let Europe instruct America, there were no satisfactory answers. Niebuhr wished to make no special concessions to American conditions. He did not reject Barth in the name of American conditions; he did not find Barth healthy even for Europe. The social struggle described in *Moral Man* and the *Reflections,* though overwhelmingly dependent upon evidence drawn from Europe, was intended to include America; Niebuhr assimilated America into the analysis by postponing the climactic struggles to one distant year or another. As a consequence of the postponement, those struggles might be less tragic and more instructive, but the basic model was the same. Nor did Niebuhr reject Marxism in the name of American conditions, but in the name of an apprehension actually fed more by European than by American facts. In sum, the empiric field that led him to the field of human nature, the field in which neo-orthodoxy flourished, was not centered on America.

Did American politics in the 'thirties testify to the nature of man in the same way? If the method of proof for neo-orthodoxy was the exclusion of alternatives, did American experience exclude the alternative of liberalism—neither Barth nor Marx—upon which Niebuhr had launched his first attacks, the liberalism of immediate as well as ultimate optimism, of "utilitarianism" mixing religion and politics into a kind of progressive social morality? This problem of the "fit"—or lack of it—between neo-orthodoxy and American conditions confronted Niebuhr, after all, in neither Barth nor Marx, who were not major alternatives for American culture at large even in the 'thirties. It confronted him in the liberal moralists, and most specifically, in the men of the social gospel.

In *Moral Man and Immoral Society*, the only men Niebuhr criticized by name who could be numbered in social-gospel ranks —William Adams Brown and Justin Wroe Nixon—were not prophets at heart, organizing their work by the social gospel, but sympathizers, cautious, unsystematic, breathing accommodation and prudence. Social-gospel idealism was nonetheless one of Niebuhr's main targets, and in *An Interpretation of Christian Ethics*, he took pains to make it clearer, mentioning Shailer Mathews, Gerald Birney Smith, the Federal Council, Francis McConnell, E. Stanley Jones—and Walter Rauschenbusch. The collection was helter-skelter. But Niebuhr here indicated that the crucial feature of the social gospel was to be found among those who recognized the social struggle and understood that something like socialism was necessary. Their error was their insistence upon tidy, nonviolent means—upon pacifism. Rauschenbusch, for instance, Niebuhr said, was a much more vigorous and realistic thinker than most of the prophets, but, squarely inside the liberal tradition, Rauschenbusch had had no conception of the class struggle and believed that the better society could be won through purely educational and moral means.[40]

In this criticism, Niebuhr was on poor ground in two respects. First, he was wrong in his notion of what Rauschenbusch had said. Second, liberal pastors reluctant to accept the harsh realism of *Moral Man* were by no means being forced to accept it by hard realities in America; they had the New Deal.

Rauschenbusch had recognized the class struggle. Nor did he, recognizing it, proceed immediately to deplore it: "Truth is mighty. But for a definite historical victory a given truth must depend on the class which makes that truth its own and fights for it." [41] Rauschenbusch had not been vague about which class he expected to make the truth of socialism its own; nor had he left more ambiguity about the verb "to fight" than was left after the involved debates of 1932 to 1934: ". . . the Christian idealists must not make the mistake of trying to hold the working class down to the use of moral suasion only, or be repelled when they hear the brute note of selfishness and anger." [42] This was a sentiment worthy of *Moral Man*, but Rauschenbusch had uttered it.

Rauschenbusch wrote in a season of pragmatic hope and confidence, certainly: socialism was to be the extension of progressivism. Niebuhr wrote in a context of pessimism: socialism was to be a rescue from disaster. But the fact remained that Rauschenbusch's conception of political strategy was not an appropriate windmill for Niebuhr's tilting. Where then did their differences lie?

The issue between them lay not in politics as such, but in the relationship between politics and religion. Rauschenbusch's effort to domesticate the concepts and vocabulary of religion to the field of politics, or better, to the field of social morality, his effort to equate salvation with morality, was what Niebuhr's criticism really caught. The price Rauschenbusch paid for this effort cost him much more on the side of religion than on the side of politics. Insisting, like Niebuhr, upon equality as the goal of politics, Rauschenbusch did not, as did Niebuhr, radically distinguish equality—justice—from perfect mutuality, or the Kingdom; he identified it with the Kingdom. Rauschenbusch, with his synthesis of religion and politics, differed from Niebuhr more on the side of religion than on the side of politics.

The similarity of his politics to Niebuhr's did not mean that their religious differences were irrelevant to politics. Under certain conditions, such religious differences told politically. But what were those certain conditions? They were only the conditions Niebuhr had dwelt upon in *Moral Man* and the *Reflections:* "hard realities," the "almost dogmatic" certainty of an hour of decision, class struggle, flirtation with disaster. When men who lived by the social-gospel fusion of religion and politics faced such conditions, then they could go only in one of two ways. They could go the way of Kirby Page, into pacifism at the expense of relevance, or the way of Harry Ward, into revolutionary myth, the one a kind of nonpolitics, the other a kind of absolute politics.

But the American scene did not force the vision of *Moral Man* upon the liberal pastors. The liberal pastors had available to them liberal politics that averted disaster, held back hard realities, finessed class struggle, ignored hours of decision, in a word, stole the ground from under both Barth and Marx. The 'thirties in America were not giving political illustration that essential homelessness to which neo-orthodoxy was a response. America still remained "home," the "moral society" that had already been both hope and reality in the social-gospel synthesis. In such a situation, how was neo-orthodoxy to be argued? When liberalism was a political success, the "conservative" religion Niebuhr had recommended might appear as groundless as his "radical" politics. Why call man a sinner when the center still held?

The New Deal faced all the pastors with a complex of dilemmas. In some instances these dilemmas were simply finessed. This was the course of the sectarians, such as Page and Ward, in their opposite ways. For them, trying to conserve pure religious logic in their politics, the facts and fortunes of the New Deal did not play upon theory, to instruct it, modify it, enrichen it, perhaps convert it. They were, as sectarians, anesthetized against the pragmatic present. Niebuhr and those, roughly, of the Fellowship of Socialist Christians, also exhibited some anesthetization. But although the pages of *Radical Religion* displayed a kind of dogmatic intransigence in discussion of the New Deal, this was grounded not in a will to save religious politics, but in a will to prove the necessity of realism. Anesthetization was least, sensitivity highest, where the old social-gospel logic was still rooted in the culture-community of the church, and still responded to prudent, defensive interests. Here the New Deal was anxiously followed as a defense against breakdown as well as a way to justice, and here, in the *Christian Century* and the Federal Council, the oldest danger reappeared, the danger of emptying religious vocabulary of its ideal meaning in the process of lending it to support utilitarian achievements.

In the first years of the New Deal, socialist criticism actually had two targets. On the one hand, there was the New Deal itself. On the other hand, there were certain attitudes about the New Deal. Logically the two were not necessarily superimposed. An editorial in the *World Tomorrow* in August, 1933, made the division neatly. "An easy method of determining the cast of mind of students of politics . . . is to note their attitude toward the N.R.A." [43] Those who hailed a victory for "the principles of social control," those who prophesied recovery, those who rejoiced over business coöperation with the program—all such were liberals, and unrealistic. On the other hand, there were distinct gains in the substitution of state capitalism for the anarchy of laissez faire, and only radical romantics could imagine that radicalism in the United States possessed morale enough and power enough to profit from a collapse.

Clearly distinguished here from the Chicago Call-to-Action apocalypticists (who wished to "foment discontent"), from Ward, and from the Revolutionary Policy Committee of the Socialist party, all of whom hearkened to the rumble of an impending hour of decision as though they were prepared for it, this judgment hinged, actually, not so much on the rescue-action aspect of the New Deal as upon a tacit estimate that social collapse had not been quite as close as these others believed. It was always to Niebuhr's polemical interests as against the liberals to insist upon the gravity of a situation, but it was also to his interests not to let pessimism become free-floating and thereby justify romantic perfectionist revolutionaries and despairing sectarians. Thus, this judgment was followed by his comment that a social system in its heyday in 1929 would not be supplanted by 1935 or 1945 without intermediate stages. The New Deal was such an intermediate stage. It was an intermediate stage, not fascism. Unlike Harry Ward, the socialist realists never charged fascism against the New Deal; the possibility that fascism might emerge depended, they declared, upon further, future events; the New Deal itself was neither seed of fascism nor its herald.

Such criticism, distinguishing between right and wrong appreciation of the New Deal, remained a line perfectly compatible with both Niebuhr's ethical realism and his socialist tactics. In fact, however, the line he chose and followed through Roosevelt's second term was that of attack on the New Deal itself. While he never failed to interrupt his criticism to help support the New Deal against its critics on the right—whether laissez-faire ideologues of the National Association of Manufacturers, spokesmen for the new sophisticated businessmen, conservative Democrats, conservative Supreme Court judges, or the Republican-voting middle-class Protestant congregations—he did not develop anything like the line of "loyal criticism" potential in the concept of the New Deal as an intermediate stage.

This was related, of course, to his apparently purely pragmatic estimates of the scene. In 1933 and 1934 his sense of crisis was at its sharpest; this was the period of his fullest use of Europe to instruct America, his fullest use of Marxist analysis (though not Marxist mythology), and his clearest rejection of American exceptionalism, in *Reflections on the End of an Era:* nothing was gained, either in analytic clarity or in political effectiveness, by taking what was different in America and using it to argue that America could escape the logic of the end of the era. In 1935 and 1936 he remained optimistic about prospects for the Socialist party itself, and thereafter about prospects for a new mass party. In addition, Niebuhr estimated that the chances for shaking down the Democratic party into a party of liberal policy—let alone anything more—were faint. Roosevelt's defeats in 1937 on the Supreme Court bill and on wages and hours highlighted, Niebuhr said, the strength of the party's Southern and Eastern conservatives. A year later, after congratulating the President upon the honesty of his efforts to unshackle himself from the Southern conservatives, Niebuhr concluded: ". . . the impossibility of ridding the Democratic party of its dependence upon southern landlordism and northern municipal corruption will probably result in the formation of a new party sometime after 1940." Finally, early in 1939, the decline of Roosevelt's star in Washington was apparent, Niebuhr thought. No plausible candidate had appeared to succeed him, the right-wing Democrats therefore no longer feared to oppose him, and for 1940, either a Republican or a conservative Democrat could be expected in the White House.[44]

Actually, undoubtedly in face of this prospect, a shift in the tone and manner of Niebuhr's criticism was already in progress. There had always been some degree of "unattached" feeling in his criticism from the first, only loosely—if at all—organized into socialist analysis, drawing essentially upon the impatience of the idealist, always liable to eschatological outbursts. Thus, in 1935, Niebuhr carefully pointed out the failure of all the supposed left-wing influence in the administration to bring about any "essential change in the division of the total national income between the owners and the workers of the nation."[45] As a test of less than two years of power, this withdrew what the editorials of 1933 had conceded, that there was a virtue in interim policy. Desperate situations were sought out to emphasize the meagerness of achievement; thus, the lot of the Southern workers was used to goad the readers of *Radical Religion,* a lot which, with the cotton-picking machine, "will probably become the most desperate situation faced by any group of workers in the civilized world."[46] Roosevelt himself drew fire: the nation "has chosen a messiah rather than a political leader, committed to a specific political program; and unfortunately the messiah is more renowned for his artistic juggling than for robust resolution."[47] As late as 1938, Roosevelt—though patently better than his reactionary critics—did not know where he was going: ". . . no final good can come from this kind of whirligig reform. Sooner or later it will produce a violent reaction."[48] The New Deal was merely insulin, warding off death without giving the patient strength.

Nevertheless, Niebuhr had already credited the President with carrying the Democratic party further to the left than anyone had thought possible, and in the pessimism of 1939 he spoke of holding to what had been gained. There was one critical gain:

"The Wagner Act is the Czechoslovakia of our domestic politics. If this gives way, it will be difficult to stem the tide of reaction." [49] Apparently it had not all been insulin and whirligig. Then, after once more reënsuring himself against illusions ("We must not be beguiled by Mr. Roosevelt.") Niebuhr found contemporary history in the fall of 1939 teaching the importance of short-range tactics as well as of long-range strategy, and during the campaign hopefully anticipated the President's freedom of action after the election.[50]

For Niebuhr, as for the social passion generally, the campaign of 1940 was dominated by the debate over foreign policy, soon to become bitter, soon to become a new line of fracture within the passion. The campaign offered reason, and also an excuse, for abandoning the Socialists for Roosevelt. Not only was it, after three votes for Thomas as a Socialist, not possible to vote for Thomas as an isolationist, but the Socialist party had become too insubstantial, too merely strategical, and the New Deal and Roosevelt too concrete, practical, and tactical. Niebuhr believed the President had shown more foresight in his preparedness program than his critics—Niebuhr included. But more than that, in the spring of 1941 the whole perspective on eight years was shifted. The President, Niebuhr now wrote, was putting up a heroic fight to keep the planned economy of the defense program under democratic control. He had made collective bargaining mandatory at a time when there were no labor partners to such bargaining. He had set Sidney Hillman in defense councils at a time when labor was spending itself in internecine war and blocking defense measures.

> For eight years now the democratic will of the Administration has shown more strength than the democratic forces in the country as a whole—a most paradoxical situation, a blow in the face of the easy theory that government is a committee of the ruling class for keeping down the ruled.[51]

This was the record—one of supersensitive, jealous fear of being taken in ("We must not be beguiled. . . .")—concluding in generous reappraisal. Even then, for several years, Niebuhr continued to hanker after a new party altogether, but not because the New Deal had been nothing but insulin and whirligig.

What must be seen in this record is that much more than purely pragmatic judgments were involved. Once he began to expound neo-orthodoxy, Niebuhr had polemical commitments to which the New Deal posed exasperating difficulties. *Moral Man* was intended as a demonstration of the inadequacy of the politics of the liberal moralists; neo-orthodoxy was intended as a theology adequate to the hard realities of politics—as well as of human existence generally. Niebuhr had made the association perfectly explicit in his *Reflections:* "In my opinion adequate spiritual guidance can come only through a more radical political orientation and more conservative religious convictions than are comprehended in the culture of our era." [52] The New Deal thus jeopardized the argument for the new religious Word itself. Enveloped in a fog of moralistic illusions among its supporters, guided by unstrategical, untactical, opportunistic thinking, the government program seemed another manifestation of a culture blending religious and political morality into utilitarian harmony. It frustrated the urgency for disentangling the religious from the ethical altogether. Supporting the New Deal, liberals could resist the religious turn to the right along with the political turn to the left.

This extrapragmatic charge in Niebuhr's criticism of the New Deal could be seen directly in the fact that he strained his own principles of political realism. At this point, the New Deal, quite apart from its liberalism, challenged both Niebuhr and the whole tradition of the social gospel. The deepest polemic in *Moral Man* had not been against poverty or injustice or selfishness; that had been taken for granted. It was against irresponsibility. The moralists, Niebuhr was saying in effect, tried to live in an ideal future. They were asking that the present become the future before they would do anything about it. To be responsible, however, is to be able to make choices in the present, no matter how hard they may be. Throughout the 'thirties, unfortunately, the Socialist party was little occupied with formulating responsible alternatives to New Deal policies. Socialists could not responsibly content themselves with complaints that the President did not institute socialism. As socialists, they knew that the hour for socialism had not come; as democrats, they were not anxious to pretend to be forcing the hour and thus risk giving over the future to a righteous revolutionary handful. Their complaints could properly be directed mainly at the political public; their task could properly be to reconstitute that public. A proper part of this basically educational and not political task was of course to puncture illusions about the New Deal, to resist beguilement. But, stopping here, this left the socialist in the position of having nothing to say about responsible politics in the present. What should have guided the responsible Christian statesman in the 'thirties? Socialism had no answer. It had an answer only for the 'fifties or 'sixties, perhaps. Even so, the claim of socialist politics to responsibility might have been maintained, through unremitting, concrete illustration of the probability of its predictions. If it was living for the day when it could bear responsibility, it should at least try by every possible means to prove that such a day really was coming. Niebuhr, however, for one, indulged in no such proofs. He simply settled for the "inevitability" preached in Marxism, and the eschatological expectation generated in the atmospheric anguish in 1931, 1932, and 1933.

In those years, his inspection of middle-class sentimentalism, labor ignorance and impotence, and oligarchical intransigence provoked him to conceptions of the United States sweeping everything into despair: "We are merely a vast horde of people let loose on a continent with little to unify us by way of common cultural, moral, and religious tradition." [53] Given society as a "horde," it was easier to rise above the problems facing those who did have responsibility for acting in the immediate pragmatic present. It was easier to assume that some kind of "inevitable" historical "logic" had taken over beyond what anyone might do to change or stop it, and to argue therefore that realism meant trying to understand this logic and prepare for the day when those who understood it would have the responsibility of leadership. Yet the New Deal constituted leadership most subtly attuned to cultural, moral, and religious—as well as economic and political—

traditions that did exist in American society, and its leaders were able to intervene in the historical logic. The New Deal itself was no "inevitability," and was able to get on with its work without the advice of those who understood what was "really" happening.

In truth, the whole weight of Niebuhr's realistic religion bore against the sort of thinking behind the third-party socialists. In all the differences between short-range and long-range tactics, between major mass-party action and third-party action, between coalition party and ideological party, there were critical issues, not merely of political tactics, but of ethics and, in the last analysis, of theology itself. Thus, to claim responsibility for the long-range, ideological party was to make certain assumptions about the nature of history, about human nature, and about the power of human reason, all of which neo-orthodoxy tended to discount.

Implicitly, Niebuhr responded to these tensions in his own position, in the fact that he did not move to the left politically through the 'thirties after all. His original turn, around 1932, was a leap, a leap out of the utilitarian middle, where religion and politics were synthesized in social morality, into the dialectic, where religion and politics criticized each other. From then on, he remained stationary, increasingly critical of the true believers on the communist and revolutionary left, until, late in the 'thirties, he began moving back to the right. He was not to stop, as far as his style of political analysis was concerned, until he had reached the conservatism of Burke and Augustine, a true expression of the neo-orthodox analysis of human nature. Once there, he could defend the New Deal, not as a triumph of liberalism, but as a manifestation of the "realism" of conservatism.

In the meantime, however, he could not make his return without jeopardizing the argument for religious realism. He was in danger of losing his political arguments for neo-orthodoxy. Niebuhr's way out was to transfer his polemic, intact, from domestic affairs to foreign affairs. Thereby he could continue to convict liberalism through its political failures.

By so doing, however, he remained exposed to the same danger he faced in the New Deal. What if politics under liberal auspices should succeed in checking disaster internationally as had the New Deal nationally? In that case, neo-orthodox arguments would once again be frustrated by the same problem—liberalism's practical success. In any event, the success of the New Deal remained. It had kept the United States exceptional; it had held off hard realities; it had deprived the neo-orthodox of any political demonstration of that essential homelessness by which alone neo-orthodoxy made sense.

Were there other ways for neo-orthodoxy to argue its case?

XV

Religion and the American Scene

Of course the New Deal proved the case for neither liberalism nor neo-orthodoxy as religions. Somehow, nonetheless, the neo-orthodox and all those with a will to realism had to get around it. Otherwise liberal philosophy would simply take its stand on American culture, which in the New Deal had appeared to demonstrate the vitality of the center against all extremes. Basically, the only way to get around it would be to go beyond efforts to link the neo-orthodox Word directly with politics. This would be to expand the field of evidence, from politics narrowly construed to the field of culture at large. Not only justice, but the quality of life, was what mattered at the pinnacle of imagination, and while from this perspective the New Deal might appear as a fortunate tactic on pure political and economic grounds, at once advancing justice a little and holding off breakdown, it might not appear to be touching more fundamental levels. Such fundamental levels had of course been the intended concern of the social gospel, and it was only on such levels that the religious argument could be finally joined, in a nation where politics had not after all come to disaster.

This expansion was an extremely difficult course to take. Three articles appearing in *Radical Religion* in 1936, 1937, and 1938, written by a New York Episcopalian, Richard Day, who was a member of the Fellowship of Socialist Christians, rather neatly marked some of the difficulties as Day strove for his own re-orientation.[1]

In the first, a review of James Truslow Adams's *The Living Jefferson*, Day examined the "American Dream," with its ideals of liberty, equality, private property and material progress. He found it a kind of religion itself, gathered up into a semimystical notion of American destiny. "Its ideals have little or no relation to the present objective conditions, but as a religion it will again lend itself readily to the drugging of the people." Day's anxiety here was primarily political, like Niebuhr's. The American Dream, he argued, would lead a people substantially propertyless to defend small property, and in so doing to shackle themselves to big property and the corporate state of the future.

In his next article, "American Christianity and Christian Americanism," Day examined the turn, among those repudiating the naturalistic and moralistic liberalism of the American churches, to English and European traditions. This could not be fruitful, he believed. A theology grown on foreign soil and wedded to a foreign conception of the Church had nothing to offer to American conditions. The correct response to the season of pressure for Americans was to plumb more deeply into native tradition. But Day still found the American Dream itself an opiate of the people, hiding the harsh realities of economics and politics. It was precisely to repudiate this culture-religion that our tradition should be plumbed again, he insisted, and a sense for prophetic religion revived. Here Day was beginning to pitch his analysis much more to religion and culture than to politics alone.

In "The American Dream Resurgent," in 1938, Day studied the growing return to the New Deal of radical spokesmen, as they abandoned their Marxism and went so far as to accept and work out ideas of a revised, reformed capitalism. An economy combining laissez faire and planning, private and public enterprise; democratic political power exercised by means of indirect controls in a multicentered economy; justice advanced less through sharp class politics than through pragmatic coalition politics pitched to

short-term goals; social interests defined in terms given in the
present rather than in some ideal future: all these, it now appeared, comprised the religion of the American Dream. Previously, Day wrote, he had considered the dream opium, a façade
behind which predatory interests had their way, an idolatrous
culture-religion. But, he said, though these were still dangers, the
most effective appeal for the near future, the most hopeful approach, lay precisely through this dream.

In this shift, Day was in company with the *Christian Century,*
with Niebuhr, with John C. Bennett, and others, so far as it was
a shift back toward accommodation with parts of the existing
culture. Day was not perfectly happy with the position in which
he was left, however, nor could he have been. The obstacle that
he had to pass was his original notion that the disentanglement
of a prophetic religion from the pervading culture-religion
depended somehow upon politics. Upon this he recanted, but
still, in his third article, Day warned that Christians must not
confuse the American Dream with the Kingdom of God. The
American Dream might be a precious tradition politically and
economically, but it was not adequate as a philosophy of life.
Thus, although its resources were to be used, they were to be
used critically and, moreover, to be supplemented and corrected
by what the American Dream had lost—a sense for the ultimate
questions of religion.

In 1938, Day had no way to give content to this warning in
terms of politics, as he had had in 1936; lacking that, his warning
had no real content at all. Implicitly, he was pointing neo-orthodoxy into new fields altogether in its search for illustrative and
convincing demonstrations of its value, but he himself was unable
decisively to move into these new fields. Nerved in the first place
by their sense of the catastrophic atmosphere of modern politics,
the neo-orthodox were disoriented by short-range and utilitarian
successes in averting catastrophe, while yet aware that those
successes were not fundamental.

In the thought of another European of much more importance
to Niebuhr than Karl Barth, Niebuhr's appeals to Christian

doctrine were in fact offered a timely grounding that was deeper than politics. Even more intimately acquainted with the storm center of the West than Barth, Paul Tillich had long exhibited that vigorous moral activity to which Niebuhr always responded. Like Niebuhr in the 'thirties, Tillich in Germany in the 'twenties had also displayed a sense of urgency, basically a timeless spirit perhaps, but an urgency prompted also by timely details in the historical situation. This was of course the urgency defined by the "proletarian situation." Tillich, however, had not cast his commitment to the proletarian situation in those moral terms used by the liberal social-gospel pastors to justify their similar commitment, nor had he cast it in the political-economic terms used by Niebuhr. He cast it in terms of culture, including but going beyond both these others, into the area that we have found Sherwood Eddy and Harry Ward entering, and that lay implicit behind all the Protestant social passion—the area of "meaning." [2]

Tillich occupied himself above all with the problem of how men could grasp ultimate meaning in particular historical situations. His approach to the problem, though bound up with the same portrait of man Niebuhr used in *Christian Ethics* and *The Nature and Destiny of Man,* was more positive than Niebuhr's. As spirit, human nature had the capacity to transcend itself from any given moment to the next. Human existence was the rise of being along the line of freedom and self-determination; indeed, it was nothing other than this, this was its definition. But at no stage in the process was final security attainable. Claims to security defeated themselves; they froze human achievements prematurely, and thus sacrificed freedom. As the symbolic expression of ultimate meaning, the "Kingdom of God" stood permanently against all such claims.

For the Oxford Conference of 1937, the first of the great world conferences in which liberalism stood on the defensive, Tillich summarized these views succinctly:

> The meaning of history can be found neither in a final stage of historical development—the ultimate fulfillment of all historical potentialities—nor in an infinite approximation to a fulfillment which can never be reached, nor in a continuous change of historical growth

and decay as found in nature, nor in a transcendent supra-nature unconnected with history.[3]

The social-gospel pastors had espoused the first—in their moments of more uncautious optimism—or the second. Both Niebuhr and Tillich understood Barth and historic orthodoxy to be trapped in the fourth. (Men like Spengler—of little significance in the American debate—represented the third.) These false meanings located, true meaning remained to be formulated. Tillich continued: "The ultimate meaning of history is the suprahistorical unification and purification of all elements of preliminary meaning which have become embodied in historical activities and institutions." Insofar as this unity and purity transcended history, the meaning of history lay "beyond" history; so far as nothing was contained in them that was not generated in history, meaning was "in" history.

Though the verbal forms of this definition, these prepositional pointers "beyond" history and "in" history, provoked much annoyance and irritation in the American theological debate, it is not to the point here to question or affirm their transparent intelligibility.[4] Tillich was using the same method used by Niebuhr, that of definition by the exclusion of alternatives. The heart of his analysis of the West was his insistence that domestication of the ultimate meaning of history "in" history and not also "beyond" history was the organizing threat to the highest values *of* history —namely, human freedom, community, and personality. The West stood at the end of an era of "autonomy" in which it had been believed that these values could be finally and conclusively fulfilled. Its crisis was that of autonomous men who had become insecure in their autonomy, with nothing but autonomous answers to their problems.

Autonomy—the assumption of self-sufficiency, a closure of the open end of existence and potentiality, both through the assertion of purportedly universal principles (preëminently by reason) and through the assertion of purportedly absolute cultural complexes (such as that of middle-class capitalism)—was a function of original sin. Tillich thus was giving sin a cultural grounding. We can hardly survey its history as he saw it: on its philosophic side, from the first break in "theonomous" thinking in Thomistic thought to the last excesses of positivism; on its more purely cultural side, from Renaissance vigor drawing on a still unwasted medieval religious capital, through Enlightenment secularization, to the beginning mass disintegrations of the nineteenth century. Of interest here is Tillich's analysis of the West in the twentieth century.

At its height, Tillich observed, Western culture had disposed of the problem of meaning by placing its trust in preëstablished rationalistic harmonies in the world and the cosmos, simply secularizing, in doing so, Judeo-Christian concepts of providence. But "natural" laws of harmony had turned out to be contingent historical circumstances. Forms of power developed by the industrial West were shattering all the order and coherence of the past. Capitalism—itself a fruit of the autonomous spirit—bore the major responsibility for the violent storms of the age. In capitalism, a process of depersonalization steadily overtook more and more areas: production, consumption, communications, politics. In the chaos of depression and war that capitalism unleashed on its purely economic side, traditional symbols of ethical unifying power disintegrated, and at an accelerating rate, until depersonalization and disintegration intensified each other. The situation in Europe had come to the point of epidemic, mass disintegration of meaning, a point of meaninglessness so appalling that the myths of fascism and communism were welcome.

In the 'twenties, Tillich had thought to see the chance for a massive reversal of this process. The times were full, gathering up the stresses and contradictions of the past in such a way that at last they were accessible to action, which might initiate a genuinely new stage of culture. The opportunity was presented concretely in the proletarians. The workers bore precise judgment against the perversions of life in capitalist class society; in the forms of their rebellion and expectations, they were just such a shattering and transforming power as could open the way for restoring to culture a sense of true meaning. Religion was not to coöperate with labor and do nothing more, nor to "identify" with socialism. Proletarian socialism—that is, Marxist socialism —was in itself a form of reintegration that remained completely autonomous, unequipped to exploit the potentialities of the times. Prophetic religion, Tillich said, was to criticize and correct socialism, while affirming and advancing the judgment of socialism upon capitalism. The new stage of culture would not be the Kingdom of God; no historical era could be that. But it would be an era in which culture might once again point to and incite the life of man as man.

Thus Tillich, originally, like Niebuhr, had a reasonably clear political implementation of his religious criticism. But his religious criticism was not dependent upon such politics, and drove much deeper than politics. This became progressively clearer as Tillich himself abandoned his political strategy altogether.

By the late 'thirties, exiled from Hitler's Germany, in the shadow of the Second World War, he felt the moment of opportunity, the *kairos*, had been lost—or else, perhaps, that it had not been an opportunity after all. His views had been, he said, "slightly romantic" in that lost decade.[5] More catastrophe would be entailed in coming to a new stage than had then seemed necessary. This left Tillich in the position that Niebuhr, after his anxious hesitations of 1932 to 1934, had resisted, of discounting all measures that might at least moderate the crisis of the times. Every form of resistance to disintegration, he said, could only add to the plunge of the old era to destruction. Humanization of capitalism, socialist and communist efforts at justice and order, attempts to reintegrate through nationalism, all only contributed to the larger catastrophic process. No positive political task for prophetic religion could be imagined to stem it. With the Second World War, Tillich spoke of a "mood of the end"; in such a moment, the only task for a theology of culture was to analyze profoundly and specifically the inner emptiness of modern cultural forms, to clarify and purify the "sacred void," the atmosphere of "not yet." Men would not be prepared to meet the *kairos* that would eventually come unless they were passionately aware of their predicament.

Thus, even if socialism or any other politics halted the catastrophes of economic breakdown and war, the deeper disintegration of meaning would go on. Niebuhr too had seen this, but Tillich saw quite unambiguously that the prophetic Word would be forced to hunt out the most secret forms of false faith, of autonomy, of resistance to the cry of freedom. These were not only such political shelters as nationalistic ideologies and socialist utopianism. Therapeutic individualistic psychology was one of them as well, along with activistic flight into careers and success, humanitarian activity, and even—subtlest of all—esthetic dramatization of the state of meaninglessness itself, the last, most refined, most intellectual security of the modern soul.

Going this far, Tillich was able to go all the way and criticize liberalism's conception of its ultimate, universal, eternal value—personality. The personality celebrated by liberalism—both religious and secular—Tillich said, was itself a construct of autonomous thought when, used as a symbol for the character of God, it was identified—and God was identified—as the embodiment of human perfections. This was a reduction of God, His limitation through liberalization, and of man. The idea of God in classic theology had united personal and suprapersonal elements. To the degree to which humanistic religion had personalized God, His nonpersonal, vital, mystical sides had been negated, and He thus ceased to be the supporting and transcending center of every personal life. The self was thus opened to invasion by the "demonic," breaking up the synthetic unity of the self established in consciousness. Reality was not, after all, personal throughout; to limit God to personality was therefore to cast all else into neutrality, which never remained such but became alien, without meaning, and thus (the opposite of God) demoniacal. Such neutral (inevitably demonic) elements remained, in the liberal concept of personality, inside men as well as outside, and the worst of the demonic was the part that invaded from within. With such invasion, "the disintegration of the consciousness-centered personality is now proceeding on a terrifying scale." [6]

The implication was plain: decisive preaching of the prophetic Word had to be directed where this threat to consciousness could be made most vivid, most urgent, most immediately convincing, most "personal." The whole project of neo-orthodoxy had to be conceived from the start in terms of the self. Political, social, economic reintegrations were possible precisely at the expense of further disintegration of consciousness-centered personalities, at the expense of depersonalization, if the self tried to escape and solve its deepest problems in such reintegration.

This location of the ultimate forms of criticism and preaching in terms of the self simply confirmed Niebuhr's own analysis. Having been inspired to his doctrine of human nature by his examination of the problem of moral man and immoral society, Niebuhr had actually found the answer to the problem to lie in the fact that it was a false problem. He tried to preserve the problem in *Christian Ethics:* "Human finiteness and sin are revealed with particular force in collective relationships; but they are present in even the most individual and personal relationships." [7] But man was not really moral; society simply allowed his sin more plausible expression. Where, after all, were the most terrific social conflicts of all, but in the most intimate community of all, the self itself? What was the ultimate form of catastrophe following pretension and unbelief but suicide? No group committed suicide, as realistic ethics knew. Niebuhr's own logic implied, although Niebuhr never spelled it out, that the potentialities of individual, small-group life bracketed, not merely surpassed, those of collective, large-group life. Greater chaos and greater cosmos alike were possible in life, the more intimately it was organized. In other words, Niebuhr's move from a social-psychological description of human nature to a religious description was correlated to a shift from the social-political field of evidence to evidence drawn from the field of the self.

He himself made this explicit. "The full dimension of depth in which all human actions transpire is disclosed only in introspection." [8] This meant a shift of the field of evidence where Christian doctrine could become convincing.

In . . . an exposition of the Christian interpretation of life and history, in comparison with the modern one, it is necessary to disavow the purpose of proving the Christian interpretation rationally compelling, in the sense that such a comparison could rationally force modern man to accept the Christian faith. The Christian interpretation of life and history is rooted in a faith prompted by repentance. It will not be convincing except to the soul which has found the profoundest enigma of existence not in the evil surrounding it but in itself.[9]

Given this test, the phenomenon described by Tillich—disintegration of consciousness-centered personality—would constitute the ultimate obstacle to preaching. In this light, the deadliness of modern society followed from its increasingly intimate invasion of the individual, an invasion intensified in some cases by social crisis but by no means contingent upon social crisis. It depended upon a false notion of society in the first place, on the one hand, and upon a vulnerable inner organization of the personality on the other hand, the two being reciprocal. Here analysis had to move beyond the discrepancy between moral man and immoral society to the differences between "concrete man" and "abstract society." It was in refusing to recognize some such distinction that Harry Ward could carry, without recoil, his vision of the new social order to the annihilation of personality.

Once this field of the self was clearly established, the full positive meaning of Niebuhr's theology could have been liberated, at least theoretically. Except against the Barthian orthodox, his use of neo-orthodoxy had remained critical, emphasizing the limitations that modern philosophies tried to ignore. The positive meaning came perfectly clear, however, in *The Nature and Destiny of Man*, articulating what had always been presumed (and half-stated) behind his criticism. At the center of the portrait of human nature was freedom. Anxiety was the permanent concomitant of freedom, and sin was one issue from anxiety. But it was not the only issue. Creativity was the other. Everything that liberalism took as slander and discouragement laid upon man—the denial of man's self-sufficiency, the denial of meaning immanent in history, the location of the center of meaning "beyond" history, the doctrine of original sin, the doctrine of grace, the doctrine of the supramoral character of God—served to defend a human destiny of freedom. These all served to break

up claims to eternal significance for ends that had no eternal
value, to explode premature satisfaction, to criticize and break
up imperial pretensions. They all acted to keep history open.

It was in driving criticism into the cultural foundations, in
Tillich's fashion, that neo-orthodoxy was clarified as a religion
geared to the enigmas of self. But such criticism sharpened the
temptation of a Barthian-style sectarianism, which Niebuhr always
rejected. Tillich and Niebuhr themselves divided at this point.
"America," Tillich wrote, "lives still in a state of happy backwardness." [10] At a 1938 meeting of the Fellowship of Socialist
Christians at Bound Brook, New Jersey, Tillich, evoking the
specters of Europe, advised that religious socialists should be
prepared to go "underground," keeping the flames of prophetic
religion alive until breakdown and chaos were ended.[11] But this
did not seem good advice for America, advice calculated to
exploit the situation of backwardness. America's "backwardness,"
as Tillich saw it, consisted of the fact that the process of mass
disintegration had not proceeded as far there as in Europe. Was
it therefore in America that the prophets should go underground?
Tillich did not explain. Would America necessarily and inevitably
undergo the further stages of disintegration already suffered by
Europe? More important, *should* America undergo those stages,
must it undergo them, in order to have *kairos?* Tillich did not
clarify.

At the same meeting, Niebuhr, although admitting the gravity
of the times, judged that America, with its long training in
democracy, its horror at the use of unrestrained power abroad,
and the extra time available to it in its backwardness, could be
saved from the worst, and he urged American radicals to stay
within the American cultural tradition. Nothing was to be gained
by going underground. Niebuhr was here beginning to recant his
rejection of any American exceptionalism in *Reflections on the
End of an Era*, but he did not confront the opposite problems.
How was the neo-orthodox Word to be heard in America if the
need for it was not felt as sharply as in Europe? In *The Religious
Situation*, Tillich had written that in America, the spirit of the
Calvinist churches still worked, preventing capitalism from turn-

ing into a mere brutal naturalism, and thus allowing Americans to believe that capitalist humanism was the realization of Christian ideals. In the face of such beliefs, he said, revolt on American soil against the essential capitalist spirit was almost impossible. Niebuhr proposed no way out of this dilemma.

The dilemma had already been sharpened by one of the most striking books of the attack upon liberalism during the 'thirties, *The Church Against the World.* In this volume, two Americans joined a European in an exposition wholly consistent with the spirit of neo-orthodoxy, except that they concluded in defense of a policy of withdrawal.

Wilhelm Pauck, who, like Tillich, had been associated with the religious socialism of Germany in the 'twenties, traced the historical and intellectual foundations of that liberal mystique in which religion consisted of the "social quest to find satisfactory values for all mankind," a view culminating in simple humanism. The particular American version of such modernism was the most complete, indebted as it was to the circumstances of the American scene for an optimistic activism turned into programs for transforming society. The modern church, Pauck said, infiltrated by this secular religion, unable to distinguish its own identity, had come to sanction and even identify itself with centers of self-sufficient meaning and autonomy. It had become a captive.

Francis Miller, chairman of the World Student Christian Federation and secretary of the Foreign Policy Association, struck at one of the leading forms of this captivity—nationalism. Were the different Protestant communities, he asked, to become the spiritual and ethical facets of their respective national cultures, or were they to stand as reliable witnesses to the Christian faith everywhere, at all times? With specific reference to America, Miller questioned whether American theology, hinging on human values and ideals and dedicated to their social realization, represented a universal faith, true and good for all men, or the expression simply of the highest spiritual insights of our particular culture. Miller felt that John Dewey was the true prophet of this American, natural, national religion; Dewey's reliance upon ideals grasped by imagination had no universal foundation; his appeal to imagination meant in practice appeal to one national frame of reference. It was essential for Protestantism to distinguish between primary and secondary ends; realization of the special ends of American culture was secondary.

Richard Niebuhr examined the captivity to capitalism. A faith and a way of life in itself, the capitalist doctrine that man's most important activity was the production of economic goods organized all else: nature, love, life, truth, beauty, justice, the laws, education, government, even the family. As its dependence upon endowments, its debt structure, and its gifts from the privileged proved, the church's entanglement was profound. This captive church sought to justify itself by its "usefulness" measured by the demands of the system.

Nationalism and capitalism: the old captors. But nationalism and capitalism, as these men emphasized, were variants only of the larger faith: anthropocentrism. The indictment here struck on that new level established by Reinhold Niebuhr and Tillich. The basic sin of capitalism, in the eyes of the social-gospel prophets, was its antipersonalism, its antihumanitarianism; in the eyes of the neo-orthodox, the basic sin of capitalism was its self-sufficiency. The locus of the evil for the social gospel was the capitalistic system; for the neo-orthodox it was modern culture, the spirit of which capitalism reflected and reinforced. And so, hearkening to what he hoped was an inchoate discontent within the church against the secular order—the church, he believed, whatever its weaknesses, being most shot with rebellion against that order—Richard Niebuhr proceeded on to warn against identification of the church with the merely anticapitalist strategies of radical politics, whether proletarian or nationalistic. Amalgamation of the gospel and politics in Christian socialism was no escape. The church should not take up the role of self-sufficient messiah. "If the church has no other plan of salvation to offer to men than one of deliverance by force, education, idealism or planned economy, it really has no existence as a church and should resolve itself into a political party or a school." [12] The church's declaration of independence could begin only with the truth that it and all life depended on God, that loyalty to him was the condition of life. In the circumstances, such a declaration meant "the church against the world."

There were elements in this appeal that were not uncongenial to Reinhold Niebuhr, or indeed to the social-gospel pastors themselves. In a remarkable article appearing in 1925, just after the high tide of the unreconstructed social gospel was breaking, Richard Niebuhr had proposed that Protestantism revive simplicity and hardness, martyrdom and mysticism, the virtues of monasticism. The ascetic ideal was in the air, he said, and Christianity should adopt it. The ideal man of the social gospel was certainly to be ascetic too, though no more so than the ideal man of neo-orthodoxy. But in these two cases asceticism was to be a direct contribution to social justice, part of a policy of boring from within the culture, whereas for Richard Niebuhr it was intended simply to restore the meaning of the religious Word.

> Segregating itself from the world, [Christianity] might recover its integrity for awhile until, confronted with another Calvary, it either suffered crucifixion or made its uneasy compromise with pharisee and sadducee. There is nothing unsocial about this attitude. It is not for love of self that the monk retires from the world but for the love of his brethren who may be saved by no other means.[13]

Equally anxious to liberate the religious world from liberal ethos, Reinhold Niebuhr could not subscribe to such strategy. His intention remained to redirect, not deny, the intention of the social gospel to make religion relevant to "the immediate problems" of social justice, and to politics and culture generally. Actually, withdrawal was conceived of by Richard Niebuhr as a "timely" policy, tailored to an era, and not simply as a timeless, abstract ideal. In 1925, and again in *The Church Against the World,* he likened modern times to the times of the prophets, of Augustine in Rome, and of the sixteenth century: "The last appeal beyond all finite principalities and powers must soon be made. It cannot be an appeal to the rights of man, of nations or religions, but only an appeal to the right of God." [14] Similar in spirit to Tillich's sense of the times in the late 'thirties, this strategy differed from Tillich's at one crucial point. Tillich made it clear that, even if the only strategy was to go underground, the prophets would have to remain passionately aware of all the issues in the culture in all their immediacy so that the crisis could be superseded by a new era. They could not withdraw from the world without abandoning the world, whatever their love for their brethren. Richard Niebuhr's strategy thus seemed not only to ignore the issues involved in the fact of American success in moderating the political and economic crisis; it ignored the whole point of Reinhold Niebuhr's realism, that religion must think about politics, culture, and history in general in terms of power, that is, the interests that are already established, and work from there. As a consequence, Richard Niebuhr again seemed to be falling back into the error Reinhold Niebuhr had originally charged against the social gospel. He appeared to be recommending his pure religious asceticism as a substitute for, rather than as a supplement to, political morality. "The best way to conserve Christian culture is to forget about it and to let it be built from within in consequence of aspiration after a salvation that lies far beyond it." [15]

It was then perfectly possible to criticize liberal culture for more than its political failures, but apparently this could lead all too easily to ignoring politics. So far as timely issues were concerned, Reinhold Niebuhr, whatever his gradual reconciliation with the New Deal implied, found no reason to give up all sense of immediate crisis. So far as timeless issues were concerned, he was interested not only in rescuing the religious Word from the confusions of the utilitarian middle. He was interested in establishing a new relationship between religion and politics, by which each clarified the other; no man could choose one against the other. He still faced the problem, however, of how to justify the neo-orthodox protest against the liberal synthesis.

His solution was to continue to concentrate on the field of politics. This he could do because the depression was hardly the last crisis for America or the West. Even if it could have been argued that through the New Deal the nation was on the way to learning how to solve problems of mass consumption and of rough economic justice, there was still the great world outside. Realism was necessary in the politics of war, and it remained to be proved that the national religion of liberalism was capable of rising to a coherent and adequate international policy.

By continuing to seek the weaknesses of liberalism in politics alone, Niebuhr saved himself polemically for a season, but at the same time inhibited himself from moving his argument for neo-orthodoxy onto new ground that might allow the frustrations posed by the New Deal to be finessed. In Tillich, in the analysis of *The Church Against the World,* and by the deepest canons of Niebuhr's own neo-orthodoxy, it was clear that the decisive field for justification of the new Word was not politics. The decisive field was, ultimately, the self, and even politics adequate not only to the domestic but also to the international perils of the nation would not guarantee the recovery of the self. If, then, the American political situation appeared to dampen the urgency of the new Word, that Word had to seek out conviction elsewhere. Inspired by politics, neo-orthodoxy would have to learn to speak of more than politics—of, for instance, the family and the church and the school, of art, of science and play, of more intense centers of human creativity and human love than were offered in the great abstractions of modern society. The final upshot of the social gospel was that the gospel had to be more personal.

Somewhat paradoxically, this necessity that the religious debate drive beyond politics received one final illustration, in the 'thirties, in one more failure in the political debate itself. By adopting crisis as the context of his political thinking, Niebuhr neglected the side of social-gospel imagination that had in fact considered the system in terms of personality. The overriding danger was chaos, the breakdown of depression and war in which desperation took over, nourishing political religions. So, also, had most of the social-gospel pastors themselves yielded up that side of their imaginations, as they supported socialism or the New Deal as restoration of order. As a rescue action, the New Deal had little to do directly with those visions of industrial democracy, of the factory as church, and of unalienated economic life which had featured the 'twenties. Its coherence depended on the perspective

of straight economic recovery, an external achievement guaranteeing nothing in the direction of personalization.

A few pastors in the 'thirties continued to speak in the old
terms. One was A. E. Holt, of the Chicago Church Federation;
Holt had had something of a labor church of his own in Pueblo,
Colorado, years before. He affirmed the basic principle of realism:
"There can be no ethics without power, and power must return
to the disinherited and power must be taken away from those who
have appropriated more than their share of it." [16] But Holt was
perfectly clear in his own mind about the new pattern of power.
Socialization was inevitable, he said. But responsible living would
not be restored through government regulation. Farmers and
labor should organize into effective groups acting in their own
interests and on their own responsibility—not to get governmental
intervention in their interests but to win direct control over their
own productive areas.

Justin Wroe Nixon, who moved from his Rochester pastorate
to Colgate-Rochester Seminary in the 'thirties, also spoke, as we
have already noted, against centralization of power in the state
and for a mixed economy.[17] Nixon, unlike Holt, had been highly
insensitive to labor tactics in the 'twenties and early 'thirties. It
might have seemed that his suspicion of state power was essentially part of the Republican party orthodoxy of the times. Yet
it was not. His vision of mixed economy, giving large areas over
to coöperatives and socialization, was hardly part of that orthodoxy.

These men were opposed not to the New Deal, but to dangers
beyond the New Deal. This position was expressed precisely by
F. Ernest Johnson of the Federal Council, who supported the New
Deal precisely because it avoided undue concentration of power
in the state. In 1940, in his "re-examination" of the social gospel,
Johnson conjured up again the vision of decentralized economic
democracy, the vision of democracy in detail, measured by the
old personalist criteria in all literal intent.[18]

Finally, in 1940, in *Can Christianity Save Civilization?* Walter
Horton argued his own solution to the ails of capitalism. The
social-credit plan of Major Douglas was, he knew, regarded in

many circles as a panacea, but Horton nevertheless defended it as a means of avoiding power centralized in the state. Horton was nearly alone in referring his fears to the New Deal itself. "Even the mild experiment in socialism and national planning which we call the New Deal has done much to create a centralized bureaucracy, undermine local initiative, and make us sing, 'Praise government from which all blessings flow.' " [19] Horton was speaking for a kind of socialism on the model of what he understood to be Swedish, highly pragmatic, nonideological, decentralized.

Here were four men who had not subordinated the "personalistic" side of the social-gospel imagination to the crisis. What happened to this tradition in the 'thirties? Primarily, it got lost in the anxiety of the arguments over crisis. That is, it got cut off from the debate over means, as that debate was hammered home by Niebuhr in *Moral Man and Immoral Society*. The vision of decentralized industrial democracy never had been, and now was still less, well anchored in any strategy for bringing it to pass.

Two of these four men themselves had no coherent interest in the forces that might protect and even embody their ideals. Nixon had simply saddled his ideals onto whatever backs seemed available at any given time—businessmen, middle classes, labor —as though the ideals were already immanent in the whole culture. Horton, with his social-credit plan, was looking for a way out of power analysis through "technique." Here democratic socialism found itself as nothing but pious wish.

The other two were not so indifferent. Arthur Holt was a kind of neo-Populist, his imagination wedded to the "agricultural hinterlands" exploited by the "predatory bourgeoisie," even as he lent an unaccustomed support to labor.[20] *This Nation Under God* was a tract in the old style, directed at the traders, Wall Street, and monopoly capitalism with all the fervor of essentially preindustrial and rural Protestantism. Even so, this was a link between the vision and the tactical means, and this realism might have been developed by others to interesting effect, contrasting with and even compensating for the rather exclusive emphasis upon labor among the neo-orthodox realists. But the religious debate frustrated any such development. The situation was nicely illustrated by the fourth of these men, F. E. Johnson. Johnson supported the New Deal, insisting at the same time that it must lead toward industrial democracy, not a state economy, and he associated his views with his vigorous defense (against Niebuhr) of religious liberalism, rejecting the crisis atmosphere as "European," arguing that evolutionary progress was more normative and insisting that the neo-orthodox "crisis theology" would pass with the crisis. Here the personalistic values conserved in the vision of decentralized industrial democracy were linked with a defense of liberal theology. The same thing was true of Walter Horton, his suspicion of the New Deal aside. Horton had not moved beyond his positions of 1934 in *Christian Realism*. His book of 1940 announced that it was time to reverse signals, from the note of judgment to the note of hope. The iron had entered men's souls enough, liberalism had been corrected enough.

Niebuhr's substitution of justice as the goal proper to politics, in his attack upon liberalism, simply undercut the personalistic level of analysis. He neither praised nor blamed the New Deal on that level. He recognized the problem this left when, in *Reflections on the End of an Era*, he warned that justice might be achieved without checking the depersonalization of society. But this observation was critical—an attack upon Marxist utopianism ready to sanction centralized power—rather than positive—a defense of the old vision.

What was missing in Holt and Johnson, as in Nixon and Horton —as it had been missing in Walter Rauschenbusch—was a plain explanation of why the centralization of power they feared in the state—a centralization that Rauschenbusch, Holt, and Johnson feared just as much in private industry—was bad. Niebuhr had such an explanation, in grounding his discussion of social power in the doctrine of original sin and then turning to attack liberal theology for its illusions. Power unchecked by other power would always be used imperialistically, in an effort to alleviate the anxiety all men felt. He made this explanation by emphasizing the crisis, by insisting upon the disentanglement of political morality from religion, and by insisting that justice, not love, was the political goal; thus, however, the personalistic values gathered up in the liberal concept of "love" were forced to the periphery of the debate.

Actually, liberals who tended the vision of democratic socialism had, at least implicitly, a positive case for their ideal. How was human nature to be exercised most fully in the ways of love except with the widest distribution of power? Whether or not power corrupted, it could be argued that the centralization of power reduced the possibilities for love, and this would be enough to discount it. In such an argument, the neo-orthodox portrait of man would not be needed. But men like Johnson were as frustrated polemically as was Niebuhr. Johnson, as will be explained more fully in chapter xvii, tried to appeal precisely to American conditions against both neo-orthodoxy and Marxism. For him, the New Deal and liberal theology were linked. But Johnson never had reason to think the New Deal was supported, either as a route to industrial democracy or simply as a rescue action, by those whom he claimed as liberals in faith, the Protestant congregations. Nor did he have reason to think the New Deal, whoever its sponsors, exhibited urges immanent in American culture toward industrial, personalistic democracy in the first place. Men like Johnson, trying to resist the neo-orthodox portrait of man while supporting the old vision of an unalienated social order, were no more able to find final justification in American conditions than were the neo-orthodox.

The whole situation stood in interesting contrast to that of another religious debate of some significance for Americans.

One of Niebuhr's important theological creditors was the passionate Dane, Sören Kierkegaard. In *The Nature and Destiny of Man*, Niebuhr made large use of Kierkegaardian logic in his discussion of sin. Niebuhr's own polemical position was not that of Kierkegaard, however. In Denmark, a vigorous and rather forgotten contemporary of Kierkegaard, Bishop Grundtvig of the established state church, had helped make way for a democratic, decentralized economy, and it was Grundtvig, among others, whom Kierkegaard had attacked. Grundtvig symbolized, for such men as A. E. Holt, Walter Horton, J. W. Nixon, and F. E. Johnson, the alternative to Marx and thereby the alternative to Kierkegaard.[21] But for Tillich, Niebuhr and the neo-orthodox, the restoration of man to himself would not be complete until religion had grasped Kierkegaard as well as Grundtvig—Kierkegaard's objection to Grundtvig's assimilation of religion into the ethical utilities of the culture, as well as Grundtvig's objection to the ethical degradation represented in laissez faire. In America, resistant to Grundtvigian reform, Kierkegaard was grasped only as Marx was grasped. That is, the crisis of laissez faire split religion and politics; the realism of Marx nerved the realism of Kierkegaard.

The fact that the two were grasped together guaranteed that Marx would no sooner be grasped than he would fall under criticism—criticism that could have opened the way to one aspect of Grundtvig, his highly pragmatic, nonideological, personalistic conception of social organization. But this was to run the risk— as Richard Day, running it, had seen—of falling back into the nation-church, culture-religion utilitarianism Kierkegaard had scorned—the risk, that is, of repeating the common pathos of the intellectual in America, being drawn back insensibly from the conceptual clarity and vitality of criticism into the terms of the all-engulfing, universally moderating national harmonies.

Refusing to follow Tillich in purifying the sacred void, Niebuhr also refused to run this opposite risk, preferring to protect Kierkegaard by continuing to look—now in foreign affairs—for the political failures of liberalism as proof of the religious errors of liberalism. Kierkegaard himself had never needed to consider this risk, since he was deaf to politics. Had he been stimulated to Kierkegaardian insights by politics, as Niebuhr had been, and had he tried to illustrate and validate his insights in terms of a politics distinguished from that of Grundtvig, he too might have had trouble.

But what Kierkegaard wished to say was that Grundtvigianism was not Christianity; it might have been a perfectly decent politics. This is what the American neo-orthodox had ultimately to learn to say, if they expected to get past the difficulty that, by their lights, American liberal politics and culture frustrated both Kierkegaard and Grundtvig—that is, frustrated the freedom of the self from society as well as the freedom of the self in society. It appeared possible that, in order to say so, it might be necessary to elevate some of the exceptionalism, some of the successes, some of the religio-political utilitarian harmonies of the American scene into systematic conceptual dignity, and to learn to praise them, not in surrender to a national culture-religion but for the sake of more effective and even more immediate religious criticism of American culture.

XVI

Neo-orthodox Man

"Contemporary atheism is the opportunity of a genuinely Protestant religion. Yes, the roots of true Protestantism are to be found more often among the unbelievers of our day than among the 'loyal churchmen.'"

Not at all alien to the spirit of Reinhold Niebuhr, this was the view of Joseph Haroutunian, professor at the Presbyterian Theological Seminary in Chicago, in his *Wisdom and Folly in Religion* of 1940. Haroutunian carried the return to classic doctrine to perhaps its extreme point, in an apology for the Calvinistic doctrine of "double election" as "the crown of Protestant piety." "The notion that God elects some for salvation and others for damnation," Haroutunian said, ". . . is the penultimate product of the Protestant spirit." He self-consciously proposed this classic spirit as "timely," the only outlook worthy of and congenial to the contemporary mind.

> Instead of being a stubborn and dogmatic optimism, our religion has to appropriate the despair and hopelessness of the modern mind. Before it sets out to give people faith and hope, it has to drink deep of the cup of contemporary anguish. It has to improve upon the pessimism of the atheist by teaching him to face the tragedy of life in all its devastating power.[1]

The difference between Niebuhr's position and Haroutunian's was clear. Niebuhr was not addressing the pessimists and the atheists. He was addressing "the moralists, both religious and secular," the optimists, those with illusions—those, basically, who believed in the perfectibility of man. These he wished to chasten. He geared his neo-orthodoxy not to improve upon pessimism, but to inject it.

Yet Niebuhr himself realized that preaching against illusions would not work. He said that the vicissitudes of history, and not mere words, "determine the time and season when illusions wax and wane." Neo-orthodoxy, in other words, did depend upon something like the atheism that Haroutunian saw as its opportunity.

> . . . there is no way of validating the truth of the gospel until men have discovered the error which appears in their final truth; and are threatened with the abyss of meaninglessness on the edge of their most pretentious schemes of meaning.[2]

The simple difficulty with Haroutunian's position was that there were few atheists in America. American politics and culture had not generated the pessimism, despair, and hopelessness that neo-orthodoxy could appropriate. Implicitly, Niebuhr solved this problem by assuming that the catastrophic course of modern history would generate disillusionment. But there were two difficulties with this. The noncatastrophic course of American history allowed illusions to persist. More important, however, Niebuhr's own final explanation of the phenomenon of immoral society stood against his hope that historical vicissitudes in themselves would lead men to discover their errors. It was in the more plausible symbols of social pretension that men could escape recognition of their true, human situation, as homeless, anxious, and sinful. Illusions of social salvation pursued at first with hopeful perfectionism would, running upon obstacles, piling up into impasses, be pursued with desperation. Wounded pretension would ram itself onward without questioning whether obstacles and impasses were not partly the fruit of its own logic. What guarantee was there that catastrophe would become instructive, and thus be checked, before the ultimate tragedy transpired, before the chaos of the end of the era concluded in some final total pretension?

Niebuhr's problems at this point were to be sharply focused in the debate on foreign policy before Pearl Harbor. The liberal pacifist isolationists he attacked all displayed a desperate wish to shelter America from the catastrophic experiences of Europe as though American liberalism, both religious and cultural, would wither under them—whereas Niebuhr plainly wished to force such experiences on America. Yet American culture itself, in the First World War as well as in its own greatest catastrophe, the Civil War, had already shown an immense capacity to rationalize tragedy into the terms of optimistic liberal moralism and a progressive interpretation of history.

What Niebuhr and the neo-orthodox had never done was to argue their case positively, not by excluding alternatives, not in terms of what it was intended to prevent, but in terms of what it was intended to defend and nourish. What this was, was perfectly apparent in Niebuhr's portrait of human nature—human freedom, the capacity for transcendence. But this Niebuhr never integrated into his discussion of politics.

What would a man postulated by neo-orthodox evangelism be like? At Edinburgh, in the Gifford lectures, Niebuhr proposed a "synthesis" of Renaissance and Reformation. By this he meant a dialectical interaction between humility and pretension. The major work of Niebuhr's life was to explain this humility. Its center was repentance, the contrition that recognized the evil within the self even before the evil outside. Its fruit was the capacity to forgive, its support a true knowledge of God possessed by grace, not by right.

Humility, however, was not equivalent to moderation, caution, or prudence. Modern culture stood on the Renaissance side of things, Niebuhr said, and he never protested the dynamic, creative motion of this spirit—as he feared the Barthians did. Indeed, he protested the stultification of this spirit by the Reformation, just as he rejected the static harmonies of the medieval vision. He always urged the vigorous pursuit of the possibilities of the moment, with all the reason, love, imagination, and will available.

It was Niebuhr's conviction, nonetheless, that the tragedies of the West followed from its unmixed Renaissance elements, and that its Renaissance character had to be checked therefore by Reformation humility. This the reformers themselves had not known how to do. The Reformation "did not illumine the possibilities and limits of realizing increasing truth and goodness in every conceivable historic and social situation." [3] It was partly a consequence of this Reformation failure to relate to history that the Renaissance spirit had become self-sufficient, with the long-range result of idolatry. Renaissance logic had committed gradual suicide, as men enslaved themselves to their own methods and successes, and then, when faced by the resulting catastrophes, to their own fantasies of historical security.

This was the ground for a criticism of Renaissance character, but it is essential to realize that neo-orthodoxy had no meaning except as it intended to instruct aspiring human energy. Without pretension, that is, without the thrust of human creative imagination, Reformation truth was literally empty. Renaissance assertion was required for recognition of Reformation truth.

> There is . . . no way of understanding the ultimate problem of human existence if we are not diligent in the pursuit of proximate answers and solutions. Nor is there any way of validating the ultimate solution without constantly relating it to all proximate possibilities. On this issue Renaissance perspectives are truer than either Catholic or Reformation ones.[4]

It was by this insistence that Niebuhr was "neo"-orthodox, transcending the long failure of historic orthodoxy to set Christianity in a vital relationship with culture. In both Catholic and Reformation orthodoxy, the attack upon sin was so exclusive that not only sin, but creative freedom as well, was swallowed up in the religious illumination. The fatal mistake was to try to check anxiety as well as sin, forgetting that anxiety was the ground not of sin alone but of human meaning also. Thus, in the "defeatism" of the Reformation, and in the "arrest" of history and culture in Catholicism—"heterodoxy" in Paul Tillich's language—man was held within bounds and limits that falsified the actual boundlessness of his nature.

In effect Niebuhr, like Tillich, was saying what neither orthodoxy nor liberalism—especially social-gospel liberalism—had ever understood: that Christianity is not a source of culture or a program for culture. It has absolutely no positive prescriptions for style and content. Man is the source of culture, and Christianity, by the light of neo-orthodoxy, is his means of remaining the source throughout history.

It is necessary to insist somewhat vehemently upon this side of Niebuhr, in view of his own original and persisting preoccupation with the illusions of idealists. Only at the point of exhaustion, of breakdown, of shipwreck, only at the point where will and aspiration finally foundered, could human nature be renewed for its destiny. The fullness of gospel truth emerges as all alternatives are excluded, cast out by hard experience. Only as there is no way of finessing the meaninglessness that overtakes the pretentious schemes of meaning in history by appeal to still more pretentious schemes will the point of gospel truth be grasped, that the source of final meaning and creative freedom is not self-contradictory. It is not grounded simply in human anxiety, with its inevitable tendency to enslave itself in bounded security, but in God—unlimited and eternal. Examined imaginatively, this point of exhaustion is in the Promethean, the Icarian, the Faustian style, and it is in life in this style that the meaning of the offer of grace, as the ground of freedom, can be most profoundly realized.

How might this style bear upon politics? Its first bearing was unmistakable: the humility, the repentance, the "creative despair" keeping the way open for creative, Renaissance energy could not exist in politics. It was precisely in politics that men found the plausible symbols of (illusory) security whereby to escape the despairing knowledge of their limitations. To use Niebuhr's words again: "Individuals may be saved by repentance . . . But the collective life of mankind promises no such hope of salvation, for the very reason that it offers men the very symbols of pseudo-universality which tempt them to glorify and worship themselves as God." [5]

Some of the reasons for this carry back to Niebuhr's own early efforts to shake off liberalism. Thus nations, classes, corporations, unions, and all the major collectivities of life do not begin to have the very organs of self-consciousness required for repentance. But the basic reason is to be understood in light of Niebuhr's religious logic, and this can be highlighted by turning once more to the dualism of moral man and immoral society.

In the Fellowship of Reconciliation debate of 1933, Richard Niebuhr had written: "We are not moral men living in immoral societies because the individual is better than society, but because as individuals we are subject to all sorts of coercions to which societies are not subjected." [6] To substitute "experiences" for "coercions" would be finally to fix the true issue. "Experiences" are the material of consciousness, and there is a sociology, or social psychology, of true experiences or consciousness. We have indicated that Niebuhr implied it from the time of *An Interpretation of Christian Ethics:* introspection is the supreme method; the self is the final field of evidence.

This is so because it is possible to repent only by excluding the alternatives to repentance, and this process of exclusion is possible in its turn just in proportion as experiences are rich in detail, in immediacy, and in variety. By their detail, their immediacy, and their variety, they inhibit escape into abstract theory, into empty futures, and into mere fantasies. Thus, proof of the Renaissance and liberal interpretations of human nature and destiny using the public experiences of science, social science, and general social progress can be refuted by the facts known to any man who sets about plumbing the full measure of his own private existence. In no matter what society of peace, progress, and justice, he will have experiences testifying to conflict, tragedy, and evil within himself.

Conversely, the further the self trusts itself to the support of system, organization, and the generalities of formal existence, the further will its experiences run thin. Its life will be alienated, evading real and immediate experience by categorizing it in standard terms given from outside. The thinner experiences run, the more will it be possible to escape knowledge of anxiety, and thus of sin. Repentance will seem uncalled for. The self, taking on the forms of pseudo-universality, will have nothing for which it understands itself to be responsible.

This would be the end of a moral man—immoral society dualism, from which the central illusions of the social gospel had stemmed, and which Niebuhr had turned against the social gospel. The illuminating contrast, as has been suggested, would be that between concrete man and abstract society, securing the argument that the fulfillment of human nature is not to be found in any particular historic human community.

Given this perspective, the positive side of neo-orthodoxy could be integrated into problems of politics. Renaissance pretension could not be allowed political expression, for there it would never experience that humility and creative despair that could save it from its own destruction in idolatry. The essential problem remained: how might men be won from the illusions—rooted in the Renaissance—that were carrying their politics to catastrophe? Niebuhr knew that the experience of disillusionment and catastrophe was by no means necessarily enough. "We do not maintain that the period of disillusionment in which we now find ourselves will necessarily restore the Christian faith. It has merely reëstablished its relevance." [7] The answer to his dilemma, absolutely demanded by the structure of neo-orthodoxy, was not that Reformation humility had to be preached against Renaissance pretension, but that Renaissance pretension had to be preached, not against humility, for none was to be found, but against the lack of pretension—which in Europe tended to be desperate, in America complacent—in the concrete life of the self.

For what was the final form of Renaissance tragedy? This Paul Tillich had specified and made central, as Niebuhr had not: the disintegration of the consciousness-centered personality. The tragic end of the Renaissance was the annihilation of the pretender by pretension. The individual was falling to the abstractions of method and of social salvation, as these abstractions, whether driven by perfectionism or desperation, grew more and more coercive, inclusive, penetrating, and scientific. Consciousness was being abolished; in its place was conditioning.

The basic defense against such disintegration could only be projects and experiences dependent upon the individual self, clustering on centers of aspiration more immediate, various, and detailed than the tempting but unmanning abstractions of society. The obvious place to begin in conceiving such projects was supplied by the basic malady of modern cultures: we are "more conscious of the relations of human communities to each other, than of the relations of individuals within their communities." [8] The neo-orthodox dialectic had to be worked out in terms drawing from the relationships between individuals, if it was to make its political relevance good; and were it to be worked out in such terms, it would have to preach pretension and aspiration before it elucidated humility. This was what modern culture had laid upon it.

Given this perspective once again, the frustrations posed to neo-orthodoxy by American culture took on new light. Tillich's "happy backwardness" was hardly adequate to integrate America into the logic of the end of an era—although it was more adequate than the oscillations Niebuhr suffered, dismissing the national culture as a thing of "hordes" at one point, only to defend it against European despair at another. With their less ideological, more piecemeal, and short-range politics, along with their providential good fortune, Americans were at least less tempted by the terrible political religions luring those who faced social catastrophe. If the New Deal sheltered liberal illusions against harsh realities, it at least prevented those illusions from becoming fanaticism. If it sheltered complacency, it at least checked desperation.

This Niebuhr came eventually to appreciate, after the war, in *The Irony of American History*. In that book, he came to praise the "ironic triumph of common sense over the foolishness of . . . wise men," but the pervading irony of the book was not intended. The "common sense" that Niebuhr opposed to liberalism did not root in any such realism as neo-orthodoxy demanded. It did not root in any self-conscious achievements—religious, political, or cultural—of American society at all. It rooted, he said, in accidents, providences, and confusions of our history that the liberal mind had misread in terms of reason, will, and "democratic faith." We had not known the source of our own strength.[9]

The accidents, providences, and confusions of our history had made America poor ground for the catastrophic political religions of Europe, but obviously this was no guarantee that the political challenges of the future, especially those in the international sphere, could continue to be met on the basis of the past. The liberal misinterpretation of our history had to be abandoned. It was not so much that Americans needed to change their political practice as to understand it; otherwise, they might foolishly change it. Niebuhr here committed himself, appropriately enough, to persist in his efforts to justify political realism, which in turn provided for neo-orthodoxy its negative proof.

If Americans were not tempted by politics of desperation, they were, however, tempted by politics of moderation—tempted to conceive it as more than politics. To meet this temptation, neo-orthodoxy was forced to discount political success, not merely political failure. Only in so doing, in turn, could it confront the religious ideals of liberalism directly, not as leading inevitably to political errors, but as constricting human experience. What was wrong with the "utilitarian middle," mingling and confusing religious and political perspectives, was not only that it blinded men to their limitations; it blinded them to their possibilities. If the security that liberal culture offered was too easy, the freedom and creative pretensions it invited were too small. If the center held against all extremes, it did so at the expense of vitality. The vitality of the individual was lost in the harmonies of his successful society.

At bottom, the tension between neo-orthodoxy and American culture derived not from the political illusions of moral men but from their religious illusions, illusions they identified with their culture. Richard Day had felt this problem, as he wrestled with the New Deal. He saw that the New Deal protected not predatory class interests, but a religious investment in history on the part of a whole culture. The American social system had long been sanctified as a realm of religious symbols, in the Puritan gospel of work, in the liberal gospel of progress, in the modern gospel of an "American way of life." America was "home," and home in religious opposition to the essential homelessness insisted upon by Niebuhr. It was "innocence," in opposition to the sin that was inevitable. "Repentance" was not an abiding pattern in the American style of experience on any level, because in the atmosphere of the pervading "utilitarian" morality, the experiences that inspire repentance were lacking. Tragedy, abysses of meaninglessness, catastrophe, the experiences by which men realize the truth of the gospel, were not necessary in lives led according to the American system, because the system was successful. The real objection of neo-orthodoxy to such lives was not that they lacked humility. It was that they were not free or, actually, real. Men let their lives be led for them, living by "outwardness" as much as though they were victims of the political religions of Europe. By no means the atheists of Haroutunian's imagination, they were moral men constricted by belief in their moral society.

This was a difficult target to attack, but it had unified the liberal minds of the social gospel, most conspicuously in the case of Rauschenbusch. Rauschenbusch had had no principles by which to criticize the established culture of the Protestant middle classes, and indeed sought for none, as he, like the rest of the liberal pastors, wished essentially to absorb all forces into that established culture. The social-gospel pastors had wished to absorb capital and labor into the church. This was the ground for their trust in a vision of the "socialized individual." Society was to be the good man writ large, and, naturally, the individual could be society writ small. This was a conceivable vision, and an endurable one, because the moral society already existed in the church-culture of the middle. As the chapter to follow will illuminate, the final critical feature of the liberal social gospel in the 'thirties was a kind of "return" to the church, precisely in reaffirmation of this sense of an established culture already available prior to any politics. One of the costs paid by the neo-orthodox for their failure to develop their positive meaning was entanglement in this return, without any effective means by which to criticize it for its lack of vitality and its essential complacency. It was a measure of Niebuhr's personal instincts that he was relatively suspicious of this return; still, he had little but political criticisms to make of it. That it lacked any support for the creative, Renaissance side of his dialectic quite as much as for the contrite, Reformation side hardly appeared.

In the postwar years, this was to leave creative Protestant thinking sadly separated, as it had been in the 'twenties, from other cultural ferment. Postwar secular criticism of the American scene, especially after the campaign of 1948, began increasingly to fix upon not politics, economic injustice, and potential disasters, but upon the captivity of the culture to ideal norms gathered up in that American Dream so ambiguously attractive and repellent to Richard Day and the authors of *The Church Against the World*. The socialized individual had become standard, supplanting the individualist for whom alone salvation could come, and his labels were "other-directed," "market-oriented," "identity-diffused," "over-steered," "over-organized"—in a word, ironically similar to that "disintegrated consciousness" analyzed by Paul Tillich. Tillich had described the contribution of social and political catastrophe to disintegration, but his analysis of the disease itself was, it appeared, as applicable to conditions of liberal success in politics as to conditions of failure. The Protestant contribution to this criticism was to be fitful and dim, as liberal pastors themselves preached harmony, and the neo-orthodox continued simply to try to prove the necessity for humility. But Niebuhr himself had made it plain that humility followed only upon creative pretension. The postwar years would make exasperating what in the 'thirties had been merely ironic, namely: that the nonreligious, pragmatic character of American politics, providing a kind of check against catastrophic political pretensions, constituted an immense opportunity for men to spend themselves in pretensions in their intimate, individual lives and their culture, in their real lives, where the catastrophes they would suffer might lead to a saving creative despair rather than to the pretensions of desperation. By an extraordinary paradox, from the neo-orthodox perspective the health of American society consisted of the fact that in America sin might be risked more imaginatively. Thus grace might be known more truly.

Niebuhr's projection of the essential experience of neo-orthodox man took the form of a philosophy of history, as alien to the sense of history among the liberal pastors as his doctrine of sin. History did not, Niebuhr insisted, accumulate grace, morality, justice, meaning. All modern philosophies of history—whether evolutionary with the liberals, or catastrophic with Marxists— were mistaken in their belief that the possibilities of chaos and evil could be progressively eliminated.

That good and cosmos could be extended, Niebuhr obviously did not deny. In fact, he insisted upon this. Love, as he presented it in *Christian Ethics*, had precisely the role of breaking up every claim to final achivement by pointing to higher ideal achievements: ". . . no fixed limits can be placed upon either the purity or the breadth of the brotherhood for which men strive in history." [10] In politics, where the competition of life with life had to be assumed, the ideal of justice had the same role. Mere growth was not progress, however, nor was it the basic pattern of history. The growth of meaning and brotherhood was rooted in human creativity, which in turn was rooted in the essential human situation of anxiety; anxiety provoked sin as well as creativity. The two were locked in permanent association.

> . . . every human advance offers new possibilities of catastrophe and every virtue has the possibilities of a vicious aberration in it . . . The conclusion most abhorrent to the modern mood is that the possibilities of evil grow with the possibilities of good, and that human history is therefore not so much a chronicle of the progressive victory of the good over evil, of cosmos over chaos, as the story of an ever increasing cosmos, creating ever increasing possibilities of chaos.[11]

"History does not solve the basic problems of human existence but reveals them on progressively new levels." [12] At the end of history awaits Antichrist.

In other words, chaos, catastrophe, tragedy are inevitable. In light of the political debate within which neo-orthodoxy emerged, it should be clear that this was not the same as to say that any particular catastrophe was inevitable. It was not to say, in one of the styles of classic orthodoxy protesting lyric perfectionism, that war is inevitable, or that the poor are always with us, or that human nature never changes. It was not to say that the catastrophes of the West in the twentieth century were inevitable. Niebuhr obviously believed in no such propositions, nor did they follow from his theology.

The reason that chaos, catastrophe, and tragedy are inevitable —by the logic of neo-orthodoxy—is that there can be no guarantee of what will be the fruits of human self-transcendence or freedom. If there were guarantees, there would not be freedom. It is in this situation of risk that the existential anxiety will issue in sinful efforts to achieve security. It follows that chaos, catastrophe, and tragedy are inevitable only where the self seeks to be a self—seeks, that is, to live by freedom. But society is not man writ large. It is not, and cannot be, the universalization of the self. Society is the condition for the existence of selves, but as such it can be understood as an artifact. Politics is an artifact, to be used as a tool for limited ends. When, however, the self accepts itself as society writ small, it seeks itself in society and politics. It turns itself into artifact, into a tool. It finds its whole integrity and meaning in the pseudo-universals offered it by society, and thus feeds into society and politics the anxiety that will make for chaos, catastrophe, and tragedy on a social and political scale.

Under what conditions does the self seek itself in this destructive way? In the final analysis, it does so when it does not realize its own true nature. That nature remains, whether recognized or not, but failure to realize it involves it in tragedies that otherwise need not occur. Its true nature is to be free, and since there is that in freedom which makes for dizziness (as Niebuhr appreciated through Kierkegaard), there is that in man which will lead him to refuse to recognize that he is, so to speak, doomed as well as destined to be free. What he will seek for in politics, then, will be a security he cannot have, and in this search he will deny himself even the limited sorts of security that politics, undistorted by religious needs, might bring. Otherwise, in moments of providential good fortune, he will pay for such security with the constriction of experience enforced by all culture religions.

Against such reduction of life, the basic religious defense indicated by Niebuhr's polemical position was not the "withdrawal" suggested by Tillich and the authors of *The Church Against the World*. It was, rather, positive collaboration with culture, such that both culture and religion might embody the dialectic between Renaissance aspiration and Reformation humility. In such a culture men could derive the symbols by which they understood themselves and their destinies from the full repertory of their experiences, not just from the abtractions of critical reflection upon those experiences. The symbols of such a culture might draw on that "full dimension of depth disclosed only in introspection." Most particularly, religion might be vitalized once again by renewed association with that side of culture inherently occupied with the individual—the humanities. All subsidence of the self into generality and adjustment, however moral, however universal, would be understood as evil. The false selves of an illusory greater stability or significance or morality which were offered men by society in place of the contingency of their actual selves would meet coherent resistance. It was open to neo-orthodoxy to state its themes more sharply by far than in its critique of politics—in a critique of sex and marriage, for instance, in modern America (not excepting liberal Protestant America), a realm of vital flux persistently betrayed in the evasions of the merely sociological. In the real life of the self, chaos, catastrophe, and tragedy will occur, but here they can be saving experiences. The self can repent, and thereby to the self alone is grace, renewing the conditions for creative freedom, available.

Such cultural vitality would be equivalent to reversing the disastrous tendency of modern society that Niebuhr observed in *Moral Man and Immoral Society*: once again men would become—as they must be to save themselves as men—more conscious of the relations of individuals than of the relations of human communities to each other. A final reversal of liberal logic would then be implied. The basic ground of human solidarity would not be the human virtues emphasized by the social-gospel pastors, but the human weaknesses emphasized by the neo-ortho-dox. United in their need, their limitations, their sufferings, and their tragedies, men are more truly joined than when united in their undeniable powers of reason and moral will. They are united on the basis of their real understanding of themselves. The frontiers, the anxieties, the exhaustion of resources every self knows would not be hidden, relegated to a kind of private and secondary sphere, but revealed. Men could thus find, in their community with one another, not the illusions and projections of security that veil their real natures, but other human beings who are also in need.

Not the least of the reasons that held Niebuhr to his political analysis was the fact that, in the debate before Pearl Harbor, he had the rare chance to approach this supremely difficult point in political terms.

At its pinnacle, in short, neo-orthodoxy did not compete with other philosophies in facing various hard realities. At its pinnacle, it was geared to discover hard realities that alternative philos-ophies did not know of in the first place. Only faith in the divine mercy, Niebuhr wrote in 1940, could ". . . disclose the actual facts of human existence. It alone could uncover the facts because it alone has answers for the facts which are disclosed." [13] Taken at this pinnacle, therefore, the intention of neo-orthodoxy was not to prove itself more adequate than the social gospel, or liberalism, or Marxism, to the task of making society more human. It was, in company with the vanguard of twentieth-century thought, to rediscover man in and save him from the abstractions of society.

XVII

The New Era and the Old Church

Springing forth from crisis, neo-orthodoxy in America was frustrated by the success of the New Deal in easing crisis. The liberal, "utilitarian" middle appeared able to hold. America's "happy backwardness" appeared to make neo-orthodox realism, both political and religious, unnecessary. This was the deep rationale for the most interesting feature of the liberal social gospel in the 'thirties: its "return" to the church. Against both sectarianism and neo-orthodoxy, liberal pastors sought more self-consciously than ever before to ground their thinking in the problem of the congregations.

It was perfectly clear that this return did not draw upon any such natural identity—half-potential, half-actual—between the church-culture and saving idealism as that upon which the social-gospel pastors had counted in the 'twenties. The social-gospel pastors did not win mass audiences any more than the neo-orthodox. By the 'thirties, it was impossible to ignore certain facts. In various straightforward sociological investigations of the churches such as those for the Institute of Social and Religious Research, the deep investment of the churches in the old, unredeemed order was demonstrated by fact, figure, and chart. Samuel

Kincheloe's *Research Memorandum on Religion in the Depression* was still more interesting. Kincheloe pointed out the "confusion" of conservative congregations faced by the similarity of the New Deal program to many of the concrete proposals of the social gospel. Ministers were reading the Lynds' investigations of Middletown and taking warning: "The church is looked to as an emotionally necessary counterweight to the swift and engulfing changes going on throughout society." [1]

The wedge driven by the crisis betrayed itself vividly in the discrepancy between the pages of the *Christian Century* and of its annex, the *Christian Century Pulpit*. For the *Century*, the depression appeared as a product of basic social causes, for practical purposes identical with capitalism; for the *Pulpit*, the failure of men to surrender themselves personally to Christ lay at the heart of matters. That the two were not necessarily contradictory was true enough, but the *Century* could not put them together. It was, perhaps, in the election year of 1936 that the pathos showed itself most poignantly: Protestant leadership gave its most concerted response to the times in the National Preaching Mission, sponsored by a gamut of agencies from Federal Council to local church, which took to the road to reap a harvest anticipated by the theory that revivals follow depression.

> . . . the population which suffers but is not severely affected economically by the depression . . . middle class and hence in our churches, especially in our Protestant churches . . . begins to feel the need of a mental and emotional security, of an inner personal need of unity, tranquillity and certainty. It therefore desires and demands a form of preaching which feeds the personal life amidst a broken and disturbed social order. [2]

This was hardly to be the personal preaching implied in Tillich, in the Niebuhrs, in Haroutunian; it did not build on the logic of sin, it did not assume the sacred void, it was not heedless of culture, it did not appropriate despair. Perhaps the Liberty League, staff headquarters for laissez-faire Republicanism, on the one hand, and the crusade-preaching of Dr. Francis Townsend and Huey Long on the other, perhaps in fact the liberal-evangelic rhetoric of Roosevelt and Henry Wallace themselves, had channeled the flood of revival into politics. In any event, the tap introduced by the Preaching Mission into the reserves of Protestant feeling did not prove to be flowing. So far as the social gospel was concerned, the only clear justification it had for itself was this failure. Some sort of political preaching still seemed to be called for.

It was of course true that some men could carry on the old pure evangelism without any concern for the dilemma. E. Stanley Jones, in his national circuit-riding and in his books, *Christ's Alternative to Communism* and *The Choice Before Us,* preached the Kingdom in all its former absolutism, in its historic possibility, and in its dependence upon simply the sanctified will of converted men. In *The Choice Before Us,* Jones addressed his "word to men of business" and his "word to men of labor" without a trace of consciousness of the class analysis that Rauschenbusch had suggested and that the realism of the 'thirties assumed. There is no need for elaborate inquiry: Jones was applying to the social gospel the methods and enthusiasm of a long career in foreign missions, and simply soared above the strategical agonies of the religious debate, following a lone course and proving that no revolution ever sweeps clean.

Everywhere else, though, more complex responses were required. One technique of meeting the problem of the church was to concede that the congregations did not make up a social-gospel majority, only in order to recoup the loss at a later stage of argument. A manifesto of 1935, *The Younger Churchmen Look at the Church,* showed that such attempts to save the old optimism were not confined to the generation passing. One of these younger churchmen, Stanley North, a New York Congregationalist, used the logic of this "false" concession quite explicitly. North began by focusing matters sharply: the prophetic radical preacher would not, he said, last beyond the first sermon in the vast majority of Protestant churches. Another kind of preaching, a "realistic" radicalism, was necessary, taking into account the fact that the majority of people are conservative. What was this realistic preaching?

> The people of the church are conservative because their back-
> grounds and experiences make them so. They will become liberal
> or radical only as their experiences change. Therefore, the realisti-
> cally radical church will be a church of new experiences . . . There
> will be a minimum of indoctrination, a maximum of illumination
> through projects centering in problems of race, industry, slums, un-
> employment, rackets on the one hand, and in recreation, art, beauty,
> the theater, music, worship on the other.[3]

Technique was the answer. The roots of the conservatism analyzed in *Moral Man and Immoral Society* would wither in
projects centering on slums and the theater.

Another of the younger churchmen, Ralph Read, chose a different argument. Read, also a Congregationalist, on Long Island,
served as president of the Conference of Younger Churchmen
and as chairman of the New York City Congregationalist Social
Service Committee, and was a member of the Fellowship of
Socialist Christians. The trouble with the social gospel, he said,
was that it was not socialism; it had preached only ameliorization,
charity, and reform. Rauschenbusch had understood the necessity
of socialism, but the social gospel had preferred "the liberal reading of economic history." "Had this mistake not been committed,
the social gospel might have become a more powerful force in
American religious life."[4] The fault was one of insight. Read gave
ground a little by calling for inner disciplinary groups within the
larger body of the church, as the vanguard for religious radicalism; but, to the extent that he dealt with the issue, he indicated
that these disciplinary groups were in truth vanguards, leaven
within the church's lump, a lump prepared to receive the leaven.

> The condemnation due the Christian Church . . . is not alone that
> its social gospel has not been adequate, but also that it has at the
> same time been unable to do that which the majority of its members
> will so vehemently insist it is the chief business of the church to do.[5]

His strange implication was that a majority that had proved unwilling to accept the social gospel would accept socialism.

Religion in this outspoken, vigorous volume remained social
morality. No one undertook to examine the possibility that the

social gospel had been heard but could not be followed. The authors believed that it had been heard and perhaps followed, but that it had not been preached scientifically enough and with enough realistic economic radicalism. It was natural, therefore, that the book be profoundly nontheological, if not, here and there, explicitly antitheological in spirit. The volume was an indication of the endless complexity of the Protestant scene: fifteen of the nineteen contributors were Presbyterian or Congregationalist. The "Methodist phase" of the passion was drawing to a close, but Methodist enthusiasm carried on quite without discrimination by lines of historic denominational descent.

The leader of the social gospel in the Federal Council, F. E. Johnson, undertook a more serious wrestle with the problem of the congregations. Johnson proposed inner-church minority groups to soften the political tensions set up within conservative congregations by social-gospel preachers, and proposed such groups perhaps more sharply than anyone else in suggesting that they be given regularized institutional recognition. Yet the rationale for these inner sects remained ambiguous. They were required in the first place because the church could not be expected to embark upon social crusades; the church was devoted to satisfaction of religious needs, and religious needs cut across the lines of ethical conviction. Johnson here was taking sides against the old social-gospel position on the "captivity" of the church. Rauschenbusch, Kirby Page, and Charles Clayton Morrison had all organized church history into two periods, pre- and post-Constantinian. But in 1934, Shirley Jackson Case, in *The Social Triumph of the Ancient Church*, argued that the Constantinian "captivity" had actually made possible the exercise of Christian influence over a wider area of the society, and called for a utilitarian ethic of gradualism in place of a perfectionist ethic suitable only for a detached, sectarian church that could have little social influence. Johnson agreed; the church, he said, was for all men and not only for saints. It would be futile and improper to try to put the church "on record" for great schemes of social reconstruction, or even for the New Deal.[6]

But the simplicity of this position was misleading, for Johnson

had misgivings even about sectarian, minority action. Entirely
too much energy had already gone into small, protesting idealistic
groups preaching radical reconstruction, he said; more necessary
were immediate realism and consensus on immediate objectives
to be pursued by the church. This was the opposite of Ralph
Read's argument, a scaling-down rather than a scaling-up of the
specific political content of the social evangel. Peculiarly, this
contradicted the strongly "environmentalist" note Johnson had
struck earlier in elucidating his doctrine of personality. He did
not wish the sectarian minorities to press directly for altering
the environment, but wanted concentration upon definite goals,
such as social insurance and labor rights, which, he thought, the
broad membership of the churches—and not only the minorities
—might be persuaded to support.

These church tactics went hand in hand with Johnson's refusal
to accept the pragmatic estimates of politics and history that
nerved neo-orthodoxy. He was ready, in *The Social Gospel Re-
examined* in 1941, to assimilate as much realistic criticism as
seemed compatible with a basic liberal view of history, but no
more. He halted sharply at the point where Niebuhr argued that
grace and regeneration could not be accumulated in history,
justifying his resistance by explicit appeal to American experience
and American congregations. Once upon a time, he said, the
classic myths of Antichrist and Resurrection, used by Niebuhr to
deny that history was progress, might have had some validity,
but no longer. At least, Johnson argued, the Christian laymen of
America did not think so. Liberal Christianity had its mythology
too, more relevant to modern conditions, part of which was the
idea of progress, of progressive consummation of the Kingdom,
a consummation—as Rauschenbusch had written—never completed, but self-validating in the pursuit. In addition, the normative character of orderly progress rather than catastrophic transi-
tions was another part of the liberal mythology, more convincing
to Americans than the crisis theology based on Europe, a theology
that would pass when the crisis passed.[7]

Johnson was sure that the liberal tendency to set the church
busy at whatever good work needed to be done was wrong. His

characterization of the church itself would have been acceptable enough to the neo-orthodox, even the Barthians: that part of the community on its knees, a "spiritual community in which people consent to endure the passing of judgment upon their own waywardness and unfaithfulness." His description of the logic of judgment was less acceptable:

> If Christianity has a true social message it is one that a community has validated in its own life . . . Truly prophetic preaching is preaching that puts into words clearer than the people can command insights deeper than they may individually have attained to, but which are so authentically in their experience as Christians that those who hear are constrained to say, "Verily, this is the word of God." [8]

The point of difference came also with the question of what these deeper insights were. Johnson in effect was denying the neo-orthodox view of politics and history, and then neo-orthodoxy itself, on the pragmatic ground that its view of politics and history was not in the experience of the American Christian community. The apparently purely technical philosophic issues dividing his liberalism from neo-orthodoxy grounded in definite social and political judgments, judgments resting essentially in the assumption that America was normative.

The crucially revealing feature of this defense of liberalism was its field of evidence. For Johnson, as for Charles Clayton Morrison of the *Christian Century*, the two leading social-gospel exponents of a kind of neo-naturalism set strongly against neo-orthodoxy, the finally decisive field of inquiry and evidence for ethics and theology was not the self. The decisive method of inquiry was not, as Niebuhr had said, introspection. Morrison gave this latter its social-gospel reading. He attacked the "subjective" God of evangelical Protestantism and spoke of a shift in the theological center of gravity from the inner life to the social order. The shift was owing to

> . . . the discovery that there is no way to conceive or define an individual which does not include his social environment, the perception that all real moral problems of individual experience are the subjective side of a situation whose objective side is social. . . . [9]

In *What Is Christianity?* Morrison demanded that the Christian's individual experience, which, he believed, Protestantism had isolated, be returned to its organic context in a living church. Perfectly proper so far as it went, this demand Morrison made quite without care to distinguish such individual experience in any degree or kind from its context. Here was again the liberal subsidence of the self into social psychology, the failure to comprehend what religious issues lay in the relation of man and society, and here was the real and only ground upon which Niebuhr and his liberal opponents could have engaged in unconfused debate. Neo-orthodox failure to move the debate decisively onto this ground left the way open for the liberal pastors to cling to their identification of the Word with American culture and the tradition of the churches.

Such identification did not save Johnson and Morrison from difficulties over the New Deal just as severe as those undergone by Niebuhr himself, however. Still men of the social gospel, they still wished to find some relevance for themselves in politics, so they could not ignore the New Deal. Moreover, if it was the American process they wished to celebrate against the crisis theology, they could hardly ignore the most dramatic feature of that process.

When Franklin Roosevelt announced in his speech in Detroit in October, 1932, that he was "as radical as the Federal Council," [10] he by no means swept into his ranks the church leaders who had written into the Social Creeds of 1912 and 1919 something like a check list of principles that the New Deal was soon to make law. We have suggested that the prophets could preach the anti-capitalist abstractions of the Kingdom more easily in terms of long-range socialism than they could preach capitalistic reforms sponsored by a Democratic administration. But the Federal Council lent the New Deal friendly support. The council's official committees, its *Bulletin,* edited by Samuel McCrae Cavert, and its *Information Service,* directed by Johnson, broadcast this support in tones temperate but firm. In a way, it was one of the most impressive testimonials to the achievements of the social gospel.

Perhaps the most vulnerable and conspicuous of the social-gospel agencies, the council was conscious of the peculiarity of its position. The favor it lent the New Deal expressed its "educational" rather than its "representative" character certainly, and there was a price to be paid: the editors of the *Bulletin* suggested in 1937 that had the council not held its ground under conservative attack, in particular upon its support for labor, it might have had twice the money from its constituents that it actually received.[11] But the council had held, and did hold, the ground. It was important that it did so. Its commitment to the Social Creed was an official commitment, and had this one most formal, most conspicuous social-gospel covenant been broken, the pressures toward sealing off the passion in sectarian enclaves and beyond institutional frontiers could have been overwhelming.

The favor it lent to the New Deal did not represent a conversion. In its emphasis upon planning in the years 1930 to 1932, lacking wholly in political specifications, the council had been receptive to tactics of stewardship and conservative paternalism as well as to tactics of liberal and labor political action. But the years 1930 to 1932 had seemed to require immediate action and the council was not in a position to propose long-range ideological standards. It could only respond "yes" or "no" to the givens of the situation. Gerard Swope and Owen D. Young were not early New Dealers, but the council had praised them not because of that; it had only been unable to criticize them. When, in 1934, the *Bulletin* found the New Deal moving toward internal crisis, as appeals to "social motive" proved insufficient in securing the ends of the program, the editors were free enough to find the heart of the program in section seven of the NRA code, specifying the right of labor to organize. They insisted that the heart of the duty of the church was to support that right. Although troubled somewhat by the rigors of the struggle, the *Bulletin* heralded a turning point in early 1937 during the CIO strikes. Nothing of this implied a new approach to political ethics, based on power analysis; nevertheless the fact remained that the council social-gospel leaders did rise to emphasize the importance of unions.[12]

Throughout all this, the council tried to maintain the old

synthesis between religion and politics. It had help. The President himself spoke at the council's twenty-fifth anniversary celebration in Washington, December, 1933, and equated the ideals of the church and the government. Henry Wallace confirmed the alliance of "Statesmanship and Religion." Later, in 1934, Daniel Roper offered his comparison of "Christianity and Economics" to the readers of the *Bulletin*.[13]

But it was not as though this fulfilled Johnson's test of loyalty to the deepest insights of the congregations. He could hardly claim that the congregations had been won over to the New Deal. Contemplating, in 1939, the contemporary impasse of the prophets, W. K. Anderson, a Johnstown, Pennsylvania, Methodist pastor, observed that the New Deal years had inspired a backwash of social reaction appealing to the old-time religion: ". . . the social gospel is in the amazing and tragic predicament of being identified with the New Deal, by the haters of the New Deal." [14] Scorn for the voting performance of the "wise" and the "good" and the "righteous" could be poured out in the pages of *Radical Religion* as its socialist, neo-orthodox editors interrupted their criticism of the Roosevelt program to hail the Roosevelt majorities, but such scorn was impossible for the council. Instead, it was forced to say:

> There are many indications that responsible leaders of business and industry, harassed by increasing costs and uncertainty as to future government policies, have been impelled toward an aggressive conservatism which is not really congenial to their sensibilities. A widespread evil in the world today is the frustration experienced by people of sensitive conscience.[15]

This did not prevent Johnson, for one, from slashing regularly at the laissez-faire preaching of the National Association of Manufacturers. But it led the council to maintain almost alone the old tradition of getting employers and labor to sit down with ministers in the coöperative spirit. The Michigan Council of Churches convened a conference during the General Motors strike of 1937 to "secure more information about industrial conflicts." In 1937 the council resolved to set afoot a Mission to Industry to promote "friendly understanding and cooperation between organized labor and employers," one of the triumphs of which was to win the attendance of the president of the NAM.[16] These were important efforts, which would have been approved by Niebuhr himself as part of the program for softening necessary conflict; but in the case of the council, not only did they not help toward freeing ethics from utilitarian domestication, they did not help win over the church offended by the utilitarian politics of the New Deal.

Council spokesmen were not embarrassed by the socialists to their left, however. Replying to an attack put forth by Senator Vandenberg, upon the dangerous expediencies and novelties of the administration, Johnson held off both sides:

> . . . it is the essence of the New Deal to *be* experimental. It commenced with two convictions: (1) that the economic arrangements existing under the capitalism of the twenties were unsound; (2) that the socialist alternative was not the way out. To find a *via media* was essentially an experimental process.[17]

Johnson associated this middle way with the vision of decentralized economic democracy that he refreshened in his re-examination of the social gospel in 1940, and we can now see a little further why that vision tended to be lost. It was associated with Johnson's anxiety to remain close to the congregations, which left him without means to hinge his vision to any existent political interests. The vision became merely exhortatory.

Johnson's New Deal politics thus left his views about "true prophetic preaching" in considerable shade. He could only hope the community would validate the New Deal—and, thereby, validate the liberal mythology he opposed to Niebuhr. It was of course a perfectly legitimate hope, but Johnson never had the chance to argue that liberal Protestant congregations shared in much of the validation provided by the nation at large.

Like most of the problems of the social gospel, that posed by the New Deal ended not in resolution but in suspension. In 1940, the council held another interfaith conference on the problem of unemployment. At the opening call to meeting, the dark suggestion was raised ". . . that a nation which has not solved its own economic problems may be tempted to divert attention toward a war psychology and armament economics." [18] This chilling prospect would seem to reflect back not only upon the council's earlier estimates of the New Deal, but more seriously upon its persistent habit of justifying whatever good order seemed likely at a given time. But nothing more was to come of it; the debate of the 'thirties was coming to its end, overwhelmed by the new terms of the debate on war.

A still more important case of support for the New Deal hand in hand with an effort to preserve the old image of saving church was that of Charles Clayton Morrison of the *Century*. The *Century* stood out among the organs of that benighted moralism castigated by Niebuhr and the socialist realists. It supported Roosevelt and the New Deal almost from the beginning; yet that support was not uncritical, and it was not in the beginning support for the New Deal as an end in itself.

Morrison's endorsement of Hoover in 1932 caused him no trouble at all: Roosevelt soon was leading where Morrison had insisted, in 1932, that Hoover, by the logic of the situation, must lead—out of the jungle of laissez faire. The first and foremost of the virtues of the new policy fixed here: laissez faire was dead. But the death of laissez faire was not enough. The New Deal represented movement in a direction, and it was the direction that pleased the *Century*. There was no fear of words: the editors said they believed Roosevelt must move toward "socialism" and they welcomed the process. The New Deal was not itself socialistic, nor did the President intend to institute socialism; the President was working within the capitalistic system and apparently he desired to keep it. But in the very effort required to shore capitalism up, reform and reprieve it, its strength was sapped by the laws of a kind of psychoeconomics.

> If, within the narrower zone left by the new deal for profit-making, the business community does not find a sufficient motive power to resuscitate itself and produce the work and goods which public welfare demands, there will be left to the President but one option, namely, the taking over of business by the government itself and the operation of it for public welfare rather than for private profit.[19]

Restriction and regularization of competition, child-labor regulation, wage-and-hour prescriptions, monetary and banking regulations—all these restricted the field for the profit motive, and without satisfaction of that motive, the system would wither. The President would then have to respond. The *Century* interpreted the elections of 1934 as a mandate: "Go left, Mr. President, go left . . . many features of the 1934 election suggest that a union of forces for a vigorous offensive in support of an avowedly radical program is not impossible." [20]

This was hardly the uncritical enthusiasm of mere liberalism. The socialist realists pointed out that the New Deal was not the end of the profit system and was not a transfer of power, and the *Century* agreed. The realists could not legitimately demand that the administration legislate socialism instantly, knowing that the time was not ripe. And again the *Century* agreed. What, then, was the difference between them? It was clear: the socialists believed the political public had to be reconstituted. The *Century* did not.

This difference came out in Morrison's suggestion of the role open to the church in meeting a peculiar dilemma raised by the New Deal. Social-gospel logic argued that a system bred men in its own image; capitalism depended upon the profit motive, its men were bred selfish and grasping. A coöperative system would call out men of coöperation and good will. But in the New Deal season of transition, what would be the effect of the old sort of man upon the new system coming to birth?

> In the long run the system itself—taking the "system" in its broadest terms as including not only the economic but the entire cultural context of the new order—will produce its own men . . . But the processes of education are too slow to count for much in meeting our imminent crisis. Some agency with immediate moral power is required.[21]

This agency was available. The church, the Christian church, had to preach forth the new economic man, else the old economic man would destroy the new order before it had time to take over the task of environmental evangelization itself.

The old and basic social-gospel tactic, set in this particular new context, stood exposed in its concrete pretensions. It looked suspiciously like a faith of desperation, yet in the *Century* it was not desperation, as its implicit estimate of the political public showed. Reviewing the Roosevelt program in 1934, the editors concluded that a revolution was in progress. "This is only another way of saying that the step from the Roosevelt system to a true and candid socialization of the economic system would be a much easier one to take than is generally realized." [22] The first step had been taken already, and the first step was the hardest.

It was not necessary for the socialist realists to deny that a first step had been taken in order to deny that the first step was the hardest. They did deny it, emphatically, in their anticipation of a "last step," that perhaps distant but "almost" inevitable hour of open resistance to the politics of justice. In this estimate of the New Deal as the critical, hardest step, Morrison was able to smother the issue of violence, and its coördinate, the issue of class. It was part of his retention of the social gospel. He was excused from the debate over coercion, from the search for a political ethic, and therefore from the search for a new religious Word to preach to the idealists on the one hand and to the congregations of the middle on the other. Yet the old rough sociology of the 'twenties was crumbled. Plainly, the Protestant middle was not carrying the ideal; it was not enrolled in the Roosevelt majorities. And the very assignment Morrison chose for the church betrayed clearly enough that neither church nor church-community provided the real driving power for social change. Its assignment was to acquiesce in the evolutionary revolution; its duty was reflexive, not creative, a defense, not a crusade. Who might actually bear the evolutionary revolution was left unspecified. The *Century* still understood the weaknesses of the AFL; it still called for an expanded labor movement.[23] But the radical future was not hinged to a more aggressive labor movement; somehow a socialist issue from the New Deal could be anticipated without reconstitution of the political audience.

The vision was a political parallel to Morrison's neo-naturalist theology, the key concept of which was "emergent evolution." The immanent processes of creation brought forth new and higher forms of meaning, genuine emergents inexplicable by mechanistic causation, revealing thereby the divine in history. It was sufficient for Morrison to read the New Deal and its future as emerging from the immanences of American life. He could not explain the fact, but the fact was enough. The anguish nerving pacifism, socialism, revolutionary absolutism, and realism was unnecessary.

Morrison's benevolent indifference to the Socialist party never wavered. In the fall of 1937 he took note of its rapid disintegration, confirming his predictions of third-party futility. Roy Burt, then executive secretary of the Socialist party, having left the ministry and his post with the Methodist Epworth League five years before for more direct action, took exception to these comments. In the course of his remarks, he referred to "the known loyalty of the *Christian Century* to capitalism." [24] The reference was disparaging. But was the *Century* loyal to capitalism then, after all, behind its verbal celebration of the socialist ideal? Was the analysis of 1933 to 1934 camouflage? Burt's comment obscured the facts: the *Century was* loyal to capitalism in 1937, but it had not been in 1933 and 1934.

Burt's accusation was directed at a *Century* that had followed the automobile strikes of the CIO in 1936 and 1937 and had hailed them as signals of "a new industrial era." Heartily approving the CIO, the *Century* approved the sit-down strike technique as well, as ". . . by far the best method of conducting industrial warfare as yet discovered." It agreed with Reinhold Niebuhr and against the Federal Council that cries about the "lawlessness" of the strikes were not to the point. The strikes were intended to establish new canons of law; old concepts of property rights were being not abolished, but expanded, to include not only buildings and machines and credit but jobs as well. Capitalism was becoming something radically different from what it had been for the generation past. The rise of the CIO symbolized the new order, in which labor would hold a position sufficient to secure its rights. And the government, led by Roosevelt, was no longer simply umpire for the game of laissez faire, but assumed responsibility for the economic conditions of the game and for its ground rules. Income and inheritance taxes, for instance, were more than revenue measures; they were directed at disparities of poverty and wealth that had subverted the old game. It was the "drastically reformed capitalism" endorsed by 51 per cent of the ministers in the *World Tomorrow*'s poll of 1934 that the *Century* here hailed.[25]

This was a rather remarkable moment. Here was the first reasonably clear evocation of the vision of reformed capitalism to appear within the social passion, as a withdrawal from or retraction of a previous commitment to socialism. The *Century*'s position reflected Morrison's own old urge to realism, the realism that had dismissed the "long-range" for the "short-range" in 1928, the realism that had found only the scholasticism of political mystics in debates over what to do in event of a fascist uprising after a parliamentary victory for socialism, what to do in event of political chaos following the breakdown of all parties, what to do in event of war. Something was happening in society: was not the study and understanding of this actuality the important job? Capitalism was not going in America as Marx had predicted: was it not better to abandon Marx rather than complain about the perversity of reality? [26]

Ironically, Morrison's affair with the New Deal amounted to something like a fulfillment of Niebuhr's basic prescription for political ethics. Morrison did not hail the new, rationalized capitalism until it appeared that capitalists would not be its only masters. He was delighted that Roosevelt asserted the responsibility of the government within the economic arena.[27] Big government and big labor had risen to take their required places alongside big capital. But the old social-gospel courage was withered, its inner hemorrhage confirmed. Morrison had not considered the New Deal an end in itself in 1933 and 1934, because the New Deal had not even intended to eliminate the profit motive and bring forth the new man. And there was no suggestion in 1937 that the profit motive stood to disappear with the new arrangements; the new arrangements were still capitalism. The new system did not require the ethic of Jesus or the socialized individual. The *Century*, however, felt inspired to no revision of social-gospel rationale; the rationale had simply silently expired. This of course did not mean that the vision of reformed capitalism was fatal to the social passion in general, as distinguished from the social gospel particularly. Eventually, the majority of the leaders of both neo-orthodox and neo-liberal positions would take up much of the kind of short-range, nonideological, mass-party politics Morrison followed in the 'thirties. Yet Morrison had unavowedly unraveled the old high identities, morality and religion, the Christianization of man and the Christianization of society, the individual and the social gospel, as Niebuhr dramatically sundered them. The sundering was creative, releasing a new energy and a new evangel, the unraveling was a retreat.

The "second honeymoon" of 1937 did not last. The *Century* continued to defend the New Deal against attacks from the right. Late in 1938, however, the President seemed to have lost his liberal zest. Unemployment remained; other vital social problems remained. This final shift in tone was bound up with Morrison's growing preoccupation with foreign policy. Once, cautiously, without pressing the line until later, he suggested what the council had suggested, that armaments policy was designed as a quick way to prosperity and employment.[28] Where such an isolationist liberal as Morrison would have wanted domestic policy to proceed, were it not to be overtaken by war, he left unsaid. Thus, on a rough average, the anti-New Deal neo-orthodox pastors were turned toward Roosevelt, the pro-New Deal social-gospel pastors against him, by the war, both leaving their judgments on the New Deal itself without conclusion.

As with Johnson, Morrison's New Deal views take on full interest in light of his strategy for the church. Morrison drove on throughout the 'thirties with the concept of the church he had set forth in *The Social Gospel and the Christian Cultus*, where he described the sixteen centuries since Constantine as apostasy. Vehement against Barthianism and all infection of American theology with European moods, the advice he gave the church nonetheless was to withdraw and align itself "against" the world. Excoriating secularized culture, he came to the point of denying that any backlog of Christian faith still remained in the secular mind and of asserting that the foundations of the West in general were hopeless. The church had to disassociate, and Morrison pointed for a beginning at the churches' financial indebtedness, their record of support for the First World War, and their acquiescence in such demands of the state as the military chaplaincy system. He despaired of finding allies. Not only did he doubt the worth of the "chambers of commerce" and the universities, he doubted labor, for which, in *The Social Gospel and the Christian Cultus,* he had in momentary heroics contemplated trading some of the bourgeois congregations. The church was quite unprepared to meet the problems of the secular world, he said; its peace movement had collapsed, it had no economic program, it had no defense against the totalitarian state. It must withdraw. The social gospel was not the church and Christian men entering the world, but the life of Christian men within the church.[29]

One way by which this could have been made consistent with the *Century's* call upon the church to send forth the new economic man who would guarantee the gains of the New Deal would have been to withdraw ultimate religious sanctions from politics altogether and locate them where Niebuhr and the neo-orthodox located them, "above" and "beyond" history, or else, as neo-orthodoxy implied, in individual, not social existence. But Morrison was not converting to neo-orthodoxy. His "church" was the ultimate symbol of a liberal American nationalism given religious stature. It pointed at that social experience of a whole culture which Johnson had used to oppose Niebuhr. Morrison's church was still the same community to which he had appealed as touchstone in 1928. It embraced essentially, as his thinking in the two years before Pearl Harbor was decisively to reveal, the community of Midwestern—and backcountry Eastern—Protestantism, progressively Puritan in personal morality, progressive in politics in the old Rauschenbusch sense, progressive and liberal in religion, wholly dependent upon a social stability for which— as it was the mark of the neo-orthodox to see—mid-twentieth-century society, even in America, provided no guarantees. His writings on the church constituted a spiritual ground for isolationism. Morrison would not hear of sectarian tactics, even such as Johnson accepted, for he was demanding sectarian purity of the whole church and, by extension, of American life; he could see divine "emergence" in both and could see it nowhere else. The withdrawal of the church from the world was effectively to mean the withdrawal of the nation from the world, and the preservation of the nation in the old Protestant image of an historical Kingdom.

In this concept of the church, Morrison symbolized more perfectly than anyone else the toughness of the nut the neo-orthodox were trying to crack. A curious passage in *What Is Christianity?* condensed the situation.

> The totalitarian states are an expression of the recoil from individualism. We currently characterize them as "demonic." Their demonic character, however, does not lie in their totalitarianism, but in the nationalistic or racial or class basis of their totalitarianism.[30]

This was to betray the deepest ground of resistance to the new word. For neo-orthodox psychology, any totalitarianism was demonic, even some imaginable totalitarianism of universal love or the American way of life—even the totalitarianism of some historical Kingdom of God. Morrison's polemic against "individualism" contrasted starkly with Niebuhr's view that the ultimately decisive field for theology was the self.

The New Deal served in all this to sustain the logically difficult but polemically natural pattern of Morrison's thinking. It acted to confirm him pragmatically in his resistance to the socialist neo-orthodox, both as socialists and as neo-orthodox. Although the New Deal was not in fact an emanation of the Protestant community, it did not appear to be threatening that community and, as Morrison was realistic enough to see, was saving it from more disastrous alternatives. He could thus safely return the social gospel into the church as a politics purer and higher than the neo-orthodox could imagine. This left the paradox that, in the two outstanding cases of support for the New Deal, both Johnson and Morrison found themselves claiming something of theological significance about American life, which they could not claim for the Protestant congregations and churches themselves.

It was a commentary upon all social-gospel history that the only reasonably systematic and persistent effort actually to penetrate a denomination was not made until enthusiasm had long evaporated and inner coherence had been mortally disturbed. It is worth while to take some notice of the sort of program that had not yet been pressed upon the liberal churches, and its fate. This was the effort made by Congregationalist leaders, who organized the Council for Social Action at the Oberlin National Council of 1934.

The Congregationalists' social-service department had been a division of the denomination's Education Society; A. E. Holt served as its secretary until 1924, Hubert Herring succeeded him. The Council for Social Action was organized as an independent body, both to intensify the work of education within the church and to sponsor direct social action. Although it received only $40,000 of the $60,000 voted at Oberlin for the biennium, the council was by all odds the best-supported social-gospel agency. With Holt as chairman, Herring as director, it was to carry out its work through several full-time secretaries assigned to various fields of social-gospel interest.[31] Trouble was threatened at the 1936 National Council. At Oberlin, in 1934, in addition to ratifying the social-action council, the National Council had passed a resolution denouncing "the profit motive" in line with old social-gospel logic. The two actions had not been concerted; the group pressing for the council had not been on the floor when the profit-motive resolution was voted; the floor had indeed been sparsely populated for that vote, 147 delegates of 764 voting it through, 130 to 17. Publicity given the Oberlin meeting tied the two together, however. In 1936, eastern laymen, from Connecticut and New Jersey in particular, came with plans for rescinding the 1934 vote on the profit motive, for some kind of affirmation of capitalism, and for restriction of the social-action council to research. With the defeat of these plans, largely through heavy clerical rather than lay opposition, the council emerged as a stable, accepted, permanent body of the denomination, drawing on the common treasury and entering the war the healthiest and most active official agency for the social faith in Protestantism.[32]

Not, like the Fellowship of Socialist Christians or the Fellowship of Reconciliation, a semisectarian society for exploration of and witness to the passion, the council was purely a taskforce for implementation of the passion. The most significant aspect of its plans was that intended to carry the social Word to the local level, through study groups within the local churches. These were to organize their own communities for action concerning slums, local unemployment, local industries, race relations, and the like. Little time was spent theorizing on the question of how such interest tied into large-scale political issues—labor action, force, socialism—on which the prophets were dividing. In actual practice, the work of the council itself came down to providing information and education on social, economic, and political matters upon which the typical parishioner typically registered his sentiments as voter, not as community activist. The council published its pamphlets and bulletins to stand in racks in church lobbies or to be used by leaders of church classes and discussion groups. *Social Action* covered key national issues and surveyed various areas of social concern, in the fashion of the Methodist Federation *Bulletin* and the Federal Council's *Information Service,* but on a considerably expanded scale.

In the first two or three years of publication, under Hubert Herring, the tenor of these discussions in *Social Action* was clear. Measures being pressed by the administration in Washington were criticized as too little and too slow. The bulletin carried no ideological line of its own, however; its pages were open to Harry Laidler of the League for Industrial Democracy, Norman Thomas, Paul Douglas, and other liberal socialists, but its criticism of the New Deal drew more upon a generalized sense of urgency than upon systematic socialist perspectives. Herring himself—together with his assistant, Alfred Schmalz—was an outspoken advocate of isolationism, a position to which a council-sponsored Peace Plebiscite in 1935 had given sanction.

Under Dwight Bradley, succeeding Herring in 1939, the

council and *Social Action* continued to cover the social and political scene, but the critical and perhaps potentially doctrinaire coloring faded. Any tactical focus upon labor and industry vanished in favor of a scatter approach, taking up race relations, coöperatives, public power, agriculture, and the rest one by one for neutral discussion. In the process, discussion of the international scene also shifted, from Herring's fervent anti-interventionism to neutral clarification of the differences dividing men on foreign policy, accompanied by a strong insistence that no position—pacifist nonintervention, pragmatic nonintervention, or intervention—could claim exclusive Christian sanction.[33]

Both of these shifts, or drifts, in *Social Action* paralleled the emergence, led by Dwight Bradley in the council, of a new religious rationale; from 1939 the council was one of the voices of neo-liberalism, laying strong emphasis upon the centrality of the sacramental church and recovery of a realistic evangelical tradition. This move in itself was commentary upon the five preceding years of effort to move the denomination by the lever of the old social gospel: it had not been moved, and now, by the arguments of the new leaders, it did not have to be moved in the way the social gospel had imagined.

In all this, the record of John C. Bennett, the most symptomatic Congregationalist spokesman for the social passion in the 'thirties, was instructive. In his contribution to the 1935 volume of the younger churchmen, Bennett stood out in two respects. He highlighted the tension between social liberalism and the congregations much more sharply than others; at the same time he more strongly emphasized qualities in the church broader and deeper than any interest it did or did not have in social liberalism. His effort to hold these two readings together was part of his neo-liberalism.

As to the first, at this time Bennett, like F. E. Johnson, advocated inner-church sectarianism. Politically liberal circles as inner-church groups would be in a position to leaven the congregations to whatever extent was possible, although that was not a great extent, Bennett agreed. Bennett wished to preserve a heavy political responsibility for the church, but he shifted it explicitly from the task of leading social reform to the duty of following it. Still a Socialist party member, he wanted church people to acquiesce in the "inevitable" revolution so that it might be a peaceful revolution. He supported the New Deal, but only as a next step toward the socialist revolution.[34]

By 1939 Bennett was supporting the New Deal in a different spirit. Revolution had given way to pragmatics. But still:

> It is uncomfortable to have no political movement in which one can have much faith, and to be left with the bare hope that out of the New Deal and the new political consciousness of labor a coherent progressive movement may come into existence.[35]

So far as the tension between congregations and political liberalism was concerned, this abandonment of socialism for the limited aims and "discomfort" of the New Deal availed no more than it had availed the Federal Council and the *Century*. The New Dealing pastor was in as difficult a relationship with his congregation as the socialist pastor, probably more so.

Bennett's increasing emphasis meanwhile fell upon those duties of the church transcending all the pragmatics of politics. This went together with his cautious assimilation of Niebuhr. Bennett was one of those, like Walter Horton of Oberlin, Henry Van Dusen of Union, and Robert Calhoun of Yale, who felt the force of the neo-orthodox attack upon liberalism, but who at the same time feared the sacrifice of certain liberal values that neo-orthodoxy, too brutally imposed, might entail. These men feared to see reason challenged too greatly by doctrines of a transcendent God, and by a too radical split between special revelation—available only to faith—and general revelation—available to reason. They appreciated the neo-orthodox revival of a sense for the "supra-moral" pinnacle in God's nature, but they were anxious that human values not be frozen on those terrific slopes. They could agree to restoration of the redeemer Christ at the "end" of history, but wished not to lose the historical Jesus. They could accept Niebuhr's criticism of theories of progress, but wished the meaning of history to remain visible.[36]

As we have suggested, it was Niebuhr's intention to provide

for such fears. But there remained a difference between Niebuhr
and, for instance, Bennett—whose *Christian Realism* of 1941
might have seemed an expression of neo-orthodoxy—even after
Niebuhr was through expressing his own objections to Karl
Barth. Niebuhr had arrived at his final position by a process of
establishing dialectical poles, Bennett by reaching out toward the
poles. Niebuhr split the utilitarian middle, Bennett tried to expand
it. This difference in methods led to a difference in destinations.
Bennett and the neo-liberals, returning to the church, effectively
abandoned the political questions that had inspired neo-orthodoxy. With Niebuhr, relatively indifferent to this return to the
church until well after the Second World War, neo-orthodoxy
preserved its high potential for criticism of the church-nation-
culture, and neo-liberalism did not.

In *Christian Realism*, Bennett argued for the church, as distinguished from the politics of world community and class justice,
on the ground of its claim to point to the redemptive activity of
God, its claim to minister to *the* problem of man. "The problem
of man is not primarily an economic or political problem. It is
finally the problem of finding meaning for his life in the face
of sin and suffering and death." [37] This left a question: no matter
how essential for the problem of man, how *did* the church involve
itself in economic and political affairs? The interesting thing was
that Bennett found himself ready to make political claims for
the church larger than those he had made in 1935. This reflected
a subtle relaxation in his sense of the immediate, American crisis,
already displayed in his turn to the New Deal, and a subtle
redefinition of the crisis as the war came on. The church, Bennett
said, might emerge as a community capable of holding all centers
of power under some degree of criticism, capable of weathering
the world storms ahead without buckling to them. It had, he
argued, real qualities for such a role. It lived by its own resources,
without state support; some social conscience had been awakened
within it; theology was reviving and driving to bedrock; a new
ecumenical consciousness, deliberately seeking to transcend all
divisions of nation, class, race, and creed, had risen. These were

objective factors, promising strength, and on their basis Bennett could rise to a new call that echoed the old social gospel.

> Today the task of the Church is to develop among its own people a mind that understands the social implications of Christianity and which seeks to make social decisions intelligently in the light of the Christian social perspective. If we cannot change the mind of the constituency of the Church, we cannot change the mind of the world.[38]

But actually, this was not the old social-gospel call. The congregations were not being asked to accept revolution or socialism or the New Deal or any particular politics. They were expected to acquiesce in the New Deal certainly; but basically, Bennett was asking them to accept the church as an organization and a symbol above and beyond and transcending all politics and political divisions. Herewith, the tension Bennett had felt between the congregations and political realism seemed to be resolved.

The peculiarity of this neo-liberalism was that, trying to avoid all extremes, it found itself back in a pre-social-gospel position, proposing a religion that would somehow serve as politics. A church that could not be persuaded to political realism could somehow incarnate a religious realism politically more adequate than the realistic politics it refused. Thus the Council for Social Action, giving up its social-gospel ways, did not then grasp the meaning of the neo-orthodox attack on the social gospel. That meaning was to set religion in a critical, "dialectical" tension with politics, and with culture generally. Neo-liberalism tended simply to obscure the political, cultural pole altogether in a new culture-religion merely somewhat more somber in hue, and again called "church."

As against the complexities of these rearrangements of the meaning of the church, the sectarian response to the 'thirties was simplicity. The sectarians persisted in tending the flame of pure intentions. Conceivably, sectarian pacifist socialism might have been transformed into pacifist support for the New Deal.

This, however, would have been a religious lapse, a religious leap backward, so to speak, and not just a pragmatic adjustment. The nearest approach to such a transformation appeared in a book published by Sherwood Eddy and Kirby Page in 1937, *Creative Pioneers*. The authors saw the New Deal as within the framework of capitalism, yet they agreed that it had made achievements of some value. Fundamental changes were occurring in public thought on economic questions, changes perhaps more drastic than any in a hundred years; the TVA alone challenged the old system of private ownership of giant industries, and perhaps would become the model for further programs. Here was the chance for a revision, not necessarily of the socialist end, but at least of the methods, the tempo, and the values of the interim. The authors, however, chose to reëmphasize urgency and anxiety:

> . . . the time element makes one apprehensive about a slow journey toward socialization. When will the American people be plunged again into the abyss of another economic collapse? How serious is the threat of fascist dictatorship in this country as a means of suppressing discontent and revolt? And every decade that passes before socialization is achieved will witness a continuance of tragic misery for the masses and increasing bitterness in the class struggle.[39]

Radical change, rapid change, pacifist change: the formula stood.

Perhaps, as the hypnotic prewar air thickened, there was no time to explore the politics of domestic social justice any further. Perhaps because of the constantly more obvious sectarianism of international war pacifism, sectarian psychology was confirmed. At any rate, in one of Page's manuals for the devotional life, published in 1941, socialism—firmly distinguished once again from Stalinism-Leninism—appeared as one of the aspects of his "prayerful spirit," quite in the old terms. The New Deal had not been a new experience. The attitudes and options of 1932 had come through untouched. The old economy of religion and politics had been preserved.[40]

It was A. J. Muste who formulated the deepest attraction of the sectarian impulse, because he had once forsaken it. In Paris, in 1936, having fled the schisms of the left, and reflecting on the lurid past, he had his vision. "Take the way of war and there is war not only between nations, classes, individuals, but war, division and consequent frustration within your own soul." [41] At Bound Brook, New Jersey, in the fall of 1936, before the national conference of the Fellowship of Reconciliation, he made his confession. "I return to the Fellowship . . . knowing from experience in the revolutionary movement that he who denies love betrays justice and murders peace." [42] Still a Congregational minister in good standing, he stepped in as head of the industrial department of the FOR; later, upon the death of Edmund Chaffee, he was pastor of the New York Labor Temple until 1940.[43] But in giving up violence, he did not give up something else. Rec-ollecting his political days, Muste observed how it had been the doctrine of "the Party," of "belonging" that had absorbed more and more interest. Lenin's doctrine of the Party quite resembled that of the True Church: it had a saving, revolutionary word, it knew itself as the only true Party, it knew it could not fail for it was the instrument of God. To belong was to know meaning, and this knowledge could not be abandoned. In Paris it had been clear to Muste that pride and tyranny had infected the one true Party-Church. How could the true True Church protect itself? Only by not protecting itself, only by never straying from love. The true believer could not stray from the True Church itself, for it was only in belonging that he could be a true be-liever.[44]

Nowhere as intense as among the explicit sectarians, the wish to be able to "believe by belonging" worked in much of the return to the church everywhere in the 'thirties. The mark of the sectarians was their lack of reservations based upon the human limitations of the visible church itself, even of the Fellowship of Reconciliation. It was a sociological eye that pierced to those limitations and, accepting them as human, proposed an ethics and a politics adapted to limitation. But this threatened the absolute, and the sectarians still wished to guarantee it once and for all.

The absolute was safe, though, only when it kept its place apart. It was precisely where sectarianism tried to pretend to work through the congregations that the most serious assault on a social-gospel agency was ever made. Harry Ward, as we have noted, spent the 'thirties as head of the League Against War and Fascism. From 1936, international politics dominated his outlook, and the New Deal as such was demoted to a secondary target. Of course, in the ideological simplicities by which the league treated of the world, there was no room for complicated revisions of judgment upon the domestic scene. "It is only when there are people's front governments in Great Britain and the United States that there can be a clear line of division between the democratic world and the Fascist world." [45]

The members of the Methodist Federation for Social Service were not followers of Ward's politics; they simply refused to draw any line; the federation itself was more nearly dominated by socialists. But in 1936 all hands suffered from having overextended their lines.

On July 29, 1935, a group of Chicago laymen organized as the Conference of Methodist Laymen in preparation for the General Conference to be held in Columbus the next year. These gentlemen drew up a definition of the purpose of the Methodist Church: it was to build Christian character through a personal individual witness. Economic systems were mechanistic and impersonal, like nature, and were not primarily concerned with man. Influence on social and economic conditions should be the work of Christian individuals; the pulpit had lost sight of its true duties when it substituted social and economic issues for the personal gospel. In light of human nature, capitalism was by and large the proper economic system, since human nature required the profit motive. Men who had made profits were members of the laymen's group. One, Henry Henschen, who served as chairman, was president of one of the Chicago banks that had collapsed in the depression. Wilbur Helm of an Illinois bond house served as secretary. Other members were Arthur Hyde, secretary of agriculture in the Hoover administration; Fred Sargent, president of the Chicago and Northwestern Railroad; Hugh Magill, head of a federation of utility investors; Burt J. Denman, manager of the United Light and Power Company; and T. W. Appleby, president of an Ohio life insurance company. Laymen's organizations were set up in two other centers, Los Angeles and New Jersey. Soon after formation of the Chicago group, the Hearst newspapers opened another of their attacks upon the social-gospel clergy, concentrating this time on Bishop Francis J. McConnell, Winifred Chappell, and Harry Ward.[46]

The laymen had three aims. They wished the General Conference to disavow the social-service federation; they wished the General Conference to disavow the social resolutions adopted by previous General Conferences; and they wished to break up the youth program of the education board. The youth program, because most accessible, was the main target. Following Roy Burt's departure from the education board for service in the Socialist party, Blaine Kirkpatrick of the Chicago Social Action Movement became secretary of the youth department, and Owen Geer, also of the Social Action Movement, assistant secretary. Both members of the federation, both men were avowed socialists. Under their direction a program, "Christian Youth Building in a New World," set the tone for a highly active youth organization, the National Council of Methodist Youth, that placed Methodism in the van of Protestant youth movements. At its first convention, in the summer of 1934, in Ernest Fremont Tittle's First Methodist Church in Evanston, Illinois, one of the nation's leading Methodist parishes, the Methodist Youth had voted through resolutions supporting pacifism, condemning capitalism, applauding the New Deal, and calling upon the administration to move further and faster.[47]

At the General Conference in 1936, the Committee on the State of the Church upheld the right of the social-service federation to use the name "Methodist." It buried a move to establish an official social-service commission in its place, while cautioning the federation to keep its unofficial relationship clear at all times. The report on social and economic questions took to generalities, in deference to the ". . . wide divergence of opinion among us as to the meaning of a Christian society as well as to the means of its realization." The Peace Commission was refused money. Instructing the Methodist Book Concern to print evangelical and other religious literature, the conference refused to instruct it to print literature on social and economic questions. Near the end of the conference, the board of bishops voted to replace Bishop Blake of Detroit with Bishop Adna Leonard of Pittsburgh as head of the board of education. Blake, along with McConnell of New York and Bishop Baker of San Francisco, was a leading patron of the youth program; Leonard sympathized with the businessmen.[48]

Seven days after the General Conference adjourned, Leonard, through the board of education, asked for and received the resignations of Geer and Kirkpatrick. In Berea, Kentucky, the National Council of Methodist Youth, meeting over Labor Day, considered secession from the official life of the denomination, but settled for a resolution in vehement condemnation of the board of education and the bishops. In 1938, Leonard purged the education department of three more officials; again the National Youth, this time meeting in Boulder, Colorado, strongly protested, without effect.[49]

The parliamentary talents of a basic Methodist middle had prevented any actual test of strength on the floor of the General Conference. The Chicago, Los Angeles, and Eastern businessmen could probably not have mustered a majority anyway. But on the other hand, for liberal clergymen to have forced through a majority for the socialist education secretaries would have been costly. The General Conference had been through one financial ordeal in 1932; it was not interested in facing another. In the upshot, the Methodist Federation was left intact, but a clear line had been drawn against its efforts to leaven the congregations. It was left clearly and only as sect, within the church but hardly of the church. There had been of course something incongruous in a socialistic Methodist board of youth education in the first place, and the federation itself had been a highly unsatisfactory rallying point for liberals, having just been taken by Ward into the League Against War and Fascism. Ward and the federation had forgotten what the congregations were really like. Those who castigated the General Conference for its "retreat" missed the point: it was not a retreat, because Methodism had never "advanced" even close to the position of the socialist secretaries who were recalled, let alone to the position of Harry Ward. The militant clergy of Chicago, Los Angeles, and New York had finally provoked reaction, ending for practical purposes in the alienation of the church from any vigorous social gospel.

In November, 1936, acting on ideas developed among members of the Fellowship of Socialist Christians and the Conference of Younger Churchmen, the social passion for the first time in its history undertook its own exclusive Protestant-wide organization. The first meeting of the United Council for Christian Democracy was held in Columbus, Ohio. The United Council was to serve as a kind of federal union for all the liberal and radical groups in the church, and more especially to organize such groups where they did not yet exist. A Presbyterian Fellowship for Social Action, led by John Paul Jones and G. S. Frye, and a Council for Social Reconstruction of the Evangelical and Reformed Church, led by John Sommerlatte and John Bollen, later by Hugh F. Klemme and Harold Wilke, were the two most successful groups enlisted into the United Council through its efforts. Congregationalists, Baptists, Disciples, and Unitarians were also organized under the United Council, as well as the interdenominational Fellowship of Southern Churchmen. The Episcopal Church League for Industrial Democracy and the Methodist Federation were the two large denominational groups from the 'twenties. As a federal organization, the United Council covered a broad spectrum of views, but its essential *raison d'être* was to provide a rallying point for all the prophets for the sake more or less of morale. It remained a highly clerical group, although its first chairman, W. F. Cochran of Baltimore, was a layman. War soon dominated its conclaves. Meeting in Cleveland early in 1940 to discuss foreign policy—with 105 Methodist delegates, 53 Evangelical and Reformed, 49 Episcopalians, 41 Presbyterians, 36 Baptists, 24 Congregationalists, 13 Unitarians, and 10 Disciples—a heavy majority supported a keep-America-out-of-war line. This majority was divided, however, among militant pure pacifists, a small group of United Front tacticians, and a larger group of pragmatic anti-interventionists, all opposed by a small pro-Ally bloc headed by Reinhold Niebuhr. The

United Council hardly survived the war in its original intended character. By 1946 only the Methodist and Episcopal groups remained, as the leadership of such United Front apologists as Richard Morford, a Presbyterian, and John W. Darr, Jr., a Congregationalist, bound the organization to unacceptable dogma. But explanations for its pale life must lie deeper: where nothing but pure intentions are bundled together, no one can draw a tight string.[50]

With respect to the church, Niebuhr, in accord with his habitual method, first split the middle, then, balancing, adjusting, measuring, tried to relate the poles back together again. This meant that he had formulated his politics without much self-conscious adjustment for church audiences, and had formulated his theology also without similar adjustment. It was implicit in both his politics and his theology that social-gospel preachments to the middle class were futile. While *Radical Religion* castigated the conservative congregations, realists understood that political behavior would follow not the lines of idealistic appeals but the lines of social interest.

Yet Niebuhr did not simply abandon the church, for, having freed politics, he had also freed religion. If it was true that social-gospel preaching at the congregations was futile, that did not mean nothing could be preached.

> In thousands of Christian pulpits the richness and breadth of the Christian gospel is lost in a moralizing radical social preaching which belabors middle-class people for not acting politically like proletarians. If the preaching is liberal moralism, rather than radical, it may be even worse, inasmuch as it gives middle-class comfortable people the illusion that they are living by the law of Christ because they have never participated in violence.[51]

> A minister who regards all the traditions and services of the church merely as opportunities to convey radical political messages ought to leave the church and enter secular political work.[52]

Let the church, Niebuhr said, recover the Christian treasures and preach them in their full religious dimensions.

This was distinct enough. But did it have anything to do with "the immediate problems of social justice"? Was it not close to the position of Barthianism, swallowing ethics in preaching the Word pure and alone? As has been indicated, what Niebuhr had to say at this juncture was much more "heedless," much less "timely" than his ethical and political thought. It appeared that a connection did remain, nevertheless, between religiously realistic preaching and social change. True, the congregations could not be made over into proletarians.[53] But, although Protestantism did not have the ear of the disinherited, it did have the ear of the privileged, and it was possible for it to carry a ministry of reconciliation to these, tempted as they were to identify their interests with eternal sanctities and the peace and good order of the established system. A ministry of reconciliation could not be carried by socio-moral appeals. It required a religio-moral fellowship in which a sense of holiness transcended all human perfections and imperfections. A sense of the total dimension in life, apprehended as judgment and mercy, contrition and grace, was the only atmosphere in which reconciliation could be advanced. In the last analysis, in fact, "every moral action is the by-product of religious tension." [54]

This was in a way to take back partially what Niebuhr had conceded—that politics followed interest. Political behavior *could* be influenced, not through preaching politics and morality but through preaching religion. Whether, however, this was an influence significant for the short range of immediate problems, Niebuhr did not spell out. Moreover, he was still leaving himself open to the difficulty that his argument for the classic Christian treasures would be undermined if the immediate problems of social justice should be solved without them—should be solved within the patterns of liberalism.

Once more it was clear that Niebuhr's thought pointed beyond the political sphere of justice in which he had begun, into culture. Niebuhr himself countered the pessimistic determinism that his attitude toward the congregations seemed to imply, on that deeper level where the issues of *The Nature and Destiny of Man* really centered. "The best antidote for the bitterness of a disillusioned trust in man is disillusionment in the self. This is the disillusionment of true repentance." [55] The problem remained of how to preach disillusionment effectively in the first place, for it was clear that such disillusionment could not be preached effectively in political terms. It could not be left in bare abstraction. It demanded exemplification and convincing translation in terms of the real lives of real selves in particular times at particular places.

So far as the conservative congregations were concerned, Niebuhr left his religious Word in abstraction. They would not listen to political preaching, and beyond the bare insistence that the religious dimensions could be preached, Niebuhr did not explore the terms of such preaching as it might relate to the broader field of culture and the deeper field of the self among those congregations. The next chapter will exhibit how he sustained his religious argument on the political level, in the debate on war. In addition, however, in the face of the problem posed by the middle-class church, he searched eagerly for other sorts of congregations altogether, ones that might in fact, after all, accept the Word of realism—in both its religious and its political implications—on the basis of their own social interests. Thus, farmers and elements of the lower middle were still in the churches. Less aware of the technical realities of the economic crisis than labor, they were yet among the economically and socially disinherited, and—Niebuhr now, in 1936, revising earlier views—their experiences could conceivably be interpreted to them in such a way as to enroll them as active bearers of social reconstruction.[56]

This idea took its most definite shape when pitched to the South. In the calculations of the social gospel in the past, the South had simply been missing. This most solidly Protestant section of the country had provoked no reflections upon its peculiarities and its possibilities. Implicitly, the social gospel had assumed that Southern Protestantism had to be liberalized before it could be social-gospelized. But Southern leaders were beginning to speak out in the 'thirties. Paul B. Kern, Methodist bishop for the Carolinas, felt that, through the New Deal, the nation was being awakened to the intolerable character of the old order of selfish, prideful, ruthless capitalism, with its disparities of wealth and its control of politics. On the other hand, looking back in 1939, E. M. Poteat, a Southern Baptist who had been a missionary in China in the 'twenties and had moved to Cleveland, felt that the promise raised in 1933 had been unfulfilled or betrayed, whether by the Supreme Court, by ideological failures, or by human weakness. Whatever the case, Poteat was thinking of more vigorous social changes than the New Deal.[57] J. E. Gilbreath, of the Southern Methodists, in *The Vision of God and the Social Order in 1936*, repeated ideas and rhetoric typical of the prophets of ten and twenty years before, but without blurring an indictment of capitalism and a defense of efforts along the lines of socialism.

Southern denominations themselves were speaking. The Baptists in 1933 set Poteat of Raleigh at the head of their social-service research bureau, which they made a permanent part of the denomination machinery. The Methodists, at Jackson in 1934, deplored the profit motive, endorsed social planning and economic control as well as minimum wages, and spoke for social insurance. Methodists also formed a council on a Christian Social Order, which probed into Southern agriculture, race relations, and, in 1938, industrial matters. Southern Presbyterian ministers, at Montreat, North Carolina, in 1935, witnessed against economic inequalities in industry and for economic security for all men. One of the most conservative denominations in America, the General Synod of Associate Reformed Presbyterians, transformed, in 1935, its Committee on Reform into a Commission on Social Regeneration, while filing a report condemning the economic system, its rules, and its players.[58]

Nothing could be taken as certain from all this, especially respecting the Southern Baptists, whose extreme congregationalism made every annual meeting a thing unto itself. Meeting in St. Louis in 1936, with a consequent disproportion of delegates from the most conservative areas of the denomination, the Baptists tabled the recommendations of Poteat's commission, which asked for an enlargement of the social-service commission, to the accompaniment of speeches that the correspondent of the *Christian Century* thought would be pleasing to W. R. Hearst. Southern radicalism was always hard to identify. In 1933, Alva Taylor, himself from Nashville, wrote in praise of a "social-gospel preacher" in Shreveport, who had been preaching an impassioned message of social justice for two years to a growing radio audience, who had withstood the demand of the largest contributor to his church that he resign because of his attack upon certain utility interests and his support of local unions, and who had become an honorary member of several unions as a consequence—a minister named Gerald L. K. Smith.[59]

But, as usual, the cutting edges were not to be found in the denominations themselves. The Fellowship of Southern Churchmen was formed in 1934, and symbolized the kind of nexus the Northern urban prophets hoped to find. One of its leaders was Howard Kester from Nashville. A student at Union Theological Seminary for a year, completing his divinity studies at Vanderbilt, Kester plunged immediately into political work before receiving Congregational ordination in 1936. His work included a leading role in organization of the Southern Tenant Farmers Union (STFU), particularly in Arkansas, where Kester risked lynching in a season of violence. There was a certain analogy with Muste at Lawrence in 1919: Kester was a secretary of the Fellowship of Reconciliation. The first organizer of the STFU to be whipped and arrested was a Negro minister. Six of the fourteen members of its national executive council were preachers, the vice-president a Southern Baptist socialist. Kester believed that the religion of escape followed by the great masses of more or less unchurched white farmers in the South could be turned into the channel of social revolution. In the same spirit, T. B. Cowan, a Chattanooga Presbyterian, wrote that the Bible was still the best textbook for the labor firing line; Gospel journalese, with the fire of the prophets and the pointedness of Paul, was the language for popular prophetic preaching. Kester also worked out of a base on Cooperative Farm No. One at Hillhouse, Mississippi, where Sam Franklin, after five years in Japan as a Presbyterian minister, managed a plantation farmed by dispossessed share-croppers, white and Negro, on the basis of share-and-share-alike.

The Fellowship of Socialist Christians followed and supported such activities with utmost attention. Sherwood Eddy, along with the Rust brothers, inventors of the Rust cotton-picking machine, led in providing funds for the Hillhouse farm. The fellowship itself voted $250 to an Institute of Southern Preachers held at Hillhouse in 1936 and 1937; Niebuhr headed a national committee supporting Kester as counselor for the STFU. Cowan was voted funds for a preaching mission in 1938. Niebuhr, Eddy, and Alva Taylor served on the advisory committee and Kirby Page was treasurer of the Highlander Folk School in Monteagle, Tennessee, organized in 1932 for training rural and industrial leaders in the Southern mountain country.[60]

The most radical leader was Claude Williams, with his "socio-religious" groups in western Arkansas in 1933 and 1934. The majority of his Paris, Arkansas, Presbyterian church members, sympathetic to his work, could not prevent the church board from ousting him. Williams then organized a New Era farm and school, and helped organize the unemployed into a Workers Alliance, sponsored by the STFU and the Socialist party, before going into Commonwealth College, a Southern version of Brookwood. Williams left the south for Detroit, as Southern workers moved up into war jobs, where he combated the Southern itinerant preachers bringing their anti-Negro and anti-union views into a tense city—working now through his People's Institute of Applied Religion.[61]

Of the Southern Tenant Farmers Union, Niebuhr wrote: "Here is a symbol of the fact that the only Protestant proletariat is in the south." Of the potentialities in general: "Here is an undissipated religious inheritance which might achieve a high degree of potency if some degree of training could perfect the native resource." [62] This was Niebuhr's answer to the problem of the conservative congregations in the mid-'thirties: find and perfect the proletarian congregations. This attention to the South as a seed-bed for genuine radical Protestantism was an interesting extension of the judgments of the Northern socialists upon the American scene: the South was not destined simply to follow the earlier stages of economic and social development in the North and West. Southern economic problems could be solved only through coöperative agriculture, for instance. Southern economy and Southern Protestantism, alike and together, would skip the stage of liberalism, passing from conservative fundamentalism to radical neo-orthodoxy directly.

This was one of the more fascinating expectations of the times. Neo-orthodoxy had grown from liberal soil; it had corrected, it had not destroyed, liberal humanism, rationalism, and dynamism. Would it look the same transplanted into the preliberal soil of the sectarian orthodoxy of Southern Baptism, Methodism, and Presbyterianism? By the canons of sociological realism as adopted by Niebuhr and some of the chastened liberals, one thing was clear: economic history would go very far indeed toward determining the extent to which this expectation would be fulfilled. A South gathered into the middle-class synthesis would exhibit a slackening of the tensions, both social and religious, from which any natural Protestant proletarian theology might spring. And perhaps TVA was likely to mean this; perhaps TVA was more likely to generate Southern Protestant liberalism in theology than Southern neo-orthodoxy. Perhaps here again the New Deal would frustrate the new Word.

In any event, in these hopes for the Southern church, Niebuhr was following the same instincts as in his hopes for the Socialist party. In each case, he followed the chance to finesse the problem of liberal culture—in the New Deal and in the standard middle-class church that preoccupied men like Johnson, Morrison, and even Bennett. He followed the chance that politics would provide the bearers of neo-orthodoxy, relieving neo-orthodoxy of the necessity of justifying itself in the face of a successful liberalism.

It was a chance conceived out of need, not out of cool inspection of the American scene. In still another sector of the Protestant community, like the South ignored by the social gospel and the neo-orthodox alike, the true state of affairs was perhaps still more clearly indicated. In 1936, for the first time in its history, the

United Lutheran Church went through genuine and serious debate over the report of its committee on moral and social welfare, as Eastern laymen fought for resolutions on world peace and industrial relations. In 1938 the United Lutherans organized a Board of Social Missions that, polling the pastors the following year, found a preponderant sentiment for active concern with social questions. A Philadelphia League for Protestant Action was headed by the editor of the *Lutheran*, Nathan R. Melhorn. The change among the Lutheran clergy from the position they had occupied in the *World Tomorrow* polls of 1931 and 1934 was marked.[63] Certainly this was a change hardly based on proletarian awakening. It was not the emergence of radicalism in an orthodox communion. It was the permeation, long resisted, of the Lutheran community by liberalism, by the bland, sect-dissolving waters of the utilitarian synthesis. This was another question for the future, whether the liberalization of Lutheran orthodoxy could profit from and be instructed by the criticism of liberalism offered by the neo-orthodox; but plainly, the Lutherans did not offer that conjunction of religion and politics for which Niebuhr persistently longed.

The "church-consciousness" of the 'thirties, then, gathered up a curious collection of stresses. At once a sociological and a theological concept, "the Church" offered both an escape from and further answer to hard problems the social gospel had come upon.

As an essentially religious and theological concept, "the Church" registered the resistance of most of the liberal pastors to the temptation of identifying their religion with a practical politics. This was the temptation of sectarianism, whether that of the means, with the pacifists, or that of the ends, with the revolutionary socialists. Under the urgency of the 'thirties, the social gospel did not transmute into a secular religion, as Harry Elmer Barnes had urged and orthodox critics had predicted.

At the same time, in no liberal circles did this church-consciousness constitute anything like the extrication of religious perspectives from the utilitarian synthesis of religion and politics, religion and culture, intended by the neo-orthodox. Instead, it offered a way of dissolving both political and religious questions otherwise impossible to meet. Thus, Johnson did not criticize neo-orthodoxy on either the political or the existential grounds occupied by Niebuhr. He answered both the political and religious challenges of neo-orthodoxy simply by referring to the majority feelings of the congregations. Here an obviously sociological meaning was mixed with a rather imprecise religious meaning in the concept of "Church." Charles Clayton Morrison's church even more clearly fused social and theological characteristics. With John Bennett, the church on its religious side emerged somehow as a kind of conscience for the society, transcending parochial boundaries in its own imitation of justice, an imitation that, Bennett believed, endowed it with a social, political meaning he had previously discounted.

In this amalgamation of social and religious definitions of the church, the pastors were reacting again to one of the crucial puzzles of the American Protestant heritage (and, to that extent, of American life). On what grounds, from what perspective, is criticism to be exercised in democratic society? For the social-gospel pastors, as for the neo-orthodox, religion constituted a principle of tension. Religion, to be meaningful, could not fail to criticize and judge. But by what standard was judgment itself to be judged? How was prophecy to be legitimized? It was on this question that the liberal pastors felt themselves drawn back into the community of the church. They wished to argue that the only judgments that were justified were those generated in the experience of the community. This was of course to renew an original impulse of the social gospel itself—to expand the established church community outward to embrace all sectors of the society. It was also, more deeply, to obey one line of democratic logic. The critical, prophetic, transcending elements of a religion —and a culture—were not to be assigned to separate institutions or separate individuals or castes. He who is judged is himself to be the judge. The people judge themselves. Every individual and all institutions must presumably incorporate the critical and transcending elements within themselves. Every man is to be his own prophet as well as priest.

Actually, of course, in their insistence upon a special role for "Church," the liberal pastors were betraying their reluctance to go the whole way with this logic. To have gone the whole way with it would have been to reopen an older choice between society *or* church. But at the same time, by fusing religious and social concepts of the church, by effectively identifying their church of religious principle, the invisible church, with the visible church of the congregations, they were absorbing the logic into the church. Thus, although the liberal pastors recoiled from Harry Ward's vision of society-as-church, because Ward's new society ignored the old church, they tended back toward Morrison's vision of the church-as-society.

In declaring that some people literally will not and cannot hear certain words of judgment, Niebuhr was rejecting these concepts. On the other hand, in saying that those deaf to the political word of judgment might hear the religious Word of transcending holiness, he appeared to be accepting such concepts on a new level. Actually, his position implied new ground. The judgment to be awaited, by neo-orthodox logic, was not, as Johnson and Morrison had it, judgment generated in the ongoing experience of the people, not even the people on their knees. It was judgment truly from "above" and "beyond," power truly "breaking in," as much a mystery as the mystery of grace. In this light, the church would be not that communion where men evolved their highest ideals, developed their fullest powers, and, through self-criticism, on their knees, renewed their deepest insights, but that communion wherein they awaited the shattering force of God. Only by the acceptance of such an experience would it be guaranteed that the ideal forms of a culture were accessible to criticism. The church would constitute a kind of channel—an open wound, so to speak—in the body of society, through which the renewing power of Being itself might enter. The church would exist primarily to receive, and only then to act and give.

Niebuhr, for one, never defined such a church. Beyond the bare abstraction of his insistence that it should hold witness to transcending holiness, he said nothing as concrete as the liberal pastors offered. He himself, in his eagerness over the Southern congrega-

tions as well as over labor, exhibited the profound tug of the
American climate away from any judgment and prophecy which
lacks a constituency. It was in the Barthian church that men
"merely" awaited God—and, according to Niebuhr, lost touch
with the substance of salvation, history. Rejecting the tendency
of the liberal pastors to allow religious insights to be controlled
by congregational majorities, he also continued to reject all
tendencies toward a church "against" the world. He could not,
however, close on the position of the liberal pastors, for the
reason we have indicated already: American politics did not
provide the sort of experiences that could bring conviction in the
religious debate.

As a consequence, the "return" to the church did not define
a new stage in the revival of religious self-consciousness. It was
rather a new postponement of decision on the issues aroused in
that revival. How can a society be saved from worshipping itself?
How can men be saved from the pseudo-universals that tempt
them in the society established around them? For religious men,
the most tempting pseudo-universal was the church-as-society.
In the debate on war in the two years before Pearl Harbor, the
fusion of church with America stood forth starkly as the utilitarian
synthesis Niebuhr was trying to split.

XVIII

The Tragic Choice: War

"By far the most difficult area in which the Christian must make social decisions is where every possible decision is so evil that whatever we do we are involved in a tragic compromise." [1] John C. Bennett was thinking here, in 1941, of the "area" of war. Actually, not even in the politics of war could a theological case be finally grounded. Bennett himself was still thinking of the evil with which men "became involved," the evil entangling them from "outside." Niebuhr's dictum remained, that the convincing evil is the one that men find within themselves. Such evil is to be understood as a factor in a drama, which must be taken for what it is.

One way to avoid accepting the tragedy of all choices in war would be to transfer attention to the future, beyond the drama. Nevertheless, in the debate over war, religious arguments were more closely joined than they yet had been. American domestic politics in the 'thirties, unlike European politics, had not been adapted for vivid illustrations of the theories of neo-orthodoxy, but in the season preceding Pearl Harbor, the social gospel stood at bay. It was forced to argue that, in 1940 and 1941, America had a choice that was not tragic.

Protestant debate during those years, unsmiling, vehement, finally bitter, testified to the power of a wounding memory. The loss to the social gospel, and to Protestantism generally, in its failure to accept the First World War as a test of idealism would be hard to overestimate. As it had all Americans, the war had caught the liberal churchmen unprepared. Their prewar logic had not been adapted to the interpretation of international politics. It had been a radically American logic, confirmed by fifteen years of the fervor of progressivism. When the arguments and pressures for intervention appeared, no one knew how to evaluate, judge, and choose. Protestant support for the war was in consequence not only almost unanimous but also almost unquestioning. It was in addition, often enough, excessive. In 1933, Professor Ray Abrams published his *Preachers Present Arms,* highlighting the excess, resurrecting the old wartime sermons and resolutions at a time intended to redouble the churchmen's conviction that in 1917 they had sinned their greatest sin, they had allowed the church and the Word of God to be captured for unholy ends.[2] Disillusionment had begun immediately, with the diplomacy at Versailles. The tableau of a gallant Wilson ensnared in the toils of a wily Clemenceau and a worldly Lloyd George became a fixture of social-gospel mythology. There was from the beginning a slight flaw in the logic of this disillusionment. It justified the cry for redemption of the church from its captivity to the state; but Wilson of course had been captured too. The truth was that America as a whole had been deluded. Neither the church nor America bore responsibility for Versailles, for America had believed the high words of Wilsonian idealism and would not have fought had she realized the "age-old realities" they cloaked. Publication of the European archives, with the work of the historians—Gooch, Barnes, Schmitt, Fay—measuring war guilt and war interest, deepened and justified the revulsion.[3]

Part of a general national recoil from the nation's first venture into major-league world politics, the peace movement (and especially its religious wing) gave that recoil a special sharpness. From the beginning, in the circles of the Fellowship of Reconciliation, in the Federal Council, in the liberal journals, the revulsion generalized beyond a pragmatically confined disavowal of Versailles to a disavowal good in all instances. The issue came to be defined as a choice for or against war as such, the essential task of reform understood as the cultivation of men's preference against war, for peace. A memory of the enthusiasm for war, of the "psychology" of 1917, instructed the peace tactics. The will had to be prepared to resist temptation, and more: temptation itself had to be eradicated.

Those statistics of slaughter and devastation, those memoirs exposing subterfuge and selfish material interests with which Kirby Page filled his tracts helped prepare the will; resistance to militarism in the schools, the press, the government, opposition to mobilization days and to superpatriotic chauvinism helped. There was a great sense of "the power of the promise." Morrison of the *Century* wrote that the first, hardest half of the outlawing of war had been achieved, because in the Kellogg Pact men had put down on paper their renunciation, they had promised.[4] One of the leaders of the postwar War Resisters League, reflecting on means to avoid another collapse of antiwar sentiment like the collapse of 1916 to 1917, concluded: "What we must bear in mind, not only in justice to [those who had collapsed], but in considering our plans for the future, is that *they violated no promises, for none had been made.*"[5] The climactic period of promises followed the first open tremors in the ground of postwar international arrangements, caused by the Japanese invasion of Manchuria. Few focused upon Manchuria itself; it was as though men felt some vague chill passing through warm and vaporous interior airs, precipitating out a flurry of commitments. Kirby Page organized a testimony meeting in a *World Tomorrow* poll of 1931; 10,000 ministers—of 19,000 replying to the poll— affirmed that they could not and would not, as individuals, sanction any future war. The poll of 1934 numbered 13,000—of 21,000 replying—offering the same promise.[6] And what was the power of a promise? We are dealing here with men for whom it was a very deep thing to make a commitment, to take a pledge. To pledge oneself, to commit oneself, to promise: this was—still even in 1931 and 1941—the type-act, the basic deed, the central and essential gesture of the evangelical Protestant soul.

The will had to be prepared to resist temptation; the meaning this notion came to carry in liberal Protestant history was that the temptation itself had to be abolished. There must be no war. Elimination of the temptation was therefore a hidden condition for any unconditional promise to resist temptation, for these were still men of the social gospel, filled, unlike the pacifists of the traditionally pacifist sects, with a faith about not only themselves and their own readiness but also about the world and its readiness. It followed that the way to eliminate war was to support every policy consistent with absolute peace, oppose every policy and measure that accepted even the possibility of war. This was the support for disarmament. This was the rationale for Page's support of the League of Nations but "with reservations," reservations against the League's power to apply sanctions. This was also the rationale for opposing the extension of American interests outside the continental boundaries, opposing military investments in Latin America, opposing possible military investments in the Far East. Although this was on its own avowal an "internationalist" and not an "isolationist" mystique, the peace movement placed special emphasis upon keeping America in the moral and unentangled way, with the understanding implicit that America should be kept so whatever the state of other nations. Morrison of the *Century* argued that Senator Borah of Idaho, who led the outlawry forces in the Senate to the final victory of 1928, the Kellogg Pact, was a model of the American internationalist.[7] "Isolationism" in the 'twenties was a doctrine of Fortress America, preached most loudly by superpatriotic societies placing their faith in a supernavy sealing off the Western Hemisphere for American imperial fulfillment.[8] Internationalism was a necessary article in the mystique of peace, in any case. Deliberately, coldly, explicitly to have circumscribed the moral task as that of peace for America and for America alone, would have confounded calculations on the level of morality and psychology with those of power: if the possibility of war in the world was to be conceded, reasonable argument might have it that America ought to calculate and prepare her defenses. The logic of defensive preparation led to the logic of defensive war, however, and the logic of defensive war was the supreme casuistic snare and delusion.

With Manchuria, the peace movement began to sort itself out along the lines of its suppressed inner divisions. Collective security and sanctions, whether applied by the League of Nations or not, lay in one direction. Mandatory neutrality and over-all embargo applied unilaterally by the United States lay in the opposite direction, and there was no way to follow them both. Neither direction could in itself satisfy the few observers appearing in the 'thirties who believed the hope for peace was geared to hope for economic reconstruction, between nations and within nations. In the face of these complexities coming to disturb the simplicities of the 'twenties, the pacifist and neutralist churchmen fell back upon the argument that, it was understood, underlay all divisions, then and forever: war gained nothing, war was worse than anything, always. Published in 1933, Abrams' *Preachers Present Arms* recalled the old failure. At a time when distinctions were beginning to be drawn between different strategies for peace and between the reasons men fought, his was a book without distinctions, without inner lights, in many ways a model of the moral mercilessness of technically "objective" history, and a model of its errors. Abrams simplified the pathos and complexity of the apostasy in a kind of double-entry account-book: in one column the peace words of 1915 and 1916, in the other the war words of 1917 and 1918. The moral was plain: fortify yourself; do not be caught again unaware; expose all temptations beforehand; reduce all temptations; remember that you have promised. Abrams' book, Page's *World Tomorrow* poll of 1934, and Walter Van Kirk's *Religion Renounces War*, published in 1934, all constituted anxious announcements that the fortress of the will was complete. In his volume, Van Kirk, secretary of the Federal Council's Department of International Justice and Good Will, collected all the pronouncements, resolutions, proclamations, and high renunciations registered by the Protestant denominations and religious peace groups through fifteen years, especially after

1930.[9] He seemed to say, in piling up this collection, that the collection was indeed a fortress: the sword had been distinguished from the Cross, war had been recognized as sin, and men of religion were choosing against it.

Such reminders that the promise had been made, together with recollections of the surrender of 1917, were key weapons of the defenders of the will from 1934 on. "The Psychology of 1917 Begins to Operate," Morrison warned as early as 1935, primarily because Sherwood Eddy had defended, during a meeting of the FOR, the use of economic sanctions against aggression. In 1936, Methodist Bishop James Baker, of the San Francisco Conference, released still another poll of the ministers, 56 per cent of 13,000 reregistering their will to sanction no war. A warning of the parallels arising between 1916 and the situation of 1937 and 1938 formed the heart of Hubert Herring's frightened and angry book, *And So To War*, published in 1938. Beginning in November, 1939, the *Century* reprinted sections of Abrams' book. In 1939, a Ministers' Peace Covenant Group headed by Allan Knight Chalmers of the Broadway Tabernacle drew up an Affirmation of Christian Pacifist Faith, which was distributed to the leading clergy of the nation and won a thousand signatures. The FOR circulated a similar pledge in 1941. Men who shifted ground were labeled with terms learned from 1917: "victim" of war hysteria, victim of "war psychosis." In 1941, George Gibson of Chicago's Hyde Park United Church asked how the great men who had apostasized from pacifism—including such as Karl Barth and Reinhold Niebuhr—could reconcile their apostasy with the responsibility they themselves held for a generation of youth groomed to understand, resist, and renounce the evil of war.[10]

In 1940, Harold Fey, a secretary of the Fellowship of Reconciliation, referring to his five years' friendship with Reinhold Niebuhr, explained why not all friendships survived the times. "I still do [value Niebuhr's friendship] regardless of the fact that he seems to me to have more influence than any other man in leading the church into another repudiation of its mission in compromise with the state on the war issue." [11] Fey here illustrated succinctly the problem Niebuhr still faced: throughout his career Niebuhr insisted that no politics could claim identity with the Word, but in Fey, in the pacifists and many of the neutralists, he faced men who still had an ideal politics they identified with the Word and who imagined therefore that Niebuhr claimed a perverse identity for his own. Niebuhr in this situation also faced the supreme polemical opportunity of his career: the chance to demonstrate tragedy as a basic form of political and social life, a chance to demonstrate that the will could not evade it.

In 1928, writing in the symposium *Pacifism and the Modern World*, Niebuhr had put himself on record like many others with that unconditional disavowal of war conventional as a minimum prerequisite to the name "pacifist."

> [War] is morally so impotent and so perilous chiefly for two reasons. One is that force in an international dispute is used by parties to a dispute and it therefore aggravates rather than solves the evils and misunderstandings which led to the dispute. . . . The other reason is that the use of force in international conflicts inevitably issues in the destruction of life, and, what is more, in the destruction of the . . . innocent. . . .[12]

Unconditional in the sense that it applied to all war, still it applied because pragmatics justified no war, not because war violated the Way of the Cross or the example of Jesus. But in 1928 the working meaning of Niebuhr's pacifism was the same as that of the absolute pacifists, such as Page, with their half-concealed absolute.

It took ten years before this unconditional character of Niebuhr's renunciation of war was wholly dissolved. Its pragmatic character allowed the renunciation to survive the onslaught of *Moral Man* against absolutist ethics in general. In the chapters on national and class morality in *Moral Man*, ideology was stripped away to reveal the interests hidden behind; this led to a calculation of how to harness class interests and power for social justice, but there were no such calculations about national interests. The chapter and the book contained no hint that realistic ethics might glimpse a logic of justice in the chaos of international conflict.

Consequently, after the storm of debate within the FOR late in 1933, after Niebuhr's resignation from the council of the fellowship, he eventually decided to remain as a member, since "pacifist" testimony against war still was needed. In the same fashion, his discussion in *An Interpretation of Christian Ethics* concentrated once more upon the ethical conundrums of domestic politics; the conundrums of war came into view not at all. The ethical—and the religious—issues between semiabsolutist war pacifism and Niebuhr's own pragmatic pacifism were precisely the same as the issues between semipacifist class politics and his own class politics. But on the field of international politics, there appeared to be no pragmatic fruits to be won from the battle of theory. He had no argument that one nation or another might be, like labor, the bearer of justice.

If it was not until 1939, however, that Niebuhr suggested a moral equation in which war was the best of all choices, his pragmatic departure from a minimum war pacifism had nevertheless begun well before. During the Ethiopian crisis, in an argument brought against John Nevin Sayre of the FOR, Niebuhr supported sanctions to be laid by the League, as well as American neutrality legislation geared into League action. Did this include support for military sanctions? Yes. The issue, Niebuhr said, had been posed clearly by Mussolini's threat of war against an oil embargo. Clearly, Niebuhr argued, unqualified disavowal of military sanctions would leave the embargoing powers helpless against such threats. Niebuhr here was willing to accept a risk of war. This rested on a general rationale: ". . . unwillingness to run some risk of war in the present moment, means certain war in the future." [13]

There were two parts to his apology. By implication, the "certain war" of the future would be a certain war that would also be "greater" and "worse" than the immediate war that sanctions might provoke. And Niebuhr covered his flank by denying that Mussolini's Ethiopian adventure could advance the cause of justice in the world. If relative injustice among nations provided the ultimate explanation of the war potential in the world situation, it nevertheless remained that war mounted by the fascist powers, however deprived they might be, would only snuff out the last chances for democratic justice within those nations where a possibility of winning it remained. Here was an economic, implicitly socialist unification of domestic and international politics. If the fascist powers were prevented from escaping their internal problems by external aggression, Niebuhr argued, "their fascistic political systems will probably be destroyed by internal combustion."

What this argument did not explain, of course, was how isolation of fascist Italy, leading to an internal destruction of fascism in Italy, would lead to economic justice or fair shares for a hypothetical future democratic Italy. The omission was important in the polemical situation, for the anti-interventionists were able to fix upon this inability of the sanction policy to claim to serve positive international justice as proof of its moral unacceptability.

Niebuhr had supported economic sanctions against Japan in 1931; was not that, then, the point of his departure from the pacifist logic? It has been noted that his resolution against war was not finally dissolved until 1939: but was not his acceptance of war risk in 1935 that final dissolution? The answer in each case is "no," because of one more distinction suppressed in the mystique of peace. In 1934, Niebuhr asked, "Shall We Seek World Peace or the Peace of America?" War was probable, he wrote. It would involve destruction such that all reasons for waging it would be lost in confusion. The standing order might be destroyed in the process, but no guarantee could be imagined that the destruction would be followed by a new order of justice; fascist feudalism was more likely. Therefore the answer to the question was: the peace of America. Let America hold out as an island of sanity in an insane world, a preserve of comparative peace in a world that was sick; let America withdraw behind the strictest neutrality legislation.[14]

The war Niebuhr contemplated here was not the war he contemplated next year in discussing sanctions against Italy. One was unlimited world war, the other was limited contained war. In Sayre's mind, during the discussion of sanctions (and in the minds of pacifists generally), no such distinction was conceded. But Niebuhr made the distinction; in 1931 he had in effect believed there was no war risk, but his logic had been set to accept the chance of a limited action anyway. Asking his question of 1934, he was thinking of world war and spoke for strict neutrality. But he had not purged himself, despite the deep pessimistic determinism in his answer, of the idea that there were after all still chances for world peace, and in 1935 calculated once again in terms of limited action. His pragmatic absolute would not be wholly dissolved until it was world war that reëntered the realm of relative choices.

This had not yet happened when his somewhat unfocused, abstract, and rhetorical prophecies of world war became clear and steady. Between 1931 and 1936, with the exception of such moments as the one in 1934 that has been noted, he felt the economic power of the democracies sufficient to stop the fascist powers. But there was a fatal flaw: "The democratic nations are also the great capitalist nations. They have the economic power to stop fascist nations by the simple use of economic pressure. But this economic power is devoted to the cause of capitalism rather than to the cause of democracy." [15] Explanations for the failure of the democracies to act were more complex than this, as Niebuhr regularly spelled them out in the pages of *Radical Religion;* but the failure in Ethiopia had been decisive in any case. From late 1935 on, he felt that the ground of the effort to prevent war was shifting from the use of sanctions to the construction of alliances—and this ground he was sure would crumble also. "Since none of the alliances will be powerful enough to coerce the unruly continent into a semblance of order, they will tend to aggravate the anarchy rather than avert it. In a sense these alliances are no more than the beginning of mobilization." [16]

Conceivably, given this inevitability, he was ready for the policy of strict isolation for America. "If there is a lesson in this picture of unrelieved darkness, it is that it is more important to lay the foundations of a new society than to seek to preserve an old one." [17] He had already written, a year earlier, that in Europe Christianity was only an ark that might save the highest Christian treasures two by two in the flood of communist and fascist spiritual anarchy, but an ark could not prevent the flood.[18] Conceivably, here was rationale for Christian isolationism even in Europe, a withdrawal to wait out the storm. But the pessimism in these years remained free floating, displaying the extra-pragmatic drive of Niebuhr's mind. His was a pessimistic imagination, but such an imagination, even when powerful, does not really accept a postulated "inevitability" of catastrophe, or grasp by anticipation its living reality, so far as to paralyze the will. Niebuhr continued to oppose mandatory neutrality legislation and over-all embargo provisions, the heart of isolationist programs; he supported embargo against Japan, reasoning that if Japan could be bogged down in China, she would be a poor ally for Germany and Italy.[19] He never proposed a politics adapted for inevitable final tragedy; in effect, he was arguing that if the United States, by bringing what pressure it could to bear, economically, was able to delay the tragedy, and perhaps arrange it to the advantage of its friends, perhaps it might not be a final tragedy.

Munich was his point of no return.

In the depths of the crisis, and before its settlement, Niebuhr faced the "horrible prospect" of Nazi hegemony. It was indeed horrible. But:

> On the other hand it is cheap heroics, particularly from the comparatively safe vantage point of America, to say that a war would be better than such a capitulation before Nazi terror . . . on the other side of that war lies disintegration of every kind. Certainly there is no certain hope of the victory of either democracy or socialism in the impending war.[20]

The point at which this text gave way was the word "certain." The demand for a "certain" hope was not a responsible demand within the situation; it was Niebuhr's last gesture, in the manner of the pacifist mystique, demanding that war issue in a positive, "redemptive" achievement, that it carry a "solution" for problems defined by the ideal. His comments following the settlement at Munich were the break:

We can't really understand in what sense the peace of Munich is to be celebrated because "at least it postponed the war." Is it really true that to postpone a war is to add to the chances of its ultimate avoidance? Is that true if the enemy who intends to make war upon you grows stronger rather than weaker by your concessions and rejoices that he has once more proved "western democracies" to be moribund and weak? There is no peace in Europe. There will be either war or a capitulation to barbarism which will really persuade some of us to regret our words during the crisis that there was little to choose between the anarchy of war or the tyranny of the Nazis.[21]

In this text, the play of the word "really" cannot be missed. The immanent principle of "hope" was finally burned away; reality, "otherness," had to be faced, without distortion.

From Munich on, Niebuhr, excoriating liberal and pacifist isolationism, supported an American policy of aid for the Allies, and spoke for a growing number of churchmen abandoning pacifist and social-gospel positions. A declaration on "The American Churches and the International Situation" was released in January, 1940, a statement on "America's Responsibility in the Present Crisis" in May. The thirty-two signers of the first included John C. Bennett, William Adams Brown, H. S. Coffin, Sherwood Eddy, J. W. Nixon, H. P. Van Dusen, and Niebuhr. Churchmen supported the William Allen White Committee; an "Interfaith Committee for Aid to the Democracies" acting in coöperation with the White committee included Coffin and McConnell, as well as the secretary of the Church Peace Union, Henry Atkinson, for whom McConnell had written a report calling for whatever aid was necessary to stop aggression. On February 10, 1941, the first issue of *Christianity and Crisis* appeared, directed specifically against pacifism and neutralism within the churches, with Niebuhr as editor. The editorial board included Van Dusen and Francis Miller; sponsors included Bennett, Brown, Coffin, McConnell, and Nixon, among many other leaders of the church at large.[22]

Although refusing to hinge American policy to the single aim of staying out of war, Niebuhr himself never called for direct, open American military intervention before Pearl Harbor. Why he did not will be discussed later in this chapter. There were churchmen who did, those on the national committee of the Associated League for a Declared War. A clergymen's Fight for Freedom Committee was formed in 1941; Van Dusen was a member. But, by and large, those who led in the debate against neutrality and pacifism, and who had also been leaders of the social passion, had not moved this far by December 7. Episcopal Bishop Henry Hobson and Methodist Bishop James Cannon were two of the leading interventionists; neither had ever been among the social prophets. Episcopal and Southern clergy were most prominent in general in support of outright intervention; from these men, unmodulated, unconditional apology for Britain flowed easily, and attacks upon striking labor unions were not uncommon. These were the echoes of 1917, preaching holy war in 1941. But they, of course, had never made the promises of 1931, and it became Niebuhr's polemical duty (and difficulty) to argue his position distinct from them. He had not apostasized from the holy policy of peace; he had transcended it, as well as the logic of the social gospel, in insisting that there were no holy choices available.

The ultimate reaches of social-gospel logic were explored by the absolute pacifists before Pearl Harbor, and one man, A. J. Muste, was clearly chief of explorers. The noninterventionist party of the ministry was not exclusively pacifist; avowed absolute pacifists were rare among them. The great majority held simply to the pragmatic unconditional rejection of war, and to a concomitant pragmatic rejection of American participation in war politics. The leading spokesmen of this position, in its purely pragmatic stance, were the isolationist socialists, represented in the church by such men as A. E. Holt and Halford Luccock, isolationist not so much because of their socialism—since they were hardly dogmatic Marxian socialists—but alongside their socialism. Similarly, Morrison of the *Century*, professing admiration for pacifists and pacifism, did not count himself a pacifist and fought his implacable battle against intervention wholly on the pragmatics of peace. Some men, like A. W. Palmer of Chicago

Theological Seminary, called themselves pacifists, but supported
a policy of defensive preparations by which the United States
would set itself "like a porcupine" against potential aggressors.[23]
But the noninterventionists as a whole never abandoned a claim
to an ultimate ethical and religious ground for their position, and
it was only in absolute pacifism that the logic of this claim was
spelled out. The strain of this effort was prodigious; Kirby Page
had given way under it and preached pacifism as a sect, not as a
politics ready for immediate responsibility. But A. J. Muste,
whose life had been devoted to political extremes and who
entered the season of pressure well acquainted with the atmosphere, had not returned from the exhausting dialectic of the
Workers Party in search of political anaesthetization. Instead,
he exhausted himself again in pleading the political case for his
new—or former, renewed—absolutism. In Muste, processes of
thought universal among the semipacifists and pragmatic noninterventionists—but in them blurred, slurred, unspoken, often
unsuspected—were brought out and carried through to final
grounds; Muste, unlike the others, knew what it was to hold to a
fixed principle without secret inner concessions. The Fellowship
of Reconciliation displayed a sure sense of the demands of the
times when it brought him back, after his wanderings, as executive secretary in 1940.

For Muste, pacifism could never have been the doctrine of an
abstract norm, relevant only as a standard for the measure of all
possible choices but impossible as a choice itself. He set it forth
in conscious opposition to those, like Niebuhr and Emil Brunner,
who in varying ways denied that the ideal could be given political
realization. Muste's argumentative purpose in the political situation of 1939 to 1941 was to justify pacifism precisely as an immediate political alternative, competing on the same level with
all other alternatives offered in the situation. "Should the religious
pacifist movement think of itself . . . as a mass movement for
achieving social change . . . ?" [24] The answer was "yes," without equivocation. That is, the pacifist was not to think of himself
simply as a lonely defender of his conscience.

Muste offered a concrete political choice:

God calls nations as well as individuals to serve him. He summons this nation today to a course of Christian realism. The political expression of this course would begin with an admission that we carry a full share of responsibility for the tragic state of the world. Surely the absence of any faintest note of humility and penitence in the President's address is ominous. Christian realism would lead us to renounce war preparation and war as obviously suicidal; to offer to surrender our own special privileges; to participate in lowering tariff walls, in providing access to basic resources on equitable terms to all peoples; to spend the billions we shall otherwise squander on war preparations and war for the economic rehabilitation of Europe and Asia, for carrying a great "offensive" of food, medicine, and clothing to the stricken peoples of the world; and to take our full share of responsibility for building an effective federal world government.[25]

This was the pacifist alternative. This sacrificial, saving, healing act, and nothing short of it, was proposed for the pragmatic situation of 1939 to 1941 and indeed for 1945 as well—and not just for some ultimate future.

"But is not all this a fantastic kind of day dreaming?" Muste asked, magnificently. "Is it even remotely possible that the religious pacifist forces, the Christian forces, should measure up to such a challenge?"[26] Muste's answer followed basic pacifist mentality; he did not say that it was remotely possible so much as he said that no other alternative was acceptable. He faced these other alternatives. One was the victory of Hitler over the Allies. Unlike others, Muste was immune to the temptation to pick out saving elements in the post-Munich European order; revulsion at victory for the Axis he took for granted.

Allied victory was another alternative, and this required more analysis. Appealing to the evidence of 1918 and 1919, Muste argued that the Allies would demand punitive peace once again. There would be another "khaki-election" in Britain, and Britain would be represented at the peace table by another imperialist. Even so, Britain and France would not be able to police the peace they dictated, whether harsh or mild; still more exhausted than they had been after the last war, when they had been unable to police the peace of Versailles, they would be less able to police another. Victorious Britain would probably require an iron dictatorship, "possibly of a predominantly Bolshevik, possibly Fascist, hue. . . ." Meanwhile, defeated Germany would repeat defeated Russia's history, except that in a complex, industrial society, the debacle would be intensified.[27] The United States would emerge the only victor, a new colossus in world trade and power politics.

Forced into making these geopolitical forecasts by the structure of his argument, Muste obviously had to predict more about the role of the United States. So he asked: "Will the United States keep a huge army of occupation in Europe to feed starving millions until some semblance of order is restored and the ghosts of a debased Bolshevism or utter anarchy are laid?"[28] The question on the one hand was rhetorical; with the answer "no," the use of First World War history was justified. But, on the other hand, the question was also an exhortation: the United States might indeed stay in Europe, but it should not. At this point Muste evoked the image of hardheaded American realism, whereby America supported Britain in order to inherit the British Empire after the war. A third alternative then, victory policed by America, was unacceptable because it meant America's loss of moral character.

In any case, Muste anticipated, as did many of the pacifist leaders, a postwar breakup of any Allied alliances that might be made and that might contain anarchy for a time; he anticipated it with specific attention to Russia: "I confess that both prospects, a new war over what is to be done with Europe, or a sovietized Europe-Asia-Africa under Stalinist control, appall me."[29] The general moral drawn from this estimate of alternatives provided the springboard for pacifist idealism:

> In other words, there are no victors and vanquished in any important sense in modern war. It makes no difference, therefore, which side "wins." The same is obviously true if a long war ends in a

stalemate of exhaustion, with no one even able to claim a victory. In any case, the vultures will descend to tear what remains of the prostrate body of European civilization.[30]

In one of the traditional gambits of polemics, Niebuhr's opponents turned one of his fighting words against him: they themselves, the pacifists declared, were the realists; they were the ones who scorned illusions. Illusion, romanticism, baseless idealism were the marks of those who could imagine how the war might lead to anything but one of these black—equally black—alternatives.

At the end of this analysis, rising out of this darkling field where it appeared that every course promised results no more and no less dismal than every other, with all so dismal that none could be chosen, an astonishing fact emerged. Not only did the alternative of the absolute remain, but just those desperate patterns into which reality had fallen made it practical.

In one of those furies of exasperation common to the times, a Maine pastor, Edwin Buehrer of Orono, flung out against the pacifists his demand for facts: "There are no historical reasons offered, no empirical reasons, no logical reasons, no practical reasons." There was only, Buehrer cried, incantation of the magic words: "It is Christ's Way, it is the Way of the Cross." [31] We must say, distinctly and explicitly, that Buehrer was justified in more cases than not; but in Muste we are dealing with a man who tried to argue the pragmatics all the way and to justify the incantations of the others, a man who tried to stand always on facts. None of the prophets showed so dramatic a talent for finding them. Like Paul Tillich, Muste had a vision of *kairos*, of a fullness of time in which history came to a moment prepared to receive and be shaped by some decisive new action, in which ferment striving to express itself in the past would be fulfilled, the outlines and foundation for a new era of stability established. Such a moment faced the world in the mid-twentieth century. Pacifism as a whole fed on this idea. "It is the war nobody seems to want. There is nowhere any enthusiasm for it. There seems to be something elemental, deep-seated, about the shrinking of the masses from war." [32] It was to tap this great reservoir that Muste proposed the saving, sacrificial act to the United States; unlike the neutralists, Muste wanted unilateral disarmament—in 1939, in 1941, in 1942.

> I believe with all my soul that the embattled peoples of the earth looking at each other like savage witch-doctors through gas masks are waiting for a nation that would have the sublime horse sense, the divine foolishness, to break the evil spell that is on mankind, lay down its arms, and say: "Boys, this thing has gone too far; I'm going home to work and live and love; and the next time I get restless and want some excitement, I'm going fishing or to see the Marx brothers in a movie or maybe even to church." Uncle Sam and his Yankees ought to be capable of that if anyone is.[33]

Let us understand: this was a critical knot in the web of pacifist apology.

An internal curiosity lurked in the argument: if it was true the *kairos* existed, was it true that a saving act by the United States was the only way to grasp it? That is, did the *kairos* justify Muste's contention that there was one, and only one, course for America in the specific situation of 1940 and 1941? It could be doubted. The following was part of Muste's discussion of a *kairos* that had been missed, of what might have been in Russia after the First World War:

> . . . an essential feature of a revolution which follows defeat in war, as did the Russian, is a revulsion on the part of the masses against war. The soldiers lay down their arms. They turn back in masses to their homes and to the ancient peaceful pursuits of the human race . . . The old order simply collapses . . . A non-violent organization in such a situation would be in a position to take full advantage of the revulsion against war . . . It would make full use of the energies a people feel under such circumstances arising from the sense of liberation from the ancient yoke, the feeling of having entered the promised land. There is also at such moments a joyous sense of brotherhood among the masses, which causes them to embrace each other, to join in jubilant songs, to share their goods, to endure gladly the greatest sacrifices . . . what might not men who had qualities of leadership, who were technically competent, and who had the spirit of Jesus, who were prepared to build on

idealism, the abhorrence of war, the will to peace, the sense of fraternity, the capacity for sacrifice which characterize the masses in such creative moments of history—what might they not achieve? [34]

From this it would appear that perhaps more than one way to fulfill *kairos* was available. If the creative moment from which brotherhood, embracing, and sacrifice sprang was one of defeat and revulsion, perhaps there was no reason for absolute despair if the war wore on, *with* America.

And in fact the sternest objection to the policy of the sacrificial act lay just here; Muste tried to face it: "People . . . tell us that 'you can't get the United States to make such a proposal.'" He did not argue the matter; he simply asked one more moral question: "If not, what does that reveal about our own moral position? What besides our own 'interests' are we fighting for in that case?" It appeared in the end that, if there was a dilemma, it had only one horn: if the United States was to be righteous, it would not fight; if the United States was not to be righteous, it should not fight.

The literature of pacifism teemed with protests against misrepresentation of pacifist logic by its opponents. One protest bore against the charge that pacifists lived by a sentimental and magical utopianism. Muste himself registered one of the protests:

> It is not proposed that the world should wake up on some bright morning and instantaneously disarm, tear down all tariff walls, assemble the parliament of man. The trouble with the world is that it has been running headlong straight away from all these things and as a result is on the brink of hell and may pitch over it. What is needed is simply that we turn square around and begin to move in the other direction. Even small genuine steps in the new direction will swiftly alleviate the situation and surely bring us out into a new world eventually.[36]

But this did not answer the essential charge. Muste's "new world eventually" was not after all simply a reasonable postponement of the absolute. Once men had turned "square around," were there never to be lapses? Were there never to be dilemmas in the reallocation of the world's resources? Were there never to be men of avarice and men of small spirit? There would, of course, always be. Then how were these difficulties to be met that they might not feed once more into war? Once again, by love and the Way of the Cross. But in that case, had not the absolute actually appeared after all? Was this not in itself the reign of love, where somehow love, emanated by someone, could solve all things always? Was not "turn square around" the same as to enter the new life?

For Paul Tillich, *kairos* was always truly a particular moment, a true offer of history but a truly historical offer. Thus, he had discerned one in Germany in the 'twenties; it had passed. He believed it no longer existed in the 'forties. Moreover, the decisive response to *kairos* for Tillich was not love; it was recognition of sin, acceptance of finiteness, of limitation. Muste spoke straight out of the sectarian evangelical tradition, with a vision of sancti-fication at the heart. This tradition had always faced difficulties in the fact that the supreme sacrificial act upon which Chris-tianity itself hinged had not been followed by the Kingdom. Con-taining—but not disposing of—this difficulty by emphasizing the Kingdom within the individual, within the soul, it had been willing to wait for the universal reign of love. For it, politics had merely been a way of waiting. But Muste could not wait. For him, politics had to offer a clear and consecutive line of progress from the political present through to the fulfillment of politics in the absolute end, the ideal future. His *kairos* was the old *kairos* of the evangelical soul, in which absolute conversion and entrance into the new world were always immediately possible. Beyond that moment, no need for a *kairos* could arise. For Muste, politics could not be contained by the visible future; for pacifism, the ideal future alone could serve as reference, and we see what it was: a perpetual present, a perpetually present moment of absolute possibilities. In Muste, we see in one of its striking forms what politics looks like when it is eternal.[37]

But why could Muste not wait? Another pacifist protest bore against the charge that pacifism meant in practice isolationism. So far as American foreign policy was concerned, isolationism pure and simple lay behind Muste's logic plainly enough. But this was not the point. Muste himself was isolated, but it was the isolation of a fearful moral frontier, the isolation of a fearful psychic exposure. His ideas were not the rationalization for withdrawal from violence, for retreat into a psychic nest, or into fortress America. The controlling need served by his logic lay elsewhere. It was not a free choice for Muste whether pacifism should claim political relevance or not, because the pacifist—on Muste's pattern—was a man who had already centered his soul in politics and whose discovery of pacifism had come through politics. His pacifism was not a technique generalized from the life of the individual to the life of society. It was a technique demanded of society by the individual whose soul had been given over to and identified with society and politics. This man had felt what it was like to be politicalized, to lead a life vibrating with every public storm, to think and dream in categories no more and no less abstract than those of public debate. Muste was one of the extreme cases of the politicalization of middle-class Protestant idealism; he was the most perfect exemplar of the pure, unmixed, unadulterated social-gospel soul. The life of society and the life of the spirit in its individuality were indeed one. "Take the way of war, and there is war not only between nations, classes, individuals, but war, division, and consequent frustration within your own soul." [38] In the politicalized man, personality was not organized in concentric circles of identity; it was all one, all open, equally vulnerable throughout. If the shell called "citizen" fought in war, the soul fought equally. The soul could not transcend the affairs of the citizen, could not call upon resources not already committed to the conflict, could know no grace on the battlefield. And because it could not, the peace it sought in politics was not world peace only, but that inner peace that "passeth all understanding." They were identical. Sanctification depended on politics; politics could sanctify. Nor could the political soul rest in a mere refusal to join the world's wars, for this refusal meant only one more agony of inner division, and division, separation, isolation from one's warring fellows. Therefore the political soul could not withdraw in silence but was forced to cry out, calling on every citizen not to fight and to join it in communion and society once more, and to offer itself as a political example by which men could be together.

It was only at some such point as this that the old problem of the social gospel, of embracing both individual and society in a unified field of theory and practice, was solved. As suggested, there was an "eternal" quality in Muste's politics. Insofar as the finite means distinction and variation and separation and contradiction, his politics was also "infinite."

For the mystique of peace, isolationism posed a moral problem. Just in its ring, the word fitted badly in the rhetoric of brotherhood with which the movement was suffused. Muste met the problem by posing his saving act. But the saving act was religion rather than politics, and its political meaning, for all Muste's sincerity, was isolationist. That is, the politics of the peace movement at large consisted of support for the neutrality acts of 1935, 1936, and 1937, support for further neutrality acts still more severe in isolating the nation, and opposition to administration policy from the time of the President's quarantine speech in Chicago in 1937—an opposition mounting to bitterness from the passage of the neutrality act of 1939. To deny that they were isolationist, the peace advocates always accompanied this merely negative side of their policy with a positive, "internationalist" side.

Late in 1935, the National Peace Conference was formed, headed by Walter Van Kirk, as a coördinating agency for some thirty peace agencies in the field. Religious groups among them were: the Fellowship of Reconciliation, the Congregationalists' Council for Social Action, the Federal Council's Department of International Justice and Goodwill, the Methodists' World Peace Commission, and the World Alliance for International Friendship Through the Churches. The National Peace Conference served as a channel for bringing peace proposals to the attention of the government; both political parties were approached with drafts of peace planks in 1936. Some of the points included were continuation of reciprocal trade, stabilized currency, participation in the International Labor Organization, a national defense policy opposed to protection of overseas investments, government control of the munitions industry, and coöperation with the League of Nations in its social and humanitarian activities. This internationalist line persisted in progressively greater anxiety. In 1936 an Emergency Peace Campaign was organized, including many of the outstanding ministers of the nation. A. B. Coe, Albert W. Palmer (president of Chicago Theological Seminary), Theodore Hume, and Kirby Page were among the members. Harry Emerson Fosdick served as chairman. Moving out in waves, the members of the EPC preached "no foreign war" across the nation. They believed the United States should help relieve economic distress, open the channels of international trade, join the World Court and the League—on terms allowing the United States to refrain from military sanctions—and shift from preparedness to a purely defensive armaments program. This too was affirmation of "internationalism." But the word "emergency" had appeared, and the heart of the campaign was its call for mandatory neutrality legislation, with provisions for over-all embargo on munitions.[39] Similarly, from 1935 on, the *Christian Century*, rejecting the "isolationist" label, yet fought for mandatory legislation with over-all embargo on munitions, and for mandatory cash-and-carry for all other goods as well. The extreme demand included quota systems on cash-and-carry trade, based on peacetime trade, and a permanent munitions embargo.[40] All this was a flat renunciation of the old theories of "neutral rights," and this renunciation, frankly avowed, occupied a main position in the peace program—for it had been in trying to defend those rights that the psychology of 1917 had been generated. But this was not thought to be isolationism. Agonizing over the isolationist label, Hubert Herring of the Council for Social Action could harmonize his conflicting sentiments only in a black realism:

> We believe that it is only a question of time until Germany will strike for the regaining of her old preserves . . . We must prepare now to stay out. There is a second storm area—the Far East. Japan is marching South. The Open Door of China will be slammed shut

by Japan, unless all signs fail. The Philippines lie within her line of march. Where will we stand in that conflict? Again, we cannot be involved.[41]

And yet, even this was not abandonment of a claim to responsible internationalism. Agonizing over, and in the end accepting, the isolationist Nye-Clark neutrality program, the secretaries of the Social Action Council still spoke for a "positive" program as well: American membership in Court and League, and especially reduction in tariffs and war debts and leadership in international economic planning.[42]

All this was obviously long-range, and time was short. What good were the International Labor Organization and reduction of tariffs in 1939? A saving short-range formula emerged: "economic conference." In January, 1938, the Belgian statesman Van Zeeland submitted to the leading European nations his report on a program for general economic reform; later in the year Kirby Page issued inquiries as to its fate. In November, Ernest Fremont Tittle, the leading pacifist minister of Methodism, wrote of the program proposed in the report: "Such an attempt—and no other —might confidently claim the approval and support of God." Lashing out both at this identification of policy with God's will and at the pretensions of the Van Zeeland report as well—"a perfectionist return to laissez faire"—Reinhold Niebuhr attacked this species of internationalism fresh in his sense of the overriding fact of Nazi power won at Munich.[43] But it was precisely following Munich that the demand for conference grew strongest. Writing of Munich, A. W. Palmer said, "It looks as though pacifism had won a significant but dangerous victory." Palmer wanted an economic conference on a world scale to exploit the victory, fend off the danger. Edgar Dewitt Jones of the Federal Council led a delegation to the President in November, 1938, to submit the conference idea. Pressed by Morrison of the *Century* and Palmer of Chicago, council leaders approached the World Council of Churches. The World Council turned the idea down, reporting that European churchmen were fearful of any conciliatory move toward the fascist states that might be interpreted as signs of weakness. The European churchmen suggested to the Americans that the crisis had passed its economic phase and had entered political and psychological stages unamenable to the Palmer approach. But the Americans insisted, and World Council leaders finally suggested a small, unofficial meeting, without fanfare, among churchmen. Thirty-four persons, therefore, collected in the Europe of July, 1939, to discuss reallocation of the world. The Americans were: Henry Atkinson; John Foster Dulles; Professor Charles Fenwick of Bryn Mawr, a consultant on international affairs; J. H. Franklin, president of Crozer Theological Seminary; Georgia Harkness; Ivan Lee Holt; Bishop G. A. Oldham of Albany; John R. Mott; Henry S. Leiper and Roswell P. Barnes of the Federal Council; and Palmer. The thirty-four produced a statement. The *Christian Century* published it. By then war had been declared.[44]

The urge flowed from a logic too deep to be stopped by that, however. In its issue of May 15, 1940, the *Century* once again inquired, "What Can America Do for Peace?" It had done nothing yet, Morrison agreed. His article proposed that the President send a delegation of twenty American statesmen to all the neutral capitals in Europe—Riga, Madrid, Rome, Athens, Brussels, Belgrade, and so on—to assemble a peace conference that would sit until the war ended: the neutrals would be galvanized, America itself would be buoyed up, and a radically new Europe could be devised. Palmer repeated the idea a few weeks later; by then, unfortunately, there were fewer neutral capitals, and it was impossible not to wonder whether it was not, finally, too late. "Probably," Palmer wrote. The idea was a moral gesture, proving good intentions. Morrison went on, though, to the theory of the saving act, proposing, in a sermon in Rockefeller Chapel in Chicago, that America act immediately to take the lead in removing the evils of the West. "The world has long awaited for a nation to arise, which will act upon Isaiah's counsel. . . ."[45] But this was desperation.

There were, in other words, a few difficulties in maintaining the "internationalist," "responsible" side of the policy for peace. Very little excited the outrage of the critics of pacifism more than these proposals for economic conferences and neutral missions.

In the harshness of debate, Niebuhr's articles disappeared from
the pages of the *Century*, and his comment upon the plan for a
conference of neutrals was evidence enough why:

> . . . a completely perverse and inept foreign policy . . . Has it
> not occurred to you that most of [the neutrals] are shivering little
> mice waiting for the cat to pounce . . . ? Your proposal is in short a
> shocking revelation of the disposition of Americans to close their
> eyes to the magnitude of the tragedy which has engulfed Europe.
> You are still looking for a comparatively simple way out. This war
> is so terrible that everyone can sympathize with pacifists who say
> they want nothing to do with it. But if they would only let it go
> at that and not seek to combine their horror of war with fatuous
> political alternatives. Of all alternatives which have come to my
> attention your most recent proposal deserves some kind of a prize.[46]

Morrison always had an answer for every critic, and he had one
now. It was true, he said, that the proposal had come too late,
"but it is in good time, however, for the next war." This was an
ironic despair, and a certain savage cynicism in despair as well.
But, despair aside—for Morrison meant the reply as adequate—
his reply proved the fact that he was not dealing with the war
that was with the situation that he was in. He was dealing with
some other war, some other era—with, that is, the ideal future.

Despite all difficulties the isolationist churchmen persisted to
the very end in trying to stand for more than American isolation
alone. The Ministers No War Committee of 1941 included many
more of the eminent names of the Protestant clergy than did any
of the letterheads of interventionist organizations: social-gospel
figures included Palmer, A. E. Holt, Paul Hutchinson, and Ernest
Fremont Tittle—all of Chicago; Georgia Harkness, Halford Luccock, A. J. Muste, and Kirby Page. The other side of the No War
Committee was the Churchmen's Campaign for Peace Through
Mediation: Palmer, Harkness, Holt, Page, Luccock, and Tittle
were members, along with Morrison, A. E. Day, E. Stanley Jones,
and Harry Emerson Fosdick. Chalmers of the Broadway Tabernacle circulated a call for negotiated peace; Muste, Palmer, and
A. E. Day were among the six hundred signers.[47] There was,
these men believed, at every moment a table waiting somewhere

around which all men could assemble to settle the questions they were otherwise trying to settle by war. It was hard to locate this table, it was hard to find a place for it, it was hard to make out just what the solutions might be; but it was easy to have faith because it was so much harder to "believe" in war.

In the last analysis there was no chance of reducing moral anxiety about being isolationist by emphasizing the positive side of the policy for peace. The anxiety was rooted in a fear that the moral position of nonintervention would be fatally compromised were the split—steadily widening since Manchuria—between the ideal of peace and the ideal of peace for America left finally unbridged and unbridgeable. Muste's saving act was too agonized, too apocalyptic, too transcendental, too—by plain implication—sectarian; those who lacked his apocalyptic heat could not believe in conferences and negotiations without also believing in something else. It was not the saving act but the "saving island" that organized the soul of isolationism in that entire range—90 if not 99 per cent—where isolationism fell short of absolute pacifism.

Before measuring and tracing the nerve of the island policy, some mention of various pragmatic assumptions underwriting it is pertinent. The island policy rested on certain estimates of the stakes in the war, and the most important estimate was moral. But more than moral arithmetic was required where responsibility was claimed; some geopolitical arguments were needed also. On the side of economics, the noninterventionists assumed and did not trouble to prove America's self-sufficiency. Whoever won the war in Europe, the material position of America would go unthreatened. Rejecting with indignation all suggestions that America might have imperial opportunities to exploit in a postwar world, the noninterventionists assumed what most Americans had assumed since the birth of the republic, that the cornucopia of the continent was everlasting, one beyond which Americans need and ought not ever look for their well-being in this world.

This was easy. A little more than assumption was called for

in the military field. Hardly likely to propose military reasoning of their own, the churchmen were content with authority—in this instance Major George Fielding Eliot, who published *The Ramparts We Watch* in 1937, and General Johnson Hagood, whose *We Can Defend America* appeared in 1938. Both books guaranteed the hemisphere. In their feeling of security, the social-gospel isolationists went further than Eliot and Hagood, however; Eliot and Hagood demanded certain defensive preparations; most of the churchmen scorned the argument of "defensive necessity" as a fatal repetition of similar arguments in 1916 and 1917. Security was easy to believe until June, 1940; then the fall of France exposed and withered the easy assumption hidden behind the professions of neutrality: the assumption that Allied victory was a certainty. For some men, this was the moment of the breaking of the promise; John C. Bennett was one, convicting himself of illusion after the disaster. "I did not face the fact that a German victory was the real danger." [48] But the central party of the passion did not break; only, in the face of disaster, it had to be reassured. The reassurances with which the *Christian Century* hastened forward were peculiar—in fact, surprising. The English suddenly appeared as "the bulldog breed." Presumably because there was a bulldog breed, it was no time for panic in America; it was a "Time for Cool Heads." Cool heads knew the British would not collapse, and could ask, therefore, if the eight billion dollars the administration had already spent on rearmament was not enough? And were not fifty thousand planes, called for by the President, a great many? In September Morrison strengthened the British position for his readers: Hitler was going to move east, not west. In May, 1941, inquiring "How Desperate Is Britain?" he reminded his readers that the British still had the resources of India to call upon. Presumably this was not the India of Gandhi, favorite and fabled of pacifist and liberal. With Hitler's attack on Russia, the *Century* argued, nerves stretched vicariously for Britain could be relaxed.[49] The *Century* fought conscription and fought its renewal; it fought the destroyers-bases deal and Lend-Lease. Britain could hold; the immanent principle of hope was justified once more. What future

Morrison assigned to Britain will be noted shortly. What he assigned to France, which after all had already fallen and which after all had also stretched the nerves of some Americans (even some of the readers of the *Century*) will be noted in some little detail.

In addition to economic and military security, the neutralist claimed one further sort of security as well: America had nothing to fear socially from staying out of the war. Democracy at home could be cultivated and increased, "no matter what" the outcome. Here once again the neutralists argued the negative side of their case most of all: going to war *would* mean the end of democracy at home. The men who made this argument had all taken their stand for democracy. They had supported the New Deal if they had not voted to its left. And what they found in interventionism was a spirit, a logic, that wounded their liberalism. Page and the secretaries of the FOR saw dictatorial patterns in the Industrial Mobilization Act. Morrison did not miss the fact that Roosevelt's 1937 and 1938 senatorial opponents on domestic social legislation rallied to his armaments program of 1939 and 1940. There were signs enough, he felt, that a business "fifth column" was ready to seize the opportunity of the defense program to roll back democratic advances. Morrison believed, in fact, that the President had chosen the interventionist program as an escape from the intractable domestic scene, as a substitute for New Deal failure. "The party in power, unable to unify the national life at the level of its economic well-being, now turns to the war as a unifying substitute . . . [Mr. Roosevelt] is the Führer of this inchoate fascism." With supreme indignation and anxiety, in the last months before Pearl Harbor, Morrison excoriated the "American century" being merchandised by Henry Luce and the "hundred years of Anglo-American naval domination" heralded by Secretary Knox as affronts to the spirit of the republic. Albert W. Palmer called upon the nation to attend to its duty of reforming its life at home, along such lines, he proposed, as those indicated by the Congregationalist Council for Social Action.[50]

Since they did not expect Axis victory, the neutralists did not discuss the problem of advancing democracy at home in event of Axis victory overseas. Rather, they foresaw general exhaustion, followed by an outpouring from America of food, medicine, reconstruction funds, sanity, and succor.[51]

So much for pragmatics in the narrow sense and for *Realpolitik*. Given these assumptions, the social-gospel neutralists were able to focus on the moral stakes in the war without being troubled by feelings of indulging perfectionist illusions. The editorials of Charles Clayton Morrison from Munich to Pearl Harbor were the masterpieces of a mind determined to be nakedly realistic in defense of America's proper moral position, which was isolation. Morrison believed the point of America's susceptibility was its conscience, its "sentimental prompting" to rush to the aid of the Allies. Realistic instruction of the conscience, therefore, he took as his task. He argued that there was a flaw in the policy simply of aid alone, since no nation, especially America, convinced that its moral welfare was at stake, would rest content with lending aid; it would fight. And to fight would be, once again, to commit the supreme moral error, to be engulfed in confusion.[52]

The inner stresses that this mind had to contain were set out on the occasion of Munich. During the crisis, Morrison examined the President's role. He agreed that the danger of Hitler's moving was acute; he agreed that the President was trying to help block Hitler and that, conceivably, this help might be effective. The point, however, was whether the American people understood what was going on. Did they realize that America was being entangled in a European crisis? They should certainly be allowed to see that this was so, and if they did, they should not and would not approve.

Then Morrison's oscillations began. The settlement itself, he wrote (after the crisis), signaled the destruction of the European order established at Versailles, which had been morally indefensible. Yet, unable to rest easy in this dictum, he added that "[The common man] feels in his bones that his deliverance has been bought at a moral price which it may take generations of human misery to pay." This, in the *Century* of September 28, 1939.

In the issue of October 12, a swing back again: "Bad as seems the moral basis on which this new agreement has been reached, it is by no means certain that post-Munich Europe will be any more immoral in its premises, or any more doomed to disintegration, than was post-Versailles Europe." The United States should keep out until the new Europe was defined.

But then finally, the heading of an editorial of November 30: "Demonic Germany and the Predicament of Humanity." [53]

The tragedy for Morrison, and for the noninterventionists as a whole, was that the sentiments of September 28 and November 30 could not safely be indulged, even in the secret heart. The equation of Munich with Versailles was a tour de force that instinct and "sentimentality" denied; but it was a tour de force that had to be maintained.

The way to maintain it was to stress what was eternally opposed to morality:

A year ago, before Czechoslovakia was abandoned to its fate, a plausible—if superficial—case might be made out for France and Britain as custodians of the fate of democracy and opponents of fascism. But since Munich Europe has reverted entirely to the old game of power politics . . . The crisis that is gathering in Europe at present is a power politics, not an ideological crisis . . . it is simply not true that the fate of democracy in this country depends upon whether France can keep Mussolini from taking Tunis or whether Britain can escape from returning Kenya to Hitler. The fate of democracy in this country will not be settled by what happens in Europe's present unhappy game of power politics.[54]

"Power politics," "power politics," "power politics." But perhaps our stress here should bear not upon the kind of game that Morrison took as scandal, but upon the fact that it was a "game."

Morrison was the one man who tried to face in detail the implications of an Axis victory. One tack suggested turnabout as fair play. "If Germany wins and imposes terms comparable with those which were imposed upon her in 1919, the Allied nations will simply bide their time, as did France after 1870, waiting for the hour when they may strike for revenge." [55] It was a peculiarity of the tractarians of peace that the treaty of Brest-Litovsk was ejected from their recollections of the First World War—just as, for instance, Walter Lippmann's *The Shield of the Republic* failed to find a place in their bibliographies alongside Hagood and Eliot. But the prospect of a German peace demanded much more drastic defenses against perturbation than this, as the neutralists watched the new Europe being carved. Morrison had already attempted to strengthen his readers to watch the fate of Britain without sentimental urges to rush in: Britain was the British Empire and the American people did not believe in it. Britian should turn herself into another Sweden, Norway, or Switzerland, and Britain would then be in no more danger from Hitler than were they. Americans liked Sweden, Switzerland, and Norway. The British Empire was going to fall someday anyway; whether it would fall gradually or catastrophically depended upon making peace with Germany now—that is, as of late November, 1939.[56]

But this was only paper idealism. Perhaps it is possible to pinpoint the more ultimate forms of political hope in Morrison's reflections on the fall of France. Hitler, he wrote, had a social revolution; the question before Hitler, with his new triumphs, was whether he would exploit it.

> . . . we have minimized the reality and importance of this revolution because we have been revolted by its hideous brutalities and disgusted by the personalities of its leaders . . . Can Hitler give the rest of the world a system of interrelationships better than the trade-strangling and man-exploiting system of empire capitalism? We have small hope that he can, but hope must not be given up entirely until it is known what he intends to do with this victory.[57]

In the case of Muste, hope supported a complete set of geopolitical predictions; for Morrison, hope sanctioned refusal to predict; in both cases, hope meant that Americans need not act. But further:

> In a united Europe governed from the German center, with a unified planned economy covering the continent, France will be able to find compensations in terms of human values. A France which has thrown off the artificial structure of empire and of capitalistic dominion in industry, together with the intolerable burden of the vast military establishment which goes with them, may experience a new emancipation, a genuine and creative revival of economic

freedom. Such a France may be the first great modern society to pass through the gate of disillusionment concerning those values clustering about the mythical concept of the "economic man" which have hypnotized and perverted Western civilization for centuries.[58]

Morrison, that is, expected France to emerge from subjugation fairly soon; meanwhile, France was being scoured and prepared morally; the anti-alcohol, anti-divorce, anti-vice decrees of Vichy hinted at it; "There is more than regimentation for a fascist society in all this." "A France that is a product of schools which have been swept clean of secularism will be at least a France with a faith—and a faith which is incompatible with the faith of nazism." [59]

The "at least" was a pressure point, betraying the terrible costs Morrison was having to pay: the new schools he was describing were the schools into which Roman Catholicism had been returned. The political structure he thought might follow Hitler was an Italian-French-Spanish bloc, a "Latin Catholic totalitarianism." In the man who had fixed sharply upon the "short-run" issues in 1928, who had protested the Pope's "invitation to a holy war" in 1937, who had protested the Taylor mission to the Vatican, it was apparent that for him to down such bitter potion —the thirst for neutrality burned the soul.

But of course Morrison never conceded in his heart of hearts that the war might really end in fascist victory. Instead, he spoke constantly of "stalemate." This forced him to stand on an unstated military analysis, but nevertheless he discerned stalemate between October, 1939, and May, 1940; he saw stalemate once more from the summer of 1940 until the spring of 1941; after it seemed Russia might not collapse after all, he pronounced a stalemate again in the fall of 1941. All the while, his demand for negotiated peace persisted; Morrison spent long pages in 1941 analyzing the outlines of such a peace, one that should not only end the war but should also be lasting.[60]

As it was forced to endure both the excruciation of such inner rationalizations and the mounting attacks from interventionists, the peace apology colored with bitterness. Morrison, conceding nothing to his opponents, defending pacifism as well as his own nonpacifist sector of the front, the object of the most withering of the fire from interventionists, anticipated the formula by which debate was to be resumed bitterly after the war. A man not friendly to dialectical thinking, he nevertheless found the formula in paradox. With Pearl Harbor there was no choice, but this did not mean that isolationists had been wrong. "Given the background of unyielding diplomacy, war was inevitable." If necessary, however, it was "An Unnecessary Necessity." [61]

Perhaps, with his customary fortitude, taking too much upon himself, tempted perhaps too often by the facility of his own formidable polemic talents, Morrison nevertheless was a true champion of Protestant isolationism at large. What was the organizing nerve of this passion? The answer in Morrison's case was an answer good for all.

All Morrison's thinking ran back into his image of the church. His politics of peace was also in the service of his devotion to the church. We have seen his anxiety to protect the church from captivity to secular interests. The supreme instance of captivity had been the church's sanctification of the First World War. This anxiety for the integrity of the church was Morrison's key anxiety and went with him always, but now we must remember precisely what he meant by the word "church." What was always at stake when he warned of the danger of captivity was not the institutional church, or the official formal church in its separateness and independence, or the invisible church, but the synthesis of religion and culture, the investment of religion in the culture, which for Morrison meant finally religious culture itself. Actually, he raised the cry "Detach America from the Next War," [62] not "Detach the Church from the Next War." This in 1939 to 1941 was the same Morrison who had espoused the "short run" in 1928, who had read the class spectrum as capital-church-labor, who had resisted the tactic of forming liberal-radical sects within the church in favor of direct evangelization of the whole church community itself. Do not break the body of the culture: this was Morrison's cry. The *Century* in 1939, 1940, and 1941, in the desperation of its opposition to Roosevelt's foreign policy, was defending the old progressive image of the good society, the older image of America as the Promised Land, the oldest image—knitted in the sociology of the Saints of 1630—of the American Israel.

Thus it was the nation to which the *Century* directed its voice, month after month, year after year, and it was a nation unlike other nations. Everything reduced to a single imperative: let America be true to herself. Here was the self-righteousness against which Niebuhr flung some of his harshest charges; Niebuhr had learned to fling them against communists locating virtue in the "one nation" of socialism, and the charge held good directed at the location of virtue elsewhere.

> This communistic fallacy is hardly more pathetic than the vagaries of our Christian, patriotic isolationists who in one moment try to persuade themselves that America is made of different stuff from other nations and in the next moment seek to throttle every impulse of sympathy and every sense of common responsibility which might establish a common humanity among us rather than a unique guilt-lessness.[63]

Little provoked noninterventionists to more furious self-defense than this charge. But Morrison's words were definitive, as in his recoil from the President's Quarantine speech in Chicago: "America's moralism, flowering in her virgin detachment, must not be projected into the motivation of Great Britain, France, and Russia, tormented as they are by the precariousness of their several positions." Precisely in trying to refute the Niebuhrian charge, he upheld it: "We have discovered that our goodness, our moralism, is in large measure the expression of our relative detachment . . . We are no more virtuous than others. The difference is a difference in circumstances."[64] America, in other words, unlike others, had grace.

Morrison feared the results of changing the circumstances that had made America good, moral, different. Of course he tried to have his argument both ways. He argued that America should not intervene because "the results of our previous attempt at intervention forbid it." In other words, if America did intervene,

it would—and should, being America—intervene only in the
Wilsonian spirit, in the name of moralism, and to attempt to
implement the Wilsonian spirit through war would be to repeat
the Wilsonian fallacy. But his real fear was that, if America did
intervene, this time she would forsake her flowering moralism.
Here Morrison exhibited the sensitivity to power calculations of
which he was capable. Obsessed with the political and historical
ambiguities of the war, he recurred constantly to the "risk," to
the "gamble," to the inscrutable wheel of fate represented by
world politics. Like many of the neutralists, he had a drastic, almost melodramatic sense of the forces in play: social revolution
and counter-revolution in Germany, Italy, Russia; the declining
power of the nations that had policed the world for a century;
the breakup of established relations in the colonial world; and the
rise of new powers wholly beyond containment according to any
of the arrangements of the past. If America intervened without
intending to stay in the postwar world, her intervention would be
as fruitless as the last; if she did stay in the world, she would be
permanently committed to struggle with an infinitely receding
series of world problems, entangled in that realm of "power
politics" alien to her history, alien to her character. It would be
a turning point in American life, a new America, exposed to
strange duties abroad and, reciprocally, unbalanced at home. The
old arrangements of the national culture would be set, however
so slightly at first, in new directions and dimensions. There would
be a new focus for American destiny, sacrificing the old.

Those old arrangements were precious ones, and the Protestant
prophets felt that they still stood near the center of them. The old
destiny was precious, and they felt it was the one for which they
spoke. Led by pastors—rather than by professors—of suburban
and metropolitan Protestantism, supported widely in the small
towns, the mystique of peace was the fight of liberal evangelical
leadership against still further displacement in the nation's
politics and still greater loss of cultural leadership—beyond the
displacement and loss from Prohibition and the campaign of
1928, efforts of the Protestant community at large. No matter how
vigorously the prophets had excoriated and denounced the sins

of American society, their denunciations had always been compatible with the supreme priority of preserving the fair land. The sins of America were the sort of sins to which a social gospel could preach. America had been the sort of society in which pacifist idealists could imagine that they were heard.

The pacifists and neutralists knew this, Niebuhr could never disprove it. Marxist and neo-orthodox reactions to 1932 had directly challenged this liberal image of a profoundly homogeneous, pervasively moral society, highly imperfect but ultimately organized by and saturated with the sanctions of religious goodness. The vast majority of the liberal pastors had not been convinced by neo-orthodoxy even when they went socialist because they still felt the immanence of the Kingdom in the national life. The Kingdom was, as Johnson of the council steadily insisted, process—the process of American culture. The anti-interventionists saw clearly that the processes of the Kingdom had no likely relevance in the vast world outside. Techniques of persuasion, of "more scientific methods of cooperation," of socializing the individual might count for less than nothing beyond American shores. The social gospel might work at home; in the giant chaos of the world it could not even be imagined.

The anti-interventionists' opposition to any extensive preparedness program as well as to intervention itself drew not simply on their logic that to prepare meant inevitably to intervene. It also reflected their sense—indefinite, imprecise, but compelling—of where American society might well be tending—further along the way of the immense, impersonal, unreachable forces of change that had already severely undermined the Kingdom-bearing culture they knew. The liberal idealists could sense nothing but a passive, reflexive, subordinate role for their culture-community in an America given still more to the mobilizations of impersonal necessity, let alone to the exigencies of world politics. For all of them the problem was precisely what it was for Muste, a question not merely of division between nations but of division within the self. It meant schism within the self that was America, and to that extent division, separation, isolation of the self that was the church. There were definite outlines of this division, which could be exposed and admitted only in lyric cries of anguish and anger. In March, 1941, the President spoke of an America "united" for his policy. The *Century* replied:

> . . . machine dominated politics of the hysterical eastern seaboard states. The states containing a large proportion of recent American immigration, the states ruled by munitions makers, the states controlled by federal patronage, the states represented by politicians of the type of Senator Ellender of Louisiana . . . these are the President's united America.[65]

Was then the church so much less than America? Here was more than war within the self; here was self-mutilation.

By 1940, Niebuhr had nerved himself up to the full implications of an ethics of responsibility. The implications were those Bennett had specified in the passage we have set at the beginning of this chapter. Niebuhr formulated them with reference to the war itself:

> It must be admitted that the anarchy of war which results from resistance to tyranny is not always creative; that, at given periods of history, civilization may lack the resource to fashion a new and higher form of unity out of momentary anarchy. The defeat of Germany and the frustration of the Nazi effort to unify Europe in tyrannical terms is a negative task. It does not guarantee the emergence of a new Europe with a higher level of international cohesion and new organs of international justice. But it is a negative task which cannot be avoided.[66]

Drawing on Tillich again: men were not always blessed with *kairos,* were not always offered a moment swollen with potential fruits; but to refuse to act because *kairos* was lacking, to demand that history offer only the future one desired before one would act was to deny any *kairos* that might eventually appear.

Niebuhr's task in the prewar years was to keep this position clear; it was a position no one had taken in the days of the great apostasy, 1917 and 1918. In neo-orthodox circles, led by Niebuhr, and neo-liberal circles, where Bennett spoke, the argument for aid to the Allies in 1941 never scorned the feelings of 1931. It was basic to the logic of this Protestant interventionism that any identification of a political course with the name of Jesus Christ was heresy; the crusade psychology had no place in politics, because of the nature—the true and proper nature—of politics.[67]

Niebuhr always tried to locate enemies on each flank; his line against a "holy war," his rejection of the war-mystique to which American Protestantism had succumbed in 1917 and 1918, he chose to draw against the most significant opponent he could have chosen. In 1938, breaking a political silence of twenty years, Karl Barth had written his letter to the Czechoslovak soldiers urging the Czech army to fight Hitler precisely in the name of Jesus Christ. Niebuhr was not yet equipped at this time to say that war was the course he supported. But it was not the policy of war to which he objected. He rejected Barth's provision of absolute sanction for war and took Barth's letter to be further, conclusive evidence of the dangerous all-or-nothing implications of Barth's theology, its dangerous incapacity to relate to the relative, day-to-day flux of politics.[68]

Moreover, Niebuhr, Van Dusen, and the other interventionists spent little time hypothesizing a postwar world; above all, they distinctly agreed the war could not and would not fulfill idealistic aims such as had been preached in 1917 and 1918. That is, the Protestant interventionists were their own men, disdaining the utopian themes played by official and self-appointed secular interventionist intellectuals of the day. The war against the fascist powers was a "negative task," and no man who tried to palliate the hard bearing of that fact could claim the label most prized by all hands in the debate—"realism."

By and large, Niebuhr won success on this negative side. Even men who deplored his influence nevertheless did not try to picture him as a crusader on the model of the First World War. When Morrison attacked interventionist "romantics," it was Episcopal Bishop Henry Hobson of the Fight-for-Freedom Committee he singled out, not Niebuhr, Bennett, Bradley, Van Dusen, or Coffin. Hobson, with his frenetic Anglo-activism, did deal in echoes of 1917 and 1918. But it was a problem for Niebuhr that Morrison did have a target, even though it was not himself, a target much broader, much more vulnerable, than Niebuhr ever admitted. Powerful invitations *were* being issued to identify the cause of intervention with the cause of religion and the church. Morrison, acutely alert to such an appeal, found it woven in the speeches of the President. He found it in the invitation released by Fiorello La Guardia, Director of Civilian Defense, requesting all ministers to preach a sermon on the Sunday of November 16, 1941—already prepared by the Office of Civilian Defense—celebrating the symbiotic relationship of religion and democracy. True, such a symbiosis did exist; true, the canned sermon dealt with it fairly; but the implications of the request were totalitarian. Morrison heard crusade in the mouth of Henry Wallace also, who in other days had figured as one of the secular prophets of the passion.[69] Nor was Bishop Hobson alone among churchmen in his war talk. There was Bishop Manning with his Tory *Kulturanglikanismus;* there was Bishop Cannon speaking crusade from that Southern fortress of the church in which the crusade of the social gospel had so long been ignored. These were Morrison's antagonists, men for whom crusade was easy because they had never felt shame about 1917 and 1918, men who did not recognize the realities in play, who suppressed the facts of where moral responsibility for the war lay, who glossed the facts of economic injustice, who simplified the facts of the world revolution in process. The danger here was real and it faced all the prophets, but it was most threatening and difficult for Niebuhr, not Morrison, for the tragic interventionists and not the neutralists. Niebuhr's attack on Barth drew the line within the church, but did it draw the line in the larger debate? In such a document as the Atlantic Charter and in the propaganda drawn from it, for instance, the squeeze upon the neo-orthodox interventionists was most severe: if the moment in history men faced was really a negative moment, did those glowing principles for world order reflect it fairly? Could a realistic, neo-orthodox political intellectual really accept the Four Freedoms as legitimate apology for war aid and war? But, on the other hand, could he join the neutralists in attacking them as romantic delusions, if not deliberately fostered opium dreams? [70] He could say nothing. Unwilling to justify official propaganda on grounds of expediency,

Niebuhr on the other hand could not pretend to believe that his tragic spirit might be spread widely and rapidly enough to serve as the decisive rationale for interventionist policies. Consequently, he could never face the neutralist insistence that intervention, in the real world of possible choices and not the ideal world of theory, was a policy justified and defended by illusions.

Involved here was one of the important, ambiguous, and obscure thrusts potential—though not inevitable—in Niebuhr's political psychology. In one sense, all the debate between Niebuhr and the liberal social-gospel prophets was gathered up in this question: What is the good man to do in the bad world of politics? The social-gospel answer always swung to the idea that the good man should act to make other men good; whether he should convert them directly, or should convert them indirectly, through politics itself, through changing their environment, remained a mystery within social-gospel ranks; but either method ended in the same view, that all problems would end with the universalization of the good man. On one level, Niebuhr contradicted this formula; the good man, the Christian statesman, the Christian intellectual leader, must assume something like average moral behavior, neither expecting nor asking that the moral quality of political forces conform to a priori standards of goodness; he must understand and work in terms of an objective, empiric social psychology. The Christian could not, that is, define his political ends and choose his political means in terms of an universalization of himself. Now this was to open the door to Machiavellianism. Ward exemplified it perfectly in his celebration of the party. Niebuhr had to close this door by criticizing the social gospel on a deeper level: he rejected its image of the good man in the first place, righteous, sanctified, radiant with the official motives of service and coöperation. Justification, not sanctification, capped his hierarchy of the phases of life. The tragic spirit was not the product of a good man's consciousness of the disparity between himself and the world; it was the product of the honest man's recognition of his own true nature as well as that of the world. This opened up new difficulties, for Niebuhr argued that the tragic sense should have political effects, and yet he could not, in light of the evidence justifying the tragic sense in the first place, let political responsibility hinge to a universalization of the tragic sense. Was a saving majority of men infused with the tragic sense any more likely than a saving majority of good men? Here again, of course, we are interested not in evoking theoretical puzzlers for their own sake, but in following them as they developed along the lines of pressure imposed by the situation the theorist with his theory was trying to face. The puzzles here, vital for the over-all bearing of Niebuhr's thought, political and religious, had concrete expression in the specific issue of whether in 1940 and 1941 the United States should go beyond war aid into open war itself. Inspection of Niebuhr's reasoning on this issue will show also to what degree Niebuhr was trying to keep his politics rooted directly in his religious insights.

As an issue in the polemics of the times, the question of active, outright American entrance into the war was posed with Niebuhr's appearance at the national convention of the United Christian Council of Democracy, in Cleveland, February, 1940. Harold Fey of the FOR attended this convention and, returning from it, represented Niebuhr as having espoused American entry. Niebuhr vigorously denied Fey's report. He favored American credit for the Allies, he said, tied to commitments "which would ensure a just peace," but he did not support military intervention. Few men did, in February, 1940, and none of the churchmen. But Fey asked a question that summarized the problem of principles: "If we lifted the arms embargo yesterday when airplanes were needed and if we remove the credit embargo when financial aid is needed, is it likely that tomorrow when men are needed, we shall not follow with military intervention?" [71] There was nothing in Niebuhr's arguments, up to that time, that turned the point of Fey's question, and Fey could not get an answer. Morrison of the *Century* hurled the same question more generally, in a challenge to those castigating the pacifists and neutralists, to "speak plainly." Those who had signed the January and May, 1940, declarations against pacifism and neutrality told what they were against; what were they for? Did they want only moral aid to the Allies, or did they want economic aid as well? or military aid? or direct intervention? or what? Morrison's intention here was plain enough: he wished to eliminate the middle ground between neutral isolation and war. Aid-short-of-war, he believed, would lead to war, and he believed the nation would not support the aid policy once this was understood.

This challenge to "speak plainly" paralleled Morrison's more vociferous, more implacable criticism of the President. From the day Roosevelt stood on the bridge in Chicago in October, 1937, and called for quarantine, Morrison imputed to him and to his policy a deliberate will for intervention running far beyond the will of the country, and a reluctance to exercise democratic candor in pressing it. The President was, Morrison wrote—as of June, 1940—"determined to take his country just as close to the verge of war as his executive power could carry it." [72] Unlike Lincoln, McKinley, and Wilson, who had allowed the nation to generate its own war mood, Roosevelt had thrown off democratic and constitutional restraint and intended to lead his country into the conflict even if divided. Morrison proposed a "national uprising" of the peace forces to hold the President to his campaign pledges, an uprising that took shape in the last high wave of America First in the late spring of 1941, following Congressional passage of Lend-Lease. Then finally, Pearl Harbor was what Morrison "expected" from the President's policy. He had written sometime before that an "incident" was bound to occur. [73]

A small library of polemics exists devoted to the question of what was in the mind of Franklin Roosevelt in the year 1941. Clearly, however, Morrison and those on his side were not primarily driven by solicitude for national unity. Rather, the nation's lack of unity allowed them to assume something that was necessary for their arguments against the President: the nation never would, never could, choose war in the full, free exercise of its democratic will. Here "democracy" meant, for Morrison, not a process of making decisions, but a value by which the content of any decision, no matter how arrived at, was judged. No decision for war could be democratic, by definition. As a consequence, Morrison, like the rest of the President's critics then and since, refused to recognize that the President was faced with one of the permanent dilemmas of democratic leadership. Was the democratic leader chosen to lead or to represent? Obviously, for both; but the emphasis in each particular situation was a product of considerations the subtleties of which the isolationists washed out. If the President, anxious to press a policy of aid to the Allies because he believed it required by the vital interests of the nation, realized that the nation was refusing to face the risk of war that the aid policy entailed, was it his bound duty as a democratic leader to force those risks on the attention of the nation? What if—as Morrison argued—this would be to wreck the original policy of aid that he believed required by national interests? Could the democratic leader be allowed to hope that, through experience with intermediate measures of aid, the nation might learn to face and accept the risk of ultimate measures? And to go the whole way with Morrison was not to shift the problem: what if the democratic leader believed the vital interests of the nation required entrance into the war? Was it his bound duty to say so, whatever the effects of his saying so might be? What if the effect might be—as Morrison hoped—to frustrate even second-best measures short of war? Summed up: must the democratic leader always, at every moment, proclaim the whole truth as he sees it, or may he try to win general recognition of the whole truth through general experience before he proclaims it?

In a certain sense, Niebuhr also was in a position of "democratic leadership." His own judgment of the leadership of President Roosevelt was not absolutely clear; in June, 1941, he observed that the President should be neither dictator nor marionette, but should tell the truth and let the people decide. He expressed some uneasiness, some unhappiness over what he felt to be the President's overlong silence, his failure to help more in educating the nation to its perils and interests.[74] But it was not at all clear that Niebuhr himself argued policy according precisely to what he felt best, heedless of what was in the minds of his audience. Departing from the social gospel's polarization of foreign policy into the alternatives of tribal isolation or holy intervention, a simplification in which much of liberal Protestantism—and not only social-gospel circles—had invested its prestige, the neo-orthodox interpretation of the war was a profoundly new, profoundly difficult word to preach. It could not be allowed to be lost in official Washington doctrine. It could not be left mistaken for the new preachments of simple moralism being raised by other leaders, both secular and religious. An adequate discussion of the war from the standpoint of neo-orthodoxy required the most discriminating, point-by-point use of pragmatic evidence; the danger was constant of forcing the evidence beyond what the audience was prepared to receive; the danger was constant of a sudden inflation of its tragic import into appeals for righteous rather than chastened action.[75]

Therefore it could be thought that Niebuhr was not, as a responsible spokesman, free to say all he thought. Yet, it is simpler to see his hesitation not so much as discretion, but as a form of polemical paralysis, and to see this paralysis, this suspension of the will, as a profoundly revealing expression of his theology.

The *Century*'s demand for plain speaking was provoked by the first organized support churchmen lent to the aid policy by late 1939 and 1940. Firmly in support of the administration's measures, Niebuhr was conscious of the force of the challenge, and in the summer of 1940 he began to discuss the line short of war:

> We do not believe that we ought to enter the war and that entry can be avoided if we act in time . . . We believe that we ought to stay out of the war because, just as in the world war, our vital interests are only ultimately and not immediately touched by a possible Allied victory. This prevents the whole nation from feeling that coincidence of vital and ideal interests which alone prompts nations to enter such a horrible carnage with comparative unanimity.[76]

Niebuhr feared here that entrance into the war would provoke vicious political controversy at home; propaganda and coercion would be necessary to contain it. "This prospect," he wrote in the spring of 1941, "is so dismal that one must regard the effort of helping the allies to victory without war as the best possible statesmanship under the circumstances." [77] Later in the spring:

. . . it should be clear that nothing in the conflict now points to a
possible call for an American expeditionary force, whatever claims
might be made upon our help on the sea and in the air. We do not
suggest that involvement even to that extent is either inevitable or
desirable.[78]

Then, speculating upon the possibility that the nation was drift-
ing into nonbelligerent aid without a clear plan or policy for
the eventual peace, Niebuhr wrote, late in 1941: "Whether such
aid will finally be followed by actual belligerency is a question
which no one can answer. It may not be necessary for the defeat
of Hitler; and it may not be given, even if necessary." [79]

Here, questions about the theory and practice of intellectual
—as distinguished from political—leadership were at stake. What
did Niebuhr himself believe about the necessity or desirability
of actual belligerency? He commended the statesmen in Washington for their success in dealing with the conditions they faced,
a primary one of which was the national reluctance to consider
war. But the national reluctance, of course, was a problem for
the responsible national political leaders. Because the nation was
reluctant, it could be said that the President ought not be urged
to ask the Congress to declare war, as though those who might
urge him spoke for the nation. It could be said that the President
should wait, that the nation ought not intervene, until the nation
was less reluctant. This, however, was not equivalent to saying
that the nation should be and should continue to be reluctant; it
was not equivalent to saying that the intellectual leader ought to
refrain from urging his audiences to support war. The business of
the intellectual leader was not confined to advising the political
leader of the possibilities for responsible political action. It was
to help create such possibilities.

But the intellectual as well as the political leader might also
have a feeling for the limits of exhortation. Niebuhr himself now,
in his suspension of exhortation, in his role of commentator upon
the state of morale rather than of instructor of morale, was playing
out implications of his own thought. He had always tempered his
expectations of the power of "mere words," of rational instruction,
of moral appeals, of preaching, to affect men's wills and actions.

He had always visualized and affirmed the possibility that truth could be learned only through politics, through "harsh realities," through history itself—politics and history unaffected by prior exhortation. He had pointed at such a case in his analysis of utopianism: modern utopianism, he had written, would almost surely not evaporate—despite such criticism of it as his own—until it was proved false by efforts to fulfill it. "Men cannot, by taking thought, strengthen their will." [80] The theme had come down from his first book, where it had appeared as one of the dissonances in his uneasy liberalism:

> To develop the wisdom of the serpents while they retain the guilelessness of doves is the task which confronts the religiomoral forces if they would aid in the moral regeneration of society. It may be that such a task is too difficult for the resources of this or any generation of the immediate future and that painful experience must prove other strategies inadequate.[81]

Such reservations had never inhibited Niebuhr from raising every appeal for wisdom and guilelessness, from indicating precisely where he himself thought short-cuts past painful experience might be open. He had always "spoken plainly." Yet here, in 1941, in a sense he did not. The nation, he said, had not yet felt that "coincidence of vital and ideal interests" at which alone a nation accumulated the will for war. But was that coincidence of interests a fixed and determined point? It was plain enough that Niebuhr was unhappy about the lack of unity in America; it was plain enough that he wished the nation already did feel its vital and ideal interests coincidental. The point of coincidence existed, partly, as it was felt to exist, and the core of Niebuhr's analysis of the policies of Britain and France during the 'thirties had been the failure of these peoples to feel it in time. In other words, for Niebuhr himself the coincidence did already exist. Nonetheless, he never called for outright intervention. To see why is to spell out some of the farthest reaches of concern that a political decision can involve.

Unlike his procedure in *Moral Man,* in the *Reflections,* and in his political writing through the 'thirties—where he concentrated his polemic in terms of economic, social, geopolitical "power" considerations—Niebuhr directed his unhappiness in 1941 upon a moral attitude. He feared America's sense of detachment and distance from the war. He feared American complacency, an emotional attitude—complacency in a world of agony. He feared that victory would amount to a harvest reaped by America from the sacrifices of America's allies. "Are we not now in danger of consciously contriving a peace for which others will pay dearly while we pay cheaply?" [82] Americans were not giving "themselves," but only their surplus—sacrificially meaningless. Yet "we belong in the same world, are part of the same family, still have faith in God and the dignity of man, and must share with them the problems and tasks of the world." [83] It was what he felt to be this hidden lovelessness of the neutralist position that unfailingly triggered his polemic vehemence.[84] Proclaiming love, demanding love, anticipating love, the effect of neutralism was to sanction division and isolation. The neutralists could not identify themselves with the other men because of the image they held of themselves and that, concomitantly, was true because they could not find in themselves the needs and the weaknesses of other men.

Here, once again, and in still more decisive fashion, the field of differentiation between the camps in the political debate was the field of religious perspective, and this time, unlike 1933 and the schism within the FOR, the division drew out the full inwardness of Niebuhr's theology. The division in the end was religious, and it was the division between a religion climaxing in morality and a religion climaxing in mercy, a religion in which the last word was the Word of grace. Time after time Niebuhr had displaced a distinct reluctance to liberate this aspect of his religious insights, precisely for fear of the political quietism it might be used to defend. He was interested in action, and in political action; the burden of his polemic from the beginning was directed at those illusions which frustrated adequate action in light of the facts. But, on the other hand, his inquiry served to search out the facts in the first place, and it was the difference between the two sides that lay at the heart of the religious division: it was only in the discovery of certain facts that the religion of grace and mercy was justified.

The final form of these facts was a fact about the self: the self could not fulfill itself. The self could not fulfill itself and could be rescued from the doom implied in this fact only on condition it recognized it as a fact. This was the great theme of *The Nature and Destiny of Man*. In the deepest sense, Niebuhr's call for aid and his silent assent to entrance into the war amounted itself to a call for love, but, unlike the call of the neutralists, for a love that accepted the nature of the "other" as revealed in tragedy because it accepted the self as in no way different. He accused the neutralists of not understanding the religious needs of men; those needs were not defined by men of righteousness administering a politics of untragic love; they were defined by men whose politics had foundered on its lack of love and, foundering, carried away all the provisional, prideful, circumscribed, necessary treasures of meaning and integrity by which those men had tried to live. It was true that there was a time to stand apart on a high place and preach the word of love, of sacrifice, of negotiated peace and economic conference. But it was also true there was a time for weeping, comfort, and the contemplation of man, even when the means of comfort was war. It was in fact not to win men to love and peace that love and peace were preached; it was to allow men to weep, to know one another and be comforted. The neutralists always offered a policy drawn from the arsenal of righteousness. Niebuhr did not: "Will the moralists who think that it would be a simple matter to make peace with Hitler if we only called an economic conference and promised to allocate raw materials, please be quiet while we weep?" [85] "The world is mad. Someday the tragedy of our era will be dramatized by an artist of sensitive insight and power and will elicit the tears of the spectator." [86] To weep was to identify, and for the spectator —as Americans were spectators—the saving response to tragedy was to identify, knowing that he too was not loving and peaceful and that tragedy could come to him, and that the logic and vulnerability of being human were within him.

In effect, Niebuhr was asking America to give up its sense of providential blessing, its sense of being a chosen nation, its sense of being more righteous than others.

Even this is not yet to get at the heart of his hesitation, and the profundity of his position depended upon the hesitation. Here we are looking at something Niebuhr himself did not spell out, something of which he was perhaps, in any systematic sense, unaware. It is as true, however, of the work of systematic intellectuals as of literary artists, that ranges of meaning not deliberately intended by the author may exist and can legitimately be sought out. It is possible that Niebuhr hoped America would not have to cross the line dividing aid-short-of-war from war itself. It is possible that he believed Americans could grasp the nature of the struggle, and a sense of their partnership in the destiny of man, without having to enter the war. In light of his avowed views, this is improbable, but it is possible. His hesitation, however, would have followed whatever the case. Niebuhr did not believe the world wars of the West were to be explained simply as "inevitabilities" of human destiny, following from sinfulness of human nature. They were inevitabilities for the West in the mid-twentieth century, however, because Western politics had been pressed forward as though the resources of realistic religion were not needed. The constant problem in Niebuhr's thought was how to restore to culture those religious insights, the truth of which perhaps only the political failures of the culture could finally demonstrate—while trying to prevent those failures. He could not solve this problem in American domestic politics, where there were no tragedies potential, plausible, or severe enough to be religiously convincing. But in the international position of America from Munich to Pearl Harbor, there was the rare conjunction of a politics potentially fruitful in religious insight—American participation in war—yet at the same time offering direct immediate resistance to continued political catastrophe—American guarantee of Allied victory. If it were to yield its most precious fruits, however, this politics could not be urged polemically but only awaited. To bear fruits for those who did not concede its existence, tragedy had to invade the mind as an inevitability, as a necessity, as a condition that could not be resisted. It could not be chosen, as a pragmatic, prudential choice. Only those could choose it—as a sacrifice, or as resistance to catastrophe—who knew what it was already and knew what it was to be prepared. The hesitation in the last phase of Niebuhr's politics of intervention, then, was identical with the hesitation that must precede and suffuse all proclamations of the religious Word of convicting sin. In very pure, simple, and clear words, Niebuhr summed up the dialectic we have been exploring here, between knowledge and will, between insight and need. Only faith in the divine mercy of Jesus Christ could "disclose the actual facts of human existence. It alone can uncover the facts because it alone has answers for the facts which are disclosed." [87] The necessity for hesitation arose here: faith in divine resources could disclose the facts because it was prepared to face the facts; but was it certain that disclosure of the facts first would reveal the divine resources? An era that, resisting knowledge of the facts, setting aside the resources as of no need, might not be prepared to survive them. Niebuhr could not know; nothing was guaranteed; crisis might provoke panic or pride just as much as penitence. And the last possibility occurs at this point: that Niebuhr in his silence, his hesitation, his waiting, was waiting to be convinced himself, waiting to be seized by the logic of human tragedy upon which his own theology rested, that he waited as an act of faith in, as a self-imposed test of, his own prophetic career, waited as almost every American citizen waited, for Pearl Harbor.

The logic of the pacifists and holy isolationists was a fantasy of agony in the will. "Economic conference," the rising of the peoples, negotiated peace were plainly rationalizations of last recourse, but they were not functions of mere illusions. Such an interventionist as H. P. Van Dusen charged pacifists with "resolute unwillingness to face known and indisputable facts." [88] But the noninterventionists themselves took pains to sharpen some of the harshest facts. Their fantasies stemmed from religious necessity. In refusing to fall back into isolationism pure and simple, they were trying to save something of their sense of the world as a realm of God's creation. In refusing to accept Niebuhr's position, they were trying to save the only basis they had for continuing to think of the world as one of God's creation. Niebuhr was proposing a relaxation of the will, not only insofar as he recommended that the pacifists give up politics, but in his own policy, which had to reconcile itself to a tragedy from which there was no political appeal.

Niebuhr did not object to pacifism in itself. Pacifism, he agreed, expressed a genuine impulse in the heart of Christianity. Moreover:

> It is a reminder to the Christian community that the relative norms of social justice, which justify both coercion and resistance to coercion, are not final norms, and that Christians are in constant peril of forgetting their relative and tentative character and of making them too completely normative.[89]

But although this reminder had political relevance, it was not itself a political policy and could not be politics. Pacifism that advertised itself as an adequate political policy was "heretical" because it violated the testimony of the total Christian gospel— the gospel in the Bible itself and in classical theology—as these testified to the true nature of God, of man, of the Cross, and of the relations between man and the Cross. But—again revealing that it was the substance, not the method, of liberalism he attacked—Niebuhr urged a broader test of heresy as well, by which political pacifism also failed: "There are no historical realities which remotely conform to it. It is important to recognize this lack of conformity to the facts of experience as a criterion of heresy." [90]

Therefore, Niebuhr said, let pacifism "be frankly irresponsible in the social struggle as the best ascetics of Christian history were. Let it regard the problem of social justice as something which does not concern it directly." [91] In 1940, he noted that the Friends were maintaining their witness without trying to obstruct the administration in Washington; he commended them to the attention of the pacifist isolationists.

All this repeated a theme Niebuhr had suggested from the time of his first book. He had proposed an ascetic criticism of bourgeois civilization in *Does Civilization Need Religion?*, a "radical" criticism of parliamentary socialism in *Moral Man*, a criticism of justice by love in *Christian Ethics*. In each case, indicating that a perfectionist witness might be needed as a kind of fixed light by which responsible policy might steer, he had also insisted that the perfectionists must not compromise their witness by mixing it with politics. They had most of all to fear those compromises they themselves did not realize they were making. But, willing to be irresponsible ascetics and not responsible pragmatists, they had a role to play.

Unfortunately for Niebuhr's appeal, political pacifism in America had nothing to do with "the best ascetics in Christian history." Its believers could not be content merely to witness. Even at those extremes—perhaps especially at those extremes—where men like Muste grew conscious of the possibly "fantastic" character of their efforts, there was no surrender. They could not stop expending themselves against the world, even if only in imagination, to touch it, to change it, to drape it and transform it in its inmost parts. At bottom, they could not give over "the will's hard labor," "the vile pressure of the will." There are regions where we can only point, not follow. However, since these harsh words of Schopenhauer against the will caught Nietzsche's eye so sharply, it is worth noting, with a twist, a word Nietzsche himself set on the tongue of Zarathustra: "These saints did not know that God is alive again." [92] God had indeed, by the deepest insights of the social gospel, died in the laissez-faire world. His rebirth depended upon man taking control of his world, through social science, socialization of the personality, industrial democratization, politics. The political pacifists were the final exemplars of that logic, and its purest victims. With them, private and public coherence was fused. The heart was exposed, and could be defended only by remorseless responsibility for all areas where disturbance entered. Thus wishes of the heart required fantasies on a world-political scale. Simply to wait, to be open and empty of politics and techniques, to be unprovided with methods and means and answers, even for an instant, was impossible. The pacifists could not, did not know how, to give up the will in a supreme moment. What might rush in to fill the moment of openness and surrender? Without plans and programs and policies, there was no guarantee, and they were unprepared to accept it in mystery.

Niebuhr, at the pinnacle of his vision, saw the Christian heart as the heart reborn, having passed through the fires of experience into a new simplicity and innocence, which, aware of harsh realities, found unity and freedom in a piety that was saving because, in the last analysis, it took the world with nonchalance, even with humor—the humor of a St. Francis, anchored beyond both society and self—as well as tragedy.[93] America had never been ground for the flowering of such pure and hardy fruits. This of course did not reflect upon the imagination or the rigor of the perfectionist impulse in America. On the contrary, the reasons for the lack of such nonchalant and ascetic flowering testified to the depth and persistence of the impulse. The society had always seemed susceptible to indefinite moralization. The life of society in America had rarely seemed so tragic or so rigid as to force ideal dispositions of the heart to flourish cut off from the power structures of the community. As a consequence, those dispositions were always subject to the temptation to set themselves at the service of politics. The holy imagination had always been able to conceive the spread and permanence of Christian perfection as the natural possibility of the nation. To calculate the glory of harnessing power, reason, and science to piety repeatedly became the main task of the piety itself. Social-gospel idealism rarely exhibited that savage aggression against society at the heart of European utopian thought; it exhibited, rather, the unconscious sacrifice of private existence to the utilitarian perfection of the whole. An old generosity, therefore, as well as a new desperation, still persisted in the pacifism and isolationism of 1938 to 1941. Relief for such agony had to provide for its critical component, its religiously burdened will.

Niebuhr provided almost nothing here. He did not seek out the deepest wounds. He did not offer alternatives to the will. He had nothing as concrete and familiar as the holy image of America to fight for. He was himself by no means articulate in reassurance that the postwar world, even if lost to perfection, would at least remain open to pragmatic dealings; that it had neither to repeat the history of the postwar 'twenties and 'thirties, nor come to chaos, nor seduce America into straight power-political amorality. Still concentrating upon politics alone, he opened no alternatives to politics of more allure than what the bare abstractions of theology might carry. This was to run a risk. Among a people for whom it had been natural to blur the Kingdom of God with society, the anxieties provoked by world politics would drive so much the deeper. Without reassurances short of tragedy, or a meaningful reconciliation beyond tragedy, helplessness and apathy might succeed among the doves, stupidity among the serpents, and among plain citizens still interested in private life, a final indifference to prophets, a new popularity of priests offering easy shelter.

XIX

Epilogue

Shortly after the Second World War, the Federal Council (which transmuted into the National Council of Churches in 1950) set out again to study relationships between religion and economic life. The fruits of this project—six penetrating volumes—far surpassed any other such inquiry in the history of the churches.[1] Their guiding feature was that they were, for the most part, studies. They were not, like the council's 1920 tract, *The Church and Industrial Reconstruction,* blueprints for action, or, like Interchurch's report on the steel strike, intervention in the world of power. The two earlier works had issued from the spirit of 1919. There was no such year of enthusiasm after the Second World War. The council's six volumes betrayed few of the old perfectionist elements; old habits of thinking in terms of alternative "systems," of "new" social orders, of "Christianized" and "unChristianized" areas of society had faded.

The council's studies paid much attention to businessmen, much less attention to labor. These proportions expressed the situation of official Protestant idealism: it was under attack from within the churches themselves. The fitful sallies mounted by conservative businessmen against the social gospel in the 'twenties and 'thirties were succeeded by more persistent assaults in the postwar years, with new and aggressive support among pastors. Spiritual Mobilization, headed by James W. Fifield, Jr., pastor of Los Angeles' First Congregational Church, spoke regularly to thousands of clergy over the country through its journal *Faith and Freedom.* John T. Flynn's attack on Protestant liberal leaders in *The Road Ahead* was given mass circulation by the Committee for Constitutional Government. The Christian Freedom Foundation distributed its journal, *Christian Economics,* to thousands of Protestant pastors. The argument was always the same: Christianity means laissez faire.

None of the old social-gospel organizations escaped severe damage. By 1952, Harry Ward's Methodist Federation, headed and controlled by Rev. Jack McMichael after Ward's retirement in 1944, was at last sharply disavowed by the church. The federation, persisting along the line Ward had adopted, had become obviously grotesque within Methodism, and at the end had been deserted by even the warmest of Methodism's social-gospel pastors. The fact that the federation was distinguished by its excesses did not explain its fate completely. Thus, the moderation of the Congregationalists' neo-liberal Council for Social Action did not save it from the onslaught. Congregationalist businessmen of the old ethos began to find voice from coast to coast, and a Laymen's Committee Opposing Congregational Political Action attacked the Council for Social Action at the General Council of 1952. A National Laymen's Committee, headed by J. Howard Pew, Presbyterian oilman and one of the most outspoken business apologists for unreconstructed laissez faire as well as the single most important sponsor of the whole wave of Protestant economic fundamentalism, fought vigorously and with considerable success to win places of power within the new National Council of Churches itself. The social gospel had at last provoked its full-scale opposition. Its days of marginal freedom within the denominations were over.[2]

The situation had its ironies. When the laissez-faire laymen attacked the social gospel, they were not attacking just an assortment of pastors. They were attacking basic features of the postwar economy, features heavily indebted to the New Deal. Yet the social gospel had never itself been able to adjust satisfactorily to the New Deal. Certainly the New Deal had not depended on social-gospel majorities. Clearly, New Deal achievements had not built upon pure social-gospel motives. Nor did those achievements begin to embody the visions of a society organized according to the requirements of personality and of love. The postwar pastors were in the awkward position of having become defenders, no longer reformers, and defenders of what fell far short of their stated ideals.

In the circumstances this meant a revival of the appeal for enlightened business leadership, but, still more, an appeal to Protestant laymen simply to accept the new system. This was not in truth a notably high or creative mission, and it painfully fulfilled the passive reflexive role into which the old social gospel had feared the Protestant community was falling. The major escape from this becalming was to carry to completion that return to the church already beginning in the 'thirties. The church had religious purposes for transcending the immediate purposes of politics, and its purposes could never be satisfied by any politics. This was the course of that neo-liberalism men like John C. Bennett and, in a different fashion, F. Ernest Johnson had begun to stress before the war. This, they believed, was not to forget politics; somehow—the connection had never been made clear—the church's awareness of its transcending religious purposes would influence politics even if not so directly as the social gospel had intended. But let the church be the church.

The postwar years did not offer many chances to make the connection of church and politics any clearer. Although there was little evidence that Northern liberal Protestant congregations were converted to New Deal politics, there was also little evidence that they were much persuaded by Spiritual Mobilization and Christian Economics. Evidence indicated instead widespread confusions if not plain indifference to the issues involved. One of the National Council's own studies indicated that large majorities comprehended no connection at all between their professions of religious faith and their actions in the world of economics and politics.³ Indirectly, the wide postwar success of narrowly individualistic evangels testified to the same thing. It had always been a blindness peculiar in social-gospel pastors that they had never imaginatively assessed the social character of Protestant fundamentalism, and in the rather more sophisticated fundamentalism of Billy Graham they faced the same challenge once more. More important were individualistic evangels successful among the religiously liberal. Norman Vincent Peale's gospel of positive thinking was geared to provide the individual with an inner coherence without raising any questions about the coherence of the society he accepted. In fact it was geared to inhibit such questions. Doctrines of psychological self-manipulation in the interests of inner peace did testify to the widespread erosion of the old self-sufficient individualism of the nineteenth century, but the new doctrines substituted passive adaptation to the system for self-sufficiency, encouraging even less responsibility for the system than had pure laissez faire. The "faith in faith" was a faith that one had only to think about things the right way, not change them.⁴

If in addition to all this it was recognized—what Morrison had seen and resisted before the war—that the Protestant community, no matter how defined, was no longer remotely identical with the national community, then the chances to correlate political choices to church culture seemed almost to have vanished. The best the postwar pastors could expect from the churches was the least they had been willing to expect before the war—simple acquiescence in policies justified on purely pragmatic grounds.

Continued attention to politics was more congenial to the neo-orthodox. The justice and order of the system, far improved by comparison with 1932, were more comprehensible in terms of Niebuhr's power analysis than in terms of liberal evangelism. Power had been brought against power and a broader equilibrium established in the economy as a whole. The impulses behind the new power had been, from the perspective of religious motives, often secular, "bread-and-butter," indeed selfish. New Deal majorities had contributed to justice and order without having been "disinterested" majorities. Able to appreciate this without religious shock, the neo-orthodox continued therefore to pay much attention to labor and to government policies. The aim was to expose all efforts to return the economy into the hands of one group alone, to strengthen the forms of an economy in which no interest or class had its way unopposed. The Taft-Hartley Act and all succeeding efforts to check and roll back labor power gave Niebuhr clear occasion to continue to illustrate his realism, especially because such efforts found sympathy in some Protestant circles. But in this realism all that older identification with labor on the basis of moral impulse or the impulse of guilt had evaporated. The goal finally was that of the pluralistic society in and of itself. One lent one's support according to one's analysis of the balance of power.

This too was not without its ironies. To adopt the perspective of a pluralistic society for its own sake was to pretend to disinterestedness all over again—one of realistic calculation of balances of power rather than of religious love, but disinterested just the same.

Niebuhr's major discussion of the factors justifying this highly flexible realism appeared in his reassessment of the American scene in *The Irony of American History* (1952). In this book he ,argued in effect that nobody had been right about American experience since the day of such realists as John Adams and James Madison. Liberal surveys of the national story as one of democratic idealism and intelligence struggling against pessimism and apathy utterly neglected all the imponderable, unpredicted, providential, and happenstance factors shaping the story at its heart. So did interpretations based upon the wisdom of laissez faire. These views integrated with the volume in which Niebuhr's political philosophy came full circle, *Christian Realism and Political Problems* (1953), with its praise of the insights of Augustine and Burke. Niebuhr's abandonment of socialism and his support of Americans for Democratic Action and the liberal wing of the Democratic party he justified in light of these conservative perspectives, highlighting the immense complexity of every political situation, the mystery confronting every choice. By providence the errors of liberal reformers and laissez-faire ideologists had balanced each other off in the past, but this providential good fortune had nourished a sentimentality that could no longer be afforded.

Yet, as in the 'thirties, Niebuhr's postwar political discussion still contained an extrapragmatic element. In 1947 the Fellowship of Socialist Christians as a body changed its name to Frontier Fellowship, and Niebuhr's criticism of socialism in succeeding years carried him to the point of attacking not merely Marxist ideology and totalitarian communism but also the social-democratic politics of western European democracies.[5] In a sense, however, all Niebuhr had come to say about American politics was that there was value in the two major parties simply because they were the two major parties. America had survived, they had survived, and they were full of the tradition, meaning, tested methods, and providential complexity that had come to survive. But if it was realistic to criticize socialists in the United States, it was by no means realistic to castigate them equally everywhere, for, if not in the United States, perhaps in other communities socialism might still have been a responsible alternative, no more infected by liberal illusions than the ADA, and certainly no more so than the Republican party. Niebuhr's new conservatism, no matter how profound as a description of history, gravely obscured the sanctions for any vanguard action at all. Frontier Fellowship was to have the utmost difficulty locating any acceptable frontiers. Unable to praise anyone in American history for its blessings, Niebuhr was left implicitly in the position of crediting providence and providence alone. This was not to drift toward Barth and the position his brother, H. Richard Niebuhr, had taken on Manchuria in 1932, but back toward the pole of opportunism, that opportunism which the providence of America could allow to seem to be policy.

In any event, with the rebaptism of the realists as Frontier Fellowship, the old lines of political struggle in the religious debate were becoming less important. This was true despite the fact that in the vaster realms of foreign policy neo-orthodox vocabulary could hardly be challenged. Here there was no escape from a sense of politics as a field dominated by forces largely if not wholly imponderable and unplanable, as Morrison had foreboded. Who was able to argue that ideal motives, even when equipped with the latest wisdom of social science, could guarantee the future? The only escape was to sacrifice responsibility altogether by insisting upon alternatives that depended upon an ideal future. This was the sectarian impulse, and the postwar years found the two basic lines of sectarian politics from the 'thirties still intact. Pacifists—still led by Kirby Page and A. J. Muste—still argued their ideal motives as policy, in supreme projection of the personal will, while Harry Ward, along with a scattering of other pastors, continued to resign his own will to that of the Soviet Union. It was a measure of the chastening of Protestant leaders that neither sect gained strength under the tensions of the cold war. It was the business of Niebuhr and the neo-orthodox constantly to cultivate a temper prepared to sustain years of danger, indecision, and compromise, prepared to carry great responsibilities without great expectations. In the cold war Niebuhr had his final political illustration of the religious theme that anxiety is to be borne, not to be eliminated. Here the political debate had practically ended, for few men of the liberal social gospel were to be found supporting impulses to escape the tension in policies of exasperated aggression or holy isolation.

Yet this did not mean the triumph, even in debate let alone in practice, of neo-orthodox theology. The politics, both domestic and foreign, which both Niebuhr and his liberal opponents had come to praise was a politics of caution and moderation, and by all the logic of Niebuhr's argument for his theology mere moderation disguised and denied the facts upon which he ultimately rested his case. Moderation in itself continued to provide shelter for the social-gospel mind. With moderation, tensions between the church and the nation could be held to a minimum. With moderation, the national culture in its postwar prosperity remained a ground for appeal against tragic idioms. In a society where moderation was the best policy, the socialized individual could still thrive by his socialization. What was to open up the ranges of experience that might impel the religious debate further? From the 'thirties it had become gradually clearer that the justification for political moderation, and in fact for any politics, was negative. What was the deepest disaster entailed in social breakdown? It drove men to identify with the pseudo-universals of political religions. Thus they lost themselves, not to a crisis opening them to new experiences but to possession emptying them and closing them against new experiences. But neither liberal social gospel nor neo-orthodoxy achieved full resonance simply in the struggle against chaos.

As earlier, again after the war, particularly in *Discerning the Signs of the Times* (1946), Niebuhr gave passing voice to the positive side of his theology, in an explicit criticism of moderation—not of moderation in politics but of moderation as a style of life, a style of human character. The peace of both nature and mind was, he said, achieved at a high cost: it destroyed the self. Peace of mind, fulfilled in prudence, exacted the price of detachment, which was to say, of irresponsibility and, more important, less life. The life of a true self, Niebuhr indicated, is not without "heroic passion," directly expressing the infinitude of desires inherent in human existence.[6] In *The Self and the Dramas of History* (1955) he at last argued the logic of this point systematically, relating the coherence of the self to those patterns of history he had outlined since *An Interpretation of Christian Ethics* and had expounded fully in *Faith and History* (1949). There are no harmonies and unities in historical experience, he said, adequate to contain the freedom of the self. No life of moderation, calculated simply to avoid catastrophe and enjoy peace, can do justice to the potentialities of personality.

But heroic passion was plainly too dangerous in politics. Politics was too risky for risks. The religious debate was called beyond politics.

What might this mean concretely? It was not without significance that, in the pages of *Discerning the Signs of the Times* which dealt with the false peace of moderation, Niebuhr offered one of the few correlations of his ideas with a work of literature.[7] Nor was the work he chose without significance: Melville's *Moby-Dick*, in which the "answer" to Ahab's megalomaniac tragedy was not a return to landlocked caution, prudence, and peace but a kind of boundless esthetic reconciliation with the antinomies of experience, beyond security, beyond morality, beyond tragedy.

Moreover, apart from the argument of *Moby-Dick*, it was its
character as literature that was important, literature as a means
to render and evoke experience in a detail, an intimacy, and an
intensity both dangerous and almost impossible in politics. Novels
and poetry, music and art—the humanities in short—were adapted
to explicate the life of the self, and thereby to nourish theology,
with far greater precision for the individual than was available
in politics. Such possibilities for further explication were endless.
Methods for rendering the dramas of childhood, of sexual life, of
work, and of education, for instance—even of sports—were
methods for correlation with theology that could help overcome
the frustration all evangelism faced when social problems disguised individual problems, when group experience blurred personal experience. Such methods were more "responsible" moreover, now in a different sense: they could take account of more
facts than the necessary abstractions of social science could hope
to do.

The point of such realms was that they invited the self to risk
itself—in "heroic passion"—by launching itself beyond frontiers
of harmony and unity and order and peace it might already enjoy,
and thus to know itself with an intimacy and a living detail that
politics could not afford. Paul Tillich's efforts in these directions
with respect to European culture suggested the creative frontiers
in America. Here and there various writers were beginning to open
such country, seeking religious and theological correlations with
psychoanalytic psychology, with literature, with existentialist
philosophy.[8] With every such opening, the question posed to
revived Protestant self-consciousness tended to become explicit:
was theology to play only the role Niebuhr had indicated when
he recommended a synthesis of Reformation humility and Renaissance aspiration? Or was it to itself incorporate both the aspiration and the humility? This, Christian theology, not excepting
Protestant theology, had never done.

Nothing in the situation of mid-century guaranteed that these
vectors of the religious debate over politics would be carried out.
A heroic nonchalance in face of political perils was perhaps less
likely than anxious obsession or the repressed anxiety of indiffer-

ence. If neither of these had yet overtaken the Protestant social passion, it was at least partly because the men of the generation passing had exposed themselves to politics with daring and generosity. One possibility in the religious debate, however, was suggested in the increasingly important theological concept of church. Among chastened liberals, the church symbolized brotherhood transcending and, presumably, thereby softening the lines of political (and racial, national, and all other) division. Here the concept of church registered a retreat from the high social gospel vision of the church as itself society. The postwar years found Niebuhr too stressing the church as never before, but a different church. The church, he said, must be sacramental.[9] It must point to the center and ground of meaning that is not in itself, in which it shares but does not possess. Here, on a most sensitive level, was a last challenge, a "high-church" challenge to a long tradition of American Protestantism. The church was not church because it was brotherhood, for it was not yet brotherhood, but because it awaited brotherhood. The brotherhood of the church was founded on need and shaped in repentance. It was expressed in waiting. This was the ultimate ground of brotherhood, because it was the only ground that could be shattered neither by human selfishness nor by human reason, virtue, and power, nor by chance. It waited upon God.

Neither concept of church, whether of brotherhood or of sacramental waiting, suggested any impulse carrying beyond the moderation of politics. Both, peculiarly, served the prudent purposes of American society. Both expressed a leap directly from politics, from an image of society as a whole, to the church without inquiring into ranges of experience no politics or society could exhaust. If there was such a thing as a religious society, it was known by the fact that it understood that no society can realize brotherhood, whether by itself or by God. Every society lives under, not toward, the kingdom of God. No society can be adequate to human imagination. Nor—to insist upon a Protestant point—could any church.

Notes

Notes

NOTES TO CHAPTER I: *The Height of the Times, pp. 1–25*

[1] Charles H. Hopkins, *The Rise of the Social Gospel in American Protestantism, 1865–1915* (New Haven, 1940), is a solid manual of basic social-gospel data. Henry May, *Protestant Churches in Industrial America* (New York, 1949), provides the most extensive survey of Protestant social ideas in the post-Civil War period. Aaron I. Abell, *The Urban Impact on American Protestantism, 1865–1900* (Cambridge, 1943), studies Protestant responses to the urban frontier. Essentially concerned with adaptations, these works are indebted to the earlier, groundbreaking suggestions of A. M. Schlesinger, Sr., "A Critical Period in American Religion, 1875–1900," *Proceedings of the Massachusetts Historical Society,* LXIV (June, 1932). James Dombrowski, *The Early Days of Christian Socialism in America* (New York, 1936), concentrates on a narrower field. W. A. Visser t'Hooft, in *The Background of the Social Gospel in America* (Haarlem, 1928), is more interested in the ideology of the movement as an expression of "Americanism" in religion. H. Richard Niebuhr's *The Kingdom of God in America* (Chicago, 1937) is an excellent study of the hope for the Kingdom from earliest colonial days, indicating how it expanded into a social-gospel version. Niebuhr's book, unlike the others, is grounded in the religious phenomena as such.

[2] See, for example, *New Era Magazine,* I (Jan., 1919); *World Call,* I (Jan., 1919); *Christian Century,* XXXV (Nov. 14, 1918), 17; *ibid.,* XXXVI (May 22, 1919), 18; *ibid.,* XXXVI (June 19, 1919), 4.

[3] Quotes: *Christian Century,* XXXVI (July 31, 1919), 6–7; *ibid.,* XXXVI (March 13, 1919), 4–5. See *Interchurch Newsletter* for 1919, *Interchurch Bulletin* for 1920.

[4] "Press Agenting the Lord," *Nation,* CX (June 5, 1920), 346–347.

[5] *Biblical World,* LIII (Nov., 1919), 607.

[6] Joint Commission on Social Service, *Triennial Report* (New York, 1919).

[7] C. R. Brown, *Social Rebuilders* (New York, 1921).

[8] *A New Social Order* (New York, 1919), p. v.

[9] *Supplement to the Messages and Papers of the Presidents,* 2d term of Woodrow Wilson, pp. 8713–14 and 8816–20.

[10] *Nation,* CIX (Dec. 20, 1919), 188–189; *ibid.,* CLI (Nov. 30, 1940), 521–522 (ed. Freda Kirchwey).

[11] In *Christianity and the Social Crisis* (New York, 1907), chap. IV, "Why Has Christianity Never Undertaken the Work of Social Reconstruction?" is particularly revealing.

[12] Dores R. Sharpe, *Walter Rauschenbusch* (New York, 1942), chap. XVI, deals with the bitter war years. His German origins exposed Rauschenbusch to suspicion by the crusade enthusiasts, among them many churchmen, some of them friends. For an expression of his feelings, see his letter to Cornelius Woelfkin in *Christian Century*, XXXV (Aug. 1, 1918), 12–13.

[13] Ellis B. Barnes, *Christian Century*, XXXVII (Sept. 30, 1920), 11–12. Barnes was a Disciples pastor in Cleveland. Three interesting discussions of Rauschenbusch: J. W. Nixon, "Walter Rauschenbusch—Ten Years After," *ibid.*, XLV (Nov. 8, 1928), 1359–1361; A. C. McGiffert, "Walter Rauschenbusch: Twenty Years After," *Christendom*, III (Winter, 1938), 96–109; Walter Bodein, "Walter Rauschenbusch," *Religion in Life*, VI (Summer, 1937), 420–31.

[14] *Christianity and the Social Crisis*, pp. 149–150.

[15] *Ibid.*, p. 194.

[16] *Ibid.*, p. 195.

[17] *The Church and Industrial Reconstruction* (New York, 1920), p. 6.

[18] *Ibid.*, p. 18.

[19] *Ibid.*, p. 110.

[20] *Ibid.*, pp. 114–115.

[21] *Ibid.*, p. 172.

[22] *Ibid.*, pp. 191–192.

NOTES TO CHAPTER II: *The Heritage, pp. 26–54*

[1] See Joseph Dorfman, *The Economic Mind in American Civilization* (New York, 1946), vol. II, for a valuable summary of the ideas of several pre-Civil War clerical economists.

[2] See chap. III; also, James W. Prothro, *The Dollar Decade: Business Ideas in the 1920's* (Baton Rouge, 1955).

[3] The literature here is of course vast. See in particular Irwin G. Wyllie, *The Self-Made Man in America* (New Brunswick, 1954), and E. C. Kirkland, *Dream and Thought in the American Business Community, 1860–1900* (Ithaca, 1956), among recent works.

[4] Henry May, *Protestant Churches and Industrial America* (New York, 1949), has good discussions of the orthodox and of Beecher.

[5] Mark May and W. A. Brown, *The Education of American Ministers* (New York, 1934), in four volumes, present a detailed discussion of many aspects of the profession; see especially vol. III, chap. XII, for some data on backgrounds.

[6] Wellman, J. Warner, *The Wesleyan Movement in the Industrial Revolution* (London, 1930), is the standard discussion.

[7] Rauschenbusch links the churches and the middle-class community in *Christianity and the Social Crisis* (New York, 1907), p. 291.

[8] Charles H. Hopkins in *The Rise of the Social Gospel . . .* (New Haven, 1940), discusses the Bible scholarship.

[9] See L. L. and Jessie Bernard, *Origins of American Sociology* (New York, 1943).

[10] *Social Rebuilders* (New York, 1921), p. 174.

[11] See *Jesus Christ and the Social Question* (New York, 1900), pp. 295–326, for Peabody's muffled wrestle with "Environmentalism."

[12] *Christian Advocate*, CIII (April 19, 1928), 487.

[13] Files of the federation *Bulletin* are the main source for the history of the federation. Also see Milton J. Huber, "A History of the Methodist Federation for Social Action," unpublished Ph.D. thesis (Boston University, 1949); R. L. Tucker, "Twenty Years of the Social Creed," *Christian Advocate,* CIII (April 19, 1928), 488–490.

[14] Circulation was 2,000 in 1926 (*Social Service Bulletin,* XVII [Dec. 15, 1926]); it had been near 6,000 in 1920 (*ibid.,* XV [April 15, 1924]); the mailing list stood at 2,300 in 1936, 3,200 in 1940 (*ibid.,* XXX [Oct., 1940]).

[15] Spencer Miller and Joseph Fletcher, *The Church and Industry* (New York, 1930), provide an excellent survey of Episcopal social action to that date. *Paul Jones* (New York, 1942), by J. H. Melish, is a brief biography of one of the leading and rather tragic Episcopal leaders. It should be noted that the CLID was not related to the League for Industrial Democracy, the Socialist education organization headed by Norman Thomas.

[16] "Bill Spofford Hails United Front," *Protestant Digest,* I (Dec., 1938), 77–78; William B. Spofford, "What Is the CLID?," *ibid.,* III (Jan., 1940), 74–76.

[17] See G. G. Atkins and F. L. Fagley, *A History of American Congregationalism* (Boston, 1942); C. H. Hopkins, "A History of Congregational Social Action," *Social Action,* VIII (May 15, 1942).

[18] H. P. Douglass, *The Protestant Church as a Social Institution* (New York, 1935), pp. 260 ff.; *Information Service* (April 28, 1923), for mention of the Reformed; *World Tomorrow,* XVII (May 10, 1934 and May 24, 1934), provided a measure of social-gospel interest.

[19] United Lutheran Church attitude toward the social gospel could be seen in the report of its secretary, E. P. Pfatteicher, *Minutes of the Convention of the United Lutheran Church in America* (Philadelphia, 1924), pp. 260–274.

[20] E. S. Sanford, *The Origin and History of the Federal Council of Churches* (New York, 1916), and John Hutchison, *We Are Not Divided* (New York, 1940), cover general council history; Hutchison on pp. 297–316 discusses its social-gospel features. Discussions of council philosophy can be found in Samuel McCrae Cavert, *The Churches Allied for Common Tasks* (New York, 1921), and F. Ernest Johnson, *The Social Work of the Churches* (New York, 1930).

[21] *Minutes of the Convention of the United Lutheran Church in America* (1926), pp. 103–104.

[22] See *Statement of Aims* (New York, 1920). Some reports and notices on the FCSO: *Churchman,* CXXVI (Aug. 19, 1922), 8–9; Kirby Page in *ibid.,* CXXXIII (June 26, 1926), 16–17; *Information Service* (March 15, 1922, and June 1, 1922); and *ibid.,* IV (Oct. 3, 1925), V (Nov. 13, 1926), and VI (March 12, 1927), on the conferences.

[23] *Christian Century,* XLV (Feb. 2, 1928), 131–132.

[24] Files of *World Tomorrow* provide a running comment on FOR affairs; J. N. Sayre, *The Story of the FOR* (New York, 1936), sketches FOR history.

[25] Policy turns: *World Tomorrow,* XV (June, 1932), and XVII (Jan. 4, 1934). See *ibid.,* XV (Aug., 1932), on origins of magazine.

NOTES TO CHAPTER III: *The Faces of Power: Capital, pp. 55–75*

[1] *Christianity and the Social Crisis* (New York, 1907), p. 402; see also, *Christianizing the Social Order* (Boston, 1912), p. 198.

² *Christianizing the Social Order,* especially pp. 203 ff.

³ *Ibid.,* pp. 468 ff.

⁴ Interchurch World Movement, *Report on the Steel Strike of 1919* (New York, 1920). Stories and news on the report were widespread. Some of the information here given is from the report itself, which lists committee members and the authorizing bodies. In addition, see Alva Taylor, "The Interchurch Report," *Christian Century,* XXXVII (July 19, 1920), 14–15; "Who Is Holding Up the Steel Report?" *Nation,* CX (June 12, 1920), 784; *ibid.,* CXI (July 31, 1920), 120. The second volume, *Public Opinion and the Steel Strike* (New York, 1921), did not draw the attention of the first, but was as important in implementing the theory behind the whole investigation as the first.

⁵ "Press Agenting the Lord," *Nation,* CX (June 5, 1920), 346–347.

⁶ Public reaction: Alva Taylor, "The Aftermath of the Steel Report," *Christian Century,* XXXVIII (Feb. 17, 1921), 16–17; *Christian Advocate,* XCV (Aug. 5, 1920), 32. *Labor* commenced publication of the report in its Aug. 7, 1920, issue. The Iron and Steel Institute attack: Marshall Olds, *An Analysis of the Interchurch World Movement Report of the Steel Strike* (New York, 1923). Joint statement: *Information Service* (June 16, 1923); on "the twelve-hour day in the steel industry," Department of Research and Education of the FCCCA, see *Information Service* (June 23, 1923), and *Federal Council Bulletin,* VI (June–July, 1923), 4–5. James Myers, *Religion Lends a Hand* (New York, 1929), gives a short account of the report. His book is typical of the many references, found in religious periodicals and books throughout the decade, to the great work. Claims were made also that the report led in highlighting the existence and deliberate use of labor spies; soon after the report, William Hard in the *Survey* and Sidney Howard in the *New Republic* during 1920 ran series on this phenomenon. This is the element recalled also by the chief investigator, Blankenhorn, in the McConnell-celebration volume, *Religion and Public Affairs,* Harris F. Rall, ed. (New York, 1937), pp. 33–60; Blankenhorn's chapter was not, it should be noted, an account of the report.

⁷ On the character of United States Steel, see *Christian Century,* XXXVII (Aug. 12, 1920), 11. Edward Devine headed the Council delegation: *ibid.,* XXXVII (March 25, 1920), 14–16. To the speech of E. Victor Bigelow, "Mistakes of the Interchurch Steel Report" (New York, 1920), Alva Taylor gave answer in *Christian Century,* XXXVIII (Jan. 20, 1921), 14–15, and *ibid.* (Jan. 27, 1921), 17–18. On McConnell's denial, *Information Service* (Jan. 13, 1923); *ibid.* (June 16, 1923), refers to Gary's appeal. At Gary's death, the *Christian Century,* XLIV (Sept. 8, 1927), 1039–1040, characterized him as a kind of perfect negation of the social gospel: "To him money was power, religion was personal, laissez-faire was God-made, and profit was the primary motive in all material enterprise."

⁸ *Christian Century,* XXXVII (Sept. 9, 1920), 18–19.

⁹ The *Federal Council Bulletin,* VII (March–April, 1924), published part of chap. 1 of Rockefeller's book under the title, "An Industrial Creed." The leading prophet on the scene in Colorado was A. A. Heist, pastor of Grace Community in Denver. He wrote a sketch of Colorado Fuel and Iron labor relations in *Christian Century,* XLV (March 8, 1928), 324–325. On western Pennsylvania see *Federal Council Bulletin,* V (Oct.–Nov., 1922), 8. On the Western Maryland:

Information Service, VI (Feb. 19, 1927). On Stewart: *Federal Council Bulletin,* XII (April, 1929), 10; *Christian Century,* XLVI (Feb. 7, 1929), 187, and (March 21, 1929), 380–381. The *Century* registered its indignation at the condoling and congratulatory telegrams Stewart received from business leaders following his arrest: XLV (Feb. 16, 1928), 197–198. Debt: *ibid.,* XLI (March 20, 1924), 378.

[10] Heist's correspondence, as noted, and also *Christian Century,* XLVI (Feb. 28, 1929), 303–304. Alva Taylor, *ibid.,* XXXVII (March 11, 1920), 11, praised Schwab and Ford as well as Rockefeller. See also "Business Men in the New Era," *Congregationalist,* CIV (July 24, 1919), 105–106. *Christian Century,* XLIII (Jan. 14, 1926), 38, contrasted John Edgerton of the National Association of Manufacturers and Ford. Ford was described as a "practical mystic" in Jerome Davis' symposium, *Business and the Church* (New York, 1926), p. 20. W. E. Sweet's book, *The Business Man and His Overflow* (New York, 1919), expressed nicely the new "humanization" of business and business ideology. This Colorado Christian-progressive businessman was probably close to the ideal pattern. He was for a time associated with the Denver labor church, he helped finance the Methodist Federation. See Wayne C. Williams, *Sweet of Colorado* (New York, 1943). In all of this, the churchmen, and especially the council secretaries and writers like Taylor, were working within the spirit that produced a flurry of books in the first half of the decade on what might be summarized as "factory constitutionalism." Some of these reports to which they referred were: Bureau of Industrial Research, *American Company Shop Committee Plans* (New York, 1919); John R. Commons *et al., Industrial Government* (New York, 1921); Savel Zimand, *Modern Social Movements* (New York, 1921); W. Jett Lauck, *The Industrial Code* (New York, 1922); James Myers, *Representative Government in Industry* (New York, 1924). The Triennial Report for 1919 of the Episcopal Joint Commission on Social Service, Frank Crouch, secretary, contained a sophisticated review of these as well as other social experiments, with special attention—in an Anglican report—to their English proving grounds.

[11] *Christian Principles and Industrial Reconstruction* (New York, 1909), p. 14.

[12] Biographical details: *Christian Century,* XXXVIII (Sept. 29, 1921), 3; on his death, *ibid.,* XLIV (Nov. 13, 1927), 1348. See Alva Taylor, "The Golden Rule to Industrial Democracy," *ibid.,* XLI (Aug. 28, 1924); 1106–1108. *Information Service,* IV (Sept., 1925), and V (Jan. 23, 1926), on the union. Nash was mentioned everywhere, attended conferences, spoke for the FCSO. He wrote a chapter for the Davis symposium, *Business and the Church,* pp. 333–344, and his own book, *The Golden Rule in Industry* (New York, 1922). He was one of the stewardship heroes in Sherwood Eddy, *Religion and Social Justice* (New York, 1927), pp. 115–118. Matthew Josephson, in *Sidney Hillman: Statesman of American Labor* (Garden City, 1952), pp. 289–300, discusses the unionization of the Nash company. Josephson speaks of Nash as "a skypilot with a silver tongue," and quotes the opinion of an Amalgamated organizer that Nash was a "profound hypocrite." Nash was a strange man, but the fact remains that, as Hillman frankly agreed, he was responsible for the unionization. Josephson clearly does not know what to make of Nash; he notes that Nash recoiled from Cincinnati businessmen who thought of his program as an antiunion scheme, and ends up characterizing him as "a mystic in his own world of illusion." Josephson would have done better

to follow Hillman's mystified sympathy for Nash rather than the orthodox "sky-pilot" line; in any case, neither the social gospel nor the labor clichés fit.

[13] Hapgood appeared in Eddy, *Religion and Social Justice,* pp. 90–93; in the Davis symposium, pp. 287–297; in Devere Allen, ed., *Adventurous Americans* (New York, 1932), pp. 233–247. A. D. N. Holt, "An Experiment in Industrial Democracy," in the Davis symposium, pp. 271–280, gave details of the plan, as did *Federal Council Bulletin,* XII (Sept., 1930), and W. B. Waltmire, "Spiritual Issues in a Canning Factory," *Christian Century,* XLV (April 26, 1928), 534–535.

[14] *Information Service* (May 2, 1921). See also Ben M. Selekman, *Sharing Management with the Workers* (New York, 1924), based on the Dutchess plant; *Christian Century,* XLII (Jan. 8, 1925), 64.

[15] M. M. Jackson, "The Kingdom of God in a Foundry," *Survey,* LIII (Dec. 1, 1924), 255–258; *Information Service* (Jan. 1, 1922); III (April, 1924) for the will; *Christian Century,* XLI (April 17, 1924), 492–493; all on Eagan. Eagan contributed to the symposium, "The Church's Relation to Industry," of the *Annals of the American Academy of Political and Social Science,* CIII (Sept., 1922), pp. 101–104. On the Dennison Company, *The Church and Industrial Reconstruction,* p. 160. This council report discussed several types of experiment. Dix: *Information Service* (Jan. 27, 1923). Some of the issues of *Information Service* carrying other experiments: (April 15, 1922); (Jan. 22, 1923); III (Sept. 24, 1924); VI (May 7, 1927 and Nov. 5, 1927).

[16] *Adventurous Americans,* p. 229.

[17] *Information Service* (Jan. 27, 1923).

[18] "Industrial Democracy Investigated," *World Tomorrow,* XVI (Dec. 21, 1933), 678–679. Hapgood replied, protesting the conclusions of the committee of four: *ibid.,* XVII (Jan. 18, 1934), 46–47. When Hapgood's son, Powers, left the plant to become an organizer for the Socialist party, it was generally agreed that this was the more correct social strategy.

[19] *Information Service,* V (May 22, 1926). Also, *Federal Council Bulletin,* IX (Jan.–Feb., 1926), 25–26; *Christian Century,* XLIII (May 20, 1926), 655. It was William B. Spofford of the Church League for Industrial Democracy who, declaring that Nash's Golden Rule idea was "bunk," spurred the FCSO investigation headed by Paul Douglas: *Christian Century,* XLIII (June 18, 1925), 808; *Information Service,* IV (Sept., 1925). Nash of course, by his actions and his words, agreed with Spofford.

[20] "The Peril of the Stewardship Ideal," XLIII (Nov. 18, 1926), 1413–1415.

[21] Yearbook of the Federal Council, *The Churches Allied for Common Tasks* (New York, 1921), p. 123.

[22] *Ibid.,* 118.

[23] The record of these conferences has been taken primarily from the files of the *Federal Council Bulletin:* New York, III (Nov., 1920), 169; Boston, IV (Oct.–Nov., 1921), 131; Chicago, IX (Jan.–Feb., 1926), 10.

[24] The Pittsburgh Employers Association, through a letter of its general manager, William Frew Long, chose the occasion of a drive by the Y.W.C.A., which had endorsed the 1919 additions to the social creed, to attack the program of the "Y" as "destructive of the very basis of American progress and civilization"; *New Republic,* XXV (Feb. 16, 1921), 335–336. Widespread indignation

among churchmen followed: see *Information Service* (June 15, 1921), and *Federal Council Bulletin*, IV (April–May, 1921, and June–July, 1921) for summaries of church reaction. A sermon on the affair by Harry Emerson Fosdick was printed in *Christian Century*, XXXVIII (May 26, 1921), 23–24; also see "The Modern Heresy," *World Tomorrow*, IV (April, 1921), 101. The $200,000 drive netted $90,000 before Rockefeller's help. Edgerton: *Information Service*, V (Jan. 2, 1926); also (Sept. 2, 1921); *Manufacturer's Record* quoted by *Information Service*, II (Nov. 24, 1923); *New Republic*, XXVII (June 22, 1921), 342. On the Baptists: *Christian Century*, XXXVII (June 30, 1921), 25; and "Can a Denomination Be Bribed?" *ibid.*, XXXVIII (July 7, 1921), 5–7. Episcopal laymen: *ibid.*, XLII (Oct. 15, 1925), 1189–1190; *New Republic*, XXIII (July 14, 1920), 194–195. NAM: *Information Service*, V (April 24, 1926). Rosebush: reviewed in *New Republic*, XLI (Nov., 1924), 24, and XLII (Jan. 21, 1925), 53; see also Rosebush, *The Ethics of Capitalism* (New York, 1923). Sayre: reviewed in *New Republic*, XXXVIII (May 7, 1924), 272–274.

[25] "The Competitive System and the Mind of Jesus," *Christian Century*, XXXVIII (May 26, 1921), 8–10; *World Tomorrow*, III (April, 1920), 116. As in the failure of the Hapgood experiment, as in the transformation of Nash from golden rule to class-tactics, sooner or later the danger involved in the position here under discussion was bound to receive its symbolic expression also. See Judge Gary, "Higher Business Standards Developing in American Business," *Current History*, XXIII (March, 1926), 775–779: "Sooner or later the adoption of business ethics pays in dollars and cents." Babson's books, *Religion and Business* (New York, 1921), and *New Tasks for Old Churches* (New York, 1922), were the best expressions of the assimilation of, rather than a recoil from, the social-gospel rhetoric leveled against the "profit motive" into an ethic centered on the old Calvinist virtues, and their fusion in service and security for the investor.

[26] Paul Kaufman's review of Arthur Nash's *The Golden Rule in Industry* in *Methodist Review*, XXXIX (Sept., 1923), 822–823.

[27] *Religion in Our Times* (New York, 1932), p. 65.

NOTES TO CHAPTER IV: *The Faces of Power: Labor, pp. 76–106*

[1] Paul Tillich, *The Protestant Era* (Chicago, 1948), pp. 166, 181. The article on the proletarian situation appeared originally in 1931.

[2] Frank Kirkpatrick, "The Steel Strike and Home Missions," *Christian Advocate*, XCIV (Oct. 9, 1919), 1297; for the Methodist program, *ibid.* (April 3, 1919), pp. 430–431.

[3] *Ibid.* (June 5, 1919), p. 710.

[4] "Translating the Church into Our National Life," *ibid.*, XCV (April 8, 1920), 482–483.

[5] Theirs was an essentially confused voice. The *Advocate*, in deploring class-consciousness, held up the principle of the classless church: ". . . we still believe in congregations where the rich and poor may meet together, and worship the Lord as the Maker and Savior of them all." The Anthracite Mission did not meet this test. *Christian Advocate*, XCV (July 29, 1920), 1012–1013. Bishop McConnell welcomed labor churches: *Living Together* (New York, 1923), p. 97.

[6] "Charles Stelzle and a New Labor Evangelism," *Christian Century*, XLI (June 17, 1924), 781. Stelzle had written several volumes before the war, includ-

ing *The Church and Labor* (Boston, 1910) and *The Gospel of Labor* (New York, 1912). An autobiographical volume, *A Son of the Bowery* (New York, 1926), expressed his pure evangelical strain. Two of his last articles dealt with the problem: "Is the Church Slipping and Why?" *World's Work*, LIV (Sept., 1927), 504–513, and "Why Labor Deserts the Church," *ibid.*, LV (Nov., 1927), 53–58.

⁷ *Information Service* (July 15, 1921, and Feb. 15, 1922); "The Church and the Unions," *World Tomorrow*, VI (Feb., 1927), 51–53; *Christian Century*, XLVII (Dec. 3, 1930), 1470. Lackland contributed to the symposium "Industrial Relations and the Church," *Annals of the American Academy of Political and Social Science*, CIII (Sept., 1922), 117–121.

⁸ The one serious flurry of vigorous and left-oriented labor churches on the continent occurred in western Canada, especially in Winnipeg; see letter from W. Mitchell, *Christian Century*, XXXVII (Sept. 23, 1920), 16. One of the spokesmen for the Winnipeg general strike was a pastor, William Ivens. A former pastor, J. S. Woodsworth, participated and became the founder of the CCF. Woodsworth, like several American pastors of strong liberal views, left the church during the war. See Olive Ziegler, *Woodsworth, Social Pioneer* (Ontario, 1934). For a statement of the general superintendent of the Canadian Methodists, opposing the labor churches as a "cloak" for "revolutionary socialism," see *Christian Advocate*, XCV (July 29, 1920), 1012–1013.

⁹ James H. Maurer, president of Pennsylvania Federation of Labor, in Jerome Davis, ed., *Labor Speaks for Itself on Religion* (New York, 1929), pp. 29–36. See also Arthur O. Wharton, president of American Association of Machinists, *ibid.*, pp. 88–96; *Labor*, Dec. 24, 1921. *Information Service* frequently published excerpts from labor papers commenting upon the churches; for examples see July 15, 1921; Nov. 15, 1921; Jan. 15, 1922. A labor leader often called upon to hold up the other end of this conversation was Warren Stone, grand chief of the Brotherhood of Locomotive Engineers; see "Possible Cooperation between Church and Labor," *Zion's Herald*, CII (April 16, 1924), 493–494; his tribute to Bishop Charles D. Williams of Michigan and the CLID in *Labor* (April 28, 1923); a tribute to Stone upon his death, *Christian Century*, XLII (June 25, 1925), 826.

¹⁰ H. D. C. Maclachen, "A Bourgeois Church in a Proletarian World," *Christian Century*, XXXVII (April 21, 1920), 9–12. Maclachen was a Disciples' minister in Richmond. See also Orvis Jordan, "What Must the Church Do to Be Saved?" *ibid.*, XXXV (Dec. 5, 1918), 3–4, for a view that the church was middle-class only. Also see Henry Sloane Coffin, in *A Day of Social Rebuilding* (New York, 1918), pp. 6 ff., and *A More Christian Industrial Order* (New York, 1920), pp. 2 ff.

¹¹ *Federal Council Bulletin*, II (May, 1919), 130.

¹² Atlanta: *Information Service* IV (Oct. 31, 1925); Los Angeles: *ibid.*, VI (Nov., 1927); New Orleans: *Federal Council Bulletin*, XII (Jan., 1929), 22. Green: *ibid.*, IX (July–Aug., 1926), 9. AFL executive committee: *ibid.*, VI (Sept.–Oct., 1923), 8. Through the help of Arthur Nash, the council maintained a more specialized evangel. In 1925, Nash, together with a prominent Universalist layman, presented money for an industrial secretary. James Myers, an ordained Presbyterian minister, came from his post with the Dutchess Bleachery Mill, and from then on held special responsibility for contacts with labor. He endeavored

to foster the idea of industrial-relations committees in every city, representing church, organized labor, manufacturers, social workers, city administration, and so on: *ibid.*, VIII (March–April, 1925), 8, and *ibid.* (May–June), 3.

[13] This account is drawn from *Information Service*, V (Oct. 23, 1926, and Nov. 6, 1926); Hubert Herring, "Labor Has Words with the Church," *World Tomorrow*, IX (Nov., 1926), 216–218; Herring, "Business Cracks the Whip," *Christianity Century*, XLIII (Oct. 21, 1926), 1292–1294; *ibid.* (Oct. 28, 1926, and Nov. 11, 1926); *Nation*, CXXIII (Oct. 20, 1926), 387–388. Green had offered his irenic statement at the Baptist National Convention in Washington only five months before.

[14] The year 1920: *Christian Advocate*, XCV (Aug. 26, 1920), 1152–1153; 1923: *Federal Council Bulletin*, VI (Sept.–Oct., 1923), 7–8; 1926: *Information Service*, V (July 24, 1926); 1927: *ibid.*, VI (July 30, 1927); 1929: *Federal Council Bulletin*, XII (Oct., 1929), 20; 1930: *Information Service*, IX (July 26, 1930). The 40,000 circulation of 1929 was not a record, however; in the enthusiasm of 1919, 115,000 copies of both the Message and the *Church and Social Reconstruction* were mailed: *Churches Allied for Common Tasks*, pp. 108, 109.

[15] *The Baptist*, VIII (Aug. 27, 1927), 1073–1074.

[16] *Information Service* (April 15, 1921).

[17] "Is It Peace or War?" *Applied Christianity* (Boston, 1896); *Recollections* (Boston, 1909), pp. 300 ff.

[18] *Jesus Christ and the Social Question* (New York, 1900), chap. vi, especially pp. 287–299, which, beginning with the "obvious likenesses" between socialism and Jesus' teaching of the Kingdom, concluded in the discovery that socialism is the "penalty" paid by the modern world for its failure to obey Jesus. The book is a perfect example of the morass from which the later prophets were trying to extricate themselves.

[19] *Christianity and the Social Crisis* (New York, 1907), p. 239.

[20] *Ibid.*, pp. 400–401.

[21] *Ibid.*, pp. 410–411.

[22] The *Christian Century*, XLIII (Sept. 30, 1926), 1192–1193, was one of the few that stated firmly that the strike was a valid method for settling grievances. The few outright condemnations of the strike came from pacifist quarters; see, for instance, Henry J. Cadbury, *World Tomorrow*, III (May, 1920), 131–135; John Haynes Holmes, *ibid.*, III (June, 1920), 174–175. These were one side of a debate; other pacifists did not agree.

[23] There had been three such prewar reports, on South Bethlehem, Muscatine, and strife in Colorado and Michigan. Lawrence: *Report on the Strike in the Textile Mills of Lawrence, Massachusetts;* also, *Christian Century*, XXXVII (Sept. 16, 1920), 15–16. Coal in 1920: *The Coal Controversy*, Bulletin No. 2 of the Commission on the Church and Social Service; the Council published Robert Bruere's *The Coming of Coal* (New York, 1922). Denver: *The Denver Tramway Strike of 1920* (Denver, 1921), published by the Denver Committee of Religious Forces; the National Catholic Welfare Council as well as the Federal Council coöperated; see also George Lackland, "Watch the Denver Churches," *World Tomorrow*, III (Nov., 1920), 339–340. Western Maryland: *The Enginemen's Strike on the Western Maryland Railroad*, Department of Research and

Education; *Information Service,* VI (Feb. 19, 1927); also, *Federal Council Bulletin,* IX (May–June, 1926), 8. Passaic: *Christian Century,* XLIII (Aug. 5, 1926), 964–990, was an issue devoted to the strike; Winifred Chappell of the Methodist Federation for Social Service gathered most of the material. Colorado: a series of letters from A. A. Heist in the *Christian Century* covered this story: XLIV (Dec. 1, 1927), 1412–1413; XLV (Jan. 19, 1928), 79; (Feb. 2, 1928), 149; (March 8, 1928), 324–325; (March 28, 1928), 424; XLVI (Feb. 14, 1929), 240–241; XLVIII (April 22, 1931), 554; Heist had come to Grace Church in 1926, replacing Lackland, who went to the labor college at Meadville, Pennsylvania, organized by Charles C. Webber: *Social Service Bulletin,* XVI (Feb. 15, 1926). Indianapolis: *Information Service,* VII (May 19, 1928); Coal, 1928: *The Coal Strike in Western Pennsylvania,* Bulletin No. 7 of the Commission on the Church and Social Service; John L. Lewis suggested that the Federal Council make a declaration supporting the Miami resolution of the union for settlement: *Information Service,* V (May 14, 1927, and April 2, 1927). Marion: *Federal Council Bulletin,* XIII (Feb., 1930), 26.

²⁴ Albion W. Small: "The Church and Class Conflicts," *American Journal of Sociology,* XXIV (March, 1919), 481–501. Tawney: *New Republic,* XXXVIII (May 21, 1924), 331–333.

²⁵ *Zion's Herald* CII (March 5, 1924), 295.

²⁶ "What Labor Asks of the Church," *Forum,* LXX (Aug., 1923), 1773–1778.

²⁷ *Federal Council Bulletin,* IV (Jan., 1921), 26. The AFL offered commendations: *Information Service* (Nov. 15, 1921).

²⁸ John A. Fitch, "Lawrence," *Survey,* XLII (April 5, 1919), 42–46; *Christian Century,* XLI (July 24, 1919), 16–17; *World Tomorrow,* XII (June, 1929), 250–254.

²⁹ On Muste: "A. J. Muste," *World Tomorrow,* XII (June, 1929), 250–254; Devere Allen, ed., *Adventurous Americans* (New York, 1932), pp. 99–117. By Muste: a prostrike statement in the colloquium, *World Tomorrow,* III (July, 1920), 214; in the symposium, "Industrial Relations and the Churches," *Annals of the American Academy of Political and Social Science,* CIII (Sept., 1922), 112–117; Devere Allen, ed., "Pacifism and Class Wars," in *Pacifism and the Modern World* (New York, 1929), pp. 91–102, the best statement of his position; in the symposium, Jerome Davis, ed., *Labor Speaks for Itself on Religion* (New York, 1929), pp. 97–107; a discussion of workers' education in Kirby Page, ed., *A New Economic Order* (New York, 1930), pp. 199–210.

³⁰ "Pacifism in the Labor Field," *World Tomorrow,* IX (March, 1926), 81–83.

³¹ To the Kirby Page volume, *A New Economic Order,* Long contributed the chapter on the coöperative movement, pp. 211–226.

³² Seattle: Alva Taylor, "The Big Strikes," *Christian Century,* XLI (July 24, 1919), 16–17. Phillips: *World Tomorrow,* XI (June, 1928), 282; *Social Service Bulletin,* XVII (Jan. 15, 1928). Miner: "The Miner's Plight," *Christian Century,* XLIX (May 4, 1932), 530–532. Harlan: "Justice and Religion in Kentucky," *World Tomorrow,* XIV (Sept., 1931); Allen Keedy, "A Preacher in Jail," *Christian Century,* XLVIII (Aug. 26, 1931), 1068–1070.

In 1932 twenty-one ministers, mostly from New York, visited Harlan to report on civil liberties; among them were Reinhold Niebuhr, Cameron Hall, and William B. Spofford. Eleven of the twenty-one were Episcopalians: *ibid.*, XLIX (May 25, 1932), 678–679. Paterson: *ibid.*, XLVIII (Sept. 16, 1931), 1131, 1150. Brooklyn: *ibid.* (Dec. 16, 1931), 1597–1598. Springfield: *World Tomorrow*, XV (Oct. 19, 1932), 14. Danville: *ibid.*, XIV (Jan., 1931), 14; the Danville strike provoked Norman Thomas to declare that the church had lost its chance: "Religion at the End of an Epoch," *Christian Century*, XLVIII (Nov. 4, 1931), 1773–1775; one of the "praying strikes," Danville seemed to display that religious feeling in social ferment for which the prophets, and above all Ward, were alert, but to which the churches, and particularly the Danville churches, did not respond. See Helen Murray, "The Praying Strike," *ibid.*, XLVII (Dec. 17, 1930), 1559–1561, and for the praying strike in Okmulgee, Oklahoma, *World Tomorrow*, VIII (Sept., 1925), 281, and *ibid.*, IX (March, 1926), 83. Chicago preachers also advanced funds to the Southern strikers: *Social Service Bulletin*, XIX (Dec. 15, 1930).

Webber: *Christian Century*, XLIV (March 31, 1927), 394–396; Webber worked for the FOR as a strike mediator, as at Nazareth, Pennsylvania: "A Minister in a Strike," *ibid.*, XLVIII (May 17, 1931), 648–650. Hall: *Information Service*, IX (June 14, 1930). Heist's activities were reported as cited in note 23. Mathias: Charles Webber, "Clergymen Invade Industry," *World Tomorrow*, XV (Aug., 1932), 330–331. Also, on the violent Herrin County, Illinois, situation, James Coale, "Are Herrin's Churches Guilty?" *Christian Century*, XLI (Oct. 2, 1929), 1271–1273; and on the Elizabethton, Tennessee, textile strikes, A. J. Buttrey, "Salvation in Tennessee: The Clergy and the Textile Strike," *World Tomorrow*, XII (Oct., 1929), 396–398.

[33] *Christian Century*, XLIX (Dec. 7, 1932), 1520.

[34] *Congregationalist*, CIV (June 5, 1919), 715–716; *Social Rebuilders* (New York, 1921), p. 27.

[35] Vincent G. Burns, "Brother Bill," *Christian Century*, XLV (Sept. 20, 1928), 1133–1135. Simpson eventually became a recluse in the Catskills, *ibid.*, LVIII (Jan. 22, 1941), 130.

[36] The details on Passaic are taken from the Passaic issue of the *Christian Century*, XLIII (Aug. 5, 1926).

[37] New Bedford: *Christian Century*, XLV (May 13, 1928), 649; Winifred Chappell, "The Strike at New Bedford," *ibid.*, XLV (Oct. 4, 1928), 1191. See also *World Tomorrow*, XI (Jan., 1928), 3–4.

[38] *Christian Century*, XLIII (June 3, 1926), 701.

[39] William A. Smith, *Christian Advocate*, XCV (Aug. 5, 1920), 1058–1059. Thus, by 1923, Harry Emerson Fosdick considered that organized labor was already a power group the equal of business, and deserved precisely equal moral admonition: *Locomotive Engineers Journal*, LVII (July, 1923), 545.

[40] *Christianity and the Social Crisis*, p. 406.

[41] Brown: *Christianity and Industry* (New York, 1919), p. 39. McConnell, *Democratic Christianity* (New York, 1919), chap. iii. Oxnam, "The Religious Significance of the Rise of the British Labor Movement," *Methodist Review*, XXXIX (Nov., 1923), 904–920. Niebuhr, "Christianity and Contemporary Politics," *Christian Century*, XLI (April 17, 1924), 498–501. Ward, *The New Social Order* (New York, 1919), pp. 185–224.

⁴² The Mission: *Christian Century*, XLV (Jan. 12, 1928), 38–39; the failure at Passaic: *ibid.*, XLIV (Jan. 12, 1927), 37. The *Century* had noted AFL failure at Lawrence: XXXVI (Sept. 16, 1920), 15–16. The *Century* complimented Sidney Hillman's union, the Amalgamated Clothing Workers (ACWU); also, *Information Service*, VII (Feb. 18, 1928), on the evangelistic, idealistic atmosphere of the ACWU.

⁴³ On Woll: *Christian Century*, XLIV (Feb. 17, 1927), 197, and XLV (Dec. 17, 1928), 1578–1580. Ward: *Social Service Bulletin*, XVI (June, 1927); *A New Social Order*, p. 321; *Our Economic Morality and the Ethic of Jesus* (New York, 1929), pp. 81 ff.

⁴⁴ Alva Taylor, "Why the Rockefeller Plan Failed," *Christian Century*, XLII (Feb. 16, 1925), 280–282, saw that shop committees and "factory democracy" required unions. Of all the postwar reports, declarations, and pronouncements, the only one to insist upon this relationship between workers, councils and unions was the Episcopal Joint Commission on Social Service in its *Triennial Report* for 1919.

⁴⁵ James Coale in "The Church and Labor," *Biblical World*, LIV (July, 1920), 354–362, stated the dilemma in general: the church recognized class-consciousness in its own body, but yet could least afford to admit that class-consciousness existed. See also Coale, "Protestantism and the Masses," *Yale Review*, XI (Oct., 1921), 78–89. There was a double problem: Could class divisions be accepted in the church? The answer had to be "no" whether or not the church was committed to the social passion; the church excluded no man from its message. But if class divisions existed without compromising the church, then it took a commitment to the passion to find class division in itself an evil.

⁴⁶ *Christian Century*, XXXVII (Sept. 16, 1920), 8–11.

⁴⁷ XLII (Aug. 6, 1925), 993–994.

⁴⁸ *The New Social Order*, pp. 149–150: "Not long ago I picked up a labor paper . . . setting forth the fallacy that labor must follow no vision but stick to reality, and therefore must seek things and power and not ideals. Such an expression is but the echo of the dominant spirit of commercialism." The translation of this was: the "class" movement of labor must not be a "class" movement.

NOTES TO CHAPTER V: *The Faces of Power: the Church, pp. 107–117*

¹ Halford Luccock, *World Tomorrow*, X (Dec., 1927), 488.

² Walter Rauschenbusch, *Christianity and the Social Crisis* (New York, 1907), part III, is a social-gospel interpretation of Christian history along these lines. Kirby Page, *Jesus or Christianity* (New York, 1929), expanded it to a volume. Constantine was the symbol of captivity for both. Morrison, in *The Social Gospel and the Christian Cultus* (New York, 1933), p. 213, expanded the symbol: "The names of Constantine and Calvin are the symbols of the capitulation of Christianity. . . ."

³ Kirby Page, *Incentives in Modern Life* (New York, 1922), p. 45.

⁴ "Labor's Anniversary," *Christian Century*, XLIII (Aug. 26, 1926), 1055–1056.

⁵ See George Coe, "Shifting the National Mind-Set," in *Pacifism and the Modern World*, Devere Allen, ed. (New York, 1929), pp. 219–228; also his

contribution to *Religion and Public Affairs,* H. F. Rall, ed. (New York, 1937), pp. 189–210. Rauschenbusch was capable of declaring: "The ultimate power on which we stake our hope in our present political decay is the power of public opinion." *Christianity and the Social Crisis,* p. 260. This only served to illustrate the beguiling power of the concept, for Rauschenbusch also knew how to organize it under his realism: "Few are impervious to public opinion, but the only public opinion that strikes men with full force is that of their own social class." *Christianizing the Social Order* (New York, 1912), p. 31.

⁶ *Methodist Review,* XXXVII Sept., 1921), 690.

⁷ *Christianizing the Social Order,* chap. II, and elsewhere.

⁸ *Ibid.,* p. 6.

⁹ *Christianity and the Social Crisis,* p. 291.

¹⁰ F. E. Johnson, *The Social Work of the Churches* (New York, 1930), p. 114.

¹¹ *Information Service,* V (Sept. 26, 1926), and *Federal Council Bulletin,* XIII (Jan., 1930). See also, Jerome Davis, "Church Boards of Control," *American Journal of Sociology,* XXXVIII (Nov., 1932), 418–431.

¹² Edmund Brunner, *Industrial Village Churches* (New York, 1930), chaps. VI and IX especially.

¹³ Liston Pope, "Religion and Class Structure," in the symposium, "Organized Religion in the United States," *Annals of the American Academy of Political and Social Science,* CCLVI (March, 1948).

¹⁴ *Our Economic Order and the Ethic of Jesus* (New York, 1929), pp. 84 ff., and *Which Way Religion?* (New York, 1931), pp. 100 ff., for Ward's sketch of postwar Protestantism. Rauschenbusch warned in 1912 that "the present insurgent movement in the West," might be the last great rising of "the old American spirit." If it failed, the new Americans coming with the social rebellion of Europe in their hearts would have to carry on: *Christianizing the Social Order,* pp. 401 ff.

NOTES TO CHAPTER VI: *The Nonpolitics of Hope, pp. 118–129*

¹ There were, of course, articles scattered through such periodicals as the *Christian Century* and the *World Tomorrow* on specific issues; the Methodist *Federation Bulletin* and *Information Service* commented from time to time. For example, on tariffs: F. E. Johnson, "Do Tariffs Violate Christian Ideals?" *Christian Century,* XLI (Jan. 10, 1924), 41–44. The tariff issue gradually became a part of the peace program. On Mellon's tax policy: *Christian Century,* XLII (Jan. 7, 1926), 7–8. On Muscle Shoals: *Social Service Bulletin,* XV (Feb. 1, 1925).

² "In Time of Hesitation," *Christian Century,* XXXVII (Oct. 14, 1920), 3–4, and "Idealism in Politics," *ibid.* (July 22, 1920), 16.

³ Coolidge: *ibid.,* XLII (March 12, 1925), 335–336; on La Follette: *ibid.* (July 2, 1925), 847–848.

⁴ "The Coolidge Business Policy," *ibid.,* XLIII (March 4, 1926); "Congratulating the Almighty," *ibid.,* XLIV (Nov. 17, 1927), 1350–1352.

⁵ *Information Service,* III (Aug. 2, 1924), 2.

⁶ *Christian Century,* XLI (July 17, 1924), 909.

⁷ "A Moral Crisis in American Politics," *ibid.* (April 26, 1928), 530–531; *ibid.* (May 10, 1928), 594–596; *ibid.* (June 28, 1928), 818–820. A nice display of the prohibition anxiety appeared in *Zion's Herald,* CII (Oct. 1, 1924), 1257,

where the editor, L. O. Hartman, wrote announcing that he had a letter proving that both La Follette and Wheeler were dry.

[8] *Christian Century,* XLV (Oct. 18, 1928), 1251–1253. Cavert, "Has the Church a Right to Speak on Public Questions?" *Federal Council Bulletin,* VII (March–April, 1924), 29; and "The Church and Public Affairs," *ibid.* (July–Aug., 1924), 1–2. Also Charles Jefferson, *Christianizing a Nation* (New York, 1929), p. 124.

[9] *Christian Century,* XLV (Sept. 13, 1928), 1098–1099; (Nov. 1, 1928), 1315–1318. Rauschenbusch, *Christianizing the Social Order* (New York, 1912), pp. 25 ff., expected a duel between Catholicism and socialism. Niebuhr, *Christian Century,* XLV (Sept. 13, 1928), 1107–1108, agreeing that the *Century* was fair in its discussion of the Catholic question, argued that it did not make sufficient allowance for the changes in temper and policy that the atmosphere of a Protestant nation forces upon papal politics; voting for Thomas, he nevertheless applauded Smith's record.

[10] "A Political Party without Candidates," *Christian Century,* XLIX (May 25, 1932), 663–666, and succeeding issues.

[11] *Church Finance and Social Ethics* (New York, 1920), p. 80.

[12] *The New Social Order* (New York, 1919), p. 291.

[13] *The Church and the Ever-Coming Kingdom of God* (New York, 1922), p. 273. Kresge's decentralized picture did not place him on some right-to-left spectrum; it appeared in Ward, *New Social Order,* pp. 369 ff.; it would appear in Johnson (of the Council), *The Social Gospel Re-examined* (New York, 1941), pp. 237 ff. The unifying factors of the social gospel were sociological and theological, not political; the difference between "socialist" and "non-socialist" prophets was not necessarily the important difference.

[14] *Public Opinion and Theology* (New York, 1920), p. 232. Shailer Mathews in one of his early social-gospel volumes marvellously betrayed the essential ambiguity of politics for the Christian mind. "A genuinely Christian church member," he wrote, "always is material ready at hand for any rational social movement; and if a census were made of those who are effectively connected with social, municipal, and national reforms, it is no very rash statement that the large majority of such persons would be found to have come, either personally or through family example, under the influence of some church." But he knew there was something wrong; he had already written: ". . . the indifference of Christians to their political obligations is notorious. . . . the great reason why the church has had so little effect upon politics has been that the Christian voter has never sufficiently realized that politics is in the field of morals." *The Church and the Changing Order* (New York, 1907), pp. 179, 133.

[15] Kirby Page, *Jesus or Christianity?* (New York, 1929), pp. 287 ff., gave one of the many comments on the LIPA. Williams' candidacy: *Christian Century,* XLIII (May 20, 1926), 654. Sketches of and motives behind the LIPA may be found scattered in such periodicals as the *New Leader,* the *New Republic,* and the *Nation,* especially in the period surrounding the 1932 campaign: thus, Devere Allen, "A Program for Revolt," *Nation,* CXXXV (July 27, 1932), 80–82; a letter from Norman Thomas, *ibid.* (Dec. 14, 1932), 584–586; John Dewey, "The Future of Radical Political Action," *ibid.,* CXXXVI (Jan. 4, 1933), 8–9; a letter from Howard Williams in reply to Thomas, *ibid.* (Feb. 1, 1933), 122.

[16] See *Christianizing the Social Order*, part VI.

[17] The best discussion of the Socialist party is Daniel Bell's in *Socialism in American Life*, Donald Egbert and Stow Persons, ed. (Princeton, 1952), I, 213–405. On church resolution: *Christian Century*, XXXVII (Sept. 30, 1920), 6; *ibid.* (Oct. 14, 1920), 4.

NOTES TO CHAPTER VII: *The New Man, pp. 130–144*

[1] *A Theology for the Social Gospel* (New York, 1917), pp. 92–93.

[2] *Christianity and the Social Crisis* (New York, 1907), p. 309.

[3] "Such a social order would develop the altruistic and social instincts just as the competitive order brings out the selfish instincts": *ibid.*, p. 408. Others would make the implied point explicit, namely, that the ancient, endless task of trying to "change" human nature could simply be finessed: "The task before us is not the changing of human nature but the creation of situations in which the more social tendencies may more easily be given expression": Kirby Page, *Incentives in Modern Life* (New York, 1922), p. 48.

[4] *Christianity and the Social Crisis*, p. 247.

[5] *A Theology for the Social Gospel*, pp. 46–47.

[6] *Ibid.*, p. 158.

[7] *Ibid.*, p. 112.

[8] F. E. Johnson, *The Social Gospel and Personal Religion* (New York, 1922), pp. 20–21.

[9] *Ibid.*, pp. 27–28. See also Samuel McCrae Cavert, "The 'Social Gospel' or the 'Gospel for the Individual'?" *Federal Council Bulletin*, V (June–July, 1922), and "Two Gospels or One?", *World Tomorrow*, XVI (March 29, 1933), 295.

[10] It need not be said that none of the discussion of individual, personality, and self in this and following chapters is aimed at the social psychology of a man like George Herbert Mead, in *Mind, Self, and Society* (Chicago, 1934). Mead's analysis of the genesis of "self" exclusively in social experience was not at stake in the differences between the social gospel and neo-orthodoxy with respect to the relations of self and society. F. E. Johnson revealed what was at stake in such a statement as this: "The moral structure of society is what gives rise to our moral standards": *The Social Gospel and Personal Religion*, p. 18. It begins to go beyond Mead when there is no way of justifying—or even imagining—a morality "beyond" society, or a self and a meaning "beyond" morality.

[11] *A Social Theory of Religious Education* (New York, 1917), p. 145. His instinct theory here was adapted from E. L. Thorndike's *The Original Nature of Man* (New York, 1913).

[12] *The Motives of Men* (New York, 1928), pp. 82 ff.

[13] *A Social Theory of Religious Education*, p. 168.

[14] See Ward's bibliography for *Our Economic Morality and the Ethic of Jesus* (New York, 1929).

[15] *Incentives in Modern Life* (Philadelphia, 1922), p. 29. Page's emphasis.

[16] Labor Sunday Message, *Federal Council Bulletin*, XI (Sept., 1928), 24–25.

[17] Coe, *A Social Theory of Religious Education*, p. 208.

[18] *Ibid.*, p. 215.

[19] *Ibid.*, p. 215.
[20] *Ibid.*, pp. 220–221.

NOTES TO CHAPTER VIII: *Two Routes to Security, pp. 145–159*

[1] *Social Service Bulletin,* IX (Jan.–Feb., 1919). *Current Opinion* (June, 1919), pp. 380–381, carried a story of the affair. The *Christian Advocate* carried the running fight: CIV (Feb. 20, March 13, March 20, March 27, April 3, April 10, May 15, 1919).

[2] *The New Social Order* (New York, 1919), p. 245.

[3] American Civil Liberties Union, *The Record of the Fight for Free Speech in 1923* (New York, 1924), p. 27; *Christian Century,* XLI (May 29, 1924), 704; *ibid.,* XLIII (June 10, 1926), 752, 756; *Christian Advocate,* CVIII (Jan. 5, 1933), 2. More will be said on the General Conference of 1936.

[4] Ward, *New Social Order,* p. 156. Robert Whitaker and S. C. Coleman, "The Appeal for Leadership," *World Tomorrow,* III (Aug., 1920), 238–240, drove this notion of the "common life" to its extreme: man was a herd animal, an emotional, vital being, not primarily a rational being; the only justifiable leadership was that which coincided with the movement of life and interpreted it. Richard Roberts, "Unfinished Masterpieces," *ibid.,* IV (Oct., 1921), 244–245, proposed the same view, driving it against Protestant individualism. Ward also liked to insist upon "the common reason of the common people," but his vision was much more rationalistic than such sheer mysticism of the mass as that of Whitaker, Coleman, and Roberts. (Ward, *op. cit.,* p. 73.) Even so, we shall find Whitaker, like Ward, obsessed with the absolute leader who shall shape the mass so that it will not need leadership.

[5] *Ibid.*, p. 89.

[6] *Social Service Bulletin,* XVII (May 15, 1927); *Christian Century,* XLIV (May 12, 1927), 585–587.

[7] *New Social Order,* p. 369.

[8] *Ibid.*, pp. 31, 78.

[9] *Ibid.*, p. 25.

[10] *Ibid.*, p. 364; and the "educated idealists" of the middle class, *ibid.,* p. 327.

[11] *Our Economic Morality and the Ethic of Jesus* (New York, 1929), especially chap. iii.

[12] *Which Way Religion?* (New York, 1931), p. 183.

[13] "Lenin and Gandhi," *World Tomorrow,* VIII (April 25, 1925), 111–112. "Can China Be Stabilized?" *Christian Century,* XLIII (Jan. 14, 1926), 46–48.

[14] The tariff: *National Defense* (New York, 1931), p. 83. The "zones," literally, in *Danger Zones of the Social Order* (New York, 1926), written with Sherwood Eddy.

[15] *The Sword or the Cross* (Chicago, 1921), p. 9.

[16] *Ibid.*, p. 107.

[17] *An American Peace Policy* (New York, 1925), p. 84.

[18] *War: Its Causes, Consequences and Cure* (New York, 1923), p. 92.

[19] *The Abolition of War* (New York, 1924), pp. 57–59, on human nature: the abolition of dueling and slavery had not required a change in human nature. The disillusioning facts, in *War: Its Causes, Consequences and Cure,*

were all to be repeated in *How to Keep America Out of War* (New York, 1939). The program for America is in *An American Peace Policy.*

[20] *National Defense*, p. 55; *Imperialism and Nationalism* (New York, 1925), chaps. iv and v, presented an extended review of the American position.

[21] *The Abolition of War*, p. 80.

[22] *Ibid.*, pp. 78–80.

[23] *Ibid.*, pp. 91–92.

[24] *Ibid.*, p. 92.

[25] Devere Allen, ed., *Pacifism in the Modern World* (New York, 1929), containing chapters by Paul Jones, Reinhold Niebuhr, A. J. Muste, Page, George Coe, Allen, and others, provides a rather precise cross section of political pacifism in its last moments of leisure.

[26] McConnell, *The Preacher and the People* (New York, 1921), p. 158. H. F. Rall, ed., *Religion and Public Affairs* (New York, 1937), is a symposium dedicated to McConnell, including chapters by Rall on McConnell's career and by Edgar Brightman on McConnell's personalistic philosophy.

NOTES TO CHAPTER IX: *The Meaning of Jesus, pp. 160–165*

[1] Barnes, *The Twilight of Christianity* (New York, 1929), pp. v, 377–387.

[2] It was of some interest that the theological drift in the radical-liberal direction was not particularly favorable to the social gospel. Among the radical liberalizers, Gerald Birney Smith and Shailer Mathews were most interested, but were not centered there. Henry Nelson Wieman, at Chicago—like the others— was the leader of "empirical theology," and, sympathetic to social liberalism, was not one of the prophets. Nor was A. E. Hayden, the outstanding humanist "quester" at Chicago, in the prophetic ranks. Harry Ward, in his social mysticism close conceptually to the social-historical radical-liberalism of Mathews, nevertheless held to the last to what can only be regarded as an evangelical commitment to Jesus: see chap. III of his *Which Way Religion?* (New York, 1931), where he rejected Wieman and radical liberalism, and reaffirmed the centrality of the ethical Jesus.

[3] See F. E. Johnson, *The Social Work of the Churches* (New York, 1930), p. 111; three highly interesting articles by Croly, *New Republic*, XXXIX (July 23, 1924), 230–237; XLIII (July 22, 1925), 222–224; LIV (March 14, 1928), 110–112.

[4] E. A. Cook, "The Kingdom of God as a Democratic Ideal," *Journal of Religion*, I (Nov., 1921), 626–640. Books of Shailer Mathews, *The Atonement and the Social Process* (New York, 1930) and *The Growth of the Idea of God* (New York, 1931), and of Shirley Jackson Case, *Jesus Through the Centuries* (Chicago, 1932) and *Highways of Christian Doctrine* (Chicago, 1936), exemplified the increased difficulty in maintaining the evangelical identity between the mystical, sanctifying Jesus and the historical Jesus.

[5] Some recent works dealing with this rather uncharted area: R. S. Fletcher, *A History of Oberlin College From Its Foundation Through the Civil War* (Oberlin, 1943); J. L. Peters, *Christian Perfectionism and American Methodism* (New York, 1956); and Timothy L. Smith, *Revivalism and Social Reform* (New York, 1957), which deals with the twenty years before the Civil War, in addition to Benjamin Warfield's older book, *Perfectionism* (New York, 1931). The perfectionist impulse still badly needs examination, especially in its post-Civil War forms.

[6] A famous statement on the whole matter: Henry J. Cadbury, *The Peril of Modernizing Jesus* (New York, 1938). Chester C. McCown, *The Search for the Real Jesus* (New York, 1940), and Amos N. Wilder, *Eschatology and Ethics* (New York, 1939), rev. ed. (New York, 1950), provide excellent discussions of the scholarly problems over thirty years with due attention to the vested interest of the social gospel in those problems. The real situation was that scholarly conclusions about Jesus' teaching could not be derived from exegesis and scholarship alone, but depended upon settlement of larger questions. Wilder, in "The Eschatology of Jesus in Recent Criticism and Interpretation," *Journal of Religion*, XXVIII (July, 1948), 177–187, suggested this, in saying that scholarship waited upon philosophy of history for further instructions. And those instructions were to depend upon the fate of the social passion. Niebuhr, of course, was not to rely on exegesis at all; Jesus for him was the Jesus of, variously, Paul, Augustine, St. Francis, Luther, Pascal, Kierkegaard. He attacked the social-gospel use of Jesus, as in *Religion in Life*, IV (Summer, 1934). Two examples of unreconstructed social-gospel views: Henry K. Booth, *The Great Galilean Returns* (New York, 1936), and G. Bromley Oxnam, *The Ethical Ideals of Jesus* (New York, 1939).

NOTES TO CHAPTER X: *The Politics of Urgency, pp. 166–185*

[1] *Christian Century*, XLVIII (July 29, 1931), 977, for the East Liberty church; C. T. Holman, "The Breadline at Worship," *ibid.* (Feb. 4, 1931), 167–168; "Is Methodism Defeated?" *ibid.*, XLIX (June 8, 1932), 727–728.

[2] *Federal Council Bulletin*, XII (May, 1929), on the endorsement. "How the Churches Are Helping in Unemployment," *ibid.*, XIII (Dec., 1930), 8–9; conferences: *Christian Century*, XLVIII (Feb. 11, 1931), 220; *Federal Council Bulletin*, XV (Feb., 1932), 17.

[3] *Zion's Herald*, CX (Nov. 16, 1932), 1441–1447.

[4] "Can Capitalism Plan?" *Social Service Bulletin*, XXII (Feb. 1, 1932).

[5] *An Emerging Christian Faith* (New York, 1930), p. 290.

[6] Charles T. Holman, "Unemployment's Grim Reality," *Christian Century*, XLVII (Feb. 26, 1930), 271–273.

[7] *Ibid.* (March 22, 1931), 334–335.

[8] *Ibid.*, XLIX (Sept. 21, 1932), 1126–1128; *ibid.* (Nov. 9, 1932), 1766–1767.

[9] The views of the council and the *Christian Century* are discussed in chap. xvii.

[10] *An Emerging Christian Faith*, p. 289.

[11] *Protestantism's Hour of Decision* (Philadelphia, 1940), p. 92.

[12] *Information Service*, IX (Dec. 27, 1930), on bishops, Ohio: *Christian Century*, XLVIII (Oct. 7, 1931), 1227–1228. S. Cal. and Pittsburgh: *World Tomorrow*, XV (Sept. 21, 1932), 280, and *ibid.* (Oct. 5, 1932), 328.

[13] *Christian Century*, XLIX (April 13, 1932), 467, for resolution; Hogle's letter, *ibid.* (May 11, 1932); reply to his letter, *ibid.* (June 8, 1932), 341.

[14] *World Tomorrow*, XVI (July, 1933), 442, and Charles C. Webber, "Methodists Approach Socialism," *ibid.*, XVII (June 14, 1934), 303–304. Detroit: *ibid.*, XVI (Oct. 26, 1933), 580–581. New England: *ibid.*, XVII (July 17, 1934), 344. Pittsburgh: *ibid.*, XVI (Aug., 1933), 476 ff.

[15] Evangelicals: "An American Church Goes Socialist," *Christian Century*,

XLVIII (July 29, 1931), 964. Garrett: *World Tomorrow*, XV (Nov. 15, 1932), 470. Ohio: *Christian Century*, XLIX (Feb. 24, 1932), 248. Y.M.C.A.: "Student Radicalism," *World Tomorrow*, XIV (June, 1931), 180–181.

[16] The full results of this poll were published in two issues of *World Tomorrow*, XVII (May 10 and May 24, 1934).

[17] *Ibid.*, XV (Oct. 26, 1932), 402. The Conference of Younger Churchmen endorsed Thomas: *Christian Century*, XLIX (Nov. 9, 1932), 1382; some 70 New York area pastors signed this endorsement. These are only examples.

[18] The Christian Social Action Movement, *Leaders Handbook* (Chicago, 1932), p. 39.

[19] *Ibid.*, p. 58.

[20] The FSC can be followed through numerous notices in the *World Tomorrow*. See especially Reinhold Niebuhr, "The Fellowship of Socialist Christians," *World Tomorrow*, XVII (June 14, 1934), 497–498.

[21] Geer, "That Repeal Plank," *New Leader*, XIII (June 11, 1932), 6; Howells, *Christian Century*, XLIX (Sept. 21, 1932), 1141. This was the reasoning Howells offered. But the case was not quite clear, since he had been a Socialist party member previously, while a prohibitionist.

[22] Old-line socialists from the days of Debs and Berger considered this sort of thing as opportunistic dilution of true socialist principles for the sake of mere votes. For one such criticism, including Niebuhr among the sinners, see James Oneal, *A Chapter of Party History* (New York, 1934), pp. 8 ff. A. J. Muste resigned from the LIPA over the bid to Norris: *New Leader*, XII (Jan. 3, 1931). Norman Thomas, eventually critical of the LIPA as a needless dual organization, nevertheless praised the Columbus, Ohio, branch; a local pastor, J. F. Meyer, was LIPA treasurer; M. H. Lichter, Robert Tucker, G. Siegenhalter, J. H. Cotton, Henry Holt, George Willetts, all pastors, were leading members: Thomas, *Nation*, CXXXV (Dec. 14, 1932), 584–586; Columbus Branch: *Christian Century*, XLIX (Nov. 16, 1932), 1415. For a last LIPA manifesto, see the pamphlet, *Audacity! More Audacity! Always Audacity!* (New York, 1933). Ministers stood as Socialist party candidates in Illinois, Roy Burt as Socialist party candidate for governor, Owen Geer for congressman-at-large, U. M. McGuire, editor of the *Baptist*, for clerk of the Supreme Court. Burt was born in Illinois, had worked in the coal mines as a boy, graduated from Kansas University and Garrett, had held a parish in Rock Springs, Wyoming, which he made into something of a labor church, and was in 1932 superintendent of the Third Department (education of young people) of the Epworth League. After the campaign, he became a full-time speaker and organizer for the Socialist party: *Zion's Herald*, CX (Sept. 28, 1932), 1223; *World Tomorrow*, XVII (March 29, 1934), 156.

[23] Something of a manifesto, this statement appeared in substantially identical forms in: *World Tomorrow*, XII (Dec., 1929), 491–493; *New Leader*, IX (Jan. 4, 1930), 4; *A New Economic Order*, Kirby Page, ed. (New York, 1930), pp. 301–312. Page registered his own pragmatic loyalty to the Socialist party in *What Shall We Do About War?* (New York, n.d.), p. 93.

[24] *World Tomorrow*, XVII (April 12, 1934), for a statement of the RPC position. Among the 47 signers, besides Henson and Mathews, were James Dombrowski and Howard Kester. Dombrowski was author of *The Early Days of Christian Socialism in America* (New York, 1936), later to be active in the

Southern Conference for Human Welfare. Kester was the most active Southern socialist minister, a leader in the Southern Tenant Farmers Union. Niebuhr's criticism of the RPC: *World Tomorrow,* XVII (April 12, 1934), 185–186, and Page's, *ibid.,* 187–188.

²⁵ The *Christian Century* carried reports on these activities, such as Edmund Chaffee on strike and unemployment relief committees, XLVIII (Jan. 7, 1931), 32–33, and Paul Hutchinson, "Hunger on the March," XLIX (Nov. 9, 1932), 1377–1378, on the Randolph Street parade that included socialist clubs, communist representatives, representatives of churches and social settlements. Frequent, though condensed, coverage appeared in the Methodist Federation's *Bulletin:* XXI (May 15, 1931), on the work of left-wing preachers, and XXII (Sept. 1, 1932), on various unemployed leagues with religious leadership. "Towards a United Front?" *Nation,* LXXVII (Nov. 22, 1933), 40–42, on Borders' outfit. The June 1933 convention was captured by a CP-CPLA coalition.

²⁶ "Pacifism and Class War," in *Pacifism and the Modern World,* Devere Allen, ed. (New York, 1929), pp. 94–97, 99.

²⁷ On CPLA: A. J. Muste, "Labor's Left-Wing Vanguard," *World Tomorrow,* XV (Sept. 28, 1932), 306–308; "The Tactics of the CPLA," *ibid.,* XVII (Feb. 15, 1934), 90–91.

²⁸ Workers Party organization: *New Republic,* LXXVII (Dec. 27, 1933), 179, and *ibid.,* LXXVIII (May 2, 1934), 344–345. A. J. Muste, "The Battle of Toledo," *Nation,* CXXXVIII (June 6, 1934), 639–640; "Toledo Thriller," *ibid.,* CXL (May 29, 1935), 632–633.

²⁹ Daniel Bell discusses these developments in *Socialism in American Life,* Donald Egbert and Stow Persons, eds. (Princeton, 1952), I, 213–405. Bell appears to think Muste was an innocent, but Muste's reconversion to the way of love from the Leninist-Trotskyist way of violence was self-conscious: *Christian Century,* LIII (Oct. 14, 1936), 1374, and *ibid.* (Oct. 28, 1936), 1430.

³⁰ Jerome Davis, "Religion and Labor Face the Future," in *Brotherhood of Church and Factory in a People's World,* a National Religion and Labor Foundation pamphlet (1942), pp. 4–5, and files of *Economic Justice,* the NRLF bulletin.

NOTES TO CHAPTER XI: *The Final Form of the Absolute, pp. 186–202*

¹ *Social Service Bulletin,* XXIII (Feb. 15, 1933).

² *Ibid.* (June 1, 1933).

³ A notable account of united front action from 1932 to 1934 is that of J. B. Mathews, *Odyssey of a Fellow Traveller* (New York, 1938). Mathews' career was a skewed parabola—from fundamentalism through the social gospel to communism to reaction. He tended to impute his own illusions and instability to some of the people around him. Mathews' inclusion of McConnell and Niebuhr among the "decoys" or "window dressing" was a reflection of the degeneration of his ability to distinguish between uncritical and critical united-front collaboration. Niebuhr, for one, was a critic—in public, not in private—of both the Communist party and Russia.

In Eugene Lyons' *The Red Decade* (New York, 1941), Harry Ward alone of religious figures appeared prominently in the story, with Sherwood Eddy suggested as an "innocent." This is not to say that Ward was unique; there was always a united-front handful, persisting into, through, and after the war:

Spofford of the CLID, Kenneth Leslie of the *Protestant*, Willard Uphaus of the National Religion and Labor Foundation, Jack McMichael (who succeeded Ward in the Methodist Federation), were all sympathetic, among others.

⁴ *Russia Today* (New York, 1934), p. 119.

⁵ *Ibid.*, p. 124.

⁶ *Ibid.*, p. 170.

⁷ *Ibid.*

⁸ *Ibid.*, p. 127.

⁹ *Ibid.*, p. 170.

¹⁰ *Ibid.*, pp. 169–170.

¹¹ *The Challenge of Russia* (New York, 1931), p. 278.

¹² *Ibid.*, p. 193.

¹³ *Russia Today*, p. 179.

¹⁴ *Ibid.*, p. 177.

¹⁵ *Ibid.*, p. x. Eddy's options on the American political scene must be remembered. The kind of people he found pursuing the synthesis in America were in the LIPA: *The Challenge of Russia*, p. 277. He himself joined the Socialist party: *New Leader*, XII (Jan. 31, 1931), 1. Niebuhr was the prophet he hailed: *Russia Today*, p. 245. But of course it was precisely the lesson that the family ethic could not be translated into ever-broadening reaches of society, and the lesson that the security, central purpose, and inner composure of the soul could not be found in politics, that Niebuhr taught.

¹⁶ *In Place of Profit* (New York, 1933), p. vii.

¹⁷ *Ibid.*, p. 84.

¹⁸ *Ibid.*, p. 296.

¹⁹ *Ibid.*, p. 425.

²⁰ *Ibid.*, p. 403.

²¹ *Ibid.*, p. 452.

²² *Ibid.*, pp. 452–453.

²³ *Ibid.*, p. 239.

²⁴ *Ibid.*, p. 443.

²⁵ *Ibid.*, pp. 427–428.

²⁶ *Ibid.*

²⁷ *Ibid.*, pp. 96–97.

²⁸ *Ibid.*, p. 97. The appeal to the analogy of the organizing powers of war appeared also in *The New Social Order* (New York, 1919), pp. 110 ff., in *The Soviet Spirit* (New York, 1944), p. 160, and elsewhere. These appeals might seem analogous simply to James' call for the "moral equivalent." If so, that is the point. Any moral equivalent to war is no better, morally, than war. The personality is subjected to the same inner devastation, the politicalization, the inner abstraction, the ultimate annihilation as a soul—deprived, that is, of responsibility. The locus of the moral problem James, and Ward, sensed in war was not war itself, but the kind of soul that could find meaning and "eternal significance" only in war or its equivalent. It would be hard to prove that the equivalent to war must be pragmatically superior to war itself in the argument that war must, by its external devastations, accelerate the inner disintegration. It would be hard to prove, that is, that the moral equivalent provided any obstacle to war in the first place, and in the second place, that the moral equivalent provided any better

conditions for true reform. The tragedy, of course, has been that the inner devastation has never been as far advanced as its anxious critics imagined, and that they, in their search for moral equivalents, advance the inner devastation beyond what any previous war or politics had wrought.

[29] *In Place of Profit*, p. 46.

[30] *Ibid.*, pp. 449, 456.

[31] Herman Reissig was one; see his review of Ward's *Democracy and Social Change* in *Christian Century*, LVIII (Jan. 1, 1941), 19–20.

[32] "The Peace Movement," *Social Service Bulletin*, XXVIII (June, 1938); "The Price of Peace," *ibid.* (Oct., 1938). See also, "The International Situation and America's Relation to It," *Radical Religion*, IV (Summer, 1939), 22–27, where Ward displayed how the absolute drove on toward fantasy, still disguised as politics.

[33] *Social Questions Bulletin*, XXIX (Dec., 1939). (The *Bulletin* had changed its name.) Ward cautioned that this should not be allowed to feed the flames of anti-Soviet propaganda.

[34] "What Shall We Do?" *ibid.*, XXX (Oct., 1940). Refusing to follow William Spofford, the CLID had been forced to make the same decision: *Protestant Digest*, III (Jan., 1940), 74–76.

[35] *Christian Century*, LVII (Feb. 14, 1940), 201, 227; *Social Questions Bulletin*, XXX (Nov., 1940); *Christian Century*, LVIII (June 11, 1941), 786; "The MFSA Program for 1941–42," *Social Questions Bulletin*, XXXI (Oct., 1941).

NOTES TO CHAPTER XII: *The Meaning of Violence, pp. 203–216*

[1] *Christian Century*, XLIX (Aug. 10, 1932), 988.

[2] Kirby Page, "The Future of the Fellowship," *World Tomorrow*, XVII (Jan. 4, 1934), 9–11. This issue, together with the issue following (Jan. 18, 1934), contained the essential facts of the poll and statements by various interested persons.

[3] Bennett, "Christianity and Class-Consciousness," *World Tomorrow*, XV (Feb., 1932), 47–49; "That Fellowship Questionnare," *ibid.*, XVI (Dec. 21, 1933), 690–692. Allen, "The False Issue of Class War," *ibid.* (March 22, 1933), 276–279, and (March 29, 1933), 302–303. Page, "Class War and Religion," *ibid.* (March 8, 1933), 225–228.

[4] Henson, "Must We Have Revolution?" *Christian Century*, XLIX (Nov. 30, 1932), 1471–1473.

[5] Bradley, "Leaven, Not Dynamite," *ibid.* (Dec. 21, 1932), 1575–1576.

[6] *World Tomorrow*, XV (June, 1932), 173–175; *ibid.*, XVI (March 1, 1933), 210–212; and *ibid.* (April 5, 1933), 322–323. Page had offered the formula previously, in his discussion of war: "To me the use of force is non-moral; it is good or bad depending upon the motives behind its use and the effects of its application." *The Abolition of War* (New York, 1924), p. 46. An almost Niebuhrian sentiment in form, this was simply to conceal the nonpragmatic absolute more completely.

[7] "Why I Leave the FOR," *Christian Century*, LI (Jan. 3, 1934), 17–19.

[8] In *Democracy and Social Change* (New York, 1940), chap. VIII offers a discussion of the New Deal in context of the Fascist threat; the "hour of decision" appeared throughout, but its coercive influence on Ward's analysis of the

American scene was perhaps most sharply displayed in chap. X, "The Class Line-Up."

⁹ *Moral Man and Immoral Society* (New York, 1932), p. 189; "After Capitalism—What?" *World Tomorrow*, XVI (March 1, 1933), 203–205. Page's discussion of Russia in 1917: *Must We Go to War?* (New York, 1932), pp. 232 ff.

¹⁰ "Professor Niebuhr Replies," *Christian Century*, LI (Jan. 31, 1934), 155.

¹¹ *World Tomorrow*, XVII (April 12, 1934).

¹² *Reflections on the End of an Era* (New York, 1934), pp. 157–158.

¹³ "Why I Leave the FOR," *Christian Century*, LI (Jan. 3, 1934), 17–19.

¹⁴ *Ibid.*, LI (Jan. 10, 1934), 46–47.

¹⁵ *Reflections on the End of an Era*, p. 82. For examples of Niebuhr's polemic in this period, directed not against men in the FOR, but against the positions at stake in the debate, see his comments on Jerome Davis, "The Christian Cult of Violence," *Religion in Life*, III (Summer, 1933), 432–441; his review of McConnell's *Christianity and Coercion* in *ibid.*, III (Winter, 1933), 141–142.

¹⁶ George Coe, the religious educator, in "What Is Violence?" *World Tomorrow*, XV (Oct. 19, 1932), 379–380, adopted Niebuhr's argument in an interesting reflection of his departure from the apolitical idealism of his book of 1917.

¹⁷ "Is Coercion Compatible with Religion?" *World Tomorrow*, XVI (March 1, 1933), 210–212.

¹⁸ "Inconsistency of the Majority," *World Tomorrow*, XVII (Jan. 18, 1934), 43–44: "The division in the Fellowship of Reconciliation may be a family affair primarily, but outsiders are interested in it since it concerns so closely the whole problem of Christian life and conduct in the modern world. . . . To one outsider at least, three points stand out. The first is the inconsistency of the pacifist position of the Fellowship itself. The second is the consistency with the basic principle of the Fellowship of those who have left. The third point is the necessity of a consistent pacifist fellowship.

The pacifism of the Fellowship, like all modern liberal pacifism, has been secondary to moral idealism. The ethics of the movement has been utilitarian, in the sense that pacific means are regarded as a better instrument than violence for the attainment of ideal purposes. But the idealistic purpose dominated. It was not the pacifism of non-resistance but the pacifism of non-violent aggression. . . . It seems much more consistent with the fundamental idealistic principle of the Fellowship to accept the non-pacifist position of those who have left the group. If we are going to be utilitarians let us be rational utilitarians and accept the principle that what matters is the ideal and that whatever is necessary for its attainment is right. Let us also be realistic utilitarians and accept the fact that man is not so spiritual, so free, so rational an animal that he can be dealt with as though he required no coercion. If we are realistic about ourselves we know that that is not true. . . .

We are not moral men living in immoral societies because the individual is better than society, but because as individuals we are subject to all sorts of coercions to which societies are not subjected. And if violent coercions are no longer frequently necessary in the case of individuals we shall not believe that this end has been attained without violent coercion in the past. . . . Yet one cannot but retain a great amount of sympathy for the majority of the Fellowship . . . They have tied together two principles which cannot be made parts of one whole . . . If they would be "pacifists" let them follow out the whole consequence and seek out the whole basis of such pacifism; but if they would be utilitarian idealists let them go with their present opponents. It is impossible for them to be both.

A Christian pacifism, or, better, a Christian non-resistance, which we may define historically as the type of attitude we see in Jesus, rejects the dominant position of the present Fellowship—the idealistic principle of aggressive fighting for our ideals, whether by tongue and boycott or by sword. It rejects the whole humanistic faith upon which this idealism is built. It is as deterministic as communism is. But it knows that there is a divine teleology, and that the aggressiveness of righteousness runs counter to it as often as does the aggressiveness of the unrighteous. It sees that the characteristic deed of Jesus was not enacted in the temple but on Golgotha and understands that he did not say: 'Love your enemy in order that you may convert him to your point of view,' but 'Love your enemies in order that ye may be sons of your Father in heaven who maketh his sun to shine on the evil and the good.' "

[19] There were three fascinating articles: H. R. Niebuhr, "The Grace of Doing Nothing," *Christian Century*, XLIX (March 23, 1932), 378–380; a reply by Reinhold Niebuhr, "Must We Do Nothing?" *ibid.* (March 30, 1932), 415–417; and a letter in counterreply by H. R. Niebuhr, *ibid.* (April 6, 1932), 447, in which Richard Niebuhr subjected Reinhold Niebuhr's basic concept of the center of meaning "beyond" history—a concept to which he hinged his dialectic between religion and politics—to one of its earliest and most searching criticisms.

[20] *Must We Go to War?* p. 264.

[21] Among other articles: "What a Christian Cannot Do," *Christian Century*, LV (Oct. 12, 1938), 1227–1229; "How Does God Deal with Evildoers?" *ibid.*, LVIII (Sept. 10, 1941), 1109–1112.

NOTES TO CHAPTER XIII: *Reinhold Niebuhr: Political Morality, pp. 217–237*

[1] *Leaves From the Notebook of a Tamed Cynic* (New York, 1929), p. xii.

[2] *Ibid.*, pp. 64, 180.

[3] "Ten Years That Shook My World," *Christian Century*, LVI (April 26, 1939), 542–546: ". . . such theological convictions which I hold today began to dawn upon me during the end of a pastorate in a great industrial city. They dawned upon me because the simple little moral homilies which were preached . . . by myself and others, seemed completely irrelevant to the brutal facts of life in a great industrial center. Whether irrelevant or not, they were certainly futile. They did not change human actions or attitudes by any problems of collective behavior by a hair's breadth, though they may well have helped to preserve private amenities and to assuage individual frustrations."

[4] *World Tomorrow*, XI (April, 1928), for a brief account of Niebuhr's career upon his installation as editor. Also, *Federal Council Bulletin*, XII (Sept., 1929), 14.

[5] "The Nation's Crime Against the Individual," *Atlantic*, CXVIII (Nov., 1916), 609–614.

[6] "What the War Did to My Mind," *Christian Century*, XLV (Sept. 27, 1928), 1161–1163.

⁷ Niebuhr, son of German immigrants, himself bilingual, offered a second reason: "Anyone who dissociates himself from the cause of his nation in such a time as this ought to do it only on the basis of an unmistakably higher loyalty. If I dissociated myself only slightly I would inevitably be forced into the camp of those who romanticize about the Kaiser. And the Kaiser is certainly nothing to me. If we must have war I'll certainly feel better on the side of Wilson than on the side of the Kaiser." *Notebook,* pp. 14–15.

⁸ "What the War Did to My Mind," *loc. cit.*

⁹ *Notebook,* p. 22.

¹⁰ *Ibid.,* p. 42 (entry dated 1923).

¹¹ "What the War Did to My Mind," *loc. cit.*

¹² *Does Civilization Need Religion?* (New York, 1927), pp. 40–41.

¹³ *Ibid.,* pp. 44–45; also p. 239.

¹⁴ Review of Salvatorelli's life of St. Francis, in *Christian Century,* XLV (May 3, 1928), 572; also, "Why I Am Not a Christian," *ibid.,* XLIV (Dec. 15, 1927), 1482–1483. St. Francis was something like Niebuhr's favorite saint, if not his ideal Christian: see also *Beyond Tragedy* (New York, 1937), chap. vii.

¹⁵ "A Critique of Pacifism," *Atlantic,* CXXXIX (May, 1927), 633–641; "The Confession of a Tired Radical," *Christian Century,* XLV (Aug. 30, 1928), 1046–1047.

¹⁶ Three articles on Ford in the *Christian Century:* "Henry Ford and Industrial Autocracy," XLII (Nov. 4, 1926), 1354–1355 (unsigned editorial); "How Philanthropic Is Henry Ford?" XLIII (Dec. 9, 1926), 1516–1517; "Ford's Five-Day Week Shrinks," XLIV (June 9, 1927), 713–714. There were various references to the Ford plants in the *Notebook,* e.g., pp. 78, 112, 116. On the "reification" of man more generally, *Notebook,* pp. 46, 78, 112. On the general texture of American society, above and beyond explicitly capitalistic features: "We Are Being Driven," *Christian Century,* XLVI (May 1, 1929), 578–579.

¹⁷ "Can Schweitzer Save Us from Russell?" *Christian Century,* XLIII (Sept. 3, 1925), 1093–1095; a review of Joseph Wood Krutch's *The Modern Temper,* which had set something like a norm for fashionable pessimism: *ibid.,* XLVI (May 1, 1929), 586–587. Niebuhr felt that scientific determinism derived from the breakdown of metaphysics; since a unifying perspective had eventually to be restored, the philosophically untenable amateur determinisms of the separate sciences would dissolve; Whitehead pointed the way: *Does Civilization Need Religion?* pp. 10–11.

¹⁸ The liberal church was still talking Fiske and Drummond (*Does Civilization Need Religion?* pp. 8 ff.) and knew nothing of, for instance, deterministic psychology (*ibid.,* p. 206). "Shall We Proclaim the Truth or Search for It?" *Christian Century,* XLII (March 12, 1925), 344–346, for an early statement of the correlation between privileged intelligent churchmen and insensitivity to the threat of an impersonal civilization; their preachers tried to exorcise the scientists' impersonal universe. The attack upon liberal use of Jesus for his "theological simplicity" rather than for his "moral austerity" recurred constantly through the middle and late 'twenties: *Does Civilization Need Religion?* p. 68; "Can Christianity Survive?" *Atlantic,* CXXXV (Jan., 1925), 84–88; "The Rev. Dr. Silke," *Christian Century,* XLIII (March 11, 1926); a review of Harry Emerson Fosdick's *Adventurous Religion* in *ibid.,* XLIV (Jan. 6, 1927), 17–18. Fosdick

was the model of the liberal preacher at his best, in Niebuhr's view—adventurous within the limits of his age, never challenging those limits from any outer perspective.

[19] *Does Civilization Need Religion?* p. 77.

[20] *Ibid.*, p. 229.

[21] *Ibid.*, pp. 163–164.

[22] "Religion's Limitations," *World Tomorrow*, III (March, 1920), 77–79; also, "Can Religion Solve Social Problems?" *Federal Council Bulletin*, X (March, 1927), 11–12, where intelligence and technical social skills are emphasized as the key.

[23] "Henry Ford and Industrial Autocracy," *loc. cit.*

[24] "The Church and the Industrial Crisis," *Biblical World*, LIV (Nov., 1920), 588–592; see also *Federal Council Bulletin*, VII (Jan.–Feb., 1924), 23–24.

[25] "Christianity and Contemporary Politics," *Christian Century*, XLI (April 17, 1924), 498–501; "Ford's Five-Day Week Shrinks," *loc. cit.* Also, *Notebook*, p. 111: "The idea that these A. F. of L. leaders are dangerous heretics is itself a rather illuminating clue to the mind of Detroit. I attended several sessions of the convention and the men impressed me as having about the same amount of daring and imagination as a group of village bankers."

[26] "Is It Possible to Preach the Gospel in America?" *Christian Century*, XLII (June 4, 1925), 739. Also, "Henry Ford and Industrial Autocracy," *loc. cit.*

[27] "Ten Years That Shook My World," *Christian Century*, LVI (April 26, 1939), 542–546.

[28] *Does Civilization Need Religion?* pp. 124–125, on complexity; the discussion of nature was scattered: "instincts," pp. 48, 79; "resistance," p. 9; death, p. 175.

[29] *Ibid.*, p. 176.

[30] "Let Liberal Churches Stop Fooling Themselves," *Christian Century*, XLVIII (March 23, 1931), 402–404.

[31] *Ibid.*, XLIX (March 2, 1932), 287–289. Niebuhr letters from Russia during his 1930 visit appeared in five issues, beginning *ibid.*, XLVII (Sept. 10, 1930), and contrast with Harry Ward's reactions a year later. Finding robust vitality, Niebuhr also found brutality and vegeance, possible bureaucratic inefficiency, and appalling lust for power.

[32] "Property and the Ethical Life," *World Tomorrow*, XIV (Jan., 1931), 19–21; "Catastrophe or Social Control," *Harper's*, CLXV (June, 1932), 114–118.

[33] *Moral Man and Immoral Society* (New York, 1932), pp. 261–262; p. 271 for Niebuhr's key words on "utilitarianism": "The utilitarian attempt to harmonize the inner and outer perspectives of morality is inevitable and, within limits, possible. It avoids the excesses, absurdities and perils into which both religious and political morality may fall. . . . But it is not as realistic as either. It easily assumes a premature identity between self-interest and social interest. . . . It is therefore better for society to suffer the uneasy harmony between the two types of restraint than to run the danger of inadequate checks upon egoistic impulses. Tolstoy and Lenin both present perils to the life of society; but they are probably no more dangerous than compromises with human sefishness effected by modern disciples of Aristotle . . . better to accept a frank dualism in morals."

³⁴ *Ibid.*, p. 57, for justice as product of reason; pp. 59–61, of religion; p. 160, of the proletariat.

³⁵ *An Interpretation of Christian Ethics* (New York, 1935), pp. 144 ff., for the full argument on "justice" as a normative principle in social ethics, in place of the teachings of Jesus.

³⁶ *Reflections on the End of an Era* (New York, 1934), p. 24.

³⁷ The Revolutionary Movement," *American Socialist Quarterly*, IV (June, 1935), 8–13.

³⁸ Rauschenbusch, *Christianizing the Social Order* (New York, 1912), pp. 397 ff.; Spinka, *Christianity Confronts Communism* (New York, 1936), pp. 186 ff.; Jones, *Christ's Alternative to Communism* (New York, 1935), pp. 188–189; Jones, *The Choice Before Us* (New York, 1937), pp. 212, 132 ff., for an example of how the nontheological, pure evangelical mind tried to come to grips with the word "materialism"; Muste, "Return to Pacifism," *Christian Century*, LIII (Dec. 2, 1936), 1603–1606.

³⁹ Johnson, *Information Service*, XIII (April 28, 1934), in book reviews of Sidney Hook and G. D. H. Cole. In *Christianity and Marxism* (New York, 1934), a three-way symposium, H. P. Van Dusen's piece showed him as an aware liberal: undismayed by talk of dialectical materialism but ready to resist excessive economic determinism, excessive emphasis upon class struggle, and excessive "environmentalism" generally, all quite without serious effort to join issues on more ultimate philosophical levels.

⁴⁰ *Reflections on the End of an Era*, pp. 142, 147, 162, for instance.

⁴¹ "Since historic Christianity, both Protestant and Catholic, has failed to find a rightful place in its scheme of things for the industrial proletariat, and has failed even more completely to understand the fateful mission of this class in modern society, it is natural that this neglect should be revenged by a self-assertion on the part of this class in which its high mission . . . should lead to unqualified (and therefore demonic) pretensions. . . .": "Christian Politics and Communist Religion," in *Christianity and the Social Revolution* (New York, 1936), John Lewis and Karl Polyani, eds., Niebuhr's fullest criticism of Marxist utopianism.

⁴² *The Nature and Destiny of Man* (New York, 1943), II, 305.

⁴³ *Moral Man and Immoral Society*, pp. 153–154, for the "religious" logic of disinheritance.

⁴⁴ *Reflections on the End of an Era*, p. 135.

⁴⁵ *A Theology for the Social Gospel* (New York, 1917), p. 223.

⁴⁶ *The Social Gospel Re-examined* (New York, 1940), p. 72.

⁴⁷ The Socialist party split at its New York convention in 1936; Norman Thomas led the center and left, roughly the younger element. Niebuhr discerned a "new burst of energy" with the split: *Radical Religion*, I (Winter, 1936), 9–10. His hopes of this period might be contrasted with a judgment in *Moral Man*, p. 218: "The hope of establishing a third party in America on the combined strength of the farmer and the worker will remain unrealistic for many decades to come. It may never be realized." Vigorous moral activity, plus the necessity for a political exemplification of neo-orthodoxy, had generated their own sense of expectation.

⁴⁸ "A New Party?" *Radical Religion*, II (Autumn, 1937), 6–7; "SP and

Labor Movement," *ibid.*, III (Winter, 1937), 3; *ibid.*, IV (Winter, 1938), 6. When, late in 1935, the Communists switched signals and adopted united-front tactics, Niebuhr, with hesitation and misgivings, approved a "genuine and united" united front: *ibid.*, I (Winter, 1936), 3–6. He was not changing his view of Russia itself; on the Moscow trials: *ibid.*, II (Spring, 1937), 2. In 1939, after having served with George Counts as chairman of a save-the-union committee in the New York Teachers Union, which succeeded in preventing an ouster of communists, Niebuhr concluded that it had been a bad game; local Communist parties were acting solely as "black legions" of the Russian foreign office; "We cannot speak for Dr. Counts, but, as for ourselves, we are a little dubious about our handiwork." *Ibid.*, IV (Summer, 1939), 8–9.

[49] "The Socialist Campaign," *Christianity and Society*, V (Summer, 1940), 3–5.

[50] "Augustine's Political Realism," *Christian Realism and Political Problems* (New York, 1953), chap. ix; p. 72 on Burke.

NOTES TO CHAPTER XIV: *Reinhold Niebuhr: Religion and Politics, pp. 238–269*

[1] "Ten Years That Shook My World," *Christian Century*, LVI (April 26, 1939), 542–546.

[2] *World Tomorrow*, XVI (Feb. 1, 1933), 119.

[3] *Reflections on the End of an Era* (New York, 1934), pp. 274–275. In "Christianity and Redemption," printed in *Whither Christianity?* (New York, 1929), L. H. Hough, ed., Niebuhr had written that religion must include grace, here in context of an analysis of love, but this was not the grace of the *Reflections.* See also, *The Contribution of Religion to Social Work* (New York, 1932), pp. 40 ff.

[4] *Moral Man and Immoral Society* (New York, 1932), p. 276.

[5] Bennett's article was published in *Christian Century*, L (Nov. 8, 1933), 1403–1406. See Horton, *Realistic Theology* (New York, 1934), p. 38, for a good expression of the determination to be tough-minded. The book was good evidence for how difficult it was to dispel "romantic illusions," and by 1940, as we note below, Horton thought realism had gone far enough.

[6] Samuel McCrae Cavert, "The Younger Theologians," *Religion in Life*, V (Fall, 1936), 520–531; members were listed by H. P. Van Dusen in *The Christian Answer* (New York, 1945), Van Dusen, ed., p. vii.

[7] "Ten Years That Shook My World," *Christian Century*, LVI (April 26, 1939), 542–546.

[8] *Realistic Theology*, p. 56.

[9] *The Nature and Destiny of Man* (New York, 1941), I, p. 3.

[10] *Ibid.*, p. 14.

[11] *Ibid.*, p. 182.

[12] *Moral Man*, pp. 49, 225 ff.

[13] *Ibid.*, pp. 42, 44.

[14] *Reflections*, p. 9.

[15] *Moral Man*, p. 82.

[16] *An Interpretation of Christian Ethics* (New York, 1935), p. 85; also, pp. 66–67.

[17] *Ibid.*, p. 90. But it did have a history—the history of the growth of

the child, for Niebuhr of course did not believe infants were sinful. See *Radical Religion*, I (Spring, 1936), 40–41, where, reviewing Philip Leon's *The Ethics of Power*, Niebuhr took the book as psychological confirmation of his doctrine. Leon insisted that egoism was not derived from particular social situations but was an *a priori* of adult action; he traced its emergence with the emergence of intelligence. In *Beyond Tragedy* (New York, 1937), especially chap. vii, "Childhood and Maturity," Niebuhr made it clear that "inevitable" sin is inevitable as a function of growth, of becoming "more" than the child. That is, the infant certainly, and the child largely, lack the reason and intelligence to be "homeless," and thus remain part of nature and thereby innocent.

[18] *Christian Ethics*, p. 85.

[19] *Ibid.*, p. 89.

[20] *Realistic Theology*, p. 56.

[21] *Social Salvation* (New York, 1935), p. 34, for an impressionistic list of ten "roots" of social evil. See also *Christian Realism* (New York, 1941), p. x.

[22] *Beyond Tragedy*, pp. 16–17; and *The Nature and Destiny of Man*, II, 89.

[23] "Barth—Apostle of the Absolute," *Christian Century*, XLV (Dec. 13, 1928), 1523–1524.

[24] "Barthianism and Political Reaction," *ibid.*, LI (June 6, 1934), 757–759 and "Europe's Religious Pessimism," *ibid.*, XLVII (Aug. 27, 1930), 1031–1033, for his reaction during a European visit.

[25] *Nature and Destiny*, I, 220; II, 66–67, 309, 117; I, 269.

[26] "Barthianism and the Kingdom," *Christian Century*, XLVIII (July 15, 1931), 922–924; Niebuhr's reply, *ibid.*, pp. 924–925. In *Christianity in America: A Crisis* (New York, 1936), Homrighausen gave his Barthian social program, which amounted in effect to a regression to the earliest days of the social gospel itself: preaching, and preaching alone.

[27] "The Attack upon the Social Gospel," *Religion in Life*, V (Summer, 1936), 176–181. In "Can German and American Christians Understand Each Other?" *Christian Century*, XLVII (July 23, 1930), 914–916, H. R. Niebuhr said "no." His *The Kingdom of God in America* (New York, 1937) traced the American evangelical tradition that was the alternative to Barth. What H. R. Niebuhr would do with the perfectionism rampant in that tradition, and criticized by his brother, was never clear.

[28] "Christianity in Its Relation to the Perennial and the Contemporary Man," *Religion in Life*, IV (Autumn, 1935), 551–558.

[29] *Moral Man*, p. 194.

[30] *Ibid.*, p. 220.

[31] *Reflections*, chap. XIII; also, "A New Strategy for Radicals," *World Tomorrow*, XVI (Aug., 1933), 490–492.

[32] For instance: "Marxists Are Taking Stock," *Christianity and Society*, V (Spring, 1940), 8–9; Edward Heiman, reviewing H. B. Parkes' *Marxism: An Autopsy, ibid.*, V (Spring, 1940), 31–33.

[33] *Reflections*, pp. 93–94; see also "The Revival of Feudalism," *Harper's*, CLXX (March, 1935), 483–488; and "Christian Politics and Communist Religion," in *Christianity and the Social Revolution*, John Lewis and Karl Polyani, eds. (New York, 1936).

[34] *Reflections,* pp. 102–103, discussing rationalization of the family.
[35] *Christian Ethics,* pp. 98–99.
[36] *Reflections,* pp. 274–275.
[37] *Christian Ethics,* p. 122.
[38] *Ibid.,* p. 122.
[39] "Ten Years That Shook My World," *loc. cit.*
[40] *Christian Ethics,* pp. 172–186, was his most extended effort to "do justice to" the social-gospel pastors. Further comments on Rauschenbusch: "Is Peace or Justice the Goal?" *World Tomorrow,* XV (Sept. 25, 1932), 275–277.
[41] *Christianity and the Social Crisis* (New York, 1907), p. 401.
[42] *Ibid.,* p. 410.
[43] *World Tomorrow,* XVI (Aug. 31, 1933), 482.
[44] "A New Party?" *Radical Religion,* II (Autumn, 1937), 6–7; "Roosevelt Purge," *ibid.,* III (Fall, 1938), 5; *ibid.,* IV (Spring, 1939), 9.
[45] "The Revival of Feudalism," *Harper's,* CLXX (March, 1935), 483–488.
[46] *Radical Religion,* I (Winter, 1936), 12. In "Roosevelt and the Share-croppers," *ibid.,* II (Spring, 1937), 3–4, the farm relief program was criticized as stopgap; the true alternatives were coöperative farming and capitalist-corporation farming—an idea nicely expressing the urge to see the crisis severe.
[47] *Ibid.,* II (Winter, 1936), 3–4.
[48] *Ibid.,* III (Spring, 1938), 4; insulin: *ibid.,* IV (Spring, 1939), 1–3.
[49] *Ibid.,* IV (Spring, 1939), 4.
[50] *Ibid.,* IV (Fall, 1939), 3–4; *Christianity and Society,* V (Spring, 1940), 7.
[51] "Social Justice in a Defense Economy," *ibid.,* VI (Spring, 1941), 6–7; "The Socialist Campaign," *ibid.,* V (Summer, 1940), 3–5; "Willkie and Roosevelt," *ibid.,* V (Fall, 1940), 5–7.
[52] *Reflections,* p. ix.
[53] "Catastrophe or Social Control?" *Harper's,* CLXV (June, 1932), 114–118.

NOTES TO CHAPTER XV: *Religion and the American Scene,*
pp. 270–291

[1] The three articles appeared in *Radical Religion,* I (Autumn, 1936); III (Winter, 1937); IV (Winter, 1938).
[2] The comments on Tillich in this section are based on *The Religious Situation* (New York, 1932), *Interpretation of History* (New York, 1936), and *The Protestant Era* (Chicago, 1948). James Luther Adams, in *The Protestant Era,* pp. 273–316, provides a good discussion of Tillich. See also Niebuhr, "The Contribution of Paul Tillich," *Religion in Life,* VI (Fall, 1937), 174–181.
[3] Oxford Conference, *The Kingdom of God and History* (Chicago, 1938), pp. 113–114.
[4] An example: C. C. McCown, "In History and Beyond History," *Harvard Theological Review,* XXXVIII (July, 1945), 151–176. McCown collected most of the charges: the neo-orthodox neglected natural science, had allowed themselves to be infected by a period of historical distress, were dominated by a European psychosis, and had no scriptural authority. Other neo-naturalists, insisting that

the concept "beyond history" was not Biblical, declared that Niebuhr and Tillich as well as the Barthians were using a concealed idealism, probably neo-Kantian: N. P. Jacobson, "Niebuhr's Philosophy of History," *ibid.*, XXXVII (Oct., 1944), 237–268; Bernard M. Loomer, "Neo-naturalism and Neo-orthodoxy," *Journal of Religion*, XXVIII (April, 1948), 79–91. What interests us here is that these attacks fortified technical philosophical and scriptural arguments with pragmatic judgments about the nature and severity of the social crisis, and about the health of American society.

⁵ "Religion and Secular Culture," *The Protestant Era*, pp. 60 ff.

⁶ *Ibid.*, p. 133, from an article first published in 1929; on the humanistic concept of personality, "Religion and Secular Culture," *loc. cit.*

⁷ *An Interpretation of a Christian Ethics* (New York, 1935), p. 124. He came close, but could never wholly abandon the moral man-immoral society distinction as a timeless distinction. Thus, *ibid.*, p. 125: "The most terrific social conflicts actually occur in intimate communities in which intensity of social cohesion accentuates the social distance of various groups and individuals. . . . Even when [they are] less pronounced than the imperialism of groups [they] may be more deadly for operating at such close range."

⁸ *Ibid.*, p. 80. Another form of the same shift: "Every temporal fact, profoundly analyzed, leads to an infinity in terms of both sources and possibilities," "Christianity in Its Relation to the Perennial and the Contemporary Man," *Religion in Life*, IV (Autumn, 1935), 551–558.

⁹ *Faith and History* (New York, 1949), p. 101.

¹⁰ *The Protestant Era*, p. 249, from an address given in 1941.

¹¹ Correspondence from Bradford Young, *Christian Century*, LV (June 1, 1938), 705.

¹² *The Church Against the World* (Chicago, 1935), p. 151.

¹³ "Back to Benedict?" *Christian Century*, XLII (July 2, 1925), 860–861.

¹⁴ *The Church Against the World*, p. 151.

¹⁵ "The Christian Evangel and Social Culture," *Religion in Life*, VIII (Winter, 1939), 44–48.

¹⁶ *This Nation Under God* (Chicago, 1939), p. 3.

¹⁷ In *Protestantism's Hour of Decision* (Philadelphia, 1940). See also his review of Paul Hutchinson's *The Ordeal of Western Religion* (New York, 1933), in *Christian Century*, LI (Jan. 3, 1934), 22–23, for his view of the crisis as moderate and his stress on the role of the middle classes rather than of labor.

¹⁸ *The Social Gospel Re-examined* (New York, 1940), pp. 234 ff.

¹⁹ "Between Liberalism and the New Orthodoxy," *Christian Century*, LVI (May 17, 1939), 637–640. See *Can Christianity Save Civilization?* (New York, 1940), pp. 260 ff. on Douglas plan.

²⁰ See "Bigger and Better Peasant Wars," *Christian Century*, LI (June 6, 1934), 759–760, as an example of Holt's sharp concern at exploitation of the farmers. He was practically alone among social-gospel leaders in this emphasis.

²¹ In Holt, *This Nation Under God*, p. 11, and Horton, *Can Civilization Save Religion?* p. 231, the reference was specific. Grundtvig figured as one of the pioneers in Sherwood Eddy and Kirby Page, *Creative Pioneers* (New York, 1937), pp. 61 ff.

NOTES TO CHAPTER XVI: *Neo-orthodox Man, pp. 292–306*

[1] This and above quotes from *Wisdom and Folly in Religion* (New York, 1940), pp. 35, 109, 138.

[2] *Nature and Destiny of Man* (New York, 1943), II, 210.

[3] *Ibid.*, II, 204–205.

[4] *Ibid.*, II, 211.

[5] An *Interpretation of Christian Ethics* (New York, 1935), p. 89.

[6] *World Tomorrow*, XVII (Jan. 18, 1934), 43–44.

[7] *Nature and Destiny of Man*, II, 207.

[8] *Moral Man and Immoral Society* (New York, 1932), p. 276.

[9] *The Irony of American History* (New York, 1952), especially chap. V, "The Triumph of Experience over Dogma."

[10] *Nature and Destiny of Man*, II, 244 ff.

[11] *Christian Ethics*, pp. 97–98.

[12] *Nature and Destiny of Man*, II, 320.

[13] "Christian Moralism in America," *Radical Religion*, V (Winter, 1940), 16–20.

NOTES TO CHAPTER XVII: *The New Era and the Old Church, pp. 307–348*

[1] Douglass and Edmund De S. Brunner, *The Protestant Church as a Social Institution* (New York, 1935), and Douglass, in the Oxford Conference volume, *Church and Community* (Chicago, 1938). Kincheloe, *Research Memorandum* (New York, 1937), pp. 72–73. R. W. Frank wrote the warning: "The American Community and the Protestant Church," *Religion in Life*, VIII (Summer, 1939), 418–426.

[2] Kincheloe, *Research Memorandum*, p. 71.

[3] Ralph Read, ed., *The Younger Churchmen Look at the Church* (New York, 1935), pp. 138–139.

[4] *Ibid.*, p. 310.

[5] *Ibid.*, p. 308.

[6] *The Church and Society* (New York, 1935), chapters iii, iv, vii.

[7] *The Social Gospel Re-examined* (New York, 1940), pp. 65 ff.

[8] *Ibid.*, pp. 134–135.

[9] "A New Protestantism," *Christian Century*, LI (Oct. 17, 1934), 1304–1306.

[10] *New York Times*, Oct. 3, 1932, p. 4.

[11] "A New Basis for Industrial Cooperation," *Federal Council Bulletin*, XX (May, 1937), 4. "The Churches and the New Deal," *ibid.*, XVI (Sept., 1933, 3–4, and Oct., 1933, 6–7), for expressions of firm support.

[12] "The Church and Labor Today," *ibid.*, XVII (April, 1934), 4–5; "A New Basis for Industrial Cooperation," *ibid.*, XX (May, 1937), 4.

[13] *Ibid.*, XVII (Jan., Feb., and June, 1934); Information Service, XVII (Sept. 10, 1938) printed the social confession of faith of Governor Frank Murphy of Michigan.

[14] "The Dilemma of the Socially-Minded," *Religion in Life*, VIII (Winter, 1939), 49–60.

[15] *Information Service,* XVII (June 25, 1938); *Radical Religion,* II (Winter, 1936), 4, and *Christianity and Society,* VI (Winter, 1941), 8–9, on the Roosevelt majorities. Johnson: *Information Service,* XVI (Dec. 6, 1937).

[16] Michigan: *Federal Council Bulletin,* XIX (Dec., 1936), 7–8. Mission: *ibid.,* XXIII (Sept., 1940). Alva Taylor, *Christianity and Industry* (New York, 1933), was another of the tracts pressing the businessman in the old fashion, only a little less exhortatory than Jones.

[17] "Senator Vandenberg's Philosophy," *Information Service,* XVI (Nov. 6, 1937).

[18] *Information Service,* XIX (May 25, 1940).

[19] "Courage, Mr. President," *Christian Century,* L (Nov. 8, 1933), 1398–1400; "The Regimentation Bogy," *ibid.,* L (June 14, 1933), 870–872; "Mr. Hoover and the New Deal," *ibid.,* LI (Oct. 3, 1934), 1230–1232.

[20] *Ibid.,* LI (Nov. 14, 1934), 1447.

[21] "A New Economic Man," *ibid.,* L (Oct. 11, 1933), 1262–1264; in "The New Deal and the Ideal," *ibid.* (Aug., 1933), 1078–1080, Morrison pointed out that the New Deal represented social control, except at the point precisely of profit-taking; he called on the churches to persuade their members to give up profits.

[22] "An Evolutionary Revolution," *ibid.,* LI (Jan. 17, 1934), 78–80.

[23] "A New Deal for Labor," *ibid.,* LI (Jan. 7, 1934), 11–12; "Reviving the Swope Plan," *ibid.,* L (Nov. 15, 1933), 1427–1428.

[24] Burt's letter: *ibid.,* LIV (Oct. 6, 1937). For Morrison's criticism of socialists at a time he believed the New Deal would issue in socialism: "What Are the Socialists Trying to Do?" *ibid.,* LI (June 20, 1934), 820–821, and "The Socialist Dilemma," *ibid.,* L (Sept. 27, 1933), 1199–1200: in "Is the New Deal Complete?" *ibid.,* LI (May 30, 1934), 720–721, Morrison urged the administration on toward planned economy, as he detected signs of complacency.

[25] "A New Industrial Epoch," *ibid.,* LIV (March 29, 1937), 376–378; "After the Motors Strike," *ibid.* (Feb. 24, 1937), 239–241; on the FC, *ibid.* (Feb. 17, 1937), 204–205; on Niebuhr, *ibid.* (July 2, 1937), 916.

[26] "Capitalism in Transit," *ibid.,* LIV (April 7, 1937), 446–448; Morrison spoke of "the framework of a society which has already, and profoundly, been transformed in its inner character."

[27] "The Second Inaugural," *ibid.,* LIV (Feb. 3, 1937), 134–136.

[28] "Mr. Roosevelt's Lost Following," *ibid.,* LV (April 6, 1938), 424–425; "Retrospect," *ibid.* (Dec. 28, 1938), 1598–1600, for a view that the average American had begun to suspect the President's program of being a patchwork of expediencies rather than a long-range campaign; unemployment remained; the year had been wasted. "More Billions for 'Defense'?" *ibid.* (Nov. 2, 1938), 1318–1320.

[29] The hopeless secular mind: "A Modern Paul," *ibid.,* LV (Feb. 16, 1938), 200–202. Some editorials on the church: "Protestantism at the End of an Era," *ibid.,* LI (April 25, 1934), 550–552; "An Ascetic Church," *ibid.* (May 23, 1934), 687–689; "First Steps Toward a Free Church," *ibid.* (May 30, 1934), 718–720; "The Arrested Church," *ibid.,* LV (May 25, 1938), 648–650. Morrison's campaign against the chaplain system dated from the early 'twenties; among many articles, see "The Federal Council and the Chaplaincy," *ibid.,* LI (June 27, 1934),

855–857, and "Demilitarize the Chaplaincy," *ibid.*, LIII (Oct. 28, 1936), 1416–1418. Trading the bourgeois congregations for labor: *The Social Gospel and the Christian Cultus* (New York, 1933), p. 172.

[30] *What Is Christianity?* (Chicago, 1940), p. 259. The doctrinal heart of Morrison's concept of the Church provoked accusations that he did not understand Protestantism: Wilhelm Pauck, "A False Catholic Protestantism," *Christianity and Society*, VI (Spring, 1941), 9–16.

[31] *Social Action*, I (Nov. 1, 1935) and *ibid.*, II (June 1, 1936) on CSA program and officers; also, C. H. Hopkins, "A History of Congregational Social Action," *ibid.*, VIII (May 15, 1942).

[32] G. G. Atkins and Frederick L. Fagley, *History of American Congregationalism* (Boston, 1942), pp. 261 ff., on the Oberlin National Council; "Social Action and the Congregationalists," *Christian Century*, LIII (July 8, 1936), 958–960, on the 1936 Council.

[33] Herring, *Social Action*, II (May 1, 1936) and Bradley, *ibid.*, V (Dec. 15, 1939) as examples of the contrast.

[34] *The Younger Churchmen Look at the Church*, pp. 28–29. In *Christianity and Our World* (New York, 1936), Bennett laid a still heavier burden on the church of the explicitly negative order of protection against fascism.

[35] "A Changed Liberal—But Still a Liberal," *Christian Century*, LVI (Feb. 8, 1939), 179–181.

[36] Bennett, *Christian Realism* (New York, 1941); Horton, *Can Christianity Save Civilization?* (New York, 1940); Van Dusen, *God in These Times* (New York, 1935); Calhoun, *What Is Man?* (New York, 1939), variously illustrate the cautious liberal appreciation of Niebuhr. See also Bennett, "The Contribution of Reinhold Niebuhr," *Religion in Life*, VI (Spring, 1937), 268–283, and Calhoun reviewing *The Nature and Destiny of Man* in *Journal of Religion*, XXIV (Jan., 1944), 59–64.

[37] *Christian Realism*, p. 139.

[38] *Ibid.*, p. 152; on the advantages of the position of the church, *ibid.*, pp. 145 ff. See Bennett, with Robert Calhoun and Theodore Hume, in a summary of the new neoliberal outlook of the council in *Social Action*, VIII (June 15, 1942).

[39] *Creative Pioneers* (New York, 1937), p. 39. Sidney Hillman and John L. Lewis were now among the pioneers.

[40] *Living Prayerfully* (New York, 1941), pp. 95 ff.

[41] "Return to Pacifism," *Christian Century*, LIII (Dec. 2, 1936), 1603–1606.

[42] *Ibid.*, LIII (Oct. 14, 1936), 1374.

[43] In *Federal Council Bulletin*, XXI (Jan., 1938), "The Future of the Labor Temple," *Information Service*, XVI (Sept. 4, 1937), and "The Way of the Cross," *Christian Century*, LV (Dec. 14, 1938), 1541–1543 Muste registered his rededication to a purified, pacifist labor movement and a purified, pacifist, sacrificial nation.

[44] "The True International," *Christian Century*, LVI (May 14, 1939), 667–669; more generally on the church, where Muste voiced his suspicions of neo-orthodoxy: "The Situation and Program of Christianity," *Religion in Life*, VIII (Spring, 1939), 222–235.

[45] *The Fascist International* (New York, n. d.) (1936–1937), p. 6. See

also *The Development of Fascism in the United States* (New York, n.d.) (1935–1936).

⁴⁶ "Methodist Money Speaks," *Christian Century,* LII (Aug. 14, 1935), 1029–1031; *Information Service,* XV (June 6, 1936).

⁴⁷ "A Church in Peril of Its Soul," *Christian Century,* LIII (June 3, 1936), 790–792; Paul Hutchinson, "The Methodists Retreat," *Nation,* CXLII (June 10, 1936), 742–743; 1934 youth: *Christian Century,* LI (Sept. 19, 1934), 1183–1184.

⁴⁸ *Nation,* CXLII (May 20, 1936), 631; *ibid.* (June 10, 1936), 742–743; correspondence in *Christian Century,* LIII (June 3, 1936), 815–816; (July 1, 1936), 928–929; (July 15, 1936), 979. *Social Service Bulletin,* XXVI (May, 1936, and June, 1936) outlined the attack on the federation and reported the convention.

⁴⁹ 1936 youth: *Christian Century,* LIII (Sept. 16, 1936), 1212 and 1236–1237; Halford Luccock, "The Purge in the Methodist Board of Education," *ibid.,* LV (Aug. 17, 1938), 987–989; 1938 youth: *ibid.,* LV (Sept. 21, 1938), 1134.

⁵⁰ *Radical Religion,* II (Winter, 1936) and III (Winter, 1937); *Christian Century,* LIII (Dec. 9, 1936), 1635–1636, and LVII (Feb. 7, 1940), 190–192; *Information Service,* XVI (March 20, 1937), and XIX (Jan. 29, 1940). None of the new denominational organizations inspired by the UCCD grew to commanding proportions; see the *Presbyterian Tribune,* LV (Oct., 1940), 5, for a dolorous comparison of the Presbyterian Fellowship at the Presbyterian General Assemblies with the status of the CLID at Episcopal Conventions—especially pointed, since the CLID like the Methodist Federation came under sharp attack in the 'thirties, chiefly from Bishop Manning of New York and a Church Laymen's Association: *Christian Century,* LIV (Sept. 22, 1937), 1182; I. F. Stone, "The Romans Would Understand," *Nation,* CVL (Oct. 2, 1937), 345–346.

⁵¹ "Sects and Churches," *Christian Century,* LII (July 7, 1935), 885–887.

⁵² "The Radical Minister and the Church," *Radical Religion,* II (Winter, 1936), 25–27.

⁵³ But nevertheless: "Practically every radical leader of consequence in the present American scene was originally inspired by religious conviction, however anxious some of them may be to hide or deny that fact now." "Religion as a Source of Radicalism," *Christian Century,* LI (April 11, 1934), 491–494. Union Theological Seminary, in the early 'thirties, led in the production of young radicals. One was Franz Daniel, Socialist party and Amalgamated Clothing Workers organizer in Philadelphia; another was Arnold Johnson, organizer for the Ohio Unemployed League, affiliated with the American Workers party before his entry into the Communist party, U.S.A.; both were mentioned by Niebuhr in the article. See Hubert Herring, "Union Seminary Routs Its Reds," *Christian Century,* LI (June 13, 1934), 799–801, criticizing President Henry S. Coffin, and Coffin, "The Minister in Party Politics," *ibid.,* L (June 21, 1933), 810–811. Also, Herman Reissig, "Homeless Religious Radicals," *ibid.,* LIV (Aug. 4, 1937), 971–973, pointing out that most of those in the prophetic forefront did not have to face a congregation, ensconced as they were in schools and offices; Reissig had just resigned his King's Highway Congregational church post in Brooklyn.

⁵⁴ "Moralistic Preaching," *ibid.,* LIII (July 15, 1936), 985–987.

⁵⁵ *Beyond Tragedy* (New York, 1937), p. 132.

⁵⁶ "The Radical Minister and His Church," *Radical Religion,* II (Winter, 1936), 25–27.

[57] Kern, "Hope Sees a Star," *Christian Century*, LVI (March 29, 1939), 412–414; Poteat, "Searching for Greater Loyalties," *ibid.* (Feb. 22, 1939), 244–246.

[58] Baptists, 1933: *ibid.*, L (July 5, 1933), 890; Methodists at Jackson: *ibid.*, LI (May 16, 1934), 670, 678; Methodist council: *ibid.*, LIV (Aug. 18, 1937), 1012, and "The Southern Church Begins to Stir," *Radical Religion*, II (Autumn, 1937), 27–30; Presbyterians: *Christian Century*, LII (Oct. 9, 1935), 1293; Reformed Presbyterians: *ibid.* (Sept. 11, 1935), 1133–1134.

[59] Southern Baptists, *ibid.*, LIII (May 27, 1936), 774–775; Smith, *ibid.*, L (Aug. 9, 1933), 1019.

[60] *Radical Religion* carried regular reports on the conferences of the Southern Churchmen; *ibid.*, III (Fall, 1938), 44–46, for instance, where Cowan pointed out the non-Puritan roots of the Southern church; Kester, "Religion— Priestly and Prophetic," *ibid.*, I (Autumn, 1936), 23–31; a note on Kester, *Christian Century*, LIII (Nov. 18, 1936), 1540; Cowan, "A Dispatch from the South," *Radical Religion*, II (Autumn, 1937), 22–26; a similar statement by a Yale Divinity School student, Chester Hunt, "The Sharecropper Looks to God," *Christian Century*, LV (Jan. 5, 1938), 12–13; Sherwood Eddy, "Radical Religion in Action," *Radical Religion*, I (Spring, 1936), 19–25; Sam Franklin, "Adventures in Applied Religion," *ibid.*, I (Autumn, 1936), 32–36.

[61] Letter from Williams, *World Tomorrow*, XVII (June 28, 1934), 17; on his dismissal, "A Victim of Ecclesiastical Reaction," *ibid.*, XVII (July 26, 1934), 15; letter from Williams, *Radical Religion*, I (Winter, 1936), 43. "The Scriptural Heritage of the People," a 1944 People's Institute pamphlet, was an example of his work in Detroit. Kermit Eby, in *Labor's Relation to Church and Community*, Liston Pope, ed. (New York, 1947), p. 96, discusses the fundamentalist mountain preachers, often subsidized by auto companies, who helped turn wartime Detroit into a social cauldron, and whom Williams opposed. Cedric Belfrage wrote two biographies of Williams, *South of God* (New York, 1941) and *A Faith to Free the People* (New York, 1944), emphasizing and celebrating Williams' Detroit and United Front career. Williams' career interested not only Belfrage—it came to interest the Un-American Activities Committee: *100 Things You Should Know about Communism and Religion* (Washington, 1949), in which Williams was starred, along with Ward and Kenneth Leslie.

[62] "Meditations from Mississippi," *Christian Century*, LIV (Feb. 10, 1937), 183–184. In all the social gospel, there was no clear image of the Negroes' church or of its social quietude; Benjamin E. Mays, *The Negro's Church* (New York, 1933), found no social-gospel alertness whatever; occasional reports, such as Horace A. White, "Who Owns the Negro Church?" *Christian Century*, LV (Feb. 9, 1938), 176–177, indicated that the 'thirties did not bring out a prophetic note. A most interesting discussion of the relation between theology and social experience, suggesting that the neo-orthodox had no right to think southern "proletarians" would adopt neo-orthodoxy, was John B. Thompson's "Prolegomena to a Proletarian Theology," *Radical Religion*, I (Autumn, 1936), 11–18; Thompson was professor of the philosophy of religion at the College of the Ozarks.

[63] *Christian Century*, LIII (Nov. 4, 1936), 1475; *ibid.*, LVI (Nov. 29, 1939), 1460–1461; T. Brinton Perry, "Lutheran Preaching Takes a Turn," *ibid.*, LVII (May 8, 1940), 606–608. The 1936 resolutions on industry recalled the

rhetoric of the 'twenties; the serious debate was on foreign policy, with the aggressive group the isolationists: *Minutes of the 10th Biennial Convention of the United Lutheran Church in America* (Philadelphia, 1936), p. 377. The 1940 convention showed more social-gospel concern in the strict sense: *Minutes of the 12th Biennial Convention* . . . (Philadelphia, 1940), pp. 316–321. The *Lutheran*, XXII (Oct. 18, 1939, 4–5, and Oct. 25, 1939, 6–7), for attitudes of some 200 Lutheran pastors. Paul W. Spande, *The Lutheran Church Under American Influence* (Burlington, Iowa, 1943), pp. 216 ff., for an extremely conservative reaction to these mild fermentings.

NOTES TO CHAPTER XVIII: *The Tragic Choice: War, pp. 349–403*

[1] *Christian Realism* (New York, 1941), p. 90.

[2] *Preachers Present Arms* (Philadelphia, 1933). Abrams found something less than a hundred clergyman who did not conform. Universalists and Unitarians provided over one-third of the seventy men he traced as pacifists (outside the traditionally pacifist sects). Episcopal socialism provided a cluster of objectors: Paul Jones, Irwin Tucker, John Nevin Sayre, John H. Melish. There were almost no Methodists, Baptists, Presbyterians, or Disciples. The four New York Presbyterians illustrated perhaps the central nerve of this liberal protest: Norman Thomas left the ministry for the League for Industrial Democracy, William Fincke entered the labor movement, William Simpson soon launched upon his itinerant's calling; Edmund Chaffee alone remained in the ministry—at the Labor Temple. Such social-gospel leaders as W. A. Brown, Cavert, Morrison, Coffin, Eddy, Luccock, Mathews, Niebuhr, Taylor, and E. F. Tittle were among the war supporters. The Federal Council of course supported the government strongly.

[3] See an obituary editorial, "The Idealism of Woodrow Wilson," *Christian Century*, XLI (Feb. 21, 1924), 230–231. Page and Eddy drew on the historians in most of their tracts; the *Century* published Schevill, "The Postwar Histories," XLI (Oct. 23, 1924), 1365–1367, and Barnes in ten articles in the last quarter of 1925 on the theme "Was America Deluded by the War?"; a review of Fay, XLVI (Feb. 7, 1929), 199–200.

[4] *Christian Century*, XLV (May 31, 1928), 691–693; also "The Treaty Is Signed" (Sept. 6, 1928), 1070–1071. Morrison organized his arguments in *The Outlawry of War* (Chicago, 1927); Salvador de Madariaga, in *Disarmament* (New York, 1929), pp. 239–240, testified that Morrison counted on two continents as one of the inspirers of the pact. James Shotwell, in *War as an Instrument of National Policy* (New York, 1929), p. 47, commented that Midwest support of the pact reflected the "New England tradition" in religion and morals—minus New England internationalism. Morrison himself wrote that had the Federal Council not been located in New York, it would not have supported the League and the World Court, opposed by Morrison because of the sanctions power: *Christian Century*, XLIII (Jan. 28, 1926), 104–106.

[5] Jessie Wallace Hughan, *Three Decades of War Resistance* (New York, 1942), p. 5.

[6] *World Tomorrow*, XIV (May, 1931), 138–154; *ibid.*, XVII (May 10, 1934), 222–256. An indignant letter in reply from General Douglas MacArthur, *ibid.*, XIV (June, 1931).

[7] "Understanding Senator Borah," *Christian Century,* XLIII (Jan. 7, 1926), 15–17.

[8] Two examples of attacks by such superpatriotism on both pacifism and the social gospel: Leroy F. Smith and E. B. Johns, *Pastors, Politicians, Pacifists* (Chicago, 1927), and Colonel E. N. Sanctuary, *Tainted Contacts* (New York, 1931).

[9] *Religion Renounces War* (New York, 1934). Van Kirk's effort—pp. 78, 79—to explain the first debates provoked by the invasion of Manchuria was a wonderful betrayal of the ground shifting under pacifist feet: he could not prevent the ideals of peace and justice, or of peace in the Far East and peace for the United States from being split, but at the same time he could not concede that this threatened the old peace morale.

[10] *Christian Century,* LII (Nov. 6, 1935), 1396–1397; Eddy moved on toward support of aid to the Allies: "Must We Face the War Problem Again?" *ibid.,* LV (Nov. 9, 1938), 1363–1365. Baker poll: *Information Service,* XV (Oct., 1936); Herring, *And So to War* (New Haven, 1938); "Christian Pacifists Take Their Stand," *Christian Century,* LVI (March 15, 1939), 343–345, and *ibid.* (June 14, 1939); 1941 poll: *ibid.,* LVIII (Aug. 13, 1941), 1009; John C. Bennett and Van Dusen were the "victims": *ibid.,* LVII (Sept. 28, 1940), 1146–1147, and *ibid.,* LVII (June 24, 1940), 918–920; Gibson, "The Flight of Moral Leadership," *ibid.,* LVIII (June 25, 1941), 829–830.

[11] *Ibid.,* LVII (March 6, 1940), 325.

[12] *Pacifism in the Modern World,* Devere Allen, ed. (New York, 1928), p. 17.

[13] *Radical Religion,* I (Winter, 1936), 25–30; see also Sayre's contribution to a symposium with Muste and Page, *Pacifism and Aggression* (n.p., n.d.) (1936?).

[14] Sanctions on Japan: "Must We Do Nothing?" *Christian Century,* XLIX (March 30, 1932), 415–417, in the exchange with his brother; *World Tomorrow,* XVII (March 15, 1934), 132–133.

[15] "The International Situation," *Radical Religion,* III (Winter, 1937), 2–3.

[16] "The Failure of Sanctions," *ibid.,* I (Autumn, 1936), 5–6.

[17] *Ibid.*

[18] "Christianity in Its Relation to the Perennial and the Contemporary Man," *Religion in Life,* IV (Autumn, 1935), 551–558.

[19] "America and the War in China," *Christian Century,* LIV (Sept. 28, 1937), 1195–1196.

[20] *Radical Religion,* III (Fall, 1938), 1–3.

[21] *Ibid.,* III (Winter, 1938), 1–2.

[22] Declarations: *Information Service,* XIX (June 1, 1940); aid committee: *Christian Century,* LVIII (Jan. 22, 1941), 134; Peace Union: *ibid.* (July 26, 1941), 866; sponsors and statement of policy were given in the first issue of *Christianity and Crisis* (Feb. 10, 1941); Fight for Freedom Committee, mentioned in the paragraph following: *ibid.,* I (June 16, 1941).

[23] For an interesting geopolitical description of Europe as "a little peninsula which has now lost its importance in our planetary life," see the article Holt wrote with H. N. Wieman, "Keep Our Country Out of This War," *Christian Century,* LVI (Sept. 27, 1939), 1162–1164; some of Palmer's statements were, "A Decade's Spir-

itual Experience," *ibid.*, LVI (June 7, 1939), 730–732; "A Road Away from War," *ibid.*, LVII (June 19, 1940), 793–795; and his contribution to the "What I Would Do If America Goes to War" series, *ibid.*, LVIII (Jan. 2, 1941), 51–52.

[24] *The World Task of Pacifism* (Wallingford, Penn., 1941), p. 15. The notice of Brunner and Niebuhr was explicit: *Non-Violence in an Aggressive World* (New York, 1940), pp. 20–21.

[25] *Where Are We Going?* (New York, 1941), pp. 21–22. Also, "The Way of the Cross," *Christian Century*, LV (Dec. 14, 1938), 1541–1543.

[26] *The World Task of Pacifism*, p. 18.

[27] *Where Are We Going?* pp. 8 ff.

[28] *Ibid.*, p. 9, and pp. 18–19 on America as heir to the British Empire; see also a further effort to discount an American postwar patrol of the world in *War Is the Enemy* (Wallingford, Penn., 1942), p. 29.

[29] *Wage Peace Now* (Philadelphia, 1942), p. 13.

[30] *Non-Violence in an Aggressive World*, p. 139.

[31] *Christian Century*, LVI (May 17, 1939), 645.

[32] *Non-Violence in an Aggressive World*, p. 133.

[33] *Ibid.*, p. 157. Muste wanted a saving, sacrificial offer made to Germany in 1940: *Non-violence . . .* , p. 152; in 1941: *Where Are We Going?* p. 22; and to both Germany and Japan even after the fall of Singapore in 1942: *War Is the Enemy*, p. 32.

[34] *Non-Violence in an Aggressive World*, pp. 85, 87.

[35] *Where Are We Going?* p. 22.

[36] *Non-Violence in an Aggressive World*, p. 145.

[37] The interest in Tillich also was explicit: "The Situation and Program of Christianity," *Religion in Life*, VIII (Spring, 1939), 222–235. The article included further attacks on neo-orthodoxy.

[38] "Return to Pacifism," *Christian Century*, LIII (Dec. 2, 1936), 1603–1606.

[39] National Peace Conference: *ibid.*, LIII (Jan. 1, 1936, 22, and June 17, 1936, 882); Emergency Peace Campaign: *ibid.* (Nov. 18, 1936), 1534–1535, and LIV (March 24, 1937), 388–389; Hughan, *Three Decades of War Resistance*, p. 16.

[40] Kirby Page, in *How to Keep America Out of War* (n.p., 1939), p. 47, was the outstanding advocate of a quota system: sales to belligerents would be limited to a yearly volume the average of five years of peacetime trade.

[41] *Social Action*, II (Jan. 10, 1936).

[42] *Ibid.*, I (June 15, 1935), 12–14; "Keep the U.S. Out of War," *ibid.*, II (Feb. 1, 1936), 29.

[43] Page: *Christian Century*, LV (June 22, 1938), 781–782; Tittle, "God and National Policy," *ibid.* (Nov. 30, 1938), 1462–1465; Niebuhr, *ibid.* (Dec. 14, 1938), 1549–1550.

[44] Palmer on Munich: "Call a World Economic Conference," *ibid.*, LV (Nov. 9, 1938), 1368–1369; "Let the Federal Council Lead," *ibid.*, LVI (Jan. 11, 1939), 46–47. Cavert, "Toward a World Conference," *ibid.* (Feb. 22, 1939), 242–244; "Toward a World Conference," *ibid.* (March 8, 1939), 311–313; Palmer, "A Christian 14 Points," *ibid.* (Sept. 13, 1939), 1101–1103.

[45] "What Can America Do?" *ibid.*, LVII (May 14, 1940); Palmer, *ibid.* (June 19, 1940), 793–795; "Isaiah Speaks to America," *ibid.* (July 3, 1940), 848–851.

[46] *Ibid.* (May 29, 1940), 706–707.

[47] No-War Committee: *Information Service*, XX (March 18, 1941); Mediation Campaign: *Christian Century*, LVIII (May 21, 1941), 701; call for peace: *ibid.* (Feb. 12, 1941), 277–278.

[48] *Ibid.*, LVII (Sept. 18, 1940), 1146–1147; Bennett had supported neutrality as late as 1939: "Neutrality: The Christian's Dilemma," *ibid.*, LVI (Nov. 1, 1939), 1329–1331.

[49] *Ibid.*, LVII (May 22, 1940, 663–665; May 29, 1940, 694–696; Sept. 11, 1940, 1103–1104); LVIII (May 7, 1941, 614; July 2, 1941, 855–856). A fascinating note of the last editorial was Morrison's declaration that New York as well as London would be panicked at the prospect of a Russian victory; presumably Chicago would not have been panicked: first, "New York" was really not America, it was just money; second, the prospect was not real to clear eyes, the only real prospect being stalemate.

[50] Page: *How to Keep America Out of War*, pp. 39 ff.; also, Harold Fey, "Defense or Despotism," *Christian Century*, LVII (Jan. 24, 1940), 110–112; the senators: *ibid.*, LVI (Oct. 18, 1939), 1259; on business: *ibid.*, LVII (June 5, 1940), 726–727; on munition's boom: *ibid.*, LVI (Aug. 2, 1939), 942–943; on political fascism: "An Ominous Nomination," *ibid.*, LVII (July 31, 1940), 942–944, and "No Third Term" (Oct. 16, 1940), 1230–1232; "A War for Imperialism," LVIII (Nov. 26, 1941), 1463–1465; Palmer, "America and the War," *ibid.*, LVII (Aug. 21, 1940), 1025–1027, under attack from Dwight Bradley of the Council for Social Action.

[51] Examples of the politics of succor are Page, *Christian Century*, LVIII (Jan. 29, 1941), 160, and Herring, *And So to War*, pp. 170–171. This depended upon the noninterventionists' psychology of war, of course: war could be fought only in hate and to the destruction of reason; participants in war could not undertake saving actions at its end.

[52] "Not America's War," *Christian Century*, LVI (Nov. 22, 1939), 1431–1433.

[53] *Ibid.*, LV (Sept. 14, 1938, 1086–1087; Sept. 28, 1938, 1150–1152; Oct. 12, 1938, 1224–1226; Nov. 30, 1938, 1456–1458). An earlier reaction controlled by the contempt of an indefensible Versailles: "Germany Invades the Rhineland," *ibid.*, LII (March 18, 1936), 422–424.

[54] "Our Frontier Is on the Potomac," *ibid.*, LVI (Feb. 15, 1939), 206–207.

[55] "Defending Democracy," *ibid.*, LVII (June 5, 1940), 726–727.

[56] "Not America's War," *ibid.*, LVI (Nov. 22, 1939), 1431–1433.

[57] "Hitler's Victory," *ibid.*, LVII (June 26, 1940), 811–812.

[58] "The Future of France," *ibid.* (Sept. 25, 1940), 1166–1168.

[59] *Ibid.*, and "France Turns Toward Puritanism," *ibid.* (Aug. 28, 1940), 1043.

[60] Two anticipations of stalemate in 1941: *ibid.*, LVIII (Jan. 15, 1941, 79–80, and Sept. 3, 1941, 1070–1071). In his five-article series on "The Search for a Lasting Peace," see especially "A Basis for Negotiations," *ibid.*, LVIII (March 12, 1941), 351–354, where Morrison was at his highly empiric, highly pragmatic,

highly sophisticated best; in the preceding four articles, he ended with the assumption that there could be definite, world-wide peace, with universal disarmament, a world government, and viable processes for carrying all economic and social problems everywhere to rational, peaceful settlement.

[61] *Ibid.*, LVIII (Dec. 17, 1941), 1565–1567.

[62] *Ibid.*, LI (March 28, 1934), 411–412; of course, he registered both emphases; for the other, "Preparing the Church for the Next War," *Christendom*, III (Winter, 1938), 110–125; but it was through detachment of America that the detachment of the church was achieved.

[63] *Christianity and Power Politics* (New York, 1940), p. 41.

[64] "A Crisis in American Peace Policy," *Christian Century*, LIV (Oct. 20, 1937), 1285–1288. This "providential" explanation of virtue was not quite enough; later Morrison attributed American neutrality not only to her oceans, "as some say," but to rational and ethical discernment as well: "On Saving Civilization," *ibid.*, LVII (May 8, 1940), 598–600.

[65] *Ibid.*, LVIII (March 26, 1941), 415–417.

[66] *Christianity and Power Politics*, p. 29.

[67] An exchange between Morrison and John C. Bennett, *Christian Century*, LVIII (Oct. 8, 1941), 1230–1232 and 1243–1244, revealed the problem the "tragic interventionists" faced in the anti-interventionists: Morrison tried to pin Bennett by arguing that to assert the war was not holy, and then to engage in it as Bennett and Niebuhr proposed, was to tell God His will must be qualified by considerations He had overlooked when He willed it. This was to show that Morrison argued for holy politics for himself, and was a reflection of his neonaturalist theism, by which God was that (limited) part of process where values were created and sustained.

[68] "Karl Barth and Democracy," *Radical Religion*, IV (Winter, 1938), 6; also *ibid.*, IV (Spring, 1939), on Barth's pamphlet, *The Church and the Political Question of Today*.

[69] "Why We Differ," *Christian Century*, LVIII (Dec. 10, 1941), 1534–1538; La Guardia: *ibid.* (Nov. 19, 1941), 1430–1432; Wallace: *ibid.* (April 23, 1941), 550–552.

[70] Morrison on the Atlantic Charter: "Are the Four Freedoms a Delusion?" *ibid.*, LVIII (Oct. 16, 1941), 926–928.

[71] Fey's report: *ibid.*, LVII (Feb. 3, 1940), 190–192; Niebuhr's reply and Fey's question: *ibid.* (March 6, 1940), 324–325.

[72] "What Comes Next?" *ibid.*, LVII (June 19, 1940), 790–791.

[73] The comparisons: *ibid.*, LVIII (Jan. 15, 1941), 75; the uprising: *ibid.* (March 19, 1941), 385–387; on the occasion of the military occupation of Iceland, Morrison wrote that the nation's resistance to the arguments of the President proved that only an "incident" of shocking character could take the country into the war, and that the occupation set the scene for such incidents: "The President Enters the War," *ibid.* (July 16, 1941), 901–902. On the matter of anti-interventionist pastors' relations with America First, see Niebuhr's harsh attack, "Pacifism and America First," *Christianity and Crisis*, I (June 16, 1941), and Morrison's harsh reply, "A Strain on the Tie That Binds," *Christian Century*, LVIII (July 2, 1941), 853–855. Actually, although a few of the social-gospel neutralists—Morrison himself, E. F. Tittle, Palmer, Page—now and then introduced

such America First spokesmen as Senator Burton K. Wheeler and Charles Lindbergh and quoted from their mouths, social-gospel neutralism was never in danger of losing itself in the apologetics of America First. See *Christian Century*, LVI (Jan. 18, 1939), 75, for the editors' wry recognition of their common front with an old local enemy, the *Chicago Tribune;* the *Tribune* reprinted a good many of the *Century's* outcries in this period, but the *Century* did not reprint the *Tribune's.*

[74] *Christianity and Crisis*, I (June 16, 1941), 1–2.

[75] Bennett was the most sensitive to this problem, as befitted his neo-liberalism. He also called up the obvious exception to the neutralists' identification of war participation with vindictiveness, Abraham Lincoln: *Christian Realism*, pp. 109–110; see also his contribution to the series "What I Would Do If America Goes to War," *Christian Century*, LVII (Dec. 4, 1940), 1506–1507.

[76] "American Neutrality," *Radical Religion*, V (Summer, 1940), 5–7.

[77] "America's Response to the World Crisis," *Christianity and Society*, VI (Spring, 1941), 4–5.

[78] "The Crisis Deepens," *Christianity and Crisis*, I (May 5, 1941), 2.

[79] "War Aims and a Just Peace," *Christianity and Society*, VI (Winter, 1941), 1–3.

[80] *An Interpretation of Christian Ethics* (New York, 1935), p. 215; *ibid.*, p. 122 on utopianism.

[81] *Does Civilization Need Religion?* (New York, 1927), pp. 163–164.

[82] "American Doldrums," *Christianity and Crisis*, I (Sept. 22, 1941), 2; see also "Leaves from the Notebook of a Warbound American," *Christian Century*, LVI (Oct. 25, 1939), 1298–1299, in which Niebuhr reacted to the news of a war boom: "I find the news almost as hard to bear as the atrocity stories. So we will increase our wealth in the blood bath of Europe. What I dread most of all is that we will accompany this profit-taking with self-righteous thanksgivings that we are not as Europe is."

[83] "America and the Enslaved Nations," *Christianity and Crisis*, I (Oct. 6, 1941), 1–2. In "Repeal the Neutrality Act," *ibid.* (Oct. 20, 1941), 1–2, Niebuhr argued that the act was immoral because it denied community. See also, "Momentous Decision by a Narrow Margin," *ibid.* (Dec. 1, 1941), 1–2.

[84] The attack on lovelessness, "Pharisaism," and self-righteousness appeared constantly. Two pointed examples: chapter II in *Christianity and Power Politics*, "The War and American Churches"; and Niebuhr's contribution to the "What I Would Do if America Goes to War" series, *Christian Century*, LVII (Dec. 14, 1940), 1178–1180.

[85] *Radical Religion*, V (Summer, 1940), 1–2.

[86] *Ibid.*, III (Spring, 1938), 2–3. As we have suggested, there was a profound sense in which Niebuhr's thought was descriptive rather than exhortatory, a study of "what is" rather than of "what should be" or "what can be." It was precisely at this point—where description consumed all possibilities for exhortation, where everything closed in to tears—that the logic of his escape from the determinism, pessimistic and socially enervating, charged against him by the liberals was made. His words on classical Greek tragedy in *The Nature and Destiny of Man* illustrated his feeling for the affinity of classical theology and an art which was descriptive in that that art sought above all to win from its audience

an identification with what was real and not with what was ideal, a pity that was a self-recognition. Here action began once again, for in the dissolution of all alternatives in tears, there was identification with the "other," and with that identification, a new sort of will emerged, the will to use whatever freedom the self possessed to move close to the other; Americans who wept recognized the essence of European tragedy within themselves, and wished then to lend themselves as Americans. The switch from political to religious criteria for choosing a political course of action occurred at this juncture.

[87] "Christian Moralism in America," *Radical Religion*, V (Winter, 1940), 16–20.

[88] "Irresponsible Idealism," *Christian Century*, LVII (July 24, 1940), 924–925.

[89] *Christianity and Power Politics*, p. 5.

[90] *Ibid.*, p. 6; the chapter "Why the Christian Church Is Not Pacifist" was Niebuhr's definitive discussion. See Umphrey Lee, *The Historic Church and Modern Pacifism* (New York, 1943), for an historical survey demonstrating the error of the view that pacifism was "true" Christianity.

[91] "Japan and the Christian Conscience," *Christian Century*, LIV (Nov. 10, 1937), 1390–1391.

[92] Nietzsche on Schopenhauer, in *Genealogy of Morals* (New York, n.d.) (Modern Library), p. 105.

[93] We have noted Niebuhr's attraction to St. Francis: *Christian Century*, XLV (May 3, 1928), 572; and see also, again, *Beyond Tragedy* (New York, 1937), chap. VII.

NOTES TO CHAPTER XIX: *Epilogue, pp. 404–413*

[1] A. Dudley Ward, ed., *The Goals of Economic Life* (New York, 1953); Kenneth Boulding, *The Organizational Revolution* (New York, 1953); H. R. Bowen, *The Social Responsibility of the Businessman* (New York, 1953); Elizabeth E. Hoyt, ed., *American Income and Its Use* (New York, 1954); A. Dudley Ward, ed., *Attitudes and Opinions of People on the American Economy* (New York, 1954); J. C. Bennett, *et al.*, *Christian Values and Economic Life* (New York, 1954).

[2] A brief discussion of laissez-faire groups can be found in Ralph L. Roy, *Apostles of Discord* (Boston, 1953), chap. XII; for denominational troubles, see chapters xiii and xiv.

[3] *Attitudes and Opinions of People on the American Economy.*

[4] See, by this author, "Billy Graham," *New Republic*, CXXXIII (Aug. 22, 1955), 8–10, and *ibid.*, "Norman Vincent Peale's Gospel of Success," *ibid.*, CXXXIII (July 11, 1955), 8–10.

[5] See *Christian Realism and Political Problems* (New York, 1953), chapter iv.

[6] *Discerning the Signs of the Times* (New York, 1946), pp. 180 ff.

[7] *Ibid.*, pp. 190–191.

[8] For instance: W. G. Cole, *Sex in Christianity and Psychoanalysis* (New York, 1955); S. R. Hopper, ed., *Spiritual Problems in Contemporary Literature* (New York, 1952); Carl Michaelson, *Christianity and the Existentialists* (New York, 1956); all are quite without parallels before the Second World War.

[9] *Faith and History* (New York, 1949), chapter XIV. One may infer that a sacramental church also meant for Niebuhr a church in which the leaders were not so often restricted by their congregations as in most American denominations; it is indicative that he should have so greatly admired the leader of Anglican social Christianity, Archbishop Temple: see *Nation,* CLIX (Nov. 11, 1944), 584–586.

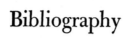

Bibliography

Bibliography

PERIODICALS

(*The following were searched systematically throughout the periods indicated.*)

Christendom, 1935–1941.
Christian Century, 1919–1941.
Christianity and Crisis, 1941.
Federal Council Bulletin, 1919–1941.
Information Service, 1921–1941.
Protestant Digest, 1939–1941.
Radical Religion (later *Christianity and Society*), 1936–1941.
Religion in Life, 1932–1941.
Social Action, 1935–1941.
Social Service Bulletin (later *Social Questions Bulletin*), 1919–1941.
World Tomorrow, 1919–1934.

(*The following were consulted upon occasion.*)

The Baptist.
Christian Advocate.
The Churchman.
The Congregationalist and Advance (later *The Advance*).
Economic Justice.
Fellowship.
Harvard Theological Review.
Journal of Religion.
Presbyterian Tribune.
The Witness.
Zion's Herald.

WORKS WITH A PRIMARY FOCUS ON SOCIAL AND POLITICAL QUESTIONS

Barker, John M. *The Social Gospel and the New Era.* New York: The Macmillan Co., 1919.
Batten, Samuel Z. *Why Not Try Christianity?* Pamphlet. Philadelphia: George H. Doran Co., 1923.
Bennett, John C. *Christian Realism.* New York: Charles Scribner's Sons, 1941.
———. *Christianity and Our World.* New York: Association Press, 1936.

Bennett, John C. *Social Salvation.* New York: Charles Scribner's Sons, 1935.

Booth, Henry K. *The Great Galilean Returns.* New York: Charles Scribner's Sons, 1936.

Brown, Charles R. *Social Rebuilders.* New York: The Abingdon Press, 1921.

Brown, William A. *Christianity and Industry.* New York: The Woman's Press, 1919.

————. *Imperialistic Religion and the Religion of Democracy.* New York: Charles Scribner's Sons, 1923.

Calhoun, Robert L. *God and the Common Life.* New York: Charles Scribner's Sons, 1935.

————. *God and the Day's Work.* New York: Association Press, 1943.

————. *What Is Man?* New York: Association Press, 1939.

Chaffee, Edmund. *The Protestant Churches and the Industrial Crisis.* New York: The Macmillan Co., 1933.

Chicago Social Action Movement. *Leader's Handbook.* Chicago, 1932.

Coe, George A. *Educating for Citizenship.* New York: Charles Scribner's Sons, 1932.

————. *The Motives of Men.* New York: Charles Scribner's Sons, 1928.

————. *A Social Theory of Religious Education.* New York: Charles Scribner's Sons, 1917.

Coffin, Henry S. *In a Day of Social Rebuilding.* New Haven: Yale University Press, 1918.

————. *A More Christian Industrial Order.* New York: The Macmillan Co., 1920.

Davis, Jerome. *Capitalism and Its Culture.* New York: Farrar and Rinehart, Inc., 1935.

Davis, Ozora. *Preaching the Social Gospel.* New York: Fleming H. Revell Co., 1922.

Dickinson, Charles H. *The Religion of the Social Passion.* Chicago: Christian Century Press, 1923.

Eddy, G. Sherwood. *America: Its Problems and Perils.* Pamphlet. New York: George H. Doran Co., 1922.

————. *The Challenge of Russia.* New York: Farrar and Rinehart, Inc., 1931.

————. *A Door of Opportunity.* New York: Eddy and Page, 1937.

————. *Facing the Crisis.* New York: George H. Doran Co., 1922.

————. *I Have Seen God Do It.* New York: Harper and Brothers, 1940.

————. *Jesus Christ: What Is His Significance?* Pamphlet. New York: George H. Doran Co., 1924.

————. *The Kingdom of God and the American Dream.* New York: Harper and Brothers, 1941.

————. *The New World of Labor.* New York: George H. Doran Co., 1923.

————. *A Pilgrimage of Ideas.* New York: Farrar and Rinehart, Inc., 1934.

————. *A Portrait of Jesus.* New York: Harper and Brothers, 1943.

————. *Religion and Social Justice.* New York: George H. Doran Co., 1927.

————. *Revolutionary Christianity.* Chicago: Willett, Clark and Co., 1939.

————. *The Right to Fight.* New York: Association Press, 1918.

————. *Russia: A Warning and a Challenge.* Pamphlet. New York: George H. Doran Co., n.d.

————. *Russia Today.* New York: Farrar and Rinehart, Inc., 1934.

Federal Council of Churches of Christ in America. *Christianity and Economic Problems.* New York: Association Press, 1922.

————. *The Church and Industrial Reconstruction.* New York, 1920.

————. *The Coal Controversy.* Pamphlet. New York, 1922.

————. *The Coal Strike in Western Pennsylvania.* Pamphlet. New York, 1928.

————. *The Denver Tramway Strike of 1920.* New York: Denver Council of Religious Forces, 1921.

————. *The Engineman's Strike in the Western Maryland Railroad.* Pamphlet. New York: Davis Press, 1927.

————. *Our Economic Life in the Light of Christian Ideals.* New York: Association Press, 1932.

————. *Permanent Preventives of Unemployment.* Pamphlet. New York, 1931.

————. *Report on the Strike in the Textile Mills of Lawrence, Massachusetts.* Pamphlet. New York, 1920.

————. *The Twelve-Hour Day in the Steel Industry.* Pamphlet. New York, 1923.

————. *The Wage Question.* Pamphlet. New York, 1922.

————. *What Is the Christian View of Work and Wealth?* New York: Association Press, 1920.

Fletcher, Toseph F. *Money-Makers and Moral Man.* Pamphlet. Milwaukee: Morehouse Publishing Co., 1934.

Gilbert, Charles K., and Charles N. Lathrop. *The Social Opportunity of the Churchman.* New York: Presiding Bishop and Council, 1922.

Gilbreath, J. E. *The Vision of God and the Social Order.* New York: Fleming H. Revell Co., 1936.

Gladden, Washington. *Applied Christianity.* Boston: Houghton Mifflin Co., 1886.

————. *The Labor Question.* Boston: Pilgrim Press, 1911.

————. *Recollections.* Boston: Houghton Mifflin Co., 1909.

————. *Ruling Ideas of the Present Age.* Boston: Houghton Mifflin Co., 1895.

————. *Social Facts and Forces.* New York: G. P. Putnam's Sons, 1897.

Gulick, Sidney. *The Christian Crusade for a Warless World.* New York: Federal Council of Churches, 1922.

Herring, Hubert. *And So to War.* New Haven: Yale University Press, 1938.

Holt, Arthur E. *Christian Fellowship and Modern Industry.* Boston: Pilgrim Press, 1923.

Holt, Arthur E., and F. E. Johnson. *Christian Ideals in Industry.* New York: The Methodist Book Concern, 1924.

————. *This Nation Under God.* Chicago: Willett, Clark and Company, 1939.

Horton, Walter M. *Can Christianity Save Civilization?* New York: Harper and Brothers, 1940.

————. *Realistic Theology.* New York: Harper and Brothers, 1934.

Hutchinson, Paul. *The Ordeal of Western Religion.* Boston: Houghton Mifflin Co., 1933.

Interchurch World Movement. *Report on the Steel Strike of 1919.* New York: Harcourt, Brace and Co., 1920.

————. *Public Opinion and the Steel Strike.* New York: Harcourt, Brace and Co., 1921.

Jefferson, Charles E. *Christianizing a Nation.* New York: Doubleday, Doran and Co., 1929.

Johnson, F. Ernest. *Church and Society.* New York: Abingdon Press, 1935.

————. *The New Spirit in Industry.* Pamphlet. New York: Association Press, 1919.

————. *The Social Gospel and Personal Religion.* Pamphlet. New York: Association Press, 1922.

————. *The Social Gospel Re-examined.* New York: Harper and Brothers, 1940.

Jones, E. Stanley. *The Choice Before Us*. New York: Abingdon Press, 1937.

———. *Christ's Alternative to Communism*. New York: Abingdon Press, 1935.

———. *Is the Kingdom of God Realism?* New York: Abingdon-Cokesbury Press, 1941.

Kresge, E. E. *The Church and the Ever-coming Kingdom of God*. New York: The Macmillan Co., 1922.

Luccock, Halford. *Christian Faith and Economic Change*. New York: Abingdon Press, 1936.

———. *Jesus and the American Mind*. New York: Abingdon Press, 1930.

Macintosh, Douglas. *Social Religion*. New York: Charles Scribner' Sons, 1939.

Mathews, Shailer. *Jesus on Social Institutions*. New York: The Macmillan Co., 1928.

———. *The Social Teaching of Jesus*. New York: The Macmillan Co., 1897.

———. *The Validity of American Ideals*. New York: Abingdon Press, 1922.

McConnell, Francis J. *The Christian Ideal and Social Control*. Chicago: University of Chicago Press, 1932.

———. *Christian Materialism*. New York: Friendship Press, 1936.

———. *Christian Principles and Industrial Reconstruction*. New York: Association Press, 1919.

———. *Christianity and Coercion*. Nashville: Cokesbury Press, 1933.

———. *Church Finance and Social Ethics*. New York: The Macmillan Co., 1920.

———. *Democratic Christianity*. New York: The Macmillan Co., 1919.

———. *Living Together*. New York: Abingdon Press, 1923.

———. *Public Opinion and Theology*. New York: Abingdon Press, 1920.

Morrison, Charles C. *The Outlawry of War*. Chicago: Willett, Clark and Co., 1927.

———. *The Social Gospel and the Christian Cultus*. New York: Harper and Brothers, 1933.

———. *What Is Christianity?* Chicago: Willett, Clark and Co., 1940.

Muste, Abraham J. *The A.F. of L. in 1931*. Pamphlet. New York, n.d.

———. *The Automobile Industry and Organized Labor*. Pamphlet. Baltimore: Christian Social Justice Fund, *ca.* 1935.

———. *Non-Violence in an Aggressive World*. New York: Harper and Brothers, 1940.

———. *Wage Peace Now*. Pamphlet. Wallingford, Penn.: Pendle Hill, 1942.

———. *War Is the Enemy*. Pamphlet. Wallingford, Penn.: Pendle Hill, 1942.

———. *Where Are We Going?* Pamphlet. New York, 1941.

———. *The World Task of Pacifism*. Pamphlet. Wallingford, Penn.: Pendle Hill, 1941.

Myers, James. *Do You Know Labor?* Pamphlet. New York: National Home Library Foundation, 1940.

———. *Representative Government in Industry*. New York: George H. Doran Co., 1924.

Niebuhr, H. Richard, Francis Miller, and Wilhelm Pauck. *The Church Against the World*. Chicago: Willett, Clark and Co., 1935.

Niebuhr, Reinhold. *Christianity and Power Politics*. New York: Charles Scribner's Sons, 1940.

———. *An Interpretation of Christian Ethics*. New York: Harper and Brothers, 1935.

———. *Moral Man and Immoral Society*. New York: Charles Scribner's Sons, 1932.

————. *Reflections on the End of an Era.* New York: Charles Scribner's Sons, 1934.

Oxnam, G. Bromley. *By This Sign Conquer.* New York: Abingdon-Cokesbury, 1942.

————. *The Ethical Ideals of Jesus.* New York: Abingdon-Cokesbury, 1941.

————. *Preaching and the Social Crisis.* New York: Abingdon Press, 1933.

Page, Kirby. *The Abolition of War.* Pamphlet. New York: George H. Doran Co., 1924.

————. *An American Peace Policy.* Pamphlet. New York: George H. Doran Co., 1925.

————. *Capitalism and Its Rivals.* Pamphlet. New York: Eddy and Page, *ca.* 1935.

————. *Collective Bargaining.* Pamphlet. New York: George H. Doran Co., 1922.

Page, Kirby, and Sherwood Eddy. *Creative Pioneers.* New York: Association Press, 1937.

————. ————. *Danger Zones of the Social Order.* Pamphlet. New York: George H. Doran Co., 1926.

————. *Dollars and World Peace.* Pamphlet. New York: George H. Doran Co., 1927.

————. *How to Keep America Out of War.* Pamphlet. New York: Fellowship of Reconciliation, 1939.

————. *Imperialism and Nationalism.* Pamphlet. New York: George H. Doran Co., 1925.

————. *Incentives in Modern Life.* Pamphlet. New York: George H. Doran Co., 1922.

————. *Individualism and Socialism.* New York: Farrar and Rinehart, 1933.

————. *Industrial Facts.* Pamphlet. New York: George H. Doran Co., 1921.

————. *Jesus or Christianity.* New York: Doubleday, Doran and Co., 1929.

————. *The Monroe Doctrine and World Peace.* Pamphlet. New York: Doubleday, Doran and Co., 1928.

————. *Must We Go to War?* New York: Farrar and Rinehart, 1937.

————. *National Defense.* Pamphlet. New York: Farrar and Rinehart, 1931.

————. *A National Peace Department.* Pamphlet. New York: George H. Doran Co., 1927.

————. *Property.* Pamphlet. New York: Eddy and Page, *ca.* 1935.

————. *The Sword and the Cross.* Chicago: Christian Century Press, 1921.

————. *The United States Steel Corporation.* Pamphlet. New York: George H. Doran Co., 1922.

————. *War: Its Causes, Consequences and Cure.* New York: George H. Doran Co., 1923.

Page, Kirby, and Sherwood Eddy. *What Shall We Do about War?* Pamphlet. New York: Eddy and Page, *ca.* 1935.

Peabody, Francis G. *Jesus Christ and the Social Question.* New York: The Macmillan Co., 1900.

Poteat, E. M. *The Social Manifesto of Jesus.* New York: Harper and Brothers, 1935.

Rauschenbusch, Walter. *Christianity and the Social Crisis.* New York: The Macmillan Co., 1907.

————. *Christianizing the Social Order.* New York: The Macmillan Co., 1912.

————. *A Theology for the Social Gospel.* New York: The Macmillan Co., 1917.

Smith, Gerald B. *Principles of Christian Living.* Chicago: University of Chicago Press, 1924.

Smith, Gerald B. *Social Idealism and the Changing Theology*. New York: The Macmillan Co., 1913.

Spinka, Matthew. *Christianity Confronts Communism*. New York: Harper and Brothers, 1936.

Taylor, Alva. *Christianity and Industry*. New York: Friendship Press, 1933.

Tittle, Ernest F. *Christians in an Unchristian Society*. New York: Association Press, 1939.

Van Kirk, Walter. *Religion Renounces War*. Chicago: Willett, Clark and Co., 1934.

Ward, Harry. *The Christian Demand for Social Reconstruction*. Philadelphia: Westminster, 1918.

————. *Democracy and Social Change*. New York: Modern Age Books, 1940.

————. *The Development of Fascism in the United States*. Pamphlet. New York: American League Against War and Fascism, ca. 1936.

————. *The Fascist International*. Pamphlet. New York: American League Against War and Fascism, ca. 1937.

————. *The Gospel for a Working World*. New York: Missionary Education Movement, 1918.

————. *In Place of Profit*. New York: Charles Scribner's Sons, 1933.

————. *The New Social Order*. New York: The Macmillan Co., 1919.

————. *Our Economic Morality and the Ethic of Jesus*. New York: The Macmillan Co., 1929.

————. *The Social Creed of the Churches*. New York: Eaton and Mains, 1914.

————. *The Soviet Spirit*. New York: International Publishers, 1944.

————. *Which Way Religion?* New York: The Macmillan Co., 1931.

Webber, Charles C. *Circuit-Riding in the 20th Century*. Pamphlet. New York, 1939.

————. *Outline of a Christian Program for Social Change*. Pamphlet. New York, 1936.

Williams, Charles D. *The Prophetic Ministry for Today*. New York: The Macmillan Co., 1921.

SYMPOSIA AND HANDBOOKS

Allen, Devere, ed. *Adventurous Americans*. New York: Farrar and Rinehart, Inc., 1932.

————, ed. *Pacifism in the Modern World*. Garden City: Doubleday, Doran and Co., 1929.

Bate, H. N., ed. *The World Conference on Faith and Order*. New York: George H. Doran Co., 1927.

Bixler, J. S., ed. *The Nature of Religious Experience*. New York: Harper Brothers, 1937.

Bower, W. C., ed. *The Church at Work in the Modern World*. Chicago: University of Chicago Press, 1935.

Cavert, Samuel McC. *The Churches Allied for Common Tasks*. New York: Federal Council of the Churches of Christ in America, 1921.

The Church Through Half a Century: Essays in Honor of William Adams Brown. New York: Charles Scribner's Sons, 1936.

Fletcher, Joseph F., ed. *Christianity and Property*. Philadelphia: Westminster Press, 1947.

Hough, Lynn H., ed. *Whither Christianity?* New York: Harper and Brothers, 1929.

"Industrial Relations and the Church," *Annals of the American Academy of Social and Political Science*, CIII (September, 1922).

Johnson, F. Ernest, ed. *A Bibliography of Social Service*. Pamphlet. New York: Federal Council of Churches, 1918.

———. *The Social Work of the Churches*. New York: Federal Council of Churches, 1930.

Knox, Edward, ed. *Religion and the Present Crisis*. Chicago: University of Chicago Press, 1942.

Lewis, John, ed. *Christianity and the Social Revolution*. New York: Charles Scribner's Sons, 1936.

Myers, James. *Churches in Social Action*. New York: Federal Council of Churches, 1935.

———. *Religion Lends a Hand*. New York: Harper and Brothers, 1929.

Niebuhr, Reinhold, ed. This Ministry: Essays in Honor of H. S. Coffin. New York: Charles Scribner's Sons, 1945.

Oxford Conference. *Christian Faith and the Common Life*. Chicago: Willett, Clark and Co., 1938.

———. *The Christian Understanding of Man*. Chicago: Willett, Clark and Co., 1938.

———. *The Kingdom of God and History*. Chicago: Willett, Clark and Co., 1938.

Page, Kirby, ed. *A New Economic Order*. New York: Harcourt, Brace and Co., 1930.

———, ed. *Recent Gains in American Civilization*. New York: Harcourt, Brace and Company, 1928.

Protestant Episcopal Church, Joint Commission of. *Reconstruction Programs: A Bibliography and Digest*. New York, 1919.

———. *Triennial Report*. New York, 1919.

Rall, H. F., ed. *Religion and Public Affairs*. New York: The Macmillan Co., 1937.

Read, Ralph, ed. *The Younger Churchmen Look at the Church*. New York: The Macmillan Co., 1935.

Sayre, John N., Kirby Page, and A. J. Muste. *Pacifism and Aggression*. Pamphlet. New York, n.d.

Schilpp, P. A., ed. *Theology and Modern Life*. Chicago: Willett, Clark and Co., 1940.

Smith, G. B., ed. *Religious Thought in the Last Quarter Century*. Chicago: University of Chicago Press, 1927.

Swift, Arthur, ed. *Religion Today*. New York: McGraw-Hill Book Co., 1933.

Van Dusen, H. P., Francis Henson, and Sidney Hook. *Christianity and Marxism*. New York: Polemic Publishers, 1934.

Van Dusen, H. P., ed. *Ventures in Belief*. New York: Charles Scribner's Sons, 1930.

WORKS RELEVANT TO THE SOCIAL PASSION, BUT OF LARGER FOCUS

Atkins, Gaius G. *Religion in Our Times*. New York: Round Table Press, 1932.

Barclay, Wade C. *The Church and a Christian Society*. New York: The Abingdon Press, 1939.

Barth, Karl. *The Church and the Political Problem of Our Day.* New York: Charles Scribner's Sons, 1939.

Brightman, Edgar S. *Personality and Religion.* New York: The Abingdon Press, 1934.

Brunner, Emil. *Justice and the Social Order.* New York: Harper and Brothers, 1945.

Cadbury, Henry J. *The Peril of Modernizing Jesus.* New York: The Macmillan Co., 1937.

Calkins, Raymond. *The Christian Church in the Modern World.* New York: The Macmillan Co., 1924.

Case, Shirley Jackson. *Christianity in a Changing World.* New York: Harper and Brothers, 1941.

————. *Jesus Through the Centuries.* Chicago: University of Chicago Press, 1932.

————. *The Social Triumph of the Ancient Church.* New York: Harper and Brothers, 1933.

Coffin, Henry S. *Religion Yesterday and Today.* Nashville: Cokesbury Press, 1940.

Eddy, G. Sherwood. *Eighty Adventurous Years: An Autobiography.* New York: Harper and Brothers, 1955.

Fitch, Albert P. *Can the Church Survive in the Changing Order?* New York: The Macmillan Co., 1920.

Fosdick, Harry E. *Christianity and Progress.* New York: Fleming H. Revell Co., 1922.

Haroutunian, Joseph. *Wisdom and Folly in Religion.* New York: Charles Scribner's Sons, 1940.

Holt, A. E. *Christian Roots of Democracy in America.* New York: Friendship Press, 1941.

————. *The Fate of the Family in the Modern World.* Chicago: Willett, Clark and Co., 1936.

————. *Social Work in the Churches.* Boston: Pilgrim Press, 1922.

Holt, Ivan Lee. *The Search for a New Strategy in Protestantism.* New York: Cokesbury Press, 1937.

Homrighausen, Elmer. *Christianity in America.* New York: Abingdon Press, 1936.

Jaspers, Karl. *Man in the Modern Age.* London: G. Routledge and Sons, 1933.

Leiper, Henry S. *Christ's Way and the World's.* New York: Abingdon Press, 1936.

Lewis, Edwin. *A New Heaven and a New Earth.* New York: Abingdon-Cokesbury Press, 1941.

Luccock, Halford. *Christianity and the Individual.* Nashville: Cokesbury Press, 1937.

Macintosh, Douglas C. *Personal Religion.* New York: Charles Scribner's Sons, 1942.

Mathews, Shailer. *Christianity and Social Process.* New York: Harper and Brothers, 1934.

————. *Creative Christianity.* Nashville: Cokesbury Press, 1935.

McConnell, Francis J. *By the Way: An Autobiography.* New York: Abingdon-Cokesbury, 1952.

Niebuhr, H. Richard. *The Kingdom of God in America.* Chicago: Willett, Clark and Company, 1937.

————. *The Social Sources of Denominationalism.* New York: Henry Holt and Company, 1929.

Niebuhr, Reinhold. *Beyond Tragedy.* New York: Charles Scribner's Sons, 1937.

―――. *The Contribution of Religion to Social Work*. New York: Columbia University Press, 1930.

―――. *Does Civilization Need Religion?* New York: The Macmillan Co., 1927.

―――. *Leaves from the Notebook of a Tamed Cynic*. New York: Willett, Clark and Colby, 1929.

―――. *The Nature and Destiny of Man*. 2v. New York: Charles Scribner's Sons, 1941, 1943.

Nixon, Justin Wroe. *The Moral Crisis in Christianity*. New York: Harper and Brothers, 1931.

―――. *Protestantism's Hour of Decision*. Philadelphia: Judson Press, 1940.

Page, Kirby. *Living Prayerfully*. New York: Farrar and Rinehart, 1941.

―――. *Religious Resources for Personal and Social Action*. New York: Farrar and Rinehart, 1939.

Rehwinkel, Alfred M. *The World Today—A Challenge to the Christian Faith*. St. Louis: Concordia Publishing House, 1940.

Reisner, E. H. *Faith in an Age of Fact*. New York: Farrar and Rinehart, 1937.

Roberts, D. E., and H. P. Van Dusen, eds. *Liberal Theology: an Appraisal*. New York: Charles Scribner's Sons, 1942.

Scott, E. F. *The Ethical Teachings of Jesus*. New York: The Macmillan Co., 1924.

―――. *The Kingdom of God in the New Testament*. New York: The Macmillan Co., 1931.

Swift, Arthur. *New Frontiers of Religion*. New York: The Macmillan Co., 1938.

Tillich, Paul. *Interpretation of History*. New York: Charles Scribner's Sons, 1936.

―――. *The Protestant Era*. Chicago: University of Chicago Press, 1946.

―――. *The Religious Situation*. New York: Henry Holt and Co., 1932.

Van Dusen, H. P. *God in These Times*. New York: Charles Scribner's Sons, 1935.

Wieman, Henry N., *et al. Religious Liberals Reply*. Boston: Beacon Press, 1947.

SOME LAY EXPRESSIONS

Babson, Roger. *New Tasks for Old Churches*. New York: Fleming H. Revell Company, 1922.

―――. *Religion and Business*. New York: The Macmillan Co., 1920.

Davis, Jerome, ed. *Business and the Church*. New York: The Century Co., 1926.

―――, ed. *Christianity and Social Adventuring*. New York: The Century Co., 1927.

―――, ed. *Labor Speaks for Itself on Religion*. New York: The Macmillan Co., 1929.

Ellwood, Charles. *Christianity and Social Science*. New York: The Macmillan Co., 1923.

―――. *The Reconstruction of Religion*. New York: The Macmillan Co., 1922.

―――. *The World's Need of Christ*. New York: Abingdon-Cokesbury Press, 1940.

High, Stanley. *The Church in Politics*. New York: Harper and Brothers, 1930.

Hutchins, Grace, and Anna Rochester. *Jesus Christ and the World Today*. New York: George H. Doran Co., 1922.

Nash, Arthur. *The Golden Rule in Industry*. New York: Fleming H. Revell Co., 1923.

Rockefeller, John D., Jr. *The Personal Relation in Industry*. New York: Boni and Liveright, 1923.
Sweet, William E. *The Businessman and His Overflow*. New York: Association Press, 1919.
Thomas, Norman. *America's Way Out*. New York: The Macmillan Co., 1931.

SOME ANTISOCIAL GOSPEL TRACTS

Bigelow, Victor. *Mistakes of the Inter-church Steel Report*. Boston, 1920.
Conant, Judson E. *The Growing Menace of the Social Gospel*. Chicago: Bible Institute Colportage Association, 1937.
Harsch, John. *Communism*. Chicago: Bible Institute Colportage Association, 1937.
Joy, Henry B. *Our Pro-Socialist Churches*. Detroit, 1937.
———. *Reference Materials, with Reference to FCCCA*, etc. Detroit, 1938.
Olds, Marshall. *Analysis of the Interchurch World Movement Report on the Steel Strike*. G. P. Putnam's Sons, 1922.
Sanctuary, E. N. *Tainted Contacts*. New York: American Christian Defenders, 1931.
Smith, Leroy, and E. B. Johns. *Pastors, Politicians, Pacifists*. Constructive Educational Publishing Co.

SECONDARY WORKS

Abrams, Ray. *Preachers Present Arms*. New York: Round Table Press, 1933.
Atkins, G. G., and F. L. Fagley. *History of American Congregationalism*. Boston and Chicago: Pilgrim Press, 1942.
Aubrey, E. E. *Present Theological Tendencies*. New York: Harper and Brothers, 1936.
Barnes, Harry E. *The Twilight of Christianity*. New York: The Vanguard Press, 1929.
Belfrage, Cedric. *A Faith to Free the People*. New York: Dryden Press, 1944.
———. *South of God*. New York: Modern Age Books, 1941.
Blachly, Clarence. *The Treatment of the Problem of Capital and Labor in Social-Study Courses in the Churches*. Chicago: University of Chicago Press, 1920.
Brunner, Edmund. *Industrial Village Churches*. New York: Institute of Social and Religious Research, 1930.
Carter, Paul. *The Decline and Revival of the Social Gospel, 1920–1940*. Ithaca: Cornell University Press, 1956.
Case, Adelaid. *Liberal Christianity and Religious Education*. New York: The Macmillan Co., 1924.
Cole, Charles C. *The Social Ideas of the Northern Evangelists*. New York: Columbia University Press, 1954.
Curti, Merle. *Peace or War*. New York: W. W. Norton and Co., 1936.
Dombrowski, James. *The Early Days of Christian Socialism in America*. New York: Columbia University Press, 1936.
Douglass, H. Paul. *Church and Community in the United States*. Chicago: Willett, Clark and Co., 1938.
———. *The Protestant Church as a Social Institution*. New York: Harper and Brothers, 1935.
Five-Foot Shelf of Pacifist Literature. Pamphlet. Philadelphia, 1942.